Exploring Nova Scotia

Sixth Edition

Dale Dunlop

Alison Scott

Formac Publishing Company Limited
Halifax, Nova Scotia

Formac Publishing Company Limited recognizes the support of the Province of Nova Scotia through the Department of Tourism, Culture and Heritage. We acknowledge the financial support of the Government of Canada through the Canada Book Fund for our publishing activities.

Library and Archives Canada Cataloguing in Publication

Dunlop, Dale, 1951-
Exploring Nova Scotia : a guide to 400+ unique adventures and activities / Dale Dunlop and Alison Scott. — 6th ed.

Includes index.
ISBN 978-0-88780-903-3
1. Nova Scotia — Guidebooks. I. Scott, Alison II. Title.
FC2307.D86 2010   917.1604'5   C2010-900749-2

Formac Publishing Company Limited
5502 Atlantic Street
Halifax, Nova Scotia
B3H 1G4
www.formac.ca

Printed and bound in Canada.

Distributed in the United States by:
Casemate Book Distributing
908 Darby Road,
Havertown, PA 19083

Distributed in the United Kingdom by:
Portfolio Books
2nd Floor, Westminster House, Kew Road
Richmond, Surrey TW9 2ND

Table of Contents

Preface   12

Part I: Introducing Nova Scotia   15
Geography   16
History   17
When to Visit   27
Before You Go   30
Getting There   32
Getting Around   33
Accommodations   33
Dining   36

Part II: What to See and Do   39
Antiques   40
Architecture   42
Arts, Crafts and Folk Art   43
Beaches   44
Bicycle Touring   46
Birding   47
Boat Tours   48
Canoeing   49
Cemeteries   50
Diving   50
Family Vacations   51
Festivals   51
Fishing   52
Geocaching   55
Golf   55
Hiking   56
Mountain Biking   58
Museums   59
Rockhounding   59
Sailing   60
Sea Kayaking   61
Theatre   61
Traditional Music   62
Walking Tours   63
Whale-watching   63
Wilderness Areas   64
Wineries   64
Winter Sports   65

Part III: Around the Province   67
Halifax/Dartmouth   **68**
    Beaches   70
    Birding   71
    Boat Tours   71
    Canoeing   72
    Cemeteries   73
    Cycling   75
    Golf   75
    Hiking   77
    Historic Sites   80
    Museums   83
    Off the Beaten Path   85
    Parks and Greenspace   89
    Sea Kayaking   92
    Special Events   93
    Special Interest   95
    Theatre   100
    Walking Tours   101
    Wilderness Areas   103
    Where to Shop   104
    Accommodations   109
    Dining   111

Lighthouse Route — Halifax to Lunenburg 125
    Beaches   128
    Birding   128
    Cemeteries   128
    Cycling   129
    Diving   129
    Golf   130
    Historic Sites   130
    Museums   131
    Off the Beaten Path   132
    Parks and Greenspace   134
    Something Different   135
    Special Events   136
    Special Interest   137
    Theatre   138
    Walking Tours   138
    Where to Shop   140
    Accommodations   141
    Dining   143

Lighthouse Route — Lunenburg to Yarmouth 146
    Beaches   151

Birding   154
Cemeteries   154
Golf   154
Hiking   155
Museums   156
Off the Beaten Path   161
Parks and Greenspace   165
Special Events   166
Special Interest   166
Walking Tours   168
Accommodations   169
Dining   171

Kejimkujik Scenic Drive   **174**
Beaches   175
Canoeing   175
Hiking   176
Mountain Biking   176
Parks and Greenspace   177
Wilderness Areas   177
Accommodations   177
Dining   179

Evangeline Trail — Yarmouth to Annapolis Royal 180
Beaches   183
Birding   184
Cemeteries   184
Cycling   184
Golf   185
Hiking   185
Historic Sites   186
Museums   187
Off the Beaten Path   188
Parks and Greenspace   191
Special Events   191
Special Interest   191
Walking Tours   192
Whale-watching   193
Accommodations   194
Dining   196

Evangeline Trail — Annapolis Royal to Halifax 199
Beaches   201
Birding   202
Canoeing   203
Cemeteries   203

Cycling 203
Golf 203
Hiking 205
Historic Sites 207
Museums 209
Off the Beaten Path 211
Parks and Greenspace 214
Special Events 215
Special Interest 215
Walking Tours 216
Wineries 217
Accommodations 217
Dining 219

Glooscap Trail — Windsor to Truro **222**
Birding 225
Golf 225
Museums 225
Off the Beaten Path 226
Parks and Greenspace 227
Special Interest 229
Walking Tours 231
Accommodations 231
Dining 231

Glooscap Trail — Truro to Amherst **233**
Beaches 236
Birding 237
Golf 237
Hiking 238
Kayaking 241
Museums 241
Off the Beaten Path 243
Parks and Greenspace 247
Rockhounding and Fossils 248
Special Events 249
Special Interest 249
Theatre 251
Wilderness Areas 251
Accommodations 252
Dining 253

Northumberland Shore — Amherst to Pictou **254**
Beaches 257
Birding 257
Canoeing 258

Cemeteries   258
Cycling   258
Golf   258
Hiking   259
Museums   260
Off the Beaten Path   262
Parks and Greenspace   262
Special Events   263
Special Interest   263
Walking Tours   264
Accommodations   265
Dining   267

**Northumberland Shore —
Pictou to the Canso Causeway**   **269**
Beaches   271
Birding   272
Cemeteries   272
Golf   272
Museums   273
Off the Beaten Path   273
Parks and Greenspace   274
Rockhounding   274
Special Events   274
Special Interest   275
Accommodations   275
Dining   275

Ceilidh Trail   **277**
Beaches   277
Hiking   278
Off the Beaten Path   279
Special Events   280
Special Interest   280
Accommodations   281
Dining   281

Cabot Trail   **283**
Beaches   286
Canoeing   287
Cycling   287
Golf   287
Hiking   288
Museums   292
Off the Beaten Path   292
Special Interest   294

Whale-watching 295
Accommodations 295
Dining 297

Bras d'Or Lakes Scenic Drive **298**
Beaches 300
Birding 300
Golf 300
Hiking 301
Kayaking 302
Museums 302
Off the Beaten Path 302
Walking Tours 303
Accommodations 304
Dining 305

Fleur-de-Lis Trail **306**
Beaches 308
Cycling 309
Hiking 309
Historic Sites 310
Museums 311
Parks and Greenspace 312
Walking Tours 312
Accommodations 312
Dining 313

Marconi Trail **314**
Birding 315
Canoeing 316
Historic Sites 316
Museums 316
Rockhounding 317
Special Events 317
Walking Tours 317
Accommodations 318
Dining 318

Marine Drive **319**
Beaches 323
Cycling 324
Birding 324
Canoeing 325
Golf 325
Hiking 326
Historic Sites 328

Kayaking   328
Museums   329
Off the Beaten Path   330
Parks and Greenspace   333
Special Events   334
Special Interest   334
Wilderness Areas   335
Accommodations   336
Dining   337

Index   **338**

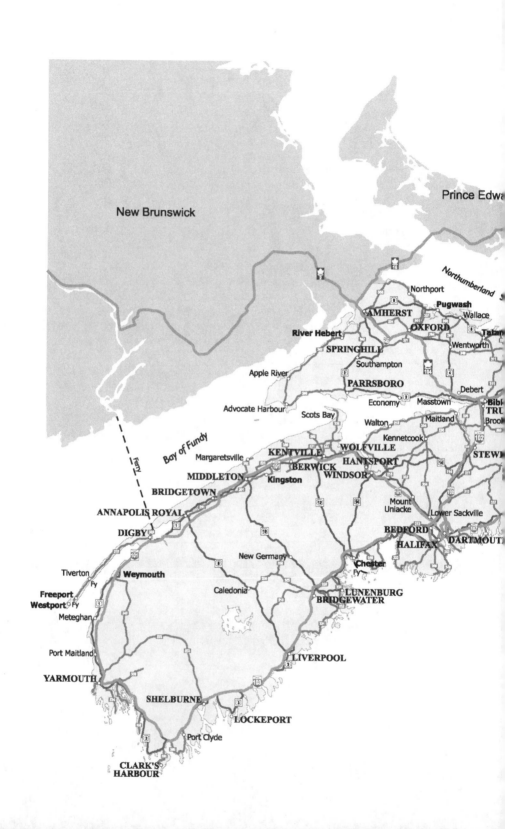

Gulf of
St. Lawrence

Island

Cape North

Pleasant Bay

Neils Harbour

Ingonish

Chéticamp

Wreck Cove

Margaree Harbour

Ferry

Inverness

Southwest
Margaree

SYDNEY MINES
GLACE BAY

NORTH SYDNEY

SYDNEY

Mabou

Baddeck

Port Hood

Eskasoni

Judique

Louisbourg

Arisaig

Havre
Boucher

St Peter's

Fourchu

ouche

PICTOU

Ferry

TRENTON

ANTIGONISH

NEW GLASGOW

MULGRAVE

PORT HAWKESBURY

ESTVILLE

STELLARTON

Arichat

Guysborough

CANSO

Dover

Upper Musquodoboit

Sherbrooke

KE

Port Bickerton

dle
squodoboit

Liscomb Mills

Sheet Harbour

Tangier

Atlantic Ocean

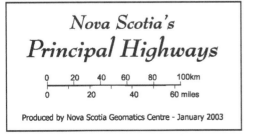

Nova Scotia's
Principal Highways

| 0 | 20 | 40 | 60 | 80 | 100km |

| 0 | 20 | 40 | 60 miles |

Produced by Nova Scotia Geomatics Centre - January 2003

PREFACE

The first edition of *Exploring Nova Scotia* was a work in progress for 20 years. On moving back to Nova Scotia in 1974, after living at various times in Newfoundland, Quebec, Ontario and Manitoba, I realized how little I knew of the province in which I was born. I was struck by the incredible variety of ecosystems and landforms in such a small province. Used to driving hundreds of kilometres out West without any great change in landscape, I was surprised to find that Nova Scotia could change completely over the space of a few kilometres. Over the past four decades, I have methodically travelled the province, from Yarmouth to Cape North and almost every place in between.

Alison was born and raised in Pictou County. Before we met in the late 1980s, her work had taken her to various parts of Nova Scotia, but only when we started travelling together did we realize what potential Nova Scotia has for adventurous couples of all ages. With the Nova Scotia atlas and the annual tourism guide in hand, we've ventured down thousands of kilometres of highways and backroads, explored the little villages and towns along the way, learned the history of still flourishing and bygone communities and hiked every type of terrain. With each trip, we've gained a greater appreciation for the beauty, diversity and usually pristine quality of the environment that make this province so special.

As the years have gone by, we've been joined by new travelling companions. My now 33-year-old son Bruce, and younger family members Lenore and Dale II have been part of the substance of all five editions of this book. Since the last edition we have had the great fortune to become grandparents twice over. This has allowed us to rediscover with them many of the places that are a joy to the young ones. Our miniature poodles have provided insight into the hazards dogs can come across on hikes, including porcupines, falling over cliffs (and surviving) and confrontations with much bigger, more aggressive dogs and owners. All in all, we've made an effort to involve the whole family, so we can share our ideas about what appeals to youngsters, teenagers, unaccompanied couples, and even pooches.

This is the sixth edition of Exploring Nova Scotia and we think it has improved considerably over the years. The second edition added addresses, phone numbers, e-mails and even a few Web sites, which back in the early 1990s were a rarity. Many people commented favourably and often with surprise at the number of things to see and do in *Exploring Nova Scotia*. Just for fun, in the third edition we decided to count these — all in all there were 455 separate entries, not including the accommodation and dining recommendations or the general information in Parts I and II. This newest edition contains even more. Some of our suggestions take only a few minutes, while others, such as a trip to Digby Neck, can take several days. We hope that with hundreds of ideas for exploring Nova Scotia, you will never run out of things to do during your stay in Canada's ocean playground. If you're a Nova Scotian, we hope this book will make you want to visit and enjoy parts of the province that you haven't visited before.

Since the first edition, the number of things to entertain and captivate tourists and residents alike has grown exponentially. Every year there are new trails to hike, museums and interpretive centres to visit, festivals to attend, restaurants and inns to check out. We do our best, between each edition, not only to explore what's new, but also to revisit the places already in the book to ensure that the information is accurate. The vast majority of the time we travel anonymously and pay our own way so we know we are getting the same treatment as the average tourist.

Undoubtedly, the biggest change since the last edition of *Exploring Nova Scotia* is the explosion of the Internet as the go-to place to plan a vacation or simply to check something out. Wherever possible we have included Web sites so that you can decide for yourself what you want to see and do. The second big change has been the worldwide economic downturn, which has resulted in the overused term 'staycations.' If you are a Nova Scotian or Maritimer, it's good to know that there are so many good reasons to vacation in your own backyard. For others, all we can say is that between us, Alison and I have travelled to every continent except Antartica and have found no place that offers more variety or better value in such a small area than Nova Scotia. We wish you good luck and much success in exploring Nova Scotia.

Dale Dunlop
Head of St. Margaret's Bay
December, 2009

Part I
Introducing Nova Scotia

GEOGRAPHY

Nova Scotia, with an area of 55,490 square kilometres, stretching 500 kilometres on a southwest-northeast axis from Cape Sable in the south to Cape North on Cape Breton Island, is Canada's second-smallest province, exceeding only tiny Prince Edward Island in size. The outstanding geographical fact about Nova Scotia is not really the land, but the sea. The province is virtually an island connected to the rest of Canada by the narrow Isthmus of Chignecto. No point of land is more than 55 kilometres from the coastline. Cape Breton is an island joined to the mainland by the Canso Causeway. It is the sea that has carved the wild and ragged shoreline of the Atlantic coast and the sea that creates the wondrous tides of the Bay of Fundy. It is the sea upon which the first European settlers arrived and the sea from which they pulled their livelihood in once-bursting nets. It is the sea for which they built ships to sail to other seas, bringing back goods rare and precious and tales even stranger. Not surprisingly, it is to the sea that Nova Scotians today are looking for new sources of wealth from offshore oil and gas. If there is one thing that most Nova Scotians know and respect, it is the sea in all its moods and incarnations.

Despite its relatively small area, Nova Scotia has an amazingly varied terrain. Technically, most of the province forms a small extension of the Appalachian chain that stretches from Alabama to Newfoundland and Labrador. While there are no true mountains and most elevations do not exceed 200 metres, in Cape Breton the land reaches an altitude of more than 400 metres, with North Barren at 580 metres being the highest point in the province. Rising directly from the sea, cliffs of up to 350 metres in height create dramatic vistas whether viewed from above or below. As well, the coastline that ranges from cliffs to sandy beaches, sheltered harbours and salt marshes, offers as many changes of scenery as one might find in any 6,500 kilometre journey, which is about how far the entire coastline would stretch if it were a straight line.

The province can be divided into three distinct physiographic regions — the lowlands, the uplands and the highlands, which in turn may be subdivided into distinct sub-regions.

The lowlands include the fertile Annapolis Valley, the low-lying areas around the Northumberland Strait and large parts of Cape Breton Island. The geology is primarily sedimentary and it is in these areas that most of Nova Scotia's rich coal seams are located. These coasts tend to be low and flat, and there are few good harbours. The shoreline is characterized by sandbars and occasional dunes. Bathers can often wade many hundreds of metres on these sandbars when the tide is out. The lowlands have the warmest waters in the province by a wide margin and are favoured by cottagers and vacationers with young children.

The Atlantic uplands comprise an area equal to half the province, from Yarmouth County all the way to Guysborough County. The uplands are a mass of Precambrian hard granite and quartzite, interspersed with belts of weaker slate. The area has been heavily glaciated; consequently, much of the soil has been scraped away and redeposited in numerous glacial formations, the most famous of which is the drumlin that forms Halifax's Citadel Hill.

The coastline of the uplands region is deeply indented, forming many good harbours, some of which are considered outstanding. Hundreds of islands dot the landscape along the Atlantic coast from Tor Bay in Guysborough County to the Tuskets near Yarmouth. Mahone Bay is famous for having an island for every day of the year, with mysterious Oak Island included among them. Reefs and shoals abound, accounting for the many lighthouses erected along this coast; of these Peggy's Cove lighthouse is undoubtedly the most famous. In many ways, the seaside regions of the Atlantic uplands validate the preconceived images of coastal Nova Scotia shared by many first-time visitors. Bare granite sheets plunging headlong into often raging surf serve to produce a sometimes awesome cataclysm between land and sea.

The highlands are those parts of the province where metamorphosed igneous and sedimentary rocks have either intruded through the pre-existing lowland sediments or resisted erosion to a better degree than the surrounding softer rock. The Cape Breton Highlands are the most notable example. The Cobequid Mountains of Cumberland and Colchester counties, the Antigonish highlands, and the North Mountain, which runs parallel with the Fundy Shore from Cape Blomidon to Digby Neck, are the other Nova Scotia highlands. Appearing as sharp ridges when viewed from below, the highlands are actually flat tablelands. This may be observed first-hand in the Cape Breton Highlands National Park. From Ingonish to Cheticamp, the Cabot Trail rises and crosses over the tablelands, several hundred metres above sea level.

The outstanding feature of the highlands is the rectilinear coastlines. In contrast with the hundreds of bays and peninsulas of the Atlantic coast, the shorelines of the Bay of Fundy and western Cape Breton are virtually straight. In the Cape Breton Highlands uplifted cliffs soar hundreds of metres directly up from the ocean to create stretches of spectacular landscape which can be viewed while driving the world-famous Cabot Trail. Less well known, but no less spectacular, are the cliffs of the Bay of Fundy, which are interspersed with fossils and unusual minerals. The cliffs at Joggins and those outside Parrsboro attract fossil hunters and rockhounds from around the world.

Anyone with a special interest in geology and geographical formations should obtain a copy of the *Geological Highway Map of Nova Scotia*, which details 92 geological and geographical features of note throughout the province. As well, information is provided on glaciation, continental drift and offshore geology as it affects Nova Scotia. Also of interest is Joanne Light's *Coastal Nova Scotia,* which gives a detailed description of much of the province's coastal geography and geology.

HISTORY

The earliest known inhabitants of Nova Scotia were Paleo-Indians, probably surviving as hunters of caribou in a land still partially covered with glaciers and much colder than it is today. However, little is known of these early people and there is a gap in the archaeological record of thousands of years between them and the later aboriginal peoples.

When Europeans first started probing the coastline in the fifteenth, sixteenth and seventeenth centuries, they found Nova Scotia inhabited by people now known as the Mi'kmaq. At one time numerous, the Mi'kmaq were once part of the Wabanaki Confederation, which included, among others, the Malecites of New Brunswick and the Penobscots of Maine. Early records report their total numbers at between 2,000 and 4,000, although the accuracy of these low estimates is doubtful and disputed. Prior to the arrival of Europeans, the Mi'kmaq followed a seasonal routine, hunting moose and caribou in the winter and migrating in the summer to the coast to undertake fishing, shellfish gathering and, occasionally, hunting seals and whales. Upon the establishment of the first European settlements, the Mi'kmaq gradually altered their way of life, redirecting their attention to the collection of furs and hides for trade purposes and abandoning many of their earlier customs.

The Mi'kmaq and the early French settlers coexisted peacefully. However, when France and England began their long and bloody fight for control of North America, the native peoples and the settlers became pawns in a conflict that lasted more than 150 years. Loyal allies of the French to the end, the Mi'kmaq did not fare well at the hands of the English. Regrettably, the mistreatment and betrayal of trust of the native peoples was a chapter of history that played out in Nova Scotia in very much the same way as in other parts of the New World. The story may eventually have a happier ending as recent Canadian court decisions have significantly expanded the Mi'kmaq's traditional rights to exploit the resources of Nova Scotia. There are very positive signs that things are turning around and that the poverty and despair that for so long characterized aboriginal life in Nova Scotia may finally be coming to an end. Anyone with an interest in Aboriginal history and culture should be sure to visit the Nova Scotia Museum of Natural History, which has excellent information and exhibits on this subject.

The first non-native sailors to land on Nova Scotia's coast were probably Norsemen, arriving some time around the year 1000 AD, when Leif Ericson was probing south from Greenland. Definite traces of Norse settlement have been found at L'Anse aux Meadows in Newfoundland, while Nova Scotia has long been considered by most historians to be the fabled Vinland or Markland, mentioned in Norse chronicles. Evidence of this is found in the many Mi'kmaq petroglyphs depicting European-type vessels. Further evidence includes a curious stone bearing a rune-like inscription that was unearthed in Yarmouth County and is now on display in the Yarmouth museum.

The next European visit to Nova Scotia is generally thought to be the John Cabot expedition of 1497, but don't tell that to followers of Prince Henry Sinclair, the Earl of Orkney, who, it is said, not only made landfall in Nova Scotia in 1398 but extensively explored the province and even built a castle there. Sinclair is a fascinating semi-mythical figure associated with the Knights Templar and Rosslyn castle, made famous in *The Da Vinci Code* as the resting place of the Holy Grail. While there is a growing body of believers in the Sinclair saga, enough to put on a serious 600th anniversary celebration in 1998, most historians take the story with a huge grain of salt.

Someone who definitely visited Nova Scotia was John Cabot, accompanied by his son Sebastian in 1497. Inspired, no doubt, by the tales of Columbus and his success to the South, Cabot, also an Italian, sailing under the flag of England for Bristol merchants, dropped anchor off the shores of Cape Breton. Although he did not find the route to India that he was seeking, Cabot did report on the rich fishing grounds of the northwest Atlantic. Within years of his return to Europe, Cabot's voyage was retraced hundreds of times annually by fishing fleets from Spain, Portugal, France and England. In 1997, Cabot's voyage was retraced once again in a replica of his small ship the *Matthew,* which touched at a number of Nova Scotia and Newfoundland destinations to commemorate the 500th anniversary of this momentous journey.

Initially, the earliest fishermen simply filled their holds and returned without landing, but as the necessity for drying and salting the fish became apparent, small settlements were established along Newfoundland and Nova Scotia's coasts. The town of Canso in Nova Scotia and the city of St. John's in Newfoundland were founded in this manner. However, it was not until more than a hundred years after the Cabot voyage that the English began to realize the value of what this transplanted Italian adventurer had discovered. Even then, it took France, England's sworn enemy, to first covet Nova Scotia before the English sat up and took notice. France had expressed an interest in North America as far back as the voyages of Jacques Cartier in the 1530s. Cartier had sailed up the St. Lawrence River as far as present-day Montreal and the French realized the economic potential of a colony that could expand inland along this mighty waterway.

Although Acadia (the French name for the territory that includes present-day Nova Scotia) did not have the economic importance of New France (Quebec) or New England, it did have great strategic value. Its many harbours and bays were able to provide shelter to naval and armed forces ready to strike north or south into the chief supply lanes of France or England. As well, the proximity to the fishing grounds was not without value. Recognizing this, the French Crown, interested in securing a more tangible foothold in the New World, granted the Sieur de Monts exclusive trade and fishing rights in the area providing he would establish a permanent settlement. In 1604, de Monts and 79 other men including Samuel de Champlain, later dubbed the "Father of New France," set sail to firmly establish the French presence in North America. Unwittingly, they were setting in motion a series of events that would make Nova Scotia one of the bloodiest battlegrounds in North America, culminating in the expulsion of the Acadians and the siege of Louisbourg.

After an initial attempt to settle on St. Croix Island on the present day

New Brunswick–Maine border, the group moved across the Bay of Fundy to the mouth of the Annapolis River and there built a habitation that they named Port Royal.

Social life at the new settlement was not what the gentlemen pioneers were accustomed to in France. Champlain, in an attempt to combat boredom, established the Order of Good Cheer, a social club whereby each of the principal gentlemen at the habitation took turns being Chief Steward for a week. It was his job to provide a feast for the others and soon a friendly rivalry developed to see who could purvey the finest, most exotic meals from what the new land had to offer. The local Mi'kmaq were welcome at these gatherings, and it was this initial hospitality and subsequent religious kinship when the Mi'kmaq accepted Catholicism, that helped cement the French-Indian alliance against the English that lasted until the final French defeat. The Order of Good Cheer is handed out by the government today as it was 400 years ago by the then government at the Habitation.

While Champlain moved on from Port Royal to found other French settlements, most notably Quebec in 1608, the English had settled first in Jamestown, Virginia, and later, further north in Plymouth and Massachusetts Bay. Concerned about being caught between the Spanish to the south and the French to the north, they conveniently remembered that in 1497 Cabot had claimed Nova Scotia for England. In 1621, Sir William Alexander, a Scotsman in the court of James I, convinced the king that New Scotland should be established in the area the French were calling Acadie. A grant was given, as was permission to establish an order of Knight Baronets who would lead settlers into this new colony. Because the grant was in Latin, New Scotland became Nova Scotia. Alexander, apparently one for attending to the proper details of pageantry, also received a coat of arms and flag for his venture. The name, flag and coat of arms are all that remain today of Alexander's colonizing efforts. No English or Scottish settlers actually made it to Nova Scotia under the guidance of Alexander.

An interesting footnote to Alexander's schemes was the fact that the investiture ceremony for the Knight Baronets required that each prospective candidate actually be in Nova Scotia when invested. As the English king had no intention of going to Nova Scotia to perform the rites, a portion of Edinburgh Castle was designated part of Nova Scotia and it was here that the ceremony took place. This small plot of land is still part of Nova Scotia and it is ironic indeed that the man who wanted Nova Scotia to be a part of Scotland succeeded only in making a part of Scotland Nova Scotian.

For the French, Acadia was always regarded as secondary in importance to New France, and no serious efforts at permanent settlement were made. The lack of colonists and the indifference of the motherland, as well as rivalry between the commanders of the various outposts in Acadia, led to minimal immigration at a time when colonies to the south and west were rapidly expanding. From 1667 through to 1750, the population of Acadia grew from 500 settlers to 10,000 persons, all living on the peninsula of present-day Nova Scotia. Settlements spread out from Port Royal along the length of the Annapolis Valley and around the fertile tidelands of the

Minas Basin and Chignecto Bay. Using techniques learned in France, the Acadians built dykes to reclaim the marshlands extending around tidal estuaries of the rivers that flow into the Bay of Fundy. They engaged primarily in agriculture, including the first extensive use of orchards in North America, as well as fishing and fur trading when the opportunity presented itself.

From 1632 to 1710 the French remained more or less in control of Acadia, extending their presence into Cape Breton and the Northumberland Strait area. Whatever peace existed between the English and French during this period was short-lived, and there was never a guarantee that raids would not take place at any time. The Acadian settlements were harassed by New Englanders who, in turn, were being attacked regularly by French-Indian war parties organized primarily in New France and present day New Brunswick. In 1710 the New Englanders, incited by recent Indian massacres in Massachusetts, decided to capture Port Royal, more because it was poorly defended than because it constituted any real threat. A group of militiamen led by Colonel Nicholson forced capitulation without much difficulty. The settlement was renamed Annapolis Royal in honour of Queen Anne and a military government imposed. In 1713, the Treaty of Utrecht formally ceded most of Acadia to England, leaving only Cape Breton Island, or Ile Royale as it was then known, under French rule. This half measure ensured that the struggle would continue.

With one last stronghold on the East Coast, France realized that it needed a base that would effectively protect the entrance to the St. Lawrence and act as a deterrent to further English expansion northward. They conceived a fortress so large and impregnable that attacking it would be futile. After careful site selection, work was begun on a massive installation at English Harbour, tactfully renamed Louisbourg in honour of the French king. Despite astronomical construction costs and inhospitable working conditions, the French managed within 25 years to erect a walled city garrisoned with thousands of troops and bristling with about 800 guns. It turned out to be France's greatest folly. Although many Acadian families did resettle in Cape Breton, they took no real interest in military affairs and chose Isle Madame and the west side of the island because of the farming and fishing opportunities available in those locales. The fortress became an isolated outpost, rampant with drunkenness, disease and mutiny. When war broke out again in 1744, Governor Shirley of Massachusetts raised an expedition to storm the fort. William Pepperell led a 49-day siege that saw every building but one damaged by cannon fire. Dispirited, the French surrendered, much to the consternation of their superiors in France who had been convinced Louisbourg could not be taken. Victory proved no blessing for the New Englanders, for more than 1,000 perished in the succeeding winter. A disastrous attempt was made on behalf of the French by Duc d'Anville to recapture Louisbourg, which ended in the loss of thousands of men and dozens of ships without a shot being fired. The French proved better at negotiating and Louisbourg was returned to France by treaty in 1748. Needless to say, the New Englanders were outraged.

Both England and France knew that the latest peace was but a respite in the continuing war. While the French rebuilt Louisbourg, the English set about establishing their own base as a counterbalance. In 1749, the settlement of Halifax was founded on a hilly peninsula that juts into one of the great natural harbours in the world and work began on the fortress that was to be known as the Citadel.

Around this time, the English governors of Nova Scotia became concerned about the high number of Acadians in the colony and the lack of English-speaking colonists. English colonists were reluctant to immigrate to a territory with an uncertain future. Incentives were therefore offered to Protestants in other parts of Europe to establish themselves in Nova Scotia. This resulted in the recruitment of German, Swiss and French Protestants, the first of whom landed in Halifax in 1750. Attracted by the promise of sizeable land grants, these settlers soon founded Lunenburg and other South Shore communities and therein began the great seafaring tradition of Nova Scotia.

The idea of expelling the Acadians was first raised by Colonel Nicholson, the capturer of Port Royal, in 1710. For the next 40 years, the Acadians remained neutral and signed the Oath of Allegiance to the British throne after being given assurances that they would not have to take arms against the French and the Mi'kmaq. However, by 1755 war once again appeared inevitable and a delegation from Grand Pré was ordered to Halifax to sign away their neutrality. They refused and Governor Lawrence and his council set in motion the expulsion order.

This Grand Dérangement is without question Nova Scotia's most widely known historical event, largely because of the popularity of Henry Wadsworth Longfellow's poem *Evangeline*. Published long after the deportation, this epic poem describes the travails of the fictional heroine Evangeline and her lover Gabriel. Separated at the time of the expulsion, the two lovers searched for one another for a lifetime, only to be reunited on his deathbed. While capturing the agony of a people torn from the only homeland they knew, the poem is inaccurate historically, placing the blame for the expulsion order on the British in London. In fact, the order to expel came from Governor Lawrence in Halifax without prior knowledge or approval of the home government. The actual expulsion was carried out largely by New Englanders who had long been amazed by the fact that foreign nationals, as they viewed the Acadians, had been allowed to occupy the best farmland in the colony. Governor Shirley (of Louisbourg fame) had repeatedly advocated some form of confiscation of Acadian lands. Regardless of who was to blame, over 6,000 of the 10,000 Acadians were loaded onto boats and deported to points throughout the American colonies. The most famous group ended up in Louisiana, where they metamorphosed into the Cajuns, a derivation of the word Acadian. Over the years, many of the deportees made their way back to their beloved Acadia. Some 900 walked from Boston only to find their farms occupied by New Englanders. Undaunted, they continued on to settle an unoccupied area between Yarmouth and Digby, now known as the French Shore.

The expulsion was an event that solidified the Acadians as a people. Over 350 years after this tragic event, the Acadians are more unified in their culture and language than any other of the founding peoples of Nova Scotia.

With the threat of Acadian resistance removed, the British were free to respond more directly to the French in Cape Breton when the Seven Years War broke out in 1756. An extension of a European conflict, the war was truly a world war, with engagements on three continents. Both France and England realized that the loser would be permanently eliminated as a power in North America. Determined to capture the walled city of Quebec, the stronghold of French power in New France, Britain knew it must first deal with the refortified Louisbourg. To this end, General Amherst and Admiral Boscawen assembled a force of 23,000 men and 40 ships in Halifax. Louisbourg itself had 8,000 defenders. In 1758, the British fleet entered Gabarus Bay to the south of Louisbourg. A series of bloody engagements followed and General James Wolfe, who later died on the Plains of Abraham after leading the British to victory at Quebec, succeeded in landing the British force with heavy losses and hand-to-hand fighting. A seven-week siege eventually forced the outnumbered and beleaguered defenders to capitulate. With Louisbourg out of the way, the British were able to strike up the St. Lawrence into the heart of New France. The French were doomed. In 1763, by the Treaty of Paris, France ceded all but her most insignificant North American possessions to England.

It is fair comment on the fortunes of war to note that after its capture, the great Fortress of Louisbourg was razed brick by brick and the land upon which it was built reverted to woods and pastures. Its deeds and men, so important in the history of North America, were forgotten for over 200 years, while Halifax, the brash and belated competitor, rose to become the largest British naval depot in the New World.

With the expulsion of the Acadians and the dispersal of many of the military personnel stationed there during the Seven Years War, Nova Scotia was virtually depopulated at a time when land was becoming scarce in New England and political oppression in Europe was forcing many to think of emigrating. A 50-year period of population growth in Nova Scotia ensued, wave after wave of newcomers settled in different areas of the province, each with their own reasons for coming and each indelibly stamping the colony with their own culture and customs.

Among the first to arrive were the New England Planters. Long familiar with, and envious of, the fertile dykelands of the Acadians, this group needed little persuasion to accept the free land grants being offered by Governor Lawrence. From 1760 on, more than 7,000 New Englanders arrived. In addition to the farmers, there were fishermen — founders of Yarmouth, Barrington and Liverpool — who relocated to be closer to their favoured fishing grounds. From Northern Ireland came Ulstermen, many of whom had stopped briefly in New Hampshire until tempted north to the Colchester County area where they established Truro and Onslow. Yorkshire farmers chose the abandoned Acadian lands of Chignecto Bay, where they mingled with the already settled New Englanders. To Pictou

County, in 1773, came the first of many shiploads of Highland Scots, piped ashore by a stowaway who had kept them amused during an arduous voyage on the ship *Hector*. These Scots, many of them tenants evicted as a result of the Highland Clearance Acts, settled first around the lowland shores of Northumberland Strait and later in Cape Breton, where the highlands reminded them of home.

The most spectacular immigration was that of the United Empire Loyalists in the years immediately following the American Revolution. Scorned in the new republic, over 20,000 shipped out of New York to Nova Scotia during a two-year period. They founded the town of Shelburne, which burgeoned to almost 10,000 people overnight. However, high hopes and hard work could not compensate for the paucity of available land and the fact that most of the Loyalists had been merchants rather than farmers or fishermen. Within a few years, a large number of the United Empire Loyalists had either returned to the United States, or moved westward to New Brunswick and Ontario.

Another group that sought refuge in Nova Scotia during this period were American blacks. Slavery had ended in Nova Scotia by 1800 and many American blacks, both freemen and escaping slaves, arrived in Nova Scotia. They were given land grants on the same terms and conditions as any other immigrants. Today, their descendants may be found in communities in all counties of the province.

If the newly arrived settlers expected that the end of the Seven Years War would usher in a period of peace in North America, they were wrong. War in one form or another continued, beginning with the American Revolution in 1775 and not ending until the War of 1812. When the War of Independence broke out many Americans, realizing that Nova Scotia was subject to the same oppressive taxation acts and lack of direct political representation that so irked the American colonists, assumed that Nova Scotia would join as the fourteenth rebellious colony. What they did not realize was that Nova Scotia was much more dependent upon the British Crown than were the other colonies. Having been very recently settled, Nova Scotia's economy was not self-supporting. As well, democratic government was a new experience in Nova Scotia and few Nova Scotians were aware of the latitude of self-government that their southern neighbours had come to expect as a right. In fact, at the outbreak of the revolution, Nova Scotia was saddled with probably the most corrupt and inept administration of any of the colonies, as had been revealed by an investigation in 1773. The British government promptly attempted to quash the findings, but the report led to the same type of unrest prevalent in New England. Indeed, there was popular sympathy with the pro-revolutionary movement among a great part of the population, particularly those who had come north from New England, many of whom had left close relatives behind. The pro-American sentiment reached a high in Cumberland County, where Jonathan Eddy and a small band of sympathizers attempted to capture Fort Cumberland in the name of "the United Colonies of America." The makeshift rebels were easily dispersed by regulars of the British Army, with few casualties on either side. Any further thoughts of Nova Scotia joining the revolution were dispelled when the British fleet and army from Boston evacuated to Halifax, making it the centre of British operations in America. With the might of the British Empire right on their doorstep, most recalcitrant Nova Scotians fell into line. This success was aided no doubt by the fact that American privateers had begun making indiscriminate raids on the entire British Atlantic coast, much to the annoyance of the residents, many of whom considered themselves neutral.

By the end of the hostilities in 1783, most Nova Scotians were staunchly pro-British. These sentiments were augmented by the large numbers of Loyalists who arrived in the province not long thereafter.

If Nova Scotians were marginally pro-British during the revolution, they became downright anti-American in the period that followed. They were angered by concessions promised to them that were granted to Americans under the Treaty of Versailles, particularly in regard to fisheries and trade. They were more angered when the United States openly sided with the French during the Napoleonic Wars, providing protection and favouritism to French privateers who preyed on Nova Scotia shipping. When the War of 1812 erupted, Nova Scotians had no doubts as to whom they would support and many welcomed the opportunity to get involved in what to them had been for some time an "undeclared" war.

Thousands of Nova Scotians served in the British forces, most voluntarily and some by impressment. The most significant role in the conflict played by many a Nova Scotian was as a privateersman. Ship owner after ship owner applied for and received letters of marque, which allowed them to capture American merchant ships and share in the booty as distributed by the Prize Court in Halifax and elsewhere. Nova Scotians, being excellent seamen, made excellent privateers. One ship alone, the *Liverpool Packet*, captured 50 prizes and caused a commercial panic in Boston.

At the conclusion of hostilities in 1814, former merchants and sailors were wealthy men, and Nova Scotia was a very prosperous colony indeed. More importantly, 1814 marked the final end of hostilities in the region, something unknown since the coming of the first Europeans. A peace with the United States was established, which remains unbroken to this day. In Nova Scotia, resentment of Americans quickly died down and the traditional links with New England were re-established, forming a friendship that is probably closer than that shared between any other part of Canada and the United States.

Peace brought no less prosperity than war. Nova Scotians embarked upon a period of seafaring and shipbuilding unexcelled in North American history. Trade had always been a bulwark of the economy, with fish and lumber being exported to Europe and the West Indies, while manufactured goods, sugar and tobacco filled the holds on return voyages.

Access to the burgeoning American market, both legal and illegal, provided another impetus for Nova Scotia to become a carrier of the world's goods. At first localized in Pictou, Yarmouth and Liverpool, the shipbuilding industry expanded to all shores. In 1854 alone 244 vessels were launched, and by 1875, Nova Scotia had 2,800 ships plying the seas from Australia to Alaska. Towns such as Yarmouth could boast registered tonnage comparable to Glasgow or Boston. Notable not only for their numbers, Nova Scotian ships were respected for their size and design. The *William D Lawrence*, the largest wooden ship ever built in Canada, was laid down at tiny Maitland on the Fundy Shore, while Donald MacKay, designer and builder of the famous clipper ships, learned his trade at the shipyards of Shelburne. The coming of the age of steam did not ring a death knell to the industry. Samuel Cunard, a native of Halifax, instituted the first trans-Atlantic steamship service, a feat that made him a millionaire and allowed him to found the White Star Line, owner of such prestigious ships as the *Queen Mary, Queen Elizabeth II* and the *Titanic*. The seafaring tradition of Nova Scotia continued well into the twentieth century, when working schooners such as the *Bluenose* were unbeatable in ocean racing.

After the American War of Independence, Britain was convinced that it had allowed the 13 colonies too much freedom of self-government and was determined not to repeat the mistake in Nova Scotia or any other Canadian colony. Nova Scotia did have an assembly of elected representatives before and after the revolution, but real power had always rested with the governor and his council, who were appointees of London and answerable to the will of Parliament. During the 1820s and 1830s, a group of reformers led by Joseph Howe, son of a Loyalist, began demanding responsible government with accountability of appointed officials. Howe's newspaper, *The Nova Scotian*, attacked the mismanagement and misuse of public funds by appointed officials, giving rise to a charge of criminal libel. Defending himself, Howe spoke for six hours, using the opportunity to showcase his views on reform and responsible government. Following his acquittal, the reform movement gained momentum until the British government, faced with increasing pressure at home from Liberals and the spectre of rebellion in Upper and Lower Canada, granted Nova Scotia self-government in 1848.

Hardly having had the time to savour the control they now had over their own destiny, Nova Scotians entered discussions with other Canadian provinces aimed at producing a confederation with a central federal government. After conferences in London, Quebec and Charlottetown, an agreement was reached, and in 1867 the Dominion of Canada was born, with Nova Scotia as a founding member along with Quebec, Ontario and New Brunswick. Prince Edward Island and Newfoundland had cautiously opted out of discussions, preferring a wait-and-see approach.

To many Nova Scotians, including Joseph Howe, confederation was a black day for Nova Scotia. It seemed more than coincidental to them that Nova Scotia entered a period of decline almost from the moment the union was entered. Certainly a good argument can be made for this point of view if only from the standpoint that the provinces of Ontario and Quebec had a vastly greater population than Nova Scotia and were able, through sheer numbers, to control the policies of the federal government to the detriment of the less-populated areas. However, this viewpoint ignores the fact that after 1867 the shipping industry declined, not only in Nova Scotia but almost everywhere. New immigration had moved the population centres and major markets for Nova Scotian goods ever westward, making the cost of Nova Scotian products uncompetitive. As well, Nova Scotia's resources were overworked and depleted in comparison to the new lands being opened in the west. Whatever the cause, Nova Scotia's Golden Age came to an end and the province went from being one of Britain's most prosperous colonies to a so-called "have-not" province in the new union.

Except for boom periods during both world wars, Nova Scotia's economy has lagged behind the other provinces throughout most of the twentieth century. The slow pace of development has had its brighter side. The unspoiled quality and tranquillity of much of the landscape that is so attractive to natives and visitors alike is largely attributable to the fact that Nova Scotia has been spared the more notorious scourges of twentieth-century progress. Pollution, unfettered land erosion, and urban blight are not the problems they are in many other North American communities, although in recent years the clear cutting of the forests has increased at a pace bordering on madness.

For the past several years, the United Nations has ranked Canada as one of the best places to live in the world, and if you ask many Canadians, they will tell you that Nova Scotia is one of the best places to live in Canada. Not only is the standard of living high, but the quality of life in Nova Scotia is exceptional. Recently, the province has attracted more and more well-educated and well-travelled newcomers who have established a variety of high-tech companies as well as work-at-home businesses such as writing, painting and direct sales. Also of note is the film industry, which has discovered that Nova Scotia's many unique and unspoiled villages are perfect backdrops for movie and television productions.

The new millennium dawned brightly for Nova Scotia when, on January 1, 2000, the first offshore natural gas was pumped into a billion-dollar pipeline to New England. Despite the recent world-wide economic downturn, Nova Scotia has remained relatively unscathed. There is no doubt that Nova Scotia is once again moving to the forefront as a place to live and work, but the truth is, it has always been a wonderful place for a vacation.

WHEN TO VISIT

Despite the fact that Nova Scotia juts into the Atlantic Ocean, its weather patterns are more typically continental than maritime. This is because most mid-latitude North American weather systems originate over the continent and travel west to east. Nevertheless, the presence of the ocean acts as a moderating influence on the continental air masses so that coastal areas show less fluctuation in temperatures through the year than do inland areas. The maritime factor also adds to the unpredictability of the weather. Any visitor from another part of the continent who regularly watches the weather forecasts while in Nova Scotia will note that they are not as reliable as elsewhere, sometimes predicting rain for days when there isn't a cloud in the sky and less fortuitously, predicting sunshine for days when only ducks could be happy with the conditions. These wild inaccuracies in forecasting are not the result of incompetent meteorologists, but rather the complexity of factors that make up the weather. Nova Scotians have come to accept this unpredictable weather with stoicism and the visitor would be well advised to make daily plans as the weather unfolds and not as it has been predicted.

If you are tempted to visit Nova Scotia in the spring, make sure you time your visit for late May or early June, as any earlier will risk inclement weather, including snow. Winter hangs on in Nova Scotia and seldom does the province enjoy a true spring. However, by the first two weeks in June you can usually be assured of mild or even hot days. One good reason to visit Nova Scotia in the late spring is to tour the Annapolis Valley with its wonderful apple and cherry blossoms.

Nova Scotian summers are not long — true summer temperatures (those in excess of 20º C) are not reached consistently until late June and only last until the end of August, although Indian Summers may stretch warmer temperatures through October. The southwest part of the province enjoys a slightly longer summer season while highland areas may not even have two complete hot months. Summer temperatures are comfortable with few days being extremely hot or cold. Coastal locations are almost always cooler than those in the interior, with the result that anyone who dislikes high temperatures can find relief by heading to the beach as thousands of Nova Scotians do on any day the mercury rises above 24º C. While July and August are both the least windy and least rainy months of the year, one can expect some measurable precipitation one of every three days on average.

Weather systems travel fairly quickly over the province and this, combined with the oceanic influence, means there are few prolonged dry spells, although if you toured the province in the summer of 1997 you would have thought this description downright ludicrous, as it did not rain for almost 45 straight days! This was a particularly bad time for the farmers, but was simply wonderful for the tourists. Alas, this summer dryness has not proven consistent since then and precipitation throughout the summer months varies from year to year. Thunderstorms are less common than in most other parts of Canada — occurring about 10 days of the year. However, no one will disagree that when it's hot and dry, the place to be is near the ocean.

Autumn is the most enjoyable season in Nova Scotia, highlighted by the turning foliage and crisp dry air. September temperatures are not significantly lower than those of July and August. The moderating influence of the ocean prolongs the autumn season well into November or even December along the coast, and in some years it is not unusual to have summer-like temperatures throughout much of October. Generally, the freezing point is reached in late November. Precipitation in the fall is greater than that in summer, but not to such a great extent as to make the weather unpleasant. The person who prefers moderate temperatures to the heat of the high summer will find autumn a rewarding time to visit Nova Scotia. For many

Nova Scotians, the authors included, this is their favourite time of year.

Nova Scotia is not a winter wonderland. While, technically, winter temperatures are not that extreme by Canadian standards, the weather is unpredictable and too often rain follows a nice snowfall. However, there are parts of Nova Scotia, most notably Cape Breton and the Cobequid highlands, where snowfall is substantial and winter recreation opportunities abound. No discussion of Nova Scotia weather is complete without at least some mention of fog. Warm continental air passing over the cold waters of the Atlantic and the Bay of Fundy have made Nova Scotia's southwest coast one of the foggiest places on the planet. In any given year, more than 90 days along this coast may well be foggy. The likelihood of fog reduces substantially as one moves inland or northward, with the warm waters of the Northumberland Strait being relatively fog free.

Fortunately, fog tends to roll inland at night and retreat offshore during the day. One should not be dismayed at being fogbound at breakfast because there is a high probability that the fog will have gone out to sea by noon. To some, fog is a sinister phenomenon that creates feelings of claustrophobia, while to others it adds a cloak of secrecy or mystery to the countryside or to a seascape. Whatever your perception, fog is as inexorably a part of Nova Scotia weather as the sun. The one real concern about fog is that it can seriously disrupt air travel plans, as it did in the summer of 2005.

It would be remiss not to mention that Nova Scotia is visited by the very occasional hurricane. Although Nova Scotia often gets the remnants of hurricanes that have been downgraded to tropical storms, with attendant rains and huge waves (much to the delight of surfers), true hurricanes are very rare. For the first time in living memory, Nova Scotia was landfall for a hurricane in September, 2003. Hurricane Juan cut a swath of destruction from Halifax to the Northumberland Strait the like of which has seldom been witnessed in Canada. Although nowhere near the magnitude of Katrina and other recent mega-destructive hurricanes, Juan did serious damage to a number of beloved places such as Point Pleasant Park and the Public Gardens in Halifax. However, over seven years after the event, recovery has been swift. Although some places were forever altered, they were not destroyed and some might say are better now than before Juan.

Lest the prospective visitor to Nova Scotia be unduly alarmed by the foregoing comments on the weather, some statistics are in order. Environment Canada estimates that over 70 per cent of days in Nova Scotia are suitable for landscape touring (the most popular pastime of Nova Scotia tourists) throughout the year. This rises to a high of almost 90 per cent in August and September, and even in January exceeds 60 per cent. Also, surprising to most, Nova Scotia was recently identified by Environment Canada as the warmest province in the country.

Listed below are the best times of year for selected activities. It will help you choose suitable dates for your visit.

1. Antiques, arts and crafts — June 15 to September 15. Many antique stores and craft galleries are seasonal operations.

2. Beaches — August. Beach aficionados will find that water and air temperatures are best during the month of August, but September is not far behind.

3. Bicycle touring — July 15 to October 1. This is the driest and warmest time of the year.

4. Birding — May 15 to October 1. Highlights include the spring and fall migrations. Sea bird colonies are most interesting in June and early July.

5. General touring, including visiting museums and historic sites — July 15 to September 15. Many of the local and provincial museums and attractions close shortly after the Labour Day weekend.

6. Golf — September 1 to October 15. The courses are in tip-top shape and usually uncrowded.

7. Hiking — July 15 to October 1. The trails are usually driest by late summer, and least crowded in September.

8. Sea kayaking — August 1 to October 1. The water temperature is warmest and the winds are mildest, especially during August.

BEFORE YOU GO

Visiting Requirements for Non-Residents of Canada

Entrance requirements to Canada are changing rapidly and getting stricter by the year. Where simple identification was once sufficient for America and most European (EU) countries, that is no longer the case post 9/11. Canada is working closely with the United States in upgrading security at the borders, which means that passports are now a necessity for all visitors, including Americans; not because Canada requires one to get in, but because the United States requires all citizens returning from Canada or elsewhere to have a valid passport. In addition, visas are required for visitors from many countries, although the United States and most EU countries are exempt. Check with Citizenship and Immigration Canada on the internet to determine whether you need a visa. http://www.cic.gc.ca/english/visit/visas.asp

What will it Cost?

Accommodations, dining and admission to attractions such as museums are generally in accord with prices throughout Canada and the United States, or perhaps a bit lower, certainly far less than most large North American urban centres. By European standards, Nova Scotia is a bargain. Most visitors from other Canadian provinces will find prices for inns pleasantly low.

Recent prolonged hikes in the price of gasoline have had the effect of keeping tourists closer to their homes and traveling less. This has had a negative impact on Nova Scotia's tourism numbers as it has elsewhere; however, the price of gas should not be a deterrent for the well-informed visitor. Gas prices in Nova Scotia are currently much closer to U.S. prices than in the past and are still well below those in most other countries. Since Nova Scotia is such a compact province with so much to see, the visitor traveling by automobile will spend far less on gas here than most other places where a drive of two or three hours or even a day between destinations is common. Finally, Nova Scotia is the type of place where you can do a lot of walking and little driving if you so wish. Halifax and Nova Scotia's many scenic towns such as Lunenburg, Chester, Baddeck, Annapolis Royal, Pictou and many others are best explored on foot and at leisure. What does make sense, with high gas prices seemingly here to stay, is to fly to Halifax and rent a car here as opposed to driving from, say, New York or Toronto. One item that we are pleased to report since the last edition is that taxes that affect tourists have decreased. In Nova Scotia, almost everything is subject to a Harmonized Sales Tax (HST). Nova Scotia and several other eastern provinces elected to unite their provincial sales taxes with the federal government's Goods and Services Tax (GST). Until recently, that tax was 15%; however, it is now set at 13%. While no one particularly likes paying taxes, it is heartening to know that we are all paying less for a Nova Scotia vacation than previously. It should be noted that foreign visitors can keep receipts and claim a full rebate on many taxable items such as accommodations. Forms for claiming the rebate are usually available at international border crossing sites. However, that being said, it would seem to make a lot of sense to include the tax in the price of goods as is done with the V.A.T. in Europe. People like to know that the price on the label or menu is the price they will pay for that item.

All in all, a vacation in Nova Scotia is no more expensive than a visit to anywhere else in Canada or many of the New England states, and it is a lot less crowded.

American dollars are accepted at virtually all places of business in Nova Scotia; however, we recommend that American visitors use Canadian dollars. While there exists a government-instituted Fair Exchange program, which virtually guarantees the proper exchange on American dollars, we strongly recommend that visitors from anywhere, including other parts of Canada, the United States and Europe, take advantage of Automated Teller Machines (ATMS), which are now found everywhere in the province. At these, you can have direct access to your account and receive the best exchange rate possible. Using ATMs also has the advantage of eliminating the worries of carrying large amounts of cash or traveller's cheques. Most credit cards are accepted universally in Nova Scotia.

Tourist Information
When the first edition of this guide was published fifteen years ago nobody had a Web site. Today virtually every aspect of the tourism industry is saturated with web content and separating the wheat from the chaff can be a problem. In this book we have attempted to identify the 'official' Web sites where possible. With respect to accommodations and dining, the web has made picking the right spot a lot easier. It is no longer necessary to give detailed descriptions of rooms, settings or menus — they are usually online for anyone to see. Choices made in advance are no longer simply good guesses. Wherever possible we

have provided web addresses so that you can see for yourselves what the various attractions, places to stay and places to eat have to offer. That being said, the Nova Scotia government annually produces some of the finest tourism materials available from any state or province. *Doers' & Dreamers' Travel Guide* is an invaluable free source of up-to-date information, including the latest accommodation rates and the seasonal opening and closing dates for all major attractions. The book is available free of charge and can be ordered online, along with many other publications, at www.novascotia.com or by calling 1-800-565-0000 in Canada and the United States and 1-902-425-5781 outside North America. The Web site is an excellent resource, on which you can book accommodations, plan your trip or take a virtual tour of the province. It is viewable in French and German as well as English.

Throughout this volume, you will see numerous references to other materials that will assist you in planning your Nova Scotia vacation. Most of these can be ordered from The Bookmark, 5686 Spring Garden Road, Halifax, NS, B3J 1H5, (902) 423-0419, www.bookmarkpei.com; or you can look for them on the web through amazon.com (US), amazon.ca (Canada) or chapters.indigo.ca, a large Canadian chain. Online is the best bet for books that are out of print. If you're looking especially for maps and travel books then Maps and More is the place. They can be contacted at www.mapsandducks.com.

GETTING THERE

Nova Scotia may hold a reputation for being off the beaten path, but it is in no way difficult to get to. Halifax Stanfield International Airport, named for a good man and honest politician, has regular direct air service to most major Canadian centres. Recently, the United States has instituted customs pre-clearance at Halifax with the result that most major American airlines now fly to Nova Scotia. Direct flights are now available to Boston, New York, Washington, Chicago and Detroit. There is daily air service linking Halifax to London, and during tourist season, regular flights to many continental cities on various charter airlines.

Most tourists that are driving enter Nova Scotia via Amherst on the Trans-Canada Highway, which links the province to New Brunswick and the rest of Canada. During the summer months, American visitors have the option of taking the ferry from either Portland or Bar Harbor, Maine, directly to Yarmouth. For those already in Canada, Nova Scotia can be reached by ferry from New Brunswick, Prince Edward Island and Newfoundland. Reservations on all of these ferries are a necessity at all but the slowest times of year. For the ferry from Saint John, New Brunswick–Digby or Wood Islands, Prince Edward Island–Caribou, try 1-888-249-7245 or www.nfl-bay.com; for Port aux Basques, Newfoundland–North Sydney, 1-800-341-7981 or www.marine-atlantic.ca. At the time of publication the government was contemplating closing the Bay Ferries between Saint John, New Brunswick and Digby, Nova Scotia service so be sure to check the Web site before making your travel plans.

A sea trip is a great way to prepare yourself for a visit to Nova Scotia and it adds a sense of adventure to your vacation. If the weather is clear there is a very real chance of seeing whales and porpoises as well as many types of seabirds.

GETTING AROUND

Nova Scotia is made for auto touring. There are ten major designated scenic routes that circle the province, plus six alternate routes that visit some of the less-known areas. No matter where you enter Nova Scotia, you can simply follow a scenic route clockwise or counter-clockwise and circle the whole province at your leisure.

The 100-series highways and the Trans-Canada Highway accommodate the increasing amount of heavy truck traffic. These highways are meant for speed and not for touring. In this book we have deliberately ignored the Trans-Canada Highway and the 100-series highways as much as possible, not only because they are not overly scenic, but because in summer they are clogged with traffic and just plain unenjoyable. Nothing is more discouraging than seeing a white-knuckled driver and family caught between two transport trucks, wondering if they are going to make it to the next exit. Let's face it, these highways generally just cause angst and are certainly not relaxing. If you accept one tip from this book, let it be this — get off the major highways and travel the scenic routes. Yes, the pace is slower, but you will actually get a chance to see and feel what the real Nova Scotia is all about. However, not to deceive the reader, some of the recommended scenic routes are not in the best of shape. While complaints of potholes are certainly not limited to Nova Scotia's roads, the number of complaints of problems on secondary roads has risen in recent years in direct correlation to budget cuts.

In Part III of this book, there is a detailed description of each of Nova Scotia's scenic routes. If one were to travel the entire circumference of the province at a leisurely pace, it would take about a week. If you wish to explore more of the side roads and attractions recommended in this book, you should allow two weeks. If you only have a few days to tour, you can circle the entire province on the scenic routes in about five days, but we recommend that you set aside about ten days to really enjoy the many distinct areas of Nova Scotia.

ACCOMMODATIONS

It is beyond the scope of this book to systematically review and rate the hundreds of hotels, motels, inns and bed-and-breakfasts in Nova Scotia. However, some comment on the type and availability of accommodations in the province is warranted. In each region we have identified our favourite places to stay, based on our experiences. Just because a place is not mentioned in this book doesn't mean we wouldn't recommend it. There are many fine places that open between editions that we just don't get a chance to visit.

While there is no shortage of suitable accommodations, neither is there an overabundance. The great majority of tourists come to Nova Scotia in July, August and September and finding a room without an advance reservation can be chancy during those months, especially in Halifax and along the South Shore. If you plan your visit for a time outside of these months, reservations, although always a wise precaution, are probably not necessary. By calling 1-800-565-0000 from anywhere in North America or 1-902-425-5781 outside North America, advance reservations can be made at many of the province's hostelries. You can do the same and get a pretty fair idea of the types of accommodations available in the areas where you might want to stay by using the Province's official Web site at www.novascotia.com and clicking on accommodation. Once in Nova Scotia, reservations can be made in person at various tourist bureaus.

Nova Scotia offers a variety of accommodations to suit most tastes and budgets. The Tourist Industry Association of Nova Scotia (TIANS) uses the Canada Select five-star rating system for accommodations in Nova Scotia. Unfortunately, the system is voluntary, with the result that it seems only the establishments that know they have the amenities to receive a high rating take advantage of the service. In Europe and elsewhere it has long been accepted that there is a need and a place for one- and two-star types of accommodation. As long as they are clean and the prices are commensurate with the amenities provided, there need be no shame in operating such an establishment. As well, we don't find the Canada Select rating system entirely reliable. There are several establishments rated as four-star that we don't think warrant it. This detracts from the credibility of those establishments that have justly earned their rating. Others, particularly inns and B&Bs, seem to get lower ratings than are called for because they might not have such amenities as satellite TV or a pool. We suspect many people choose this type of accommodation precisely because they don't have these "essential" features. The annual tourist guide does include ratings where available, but until the province makes ratings mandatory, they are not as useful as they could be.

Hotels and Motels

Over the past 20 years, the Halifax metropolitan area has benefited by the opening of several large modern hotels, most connected with national or international chains, as well as the refurbishment of a number of older classics. Rates are comparable to most Canadian cities and considerably cheaper than most North American and international cities. Outside the Halifax area, there are some fine resort hotels, notably The Pines at Digby and Keltic Lodge at Ingonish; however, most accommodations are of the motel variety. The general rule that "once you've seen one motel room you've seen them all" applies in Nova Scotia as elsewhere. Bearing this in mind, look for establishments that have a good view or an especially scenic setting that distinguishes them from the run-of-the-mill. A fairly reliable guide when choosing a motel is to inquire as to which is the newest establishment in the area. Not surprisingly, these are often the best choices.

Country Inns

If you're looking for character in your accommodations, inns are the way to go. For many years before the deluge of Where to Stay guides, Norman Simpson lauded the hospitality and tranquility of Nova Scotia's inns in edition after edition of *Country Inns and Back Roads*, which at one time was the inn-goers' bible. While not all establishments were listed by Simpson, his idyllic descriptions of Milford House or the Inverary Inn could be applied to many other Nova Scotia inns without loss of credibility. Fortunately for the discerning traveler, an increasing number of quality country inns have opened in Nova Scotia in recent years. It is now possible to spend several weeks on the road and stay at a different inn every night. It is worth noting that inn rates are comparable to, if not lower than, many other establishments that do not offer the same quality of experience.

B&Bs

Increasingly attractive to the traveler with a limited budget, B&Bs have been growing in numbers for several years all around the province. Offering simple accommodations and a hearty breakfast, B&Bs are a good way to meet people and the rates are hard to beat. A list can be obtained from most tourist bureaus.

Youth Hostels and Couchsurfing

The hostel situation in Nova Scotia seems to have been in flux the last number of years, with a number of hostels either closing or switching affiliations. Several of the universities offer very reasonable rates for dorm rooms in the summer. A list of hostels can be found at www.hostels.com/ca.ns.

If you really don't want to pay anything for accommodations you can always try couchsurfing, a relatively new phenomena whereby people, through the web, indicate a willingness to provide a bed for free in exchange for . . . well nothing really, just your company. Couchsurfers generally are young, adventurous and eager to meet new people. If this might be for you go to www.couchsurfing.org. A recent visit revealed a number of Nova Scotians of all ages willing to share their homes.

Campgrounds

With over 160 campgrounds in the province, it is unlikely that you'll have difficulty finding a place to pitch a tent or park a trailer. The majority of campgrounds are privately owned with almost all providing serviced or unserviced sites, flush toilets, firewood and whatever else campers may consider necessary. The same stricture regarding hotels and motels applies to campgrounds: some have much better locations and facilities than others, so it pays to look around. The campground locations in provincial and national parks tend to see much greater use by tenters than the private ones, many of which cater exclusively to RVs. If you plan to stay at one of the national park campgrounds, especially on a weekend, arrive early, preferably before noon. A complete list of campgrounds is contained in the annual *Doers' & Dreamers' Travel Guide*.

DINING

Despite an abundance of working material from the sea and land, not so long ago eating in Nova Scotia restaurants was a hit-or-miss affair. Good cooking did exist, to be sure, but somehow it seldom managed to make the transition from private home to restaurant without losing something in the translation. Thankfully, this has completely changed, as a new generation of chefs and restaurants strive to present Nova Scotia seafood and produce in gastronomically exciting ways. The Halifax restaurant scene is among the best of any city of its size in North America and far better than some much larger Canadian cities. The result is that dining in Nova Scotia can be the most enjoyable part of a Maritime vacation. Of course, if you are addicted to hamburgers, pizza and fried chicken, there are plenty of establishments to cater to your tastes, including most recognized national chains.

Assuming you've decided to pass up McDonald's in favour of something more traditionally Nova Scotian, the choices are numerous. Without question, seafood is the prime attraction as Nova Scotia is Canada's leading province in terms of the total value of seafood landed, something that might come as a surprise to Newfoundlanders. Without question, the lobster is the king, or queen, of the seafood parade, accounting for well over half of the value of the annual fishery. Usually considered an expensive delicacy in most places, lobster is widely available at all times of year at prices that are as low as they have been in recent memory. Anyone who likes lobster or anyone who hasn't tried it should make at least one meal of it in Nova Scotia. With apologies to Maine, Nova Scotia has the best lobster in the world. The silver lining in the cloud that makes the water so cold for swimming is that it makes for the firmest and tenderest lobster meat anywhere. Nova Scotia catches, processes and exports more lobster than any other place in the world. The lobster season varies from district to district, but you can be sure it will be open somewhere in the province so it will always be fresh.

The traditional method of preparation is to boil or steam the lobster in sea water. While recent trends have seen inventive chefs offer new and exciting ways to enjoy it, most lobster lovers prefer theirs prepared simply, served hot or cold with melted butter. Many establishments other than restaurants offer lobsters, live or pre-cooked, although neither lobster suppers nor dining at lobster pounds have caught on in Nova Scotia as they have in Prince Edward Island and Maine, respectively.

The lobster is not the only shellfish of note in Nova Scotia — scallops, oysters, mussels and clams are all readily available. A true delicacy not often found on menus outside Cape Breton, queen or snow crab is very similar to the king crab so revered on the west coast. If you see it on the menu, try it.

With the continued collapse of the offshore groundfish fishery, the price of fresh fish has skyrocketed. While there still seems to be a ready supply of fresh fish at the local markets and restaurants, you can expect to pay dearly for it. The days of great fish and chips for $1.99 are now long gone, but even at $8.99 it's still a bargain compared to a steak or lamb chops.

The most popular fish are haddock (especially good in chowders), halibut, flounder and salmon, all of which regularly grace the menus of local seafood restaurants. Occasionally available are more exotic species such as swordfish, tuna and monkfish. Two local delicacies that should be sampled are Digby chick and Solomon Gundy, smoked and pickled herring respectively. A final note on seafood; don't fail to try a bowl of seafood chowder, an East Coast favourite with as many recipes as makers.

Over the past decade there has been a growing appreciation for eating responsibly. Locally grown food is fresher, healthier and usually environmentally friendly. An increasing number of Nova Scotia producers and restauranteurs have committed to serving only locally grown or raised foods at their tables, wherever possible. A Taste of Nova Scotia is an organization formed for just that purpose. You can get a list of member restaurants by visiting www.tasteofnovascotia.com.

In terms of what to expect other than seafood, there are many other choices in Nova Scotia, which has a large and diverse agricultural history. After all, it was the Acadians who first introduced European-style agricultural practices to North America. Local lamb, pork and chicken are widely available and often deemed preferable to beef, the best of which is usually imported from the west. A host of seasonal fruits and vegetables are available throughout the tourist season, many offered at various farmer's markets around the province. Nova Scotia is the largest producer of wild blueberries in Canada and is also noted for its many varieties of apples. Many famous types, such as the MacIntosh, were first developed here. Other products uniquely Nova Scotian are specialty cheeses, smoked meats and sausages, maple syrup products and dulse, a dried seaweed that some people find irresistible. No matter where your travels take you in Nova Scotia there is no reason not to eat healthy, well-prepared meals. To assist the reader in choosing a restaurant, we have included some favourites in a variety of price ranges. As with our accommodation selections, these choices represent places we frequent and like. It doesn't mean that if a restaurant is not in this book we would not recommend it. The Nova Scotia restaurant scene is vibrant and ever-changing. Between editions, new and exciting eating establishments always spring up and unfortunately old favourites that are listed sometimes close.

Also useful is *Where to Eat in Canada* by Anne Hardy, a volume that is revised annually and is considered a standard reference for good eating by many Canadians. You'll easily save the money that this book will cost you if you avoid just one bad choice. While we don't agree with all of the choices that appear in this volume, as a rule of thumb, we find the current edition pretty reliable.

Like all North Americans, Nova Scotians have been drinking a lot more wine than in the past. Wine lists of late have expanded and prices have fallen while the level of knowledge of the restauranteurs has increased.

Nova Scotia has a thriving wine industry as more and more vintners recognize the unique microclimates that make for great growing conditions. By all means don't be afraid to try a Nova Scotian wine with your meal. They provide good value for your money. For beer drinkers, please note that Nova Scotia is where Alexander Keith's is brewed. For over 180 years, Keith's has been a Nova Scotian and now a Canadian favourite. Be sure to down at least one pint while you are here.

Part II
What to See and Do

Nova Scotia has a truly amazing variety of things to see and do that will appeal to all ages, abilities and budgets. The diverse landscape, particularly the changing coastlines, the unique historical background and the balance between urban, rural and wilderness activities partially account for why such a small place has so much to offer. What follows is an alphabetical listing of these activities. The reader is bound to find many of interest.

ANTIQUES

Until about 25 years ago, Nova Scotia was an extremely fertile source of antiques. Store owners and auctioneers seemed to be able to come up with a rejuvenated stock every season. Very few of these items were imported, almost all were found in older country and city homes, where they may have remained in use since their original purchase from a local factory, long since defunct, or an itinerant Yankee peddler selling what was then the latest in clocks or other goods from Boston or New York.

Until the late nineteenth century Nova Scotia possessed a thriving domestic manufacturing industry, producing a great variety of the household goods that are now sought after by ardent collectors, in particular glassware and furniture. Glass factories in Trenton and New Glasgow were in production until just after World War I. Originally importing master glassworkers from the eastern United States and from Ontario, these glass companies were soon turning out products that were as fine as those of any competitor. For example, in a vote on over a thousand patterns by North American dealers and collectors to find the best pressed-glass goblets, Nova Scotia patterns earned four of the top ten spots. Today, this glassware is greatly desired by collectors and, not surprisingly, Nova Scotia is a good place to find it, but be prepared to pay top dollar for pieces in mint condition.

Nova Scotia has produced fine hand made furniture since the eighteenth century, although the chances of acquiring truly rare specimens is remote, most pieces having long since found their way into museums or high-end private collections. Working in white pine, maple, birch and mahogany, Nova Scotia cabinetmakers produced chairs, chests, desks, cupboards, and so on, usually emulating the styles of the region from which they emigrated. In addition, Nova Scotia had its share of clockmakers, silversmiths and potters, whose works are now in great demand. The best places to view high-quality Nova Scotia-made antiques are the many museums located throughout the province. The Nova Scotia Museum located in Halifax and the Museum of Industry in Stellarton are particularly noteworthy museums.

Articles produced in the province are not the only attractions. While many of Nova Scotia's immigrants arrived with nothing but the proverbial shirts on their backs, many others, including the New England Planters and Loyalists, brought plentiful goods with them. Some Loyalists even brought whole homes to reconstruct. In light of the lock, stock and barrel moves of these displaced gentry, it is not surprising to find that some Nova Scotia antique stores carry a good selection of American-made antiques.

Likewise, many British officers stationed in Nova Scotia had a preference for English goods over colonial items and imported as much as they could. Most of the officers departed, but their larger belongings didn't. They were often sold to local families, where they remained until acquired by a dealer or a collector.

Another prime source of antiques in Nova Scotia has been the incessant rovings of its seafaring sons, returning from parts known and unknown, laden with souvenirs and mementos of far-off lands. These keepsakes were usually handed from generation to generation along with the stories that accompanied their acquisition. As an example, one Halifax auction featured items from around the world collected by Alexander Graham Bell on a goodwill tour early in the century.

Of interest to many serious collectors, Nova Scotia is also rich in military and Maritime artifacts. Muskets, swords, ship bells and innumerable items connected with warfare and the sea are occasionally found at auction or for private sale.

Nova Scotia's treasure trove of antiques has not remained undiscovered and for many years dealers have been taking entire truckloads of merchandise to New England and Ontario. These predations have had their effect and it would be pointless to pretend that the antiquing is as good as it used to be. However, there are still many fine antique stores throughout Nova Scotia and one never knows just what might turn up. Dealers gather at least four times a year for major antique expositions, which are always well advertised in advance. To locate an antique dealer go to www.antiquesnovascotia.com, which has a listing of dozens of dealers, many of whom now have their own Web sites. With the advent of eBay, many may forget that there is still such a thing as a real auction as opposed to a virtual one. For many, there is no substitute for the thrill of bidding in person on an item that may be very rare or very appealing. Not a summer weekend goes by in the province without at least one auction occurring somewhere in rural Nova Scotia. Sometimes held out-of-doors, these auctions more often than not represent the contents of one or more estates, with the legatees opting to sell rather than keep the items that may have had much value to their parents, uncles, aunts or friends, but little to them. Prices fluctuate wildly at these auctions. Something worth $10 may go for $100, but just as likely something worth $100 may be got for $10. There is no question that good buys can be had, but this is only part of the fun. The auction itself is the big event, attracting persons of all possible backgrounds, some with real knowledge of antiques, others less so. The country auction truly captures the down-home flavour of rural Nova Scotia. No visitor to the province should miss a chance to attend one. One family that has been synonymous with Nova Scotia country auctions for many years are the Pidgeons of Pictou County. Their upcoming auctions can be viewed at www.pidgeonauctions.com. In addition to these country auctions, there are regular antique auctions held throughout the year in the Halifax area and Colchester, Lunenburg and Pictou counties.

ARCHITECTURE

Architecture buffs will find no shortage of material to engage their fascination while touring Nova Scotia.

The traveller who arrives in Yarmouth will immediately be struck by the architectural similarities between Nova Scotia and New England towns. This is no coincidence. The main streets of the towns on both the South Shore and in the Annapolis Valley were laid out in the nineteenth century and incorporated "prefabricated" houses of Loyalist landowners as well as universally popular neo-classical-style architecture adapted for wooden construction.

No undisputed examples of pre-expulsion Acadian architecture still stand in Nova Scotia, as many buildings were razed by the English although a large stone edifice near Newport Landing in Hants County is conceded by most to be of French origin. When the New Englanders arrived to take over the abandoned Acadian farms or establish new towns closer to their traditional fishing grounds, they erected structures in the contemporary fashion using their expertise in carpentry and the readily available forests for their materials. Often the frames or even entire structures were shipped to Nova Scotia for erection, St. Paul's Church in Halifax being the most notable example. Everywhere, one sees examples of the neo-classical style of dwelling, invariably whitewashed, and less commonly, the saltbox shape that is popular in Connecticut and Massachusetts.

Some good examples of the one-room cabin or cottage first popularized in Salem and Plymouth, often with many later additions, still exist, particularly in the Annapolis Valley. Among the finest, most striking architectural achievements of these early builders are the churches, of which the Old Covenanters Church at Grand Pré is but one outstanding example.

Other influences such as the Scottish and Gothic can be seen. For the former, see especially the stone houses in Pictou. By and large, however, Nova Scotia towns have a uniformity of architecture style that bears far more similarity to Maine or Vermont than to Ontario or Quebec.

One notable exception to this is Halifax, the seat of British power in North America after the revolution. For obvious political reasons, Province House was built in a classical style developed in England in the eighteenth century. Vaguely Renaissance in appearance with its ornamental stone columns, the building has a symmetry and harmony of design that was later copied (with less effectiveness) throughout British North America. Other notable examples of British classicism in Halifax are the Town Clock and the Prince's Lodge rotunda, the only remnant of the Duke of Kent's Rockingham estate. The British classical style was not alone in influencing Halifax and environs, as the Regency-styled Government House and the Georgian-styled Uniacke House illustrate.

People with an interest in architecture should not confine their attentions in Nova Scotia solely to housing. The province contains some of the most outstanding examples of military architecture in North America. Most prominent are the Louisbourg restoration project and the Halifax Citadel, particulars of which are given later in this book. Also of note are

Fort Anne at Annapolis Royal and the Habitation at Port Royal.

A book that will make any trip around the province more enjoyable from an architectural point of view is Allen Penney's *Houses of Nova Scotia*. It is especially useful on many of the walking tours described later.

ARTS, CRAFTS AND FOLK ART

Whether it is the laid-back rural atmosphere of much of the province or something in the salt air, the fact is Nova Scotia has been attracting, as permanent residents, significant numbers of professional craftspeople from throughout North America. Since 1948, the number of individuals earning their living this way has increased tenfold, with the result that Nova Scotia is one of the best destinations in North America to buy high-quality arts and crafts. The Nova Scotia Centre for Craft and Design in Halifax is a world-class institution specializing in teaching students the intricacies of working with ceramics, metals, textiles and mixed media among other specialties. The Mary E. Black Gallery is the only public gallery in Nova Scotia that showcases contemporary crafts from around the world. The Centre publishes a free *Guide to Craft and Art in Nova Scotia*, listing more than 400 outlets, a calendar of craft events and artisans by specific craft. A copy can be downloaded at www.craft-design.ns.ca/guide.

In recent years, the Studio Rally map has become an increasingly popular way of finding and visiting crafts shops around the province. The map is worth having as a souvenir because of its many fine pictures of Nova Scotia artistry. To find out more visit www.studiorally.ca. The Web site provides detailed information on dozens of Nova Scotian artisans. If you have a serious or passing interest in almost any conceivable type of artistry or craft, the Studio Rally map is a great guide. It also provides details on when and where to meet the artisans and learn a lot more about their works.

What should the potential buyer of Nova Scotia crafts be on the lookout for? The options are numerous. First, obtain the guide and map to locate any particular places you might visit on your travels. Second, keep an eye on the newspaper for details of the many craft shows held throughout the province at all times of the year, often in conjunction with festivals of one kind or another. The larger craft shows spotlight the work of more artists than is possible for any single craft shop. Prices may be cheaper. It also provides an opportunity to meet the artisans, most of whom are more than willing to discuss their work.

What to buy is always a matter of personal preference; however, there are some areas in which Nova Scotia craftspeople seem to excel. One is folk art. For many years, fishermen waiting for the weather to turn or farmers sitting by their wood stoves at night would carve and paint objects and images familiar to them in their everyday lives. The items could be functional, such as a toy or a weather vane, or they could be whimsical, intended only for the amusement of the creator. Those artists were self-taught and their work bears little relation to the mainstream of contemporary art. In fact, only in the twentieth century has their talent and output been recognized as genuine art.

Fortunately, tradition is alive and well in Nova Scotia: folk art may be seen and purchased at various galleries and craft shops throughout the province. A painting by Joseph Norris or a wood sculpture by Collins Eisenhauer is as representative of true Nova Scotian art as one is likely to obtain, although in recent years the prices for the best artists have risen astronomically.

The more conventional arts and crafts are abundant. There are dozens of clay and earthenware studios, each producing functional and decorative pots revealing the distinctive style of the maker. Quilts and hooked rugs of both traditional and contemporary design are available at most crafts shops, as are the latest offerings from a variety of weavers and fibre artists. Candle makers, blacksmiths, leather workers, toy makers, pewter artisans and woodworkers all legitimately vie for your dollar in Nova Scotia. The list of arts and crafts is as long as the imagination of the artisans that produce them. The important thing is that Nova Scotia has been at the forefront of traditional craftsmanship for more than 50 years. Forget that plastic lobster key chain and take home a memento that will bring lasting pleasure.

Rather than recommend specific stores and artisans as we have done in some editions, in this edition we recommend towns and villages as well as areas of Halifax where there are concentrations of craftspeople who offer authentic Nova Scotia products.

BEACHES

If your idea of a great beach is sun, sand and fairly warm water, Nova Scotia is the place for you. It has some of the finest swimming beaches north of the Carolinas, particularly along the Northumberland Strait. However, if you prefer a deserted strand where you can stroll while beachcombing for shells, and driftwood or watching shore birds, you won't be disappointed. Perhaps nowhere else in North America are there so many great beaches with so few people on them. Even at the height of the summer season, with a little effort you can get away from the crowds. Whether your preference is the sound of the waves roaring over a shingle beach, or a gentle lapping of water on the shore, you will have no trouble finding what you like. Nova Scotia's 7,500-kilometre shoreline ensures that there is not only a great quantity of beaches, but a great variety as well. There is almost literally a beach for everyone, particularly since the beaches are all publicly owned.

Swimming in Nova Scotia may seem a paradoxical situation to many, for the general rule is that the further north you go, the warmer the water. This is because the Atlantic coast is affected by the cold waters of the southward-flowing Labrador current, while northern waters are moderated by the warmer outpourings of the Gulf of St. Lawrence.

Northumberland Strait

Here, the water temperature reaches 17–19° C by mid July and remains high until September, sometimes reaching 20° C. The beaches along this shore are characterized by red sandstone ledges and sandbars, which extend well out into the strait. When the tide is out, these bars and ledges are warmed by the sun and release their heat into the water when the tide rolls in. The result is deliciously warm surf that one can enjoy for hours. These beaches are particularly suitable for children because they are shallow and warm. If you like to spend a lot of time in the water, this is the area to head for. Some of the most popular beaches in this area are Melmerby, Rushton's, Cameron and Heather.

Cape Breton
Water temperature and beach conditions on the western side of the island are very similar to that of the Northumberland Strait, making for excellent swimming. On the north shore of Cape Breton water temperatures are slightly lower, but still higher than on the mainland. However, the number of beaches along this shore is limited. Not to be overlooked in Cape Breton is the Bras d'Or Lakes system, which has some fine beaches and water temperatures up to 20° C. The most popular beaches in Cape Breton are Port Hood, Inverness and Ingonish; however, if you are interested in some truly spectacular wild and deserted beaches head for the eastern side of the island where Belfry Beach and Point Michaud are marvelous.

Eastern Shore
From Canso to Halifax, there are many spectacular and often deserted beaches. Outstanding Eastern Shore beaches are Lawrencetown, Martinique, Tor Bay and Clam Harbour. The drawback is the water temperature, which seldom exceeds 18° C. This area features the highest surf in Nova Scotia, with waves breaking on finely grained sand. This is a prime location for all types of surfing, especially at Lawrencetown, although the number of days when you don't need a wetsuit are limited.

South Shore
This is a coastline dotted with probably the most beautiful beaches in the province. Evenly breaking waves on white sand is the rule here. Again, the catch is the water temperature, which is comparable to or slightly lower than that of the Eastern Shore. Most of the best South Shore beaches are located in Lunenburg, Queens and Shelburne counties and include Rissers, Crescent, Carters, Summerville and Sand Hills.

Bay of Fundy
Unless you are a member of a Polar Bear club, forget swimming in this area. It has the coldest water in the Maritimes, although there are some passable beaches in the Minas Basin area, where temperatures may get up to 18° C. The outstanding feature of the Bay of Fundy beaches is the mudflats exposed at low tides. In some places and in some conditions, the low-water mark is about 2 kilometres from the high-water mark. The mudflats make for great fun clamdigging, rockhounding or exploring a traditional fishing

weir, where just about any denizen of the sea might turn up. You have to be prepared to get a little muddy (or a lot if you're a little kid). Evangeline Beach near Grand Pré is the place to experience a Bay of Fundy beach.

Overcrowding is not a problem on Nova Scotia's beaches, although admittedly, on hot summer weekends some of the beaches in the Halifax area can get pretty busy. Nevertheless, one can be sure that by driving a little further, the crowds thin out. On weekdays, the beaches are almost always sparsely populated. As for biological dangers, swimming at Nova Scotia's beaches is about as safe as you can get, with jellyfish being about the only menace. Anyone with a good pair of eyes and legs can avoid these occasional drifters. Shark attacks are nonexistent. However, there are areas with dangerous rip tides and undertows, particularly in the Lawrencetown area. Pay attention to warning signs, use common sense at all times and if you don't know the area well never swim outside supervised areas. A final note for those who don't like getting salt water in their mouths: Nova Scotia has excellent swimming areas on its hundreds of lakes and streams.

Detailed descriptions of Nova Scotia's best beaches and their facilities are contained in Part III.

BICYCLE TOURING

Nova Scotia is one of North America's best destinations for bicycle tourists. Although small in area, the province offers an amazing variety of scenery over an extensive highway system. Any one of the official tourism trails in the province would make a great cycling vacation, although the Cabot Trail should be attempted only by those in very good physical condition. Both the Evangeline Trail through the Annapolis Valley and the Light-house Route along the South Shore pass through many interesting towns and villages, with few significant climbs or descents.

In addition to the variety, Nova Scotia's temperate climate makes it very favourable for cycling. Many of the most interesting cycling routes skirt the ocean, which provides a continuous cooling breeze, as well as frequent opportunities to stop at beaches and picnic parks along the way.

The preferred places to begin a bicycle tour of Nova Scotia are Yar-mouth or Halifax. Arriving at Halifax Airport is equally popular, as it provides a convenient central starting point from where up to a dozen different tours can be commenced. The best times for a cycling tour are June, September and October, when the weather is mild, and the traffic considerably lighter than in July or August. A tour through the Annapolis Valley in early June when the hillsides are blushing with apple and cherry blossoms can be wonderful. Likewise Cape Breton in the fall, when the leaves change colour and the skies are at their clearest, is truly exhilarating.

Although the 100-series highways are fairly straight and have paved shoulders, most cyclists avoid these in favour of the older, narrower provincial highways. These new highways are not scenic, have high-speed traffic, particularly trucks, and provide fewer interesting places to stop.

An alternative to following a designated trail is to set out from a base in one of the more interesting towns, such as Lunenburg or Wolfville, which have a variety of accommodations and dining. The days can be spent exploring the back roads and villages and avoiding the heavy traffic, while evenings can be spent enjoying the various inns and restaurants in these towns.

A number of cycle touring companies, both local and international, regularly include Nova Scotia in their destinations. We have often run into the participants on these cycling tours at various places in the province and have yet to hear anything but praise for the operators. While these tours may seem relatively expensive, they offer the real benefit of not having to cycle with 40 or 50 pounds of baggage, as well as the security of van backup in the event that your bicycle needs repair or you need assistance. They also seem to consistently pick high-quality inns and restaurants as their starting and stopping points. It appears to be a case of getting what you pay for. For further information check out www.freewheeling.ca, which is a Nova Scotian company specializing in guided and self-guided cycling tours.

If you are planning your own cycling trip to Nova Scotia, a copy of *The Nova Scotia Bicycle Book* by Gary Conrod, is invaluable. This useful book outlines 39 tours with details on what to see and do on each tour. The trails can be linked to provide a tour of the entire province. You can obtain a copy by visiting www.atlanticcanadacycling.com, which has a wealth of up-to-date information on cycling in Nova Scotia. This group also organizes regular cycling/camping trips to various parts of the province at minimal costs. It is a great way to meet fellow cycling enthusiasts in a friendly non-competitive atmosphere. The site to visit if you are interested in road racing is www.bicycle.ns.ca.

The best places for short cycling tours are described in Part III.

BIRDING

Birding is one of the fastest-growing pastimes in the world, with birding-related tourism becoming big business. Over the past 30 years, birders have come to realize that Nova Scotia, with its great variety of coastal habitats, is one of the best birding destinations in North America. Ornithological tour companies now regularly include Nova Scotia on their list of places to visit.

What is it that attracts so many birders to Nova Scotia? In the spring, unquestionably one of the biggest draws is the sea bird colonies on the many islands off the Nova Scotia coast. Visits to the breeding areas of puffins, razorbills, guillemots, petrels, terns and gulls are all possible on a birding tour of the province. A second great attraction is the fall migration of shore birds, particularly along the Bay of Fundy. Beginning in early August, shore birds by the millions return from the Arctic to stop on the food-rich mudflats of the upper Bay of Fundy, where they fatten up before continuing their long journey south. The sight of 100,000 shore birds dipping and swirling in unison, in some symmetrical pattern known only to them, is truly awe-inspiring. Also of interest to birders are the great number of bald eagles, particularly in Cape Breton.

Other birders will be attracted to Nova Scotia to visit some of the recognized hot spots, such as Brier Island or Cape Sable Island, which attract not only exceptional numbers of species, but rarities as well. Pelagic tours on whale-watching boats will usually yield a goodly number of ocean wanderers including shearwaters, petrels, jaegers, fulmars and other species seldom seen from land. These species can also be seen from the ferries that call on Nova Scotia from Maine, New Brunswick, Prince Edward Island and Newfoundland. You can start your birding before even setting foot in the province.

The competent observer can expect to see up to 200 species of birds while in Nova Scotia. Another 200 species have been reliably reported at one time or another. Don't overlook the inland areas where 22 species of warblers nest in the different forest environments.

Serious birders should obtain a copy of the recently published *Birding Sites of Nova Scotia* by Blake Maybank, an exhaustive guide to birding and wildlife sites in Nova Scotia. You can order a copy from Mr. Maybank's Web site http://maybank.tripod.com/BSNS/BSNS.htm, which contains just about everything you could possibly want to know about birding in Nova Scotia. Especially useful are downloadable birding site lists for dozens of birding hotspots in every county. There are also a number of recent publications designed with the novice birder in mind that are widely available at most bookstores. For the more advanced birder a copy of *Birds of Nova Scotia* by the iconic Robie Tufts is a must. Mr. Tufts was a friend of birding legend Roger Tory Peterson, who provided many of the drawings for this book. In print for almost fifty years, the work is the definitive guide to identifying Nova Scotia birds. A checklist of Nova Scotia's birds is available from the Nova Scotia Museum of Natural History, and both Kejimkujik and Cape Breton Highlands National parks provide a free checklist of species frequently seen in the parks. The respected ornithological tour company Victor Emmanuel Nature Tours has a regular birding expedition to Nova Scotia. Check it out at www.ventbird.com. Finally, to get up-to-date information on local birding outings or rare bird alerts visit the Nova Scotia Bird Society at http://nsbs.chebucto.org.

BOAT TOURS

For many years, much of Nova Scotia's beautiful coastline, and in particular its hundreds of small offshore islands, was accessible only to the fishermen who knew, by hard experience, the presence of every underwater reef and rock. Some of the finest beaches, most photogenic lighthouses and remotest settlements went unobserved by all but a very few. Over the past number of years, this has slowly changed as more and more ex-fishermen are realizing that the places they have taken for granted for so long are potential tourist attractions. Not only has there been an explosion in the number of excursion boats that will take people on regularly scheduled whale-watching tours, sightseeing excursions and visits to offshore bird colonies, but also the opportunity to take a customized trip to a destination of your choice is now very possible. Most of these trips are by way of

Cape Islander fishing boats, captained by former or off-duty fishermen. While the amenities available on the boats vary widely, you can be sure that the skippers are extremely knowledgeable, and they will do their best to show you or lead you to the top offshore sites they know.

Some of the seldom-visited islands that can now be reached by these services include the LaHaves, with their wonderful sand beaches; the Tuskets, famous for shipwrecks and lighthouses; McNutt Island, once home to a thriving community now long gone; and remote Seal and Bon Portage islands, where birders may find species unique to Nova Scotia, if not to North America. In recent years, it has become possible to accompany lobster fishermen as they ply their trade, hopefully with success. Fresh-out-of-the-ocean lobster is the reward for helping out. In addition to fishing excursions, whale watching, scuba diving or just relaxing sightseeing, there is always the opportunity to board a wooden sailing ship. The ultimate is a tour on the legendary *Bluenose II* out of Lunenburg, but if that doesn't happen there are several choices in Halifax. The annual *Doers' & Dreamers' Travel Guide* has a list of boat tours. No trip to Nova Scotia would be complete without at least one excursion onto the ocean that surrounds on all sides. Chances are it will be a highlight of your trip.

CANOEING

A recent publication by the Department of Tourism describes Nova Scotia as a canoeist's paradise. This is a bit of an overstatement considering the size of the province and its lack of major waterways. If you lean toward lengthy excursions through untracked wilderness, shooting whitewater rapids and portaging around raging cataracts, Northern Ontario, Quebec or Maine would be better destinations. However canoeing opportunities in Nova Scotia abound. For the less experienced, Kejimkujik National Park is a great place for family canoe trips while the nearby Tobeatic Wilderness Area is becoming increasingly recognized as an area of great natural beauty best explored by canoe. The Shelburne River, which begins in the watershed of the Tobeatic, has been designated a Canadian Heritage River and does provide serious whitewater canoeing at certain times of year, mostly late spring. One of the few companies providing guided tours of various durations (three days to three weeks or more) into these Nova Scotia wilderness areas is Hinterland Adventures and Gear. Check out their tour offerings at www.kayakingnovascotia.com.

If your interest is in taking two- to three-day trips with a minimum of portaging and a maximum of great natural and historic sites to visit along the way, then Nova Scotia has a number of great river routes, including the Annapolis, Shubenacadie, Musquodoboit and Margaree. Detailed waterproof maps of many of Nova Scotia's best routes have been produced by the province and are available from Maps and More (www.mapsandducks. com). The key to canoeing in Nova Scotia is accessibility, as almost all routes can be reached by automobile. Combine this with the availability of rental equipment, and a short canoe trip can be readily included in a longer Nova Scotia vacation.

A list of canoe rentals and outfitters can be found in the annual *Doers' & Dreamers' Travel Guide.*

In Part III, we have listed some of the most popular canoe routes, all suitable for canoeists of medium ability.

CEMETERIES

Aside from being tranquil places to reflect on life and death, cemeteries offer opportunities to appreciate the harsh conditions of early life in Nova Scotia. Old cemeteries, whether they are English or French, Loyalist or Planter, reveal early death for many children, sometimes entire families wiped out in epidemics, women's lives cut short in childbirth and stone after stone for men lost at sea or killed in mining disasters. Coming into the twentieth century, we can see how many men gave their lives in the two world wars and, in fishing communities, the continued loss of young men at sea. Yet visiting cemeteries does not have to be a depressing exercise. One can see the headstones as works of art worthy of study for more than just the inscriptions.

Early cemeteries in Nova Scotia date from the English conquest of Annapolis Royal in the early 1700s. There were no identifiable examples of Acadian cemeteries until recently when one was accidentally discovered at Falmouth, the former Acadian settlement of Sainte-Famille. The Annapolis Valley and the South Shore have many excellently preserved Loyalist, Planter and German cemeteries. Some of the best are mentioned in Part III. Those with an interest in cemeteries and headstones should pick up Deborah Trask's excellent book titled *Life How Short, Eternity How Long: Gravestone Carving and Carvers in Nova Scotia.* This is of great assistance in identifying the various types of stones and carvers who worked in early Nova Scotia.

DIVING

When Alex Storm salvaged the wreck of the eighteenth-century French pay ship *Chameau* in Louisbourg Harbour in 1965, divers took a sudden interest in Nova Scotia. The rich haul of gold and silver coins and valuable antiquities made others speculate as to what might lie concealed in Nova Scotia's remaining 3,000 documented wrecks, only a small number of which have been located. Over 40 years after the *Chameau* find, interest remains high and although no new finds of this magnitude have been made, dozens of new wreck sites have been identified and Nova Scotia's reputation as one of the best cold-water wreck diving places in the world has solidified. This was further enhanced by the deliberate scuttling of the former destroyer *Saguenay* to create an interesting and relatively safe dive site not far from Lunenburg.

Another plus for Nova Scotian divers is undoubtedly the clarity of the water, which greatly enhances underwater photography. The one serious drawback is the temperature of the water. Wetsuits of at least 3/16-inch thickness are a must, with most divers preferring the 1/4-inch thickness. Year-round diving is possible, as the coastal waters do not freeze, but June to October will be the limit for all but the hardiest.

Wreck diving in cold water is only for the most experienced of divers and carries a substantial element of risk. However, for those up to the challenge, there are a great many identified sites including some of the most famous wrecks of all time such as the SS *Atlantic*. A list of dive shops and dive operators is annually updated by the Department of Tourism and is found in the *Doers' & Dreamers' Travel Guide*. You will also find a plethora of information on Nova Scotia shipwrecks on Dave Clancy's Shipwrecks of Nova Scotia Web site at http://nswrecks.net. Whether you have an interest in wreck diving or not, you should visit the exhibit on Nova Scotia wrecks and the efforts to salvage them that is on permanent display at the Maritime Museum in Halifax.

FAMILY VACATIONS

If your idea of a great family vacation is heading to a theme park, waiting in long lines and paying hundreds of dollars for a day of entertainment, then Nova Scotia is not for you. The fact is Nova Scotia is really one great natural history park. There is no need for anything artificial or constructed. What this area offers for families is the chance to directly experience nature and our nation's history firsthand. Whether it be walking with your children on a wave-swept beach, holding on to them for dear life as you crash through the rapids on a tidal bore rafting expedition, or simply sharing with them the awesome sight of a breaching humpback whale, Nova Scotia offers an opportunity for families to accumulate memories that will last a lifetime. In addition to the chance to collect fossils and interesting rocks, hike to hidden waterfalls or catch a shiny mackerel from a fishing wharf, there are all the historical opportunities. There has never been a child who doesn't love to explore an old fort and Nova Scotia has lots to offer, from the entire fortress town at Louisbourg to the marching soldiers at the Halifax Citadel to the fur traders' post at the Habitation in Port Royal. Many of the provincial museums are especially designed with children in mind, particularly Ross Farm, the Lunenburg Fisheries Museum and Sherbrooke Village.

There is an increasing realization that family vacations mean spending time together doing interesting things, and there is no better spot to do this than Nova Scotia, and besides, it's a heck of a lot cheaper than a crowded theme park.

FESTIVALS

The latest *Nova Scotia Festivals and Events Guide* lists at least one event every weekend from April to November in one community or another. The second week of August shows no fewer than 16 separate events in as many different locations — a total of 550 in all. Obviously, for those with a predilection for pageantry, music and competition or just the plain fun of a community get-together, there is no shortage of places to indulge these interests in Nova Scotia.

The happenings come in all types and sizes, from the grandeur of the

Nova Scotia Tattoo to the laid-back atmosphere of a local fiddling contest. Many of the festivals are organized around a theme or commemorate an historical event or person, while others are little more than local gatherings at a lobster supper or clam bake. Visitors are uniformly welcome at all events, but be forewarned, these special attractions, especially the larger ones, are extremely popular. Advance reservations for accommodations are usually a must. On the other hand, many take place only a short drive from Halifax/Dartmouth or other major communities and can be attended in one day. Listed in Part III are some of the special events most enjoyed by locals and visitors alike.

FISHING

With over 7,500 kilometres of coastline, it is no surprise that Nova Scotia has excellent saltwater fishing. While the variety of fish is not equal to that of more southerly waters, the quantity certainly is. Many of the same species that have long been the backbone of the North Atlantic commercial fishery are easily caught with rod and reel. No license is required to fish for saltwater species if you go out on a charter or party boat. Despite the closure of large parts of the inshore commercial fishery, recreational fishing continues.

Groundfish — haddock, cod, flounder and halibut — are found in almost all Nova Scotia waters, and as they are usually deep feeders, it is necessary to charter a boat to get to their fishing grounds. The usual fee is approximately $250 per day and up for an entire boatload. For this the operator will supply all the equipment and bait, and with fish-finding sonar, you are almost guaranteed a successful day. Half-day excursions are also available. Many boats can provide picnic lunches or chowders on request, as well as sightseeing cruises if one prefers scenery to fishing. An up-to-date list of available charter boat captains is available from most tourist bureaus.

The usual equipment for ground fishing is fairly heavy tackle, particularly if cod or halibut is the quarry. For those who would like to try a method of fishing first used in these waters almost 500 years ago, hand jigging for cod is an experience that will not soon be forgotten. However, be forewarned, after hauling up 10 or 20 good-sized codfish, your arms will feel like lead and you will be ready for a good night's rest. On the other hand, you will also understand and appreciate some of the difficulties and pleasures of making a living from the sea. Hand-line outfits are usually available from the same operators who provide rod-and-reel fishing.

Pollock — often called the Boston bluefish — is a fighting fish and one of the easiest to catch. The larger fish, up to 35 pounds, are usually caught from charter boats, some of which have landed 600 pounds in half a day's fishing. The smaller fish of 1 to 4 pounds tend to congregate inshore, and in late summer it is no exaggeration to say that some localities teem with them. Try fishing from wharves with light spinning tackle or fly rods using lures, flies or bait — it is literally possible to catch one every cast under favourable conditions. Pollock are found in almost all coastal localities in the province; the best method of finding them is to ask a local resident.

Mackerel is a pretty silver and blue striped species that travels in schools and provides excellent sport on light tackle. If you see the surface of what appears to be a calm sea suddenly start to boil, in all likelihood it is a school of mackerel chasing minnows. It is a splendid sight and one that will provide fantastic fishing. Most mackerel fishing from boats uses the chumming method to attract the fish, but in some localities they can be caught from shore. Again, the best procedure is to ask a local resident where to fish.

Striped bass is a game fish, highly prized by American anglers. They are common along the Bay of Fundy, Northumberland Strait and southwestern shore waters.

In recent years Nova Scotia has started to gain a reputation as a striped bass hot spot. Several 50-pound-plus fish have been landed within recent years, setting both the Canadian record and a world junior record. The best method for catching bass, whether from shore or boat, differs from locality to locality. Eelskin rigs are a favourite in some areas. Bass fishing contests are held throughout the summer in Digby and Annapolis counties.

Another tough customer that has started to appear fairly regularly along the South Shore is the voracious bluefish — pound for pound one of the toughest fighting fish found anywhere. It is only a matter of time before serious fishermen start to realize that this fish is heading further north as the oceans gradually warm.

Sea-run brook trout and brown trout ascend many rivers in Nova Scotia beginning in late May. These fish are larger and more powerful than their landlocked cousins, with some browns running over 15 pounds. Fly fishing and trolling with light spinning tackle are the usual methods of catching them. Note that if you fish these species from the shore of a river mouth, a license will be required, as they are considered freshwater fish once they have started their upriver migration.

Bluefin tuna is undoubtedly one of the premier catches for anyone who likes to fish for the pelagic giants. The tremendous size and brute strength of this fish have earned it an enviable reputation among big-game fishermen, and Nova Scotia's waters are home to the largest specimens ever taken on rod and reel. First popularized by the English angler and reel manufacturer Mitchell-Henry, and later by novelist-adventurer Zane Grey, the Nova Scotia tuna fishery attained worldwide fame between 1937 and 1976, when the International Tuna Cup matches, featuring entries from many nations, were held annually off Wedgeport in Yarmouth County. But the tuna is an unpredictable fish and in recent years has largely abandoned the Wedgeport area in favour of the waters of the Eastern Shore and St. Georges Bay, where in 1976 a world-record, 1,496-pound fish was taken.

Fishing for tuna is conducted from boats specially equipped with swivel chairs and foot wells, using heavy tackle. It is an expensive and time-consuming pastime, as it may take days to get a strike and then another 8 to 10 hours of backbreaking work to land the fish. Obviously, it is not a sport for the weak of heart or wallet. For those willing to try their luck and test their mettle, a list of tuna boat operators is available from most tourist bureaus. Aside from tuna, these boats will catch shark and maybe, if you are lucky, swordfish.

Shark fishing is becoming increasingly popular in Nova Scotia with the blue shark being the usual quarry, although porbeagle (mackerel shark) and mako are increasingly found. There have been a number of shark derbies held recently off Halifax and elsewhere. Unfortunately, it seems that far too many sharks are killed needlessly and a fair controversy has arisen as to whether this is a legitimate sport or not.

Not everyone has the time or inclination to spend a day on the open waters in order to catch fish. Fortunately, good fishing is only as far away as the nearest wharf. Around every piling and breakwater is the ubiquitous cunner, a small perch-like fish that is easily caught using a piece of periwinkle or clam as bait. They can provide endless hours of amusement with their bait-stealing antics and are a great way to introduce children to saltwater fishing. Also caught from wharves and breakwaters are sculpin, small flounder and, in Yarmouth County, the tautog or black fish.

Without doubt the Atlantic salmon is the royalty of Nova Scotia's freshwater fish and the prime attraction to visitors who come here primarily to fish. The Margaree, Medway, St. Marys and Stewiacke rivers in Nova Scotia are as well known to serious salmon fishermen as the Miramichi, Matapedia or Restigouche in New Brunswick. The best part of Nova Scotia salmon fishing is that none of the waters are leased or privately owned (as in New Brunswick and many of the other good salmon waters), with the result that in Nova Scotia the best pools are open to everyone and the prohibitive cost of salmon fishing is not a factor. The angling is restricted to fly fishing only and a guide is a must, as the favourite flies vary from river to river and even from pool to pool. Some of the favourite fly patterns, such as the Deadly MacIntosh, are Nova Scotian creations probably unknown to most visitors. A list of guides is available at most tourist bureaus.

There are 31 salmon rivers and streams in the province that consistently produce. The open season varies from area to area, opening as early as May in some waters and not until September in others. Again, a guide will be of great assistance in determining the best streams at any given time.

It need hardly be said, but one cannot simply stop the car by any stream and start hauling out salmon. It is doubtful that this could be done anywhere. The salmon has been called the world's most harassed fish. For decades, conservationists have been battling commercial over-fishing, hydroelectric projects, poaching and acid rain, in an effort to save the Atlantic salmon. If Nova Scotia has not suffered the depredations and outright extirpations that some American and European rivers have, neither has it escaped unscathed. Today's salmon runs are a mere shadow of what they once were. A recent agreement ending commercial fishing in the area of the Arctic Ocean, where it is believed many Nova Scotian–spawned salmon congregate, is a hopeful sign. Nonetheless, a good many fish are taken annually. For the angler with some degree of skill, a little luck and a lot of patience, Nova Scotia rivers can still provide opportunities, at an affordable cost, to find out why Atlantic salmon is revered as the king of freshwater fishes.

While the salmon fishery has declined, it has been replaced for many by a great increase in the amount of smallmouth bass fishing available in Nova Scotia. Not too long ago the smallmouth was restricted to a small area in the southeastern part of the province. It has now expanded, whether naturally or by concerted efforts by bass fisherman, to most of the mainland. The smallmouth gives a great fight for its size, is easy to catch and has become a great favourite of some Nova Scotian anglers. Other freshwater fish that are eagerly sought are three species of trout — brook, rainbow and brown — as well as shad, which make a great migration up Nova Scotia's rivers in mid-spring. A license is required for all freshwater fishing.

GEOCACHING

When the United States military launched a series of satellites to create a Global Positioning System (GPS) that would allow anyone to pinpoint their exact location anywhere on earth within a matter of inches, little did they realize that they were also creating the world's fastest-growing recreational activity — geocaching. Usually described as a high-tech version of hide-and-seek, geocaching involves hiding, or in most cases finding, small containers that may contain any number of items, but almost always a logbook. The geocaches, as they are known, are placed by individuals who then post the exact co-ordinates of the location on the Web at www. geocaching.com. The co-ordinates can then be downloaded, along with other information, into handheld GPS units and then the fun begins. If you liked the old-fashioned treasure hunts of summer camps, you will love geocaching. It is an activity that particularly lends itself as a family activity; nobody gets more excited than the young ones to find a geocache, often in an area one might have traversed dozens of times without knowing what was hidden nearby.

Geocaching only began in 2000 when the GPS system was made available for public use. The first geocache was hidden in Oregon in May 2000, and a month later, Canada's first was hidden in Nova Scotia's Graves Island Provincial Park. At the time of writing, 865,000 geocaches existed worldwide, and there will probably be over a million by the time you read this. Nova Scotia has more than its share of geocaches; many are very easily accessible while others are in the most remote parts of the province, constituting a real challenge to find. If you are a geocacher you will not be disappointed in searching for Nova Scotia's hidden treasures and if you are not, check out the geocaching Web site to find out what you are missing.

GOLF

With a large percentage of the population being of Scottish descent, it is no surprise that Nova Scotia has many fine golf courses. What may be a surprise to those accustomed to playing in more congested areas is that all but one or two of the province's more than 80 courses are open to play by visitors. In recent years, there has been an explosion of interest in golf in

Nova Scotia, as there has been elsewhere. A number of new championship courses have opened and more are on the drawing books from the likes of such renowned golfers as Nick Faldo. The addition of championship layouts in Fox Harbour, Baddeck and Halifax has been complemented by the restoration and refurbishment of the classic Highlands Links in Cape Breton. Canada's most respected golf writer, Lorne Rubenstein, has listed this Stanley Thompson layout as one of the top five courses in the country, and in various golf publications it has been rated the best course in Canada.

Great courses by the sea are few and far between in most places and usually private, yet Nova Scotia has quite a number, from the legendary beauty of Highlands Links in Cape Breton to the Chester Golf Course overlooking the islands of Mahone Bay, to Northumberland and Fox Harb'r golf courses, from which the red cliffs of Prince Edward Island are visible. Opening in 2010, The Lakes Golf Club overlooking the Bras D'or Lakes is a Graham Cooke design that will rival the best of our resort courses. Even more tempting is Cabot Links, which will be a true links course on the outskirts of Inverness in western Cape Breton. Cabot Links was developed by the same group that made Bandon Dunes in Oregon, one of the top courses in the world. Serious golfers will want to pick up the *Nova Scotia Golf Guide* by Garvie Samson and Scott Smith. It contains details on the more than 60 Nova Scotia courses, including some we didn't know existed. Another excellent resource is http://golfingns.com, which has links to all the courses you might want to play and up-to-date information on the newest developments.

Detailed descriptions of the best golf courses in the province are found in Part III. Set out below is a suggested itinerary for many of the best courses, which would make an excellent golfing vacation for golfers of any calibre. The tour begins in Halifax, but if you are arriving by car at Amherst or Yarmouth, it can be adjusted accordingly. The tour will take you to the most scenic areas of the province including the South Shore, Annapolis Valley, Northumberland Strait and the Cabot Trail. At most you should have a 2–3 hour drive each day.

Day 1 — Arrive in Halifax. Play Glen Arbour. Overnight in Halifax.
Day 2 — Play Chester or Osprey Ridge. Overnight in Digby.
Day 3 — Play the Pines. Overnight in Wolfville.
Day 4 — Play KenWo or Avon Valley. Overnight in Pictou.
Day 5 — Play Northumberland Links or Fox Harb'r. Overnight in Pictou.
Day 6 — Play Dundee. Overnight in Baddeck.
Day 7 — Play Bell Bay. Overnight in Baddeck.
Day 8 — Play Highlands Links. Overnight in Ingonish.
Day 9 — Play Grand Portage. Overnight in Cheticamp.
Day 10 — Return to Halifax.

HIKING

If there is one tourism sector where the chance to explore Nova Scotia has increased dramatically, it has been in the number and variety of hiking trails that have been opened or expanded over the past 20 years. Perhaps only kayaking has seen a greater explosion of interest from Nova Scotians and visitors. Nova Scotia's extremely varied coastlines, combined with its distinct geographic and geologic regions, offer hiking opportunities second to none in Canada. We have hiked almost all Nova Scotia's recognized trails and can say with certainty that this healthy and inexpensive activity is one of the best ways to really discover the unique landscapes of Nova Scotia.

Most of the hikes described in this book can be divided into a number of basic categories — hikes along the coast, hikes along inland valleys often leading to waterfalls, hikes to look-offs and vistas and hikes along abandoned railbeds, usually as part of the Trans Canada Trail.

Some of the hikes described in this book are all-day treks, while others are shorter rambles, taking only a few hours to complete. For hikers desiring a longer experience, there are a number of options. One is to check out the current status of the Trans Canada Trail. This is the longest and most ambitious trail project ever undertaken anywhere. When complete, it will link all provinces and territories in approximately 21,500 kilometre pathway that will be open not only to hikers, but also to bikers and snowmobilers. The Nova Scotia section will be 700 kilometres when complete. As of 2009, 400 kilometres have been opened. When fully completed, the Nova Scotia trail will link the Acadian trail system along Cape Breton's rugged western coastline to trails on the mainland that mostly follow abandoned railway beds. Sections of the trail in Cape Breton are open from Meat Cove, near the extreme northern tip of the island, to Mabou Harbour on the western coast. This trail wanders from sea level to the highland plateau and maintains almost constant visual contact with the Gulf of St. Lawrence. It promises to be one of the most popular hiking destinations in eastern Canada. As well, substantial portions of the trail are now open along the Eastern Shore, in the Northumberland Strait area and along the South Shore where you can now go from Halifax to beyond Liverpool without interruption. By the next edition, the entire Nova Scotia segment is scheduled to be complete. Some of the portions that have been finished are described in further detail in Part III.

One thing that needs to be commented upon with respect to usage of the Trans Canada Trail is the fact that Nova Scotia, unlike almost all other Canadian jurisdictions, permits all-terrain vehicles (ATVs) on large portions of the trail. In the author's opinion Nova Scotia made a huge mistake in breaking with the Active Transportation model favoured by almost all of the other provinces and territories in Canada. The subject of a continuous ATV trail from Yarmouth to Cape Breton is a highly controversial one in Nova Scotia, with empassioned opinions on both sides. But the authors contend that in this age of awareness about the need to use energy wisely, of the benefits of physical activity and the necessity to preserve the environment, there is no place for these mechanized toys on national pathways. Not only does their very use detract from the enjoyment of walkers, bikers and skiers because of their speed, noise and exhaust fumes, and they can cause physical damage to the trail. Bridges that should last decades need repair or replacement not long after opening. Paths that have been carefully groomed so that small children on bikes or even strollers can access them are turned into rutted mounds that even mountain bikes have a hard time traversing. Frankly, we are ashamed that Nova Scotia is so out of touch with the rest of Canada, and most of the world for that matter, on this issue and has allowed the selfish desires of a few to trump the wishes of many more to use and enjoy the Trans Canada Trail in a sane and sustainable manner.

Almost as eagerly anticipated as the completion of the Trans Canada Trail has been the opening of Cape Chignecto Provincial Park. Nova Scotia's newest and largest provincial park preserves the remotest and wildest part of the Fundy coastline, with the highest cliffs and arguably the most dramatic seascapes in all of North America. The park will not be developed and facilities will remain at a minimum. An extremely rugged 50-kilometre trail circumnavigating the park has been built. Recently, the Eatonville Day Use Area opened up an entirely new area of the park to hikers and wilderness campers. It is now possible to hike to the famous Three Sisters rock formation. Altogether, there are five new scenic lookoffs that provide some of the most worthwhile reasons to hike Cape Chignecto.

There are a number of publications that focus exclusively on hiking in Nova Scotia and provide detailed maps of the hikes that space does not permit in this volume. Most notable are Michael Haynes' *Hiking Trails of Nova Scotia*, now in its 8th edition, and *Hiking Trails of Cape Breton*, which detail over 70 different hikes of all types and lengths. Also of note are Pat O'Neil's *Explore More! Cape Breton: A Guide to Hiking and Outdoor Adventure*, which has many interesting trails in the Cape Breton area not included in this book, and David Lawley's *A Nature and Hiking Guide to Cape Breton's Cabot Trail*, which has detailed information on the trails of Cape Breton Highlands National Park. Also of particular interest to those who relish waterfalls (and who doesn't) is Allan Billard's *Waterfalls: Nova Scotia's Masterpieces*. This volume describes 42 waterfalls and the trails that lead to them.

There are a number of companies that offer specialized hiking tours in Nova Scotia. Among these we recommend Scott Walking Tours, which is based in Nova Scotia and specializes in Atlantic Canadian destinations. They can be reached at www.scottwalking.com.

Every one of Nova Scotia's scenic trails has opportunities for hiking enthusiasts, and in Part III you will find details about some of our favourite routes.

MOUNTAIN BIKING

Nova Scotia, with its long history of settlement, is particularly well-suited to certain types of mountain biking. What do settlements have to do with mountain biking opportunities? Simple: settlers build roads — roads linking farms to new towns, roads to mines, lumber roads and military roads. When the mines run out, the trees have been felled or the armies move on to fight their battles elsewhere, the roads are abandoned, at least until they are rediscovered by mountain bikers.

Nova Scotia is literally covered with these old tracks and forgotten roads that lead not only to abandoned farmsteads, sawmills or mines, but sometimes entire communities that have disappeared into the mists of time. Other than hiking, mountain biking is often the only way to visit these out-of-the-way spots, but mountain biking in Nova Scotia is not by any means limited just to abandoned roads. Long before the Europeans arrived, the aboriginal peoples had clearly defined woodland paths, some of which still exist. At Kejimkujik National Park it is possible to bike some of these ancient paths along the banks of the Mersey River and Lake Kejimkujik. Finally, if your interest is in strenuous and grueling climbs followed by exhilarating downhills, then the Cape Breton Highlands has more than enough off-road trails to keep you occupied. Try the trip to Money Point at the very tip of Cape North, Nova Scotia's most northerly location, for a real killer of a ride.

Geoff Brown and Kermit Degooyer's *Mountain Bike Nova Scotia* details 18 one-day tours that cover just about every type of terrain and mountain biking experience available in this province, including the aforementioned Money Point trip.

MUSEUMS

The provincial and federal governments operate and maintain over 30 museums throughout Nova Scotia. In addition, there are approximately 75 community and privately owned museums that are open to the public, spread throughout all the counties. In any day's drive you are bound to come across at least one or two. Some, such as the Maritime Museum of the Atlantic in Halifax and the Fisheries Museum in Lunenburg are worthy destinations in and of themselves. There are thematic museums, such as the Miners' Museum in Springhill, or those dedicated to one individual, such as Hank Snow in Liverpool or Giant MacAskill in Englishtown. There are a great number of historic homes, such as Haliburton House in Windsor or Prescott House just outside Port Williams. In Sherbrooke Village, an entire era has been recreated as a living museum. Whether your interest is history, nature, education or commerce, there is a museum for you. Our favourite museums and exhibits are described in detail in Part III.

ROCKHOUNDING

This interesting activity is very popular in Nova Scotia, especially in the Bay of Fundy area, which is recognized as one of the best collecting grounds in North America. Every August hundreds of collectors descend on Parrsboro for an annual get-together where a friendly exchange of information and a general display of specimens takes place. The primary attractions here are agates and amethysts. The basalt rock of the Fundy shoreline is studded with many minerals of the quartz family as well as zeolites. Collecting is relatively easy in most locations, involving no more than a leisurely walk along the shoreline at low tide. Some locations, such as Amethyst Cove on Cape Split and Moose Island, can only be reached by boat or strenuous hiking. Those willing to go to this extra trouble are usually rewarded with better specimens. The Bay of Fundy area is not alone in Nova Scotia in providing good rockhounding territory. The Hants County area is noted for gypsum, barite, fluorescent calcite, manganese and antimony. Gold occurs in quartz veins in many locations on the mainland and as placer deposits at the Ovens in Lunenburg County. Any of the coal-bearing areas of Cumberland, Pictou and Cape Breton counties can provide good samples of jet and other coal-related collectibles including fossilized vegetation. The Joggins area in Cumberland County is particularly noted for fossils.

The equipment needed for rockhounding is minimal — a geological hammer, protective eye glasses and a good book on mineral identification. The widely available *Geological Highway Map of Nova Scotia* will guide aspiring rockhounders to likely spots, as will a real or virtual visit to Rob's Rock Shop in Kentville (www.robsrockshop.com) where the owner will be glad to assist.

SAILING

Sailing and Nova Scotia go together like bread and butter. During the summer months the coast of Nova Scotia offers unlimited scope for cruising by sail or motorboat. The nautical traditions have been preserved since the province's golden age of sail. For visiting sailors this is a boon. Facilities are well distributed, modern and relatively inexpensive, with 30 provincial yacht clubs, all of which welcome visitors from other clubs. If you are not a member of a yacht club, you are still welcome at most of them. These clubs provide mooring and launching facilities, repairs, fuel and clubhouse privileges. A list of 20 marinas offering services to the public can be found in the *Doers' & Dreamers' Travel Guide*.

Sailors who favour the wind for propulsion outnumber by a large margin those who choose motor-driven cruisers. The steady and predictable winds of Nova Scotia waters minimize the necessity of resorting to engine power, other than for getting underway and docking.

The best sailing waters are on the Atlantic coast and in the Bras d'Or Lakes. The Atlantic shoreline, indented by hundreds of sheltered inlets and coves, provides no shortage of ideal mooring locations. In 2009, St. Margaret's Bay played host to the Laser World and Laser Masters World Championship, the largest competitive sailing competition ever held in Canada. Mahone Bay, with an island for every day of the year, is a sailing paradise. The Bras d'Or Lakes are really a small inland sea connected to the Atlantic by several channels and the St. Peter's Canal, completed in 1869. Here, the highlands of Cape Breton rise dramatically from the pristine blue waters of the lake, providing exquisite vistas. The Cape Breton Development Corporation has installed mooring sites at various locations around the lake to complement the many natural mooring sites available.

Canada Customs' regulations require that all foreign pleasure-craft report to the nearest Customs Office upon arrival in Canadian waters. Here a cruising permit is obtained which is surrendered upon departure. There are 19 ports of entry in Nova Scotia, so reporting should not be an inconvenience and will provide an opportunity to obtain nautical charts and information, if this has not been done in advance.

Those more interested in day-sailing than cruising can find daily rentals at many of the yacht clubs. Experienced sailors may have the opportunity to rent full-size sloops, while novices will likely be limited to Lasers or Sunfish. Windsurfers are also available at some locations. If you are not a sailor but would like to learn, there are over 15 locations at which to do this. Sailing lessons may vary from one-day or half-day private sessions to week-long courses on the open ocean. Anyone interested in lessons or rentals may obtain up-to-date information by contacting the Nova Scotia Yachting Association at www.nsya.ns.ca. This site links to all the information that any visiting sailor will need to plan for a Nova Scotia sailing vacation. *Cruising Nova Scotia from Yarmouth to Canso*, revised in 2003, by Wayne Clark, Judith Penner and George Rogers is a detailed and informative publication that will make any sailing trip easier to plan and execute.

All in all, Nova Scotia has something for everyone in the sailing department.

SEA KAYAKING

Sea kayaking is one of the fastest-growing sports in Nova Scotia. Not long ago, a sea kayak was a rare sight, but there are a number of outfitters offering not only rental equipment and instruction, but everything from overnight to week-long guided kayaking trips to some of Nova Scotia's most beautiful and remote spots. The province is naturally inclined toward this sport, with the immense variety of habitats along its coastline and the great numbers of offshore islands, particularly along the Atlantic coast. More experienced kayakers may be interested in exploring some of the palisade-like cliffs of Cape Breton or the Fundy shore. Others will be interested in the great variety of marine life, including several species of seals, dolphins and whales that frequent bays and harbours at different times of year; bluefin tuna, swordfish, sun fish and other unusual sea creatures can also be found within the waters off Nova Scotia. While the kayaking world has discovered Nova Scotia and realizes the untold possibilities for that sport here, the islands and bays remain relatively deserted in relation to other more populated areas of North America and Europe.

Scott Cunningham, who circumnavigated the entire province in the early 1980s, has written an invaluable book, *Sea Kayaking in Nova Scotia*, a compilation of three earlier volumes. It sets out in detail a great variety of routes around the Nova Scotia coast. Serious kayakers should plan their trip to Nova Scotia with the assistance of this book. Cunningham also offers tours through Coastal Adventures, www.coastaladventures.com.

THEATRE

For many years, Nova Scotia has had a number of active seasonal repertory theatre companies throughout the province. Halifax, especially since the founding of the Neptune Theatre in the early 1960s, has been an important regional centre for the performing arts. Since being completely rebuilt in 1997, Neptune has offered consistently high-quality productions of well-known musicals and dramas as well as the occasional original presentation. Complementing Neptune in Halifax is the Shakespeare by the Sea company that puts on works by the bard and others in the outdoor setting of Point Pleasant Park.

Regional repertory theatre has always been strongly supported throughout the province, and it is possible to take in shows at half a dozen locations including Chester, Yarmouth, Parrsboro and Antigonish.

In Part III, more detailed listings appear on the repertory theatres, as well as more on Neptune and Shakespeare by the Sea.

TRADITIONAL MUSIC

Nova Scotians accept as an historical fact that the first Scots to arrive in Nova Scotia, aboard the ship *Hector*, were piped ashore by an itinerant bagpiper, who shipped out for no particular reason other than to entertain the apprehensive immigrants on that long and rough voyage to a new life. Whether the tale is true matters little, for it is an undisputed fact that since the arrival of the Scots in Nova Scotia, there has been an unbroken tradition of playing Celtic music, and playing it extremely well. Ashley MacIsaac, Natalie MacMaster, the Rankins, the Barra MacNeils — if you have any interest whatsoever in Celtic music, you've heard these names. They are all Nova Scotians, Cape Bretoners to be precise, and they are the latest generation in a heritage that dates back to the first Scottish emigration to Nova Scotia over 200 years ago.

What exactly is traditional Celtic music? It is usually played on the fiddle with accompaniment on any number of other instruments, including the bagpipes, acoustic guitar, drums and spoons. It is primarily instrumental, although many of the songs do have words, if that makes any sense. Above all it is toe-tapping, knee-slapping get-up-and-dance music. It is almost always cheerful and full of life with little hint of the many economic problems that Cape Bretoners have long been accustomed to. It is the makings of a ceilidh, that celebration of life, that makes Cape Bretoners so unique.

If you want to attend a ceilidh and hear some great traditional music, then Nova Scotia is without doubt the place to do it. Almost every week throughout the summer and fall, in small communities such as Margaree, Mabou and Inverness, ceilidhs are held and visitors are welcome amid the warmth of the local hospitality. The musicians, whether they are well-known veterans, or up-and-comers, will almost certainly surprise you with their talent. We highly recommend that you make an effort to take in a ceilidh as part of your Nova Scotia vacation. The Celtic Colours music festival, which coincides with the glorious fall colours of the Margaree Valley, provides yet another reason to make a special trip to this magic isle. At venues all across Cape Breton, not only Nova Scotia's best but the world's best Celtic musicians join forces to produce a week-long ceilidh of massive proportions. Any true lover of Celtic music should make it a point to attend Celtic Colours at least once.

Celtic music is not the only traditional music played in Nova Scotia.

The Acadians have a very strong musical legacy, which you will recognize if you are familiar with Louisiana Cajun music. The Cajuns are descended from the Acadians. Today, Acadian music is still alive and well in Nova Scotia and may be heard during any one of a number of Acadian festivals that are held throughout the summer.

While not strictly speaking traditional music, country music is also very popular in Nova Scotia, particularly along the South Shore and Annapolis Valley. Hank Snow, Wilf Carter and Carroll Baker all hail from these vicinities. If you like country music laced with old-time fiddlin', take in one of the county exhibitions along the South Shore or in the Valley.

WALKING TOURS

If you are not a "hiker" but you do like to discover new territory on foot, then you may be looking for some walking tours along your way. Nova Scotia's coast is dotted with many picturesque small towns and villages, many of which are worthy of a stroll around the main streets. Increasingly, tourists are realizing the value of not just speeding through these towns, but getting out and walking around to more fully appreciate the architecture and history, as well as absorbing the local colour.

For all the different flavour that Nova Scotia has to display, there is a wide choice of communities to explore, from the historic reconstruction of Louisbourg to the narrow, steep streets of Lunenburg or the Scottish heritage of Pictou. Many of these towns have developed their own walking tours and these are noted in Part III. The authors recommend possible routes for several interesting communities where no "official" tour has been set out. Whether your stay in Nova Scotia is a few days or a few weeks long, you'll find that a walk around town will give you a real feeling for the heart of Nova Scotia — its towns and villages.

WHALE-WATCHING

Nova Scotia is the top destination in eastern North America for whale-watching, in terms of both the variety of species that can be seen and the sheer number of whales. The warm waters of the Gulf Stream pass close by the cold waters of the Bay of Fundy, creating an up-welling of organic material, which in turn leads to plankton that attracts whales. From spring to late fall, the mouth of the Bay of Fundy is the feeding ground of some of the largest whales on earth, including fin whales, humpbacks and the extremely rare Atlantic right whale. Smaller minkes and pilot whales are common, as are a number of species of dolphins and porpoises. The odds of seeing whales on an expedition from Brier Island or Digby Neck are so good that most operators offer a money-back guarantee should no whales be seen. So far they have had to honour this guarantee only once or twice in the past few years.

The Bay of Fundy is not the only area for whale-watching. The Gulf of St. Lawrence and Cabot Strait, accessible from ports along western and northern Cape Breton, are also home to many species, especially schools of smaller pilot whales. If you have never been whale-watching before, you have no idea of the majesty of these giant creatures and the awe-inspiring effect they have on people who view them close up. You really owe it to yourself to go whale-watching at least once in your life, and there is no better place to do it than Nova Scotia.

WILDERNESS AREAS

Of all the provinces and territories, Nova Scotia has the smallest percentage of publicly owned land, most of it having been doled out in Crown grants designed to attract settlers and industry over a hundred years ago. The high concentration of private land has resulted in widespread clearcutting through the province. Knowing that once a province's wilderness heritage is lost through forestry, mining or other activity, it is virtually impossible to reclaim, in the 1990s some far-sighted people within and without government set about to achieve a goal of preserving 12 per cent of the province's landmass as protected areas. Part of that goal has been attained by the designation of 33 Wilderness Areas accounting for 5 per cent of Nova Scotia. While many of these areas are relatively small — designed to protect some unique natural feature — others, such as Tobeatic and Pollett's Cove/Aspy Fault, are huge and offer fantastic recreational opportunities for those who are prepared to rough it. In Part III we set out a number of specific things to do in various Wilderness Areas. For information on any of the Wilderness Areas visit www.gov.ns.ca/nse/protectedareas/wildernessareas. asp where you will also find a photo gallery that will whet your appetite for a visit to one of these areas.

WINERIES

For many years Canadians were not significant consumers of wine. That has changed dramatically over the past few decades as the benefits of moderate wine consumption have been widely publicized and wine sales have soared at the expense of beer and hard liquor. This has in turn sparked an explosion in the number of wineries throughout North America and Nova Scotia is no exception. Considering that Nova Scotia is, according to most historians, the Vinland discovered by the Norsemen over a thousand years ago and named for the wild grapes that were found growing here at the time, it is not surprising that there is a long association with viniculture. It is known that as early as the 1630s French settlers were growing grapes for the purposes of making wine.

The first efforts at commercial wine-making began well over thirty-five years ago in the Annapolis Valley and were not particularly successful. However, that all changed with the establishment of the Jost Winery on the Malagash Peninsula, which has produced many prize-winning wines including world-class ice wines. A second look at the Annapolis Valley revealed many distinct territories that have in turn spawned new plantings and wineries. Nova Scotia even has its own distinct white grape — the L'Acadie Blanc, which produces a wine that pairs very well with Nova Scotia seafood. In addition to wines made via the traditional grape method, a number of Nova Scotian wineries specialize in fruit wines based on blueberries, strawberries and other native fruits and berries.

There are now enough established wineries to warrant a separate book. Sean Wood, long-time wine columnist for the Halifax newspaper, *The Chronicle Herald,* has written *Wineries and Wine Country of Nova Scotia,* which provides everything you need to know about Nova Scotia wineries, with a few micro-breweries and a distillery thrown in for good measure. For online information go to the excellent Winery Association of Nova Scotia site at www.winesofnovascotia.ca, where there is information on upcoming wine festivals and events, most of which spotlight the pairing of Nova Scotia wines with local produce.

WINTER SPORTS

This is only the third edition that has included anything on winter sports, and that's probably because the last few winters have seen reliable snowfall with a minimum of rain or extremely cold temperatures. Cape Breton, the Cobequid Mountains and parts of the Annapolis Valley have had especially good snowfalls. When we do get this type of weather in winter, Nova Scotia is a wonderful place to be outside. While it is true that no one should plan a trip to Nova Scotia just for downhill skiing, there are a great number of opportunities for cross-country skiing. Both national parks keep a number of trails open exclusively for cross-country and snowshoeing. In highland areas, several tourist operators have developed trails specifically to attract a winter clientele. Some of these places are quite remote and offer some very challenging trails. For example, check out Ski-Tuonela at www. skituonela.com. For novices, the abandoned railbeds that form much of the Trans Canada Trail in Nova Scotia are great spots for an outing, in particular the sections at Mabou, St. Margarets Bay and various places along the Eastern Shore.

Although we are not enthusiasts about mechanized recreation and, frankly, despise the damage we repeatedly come across from ATVs, there is some appreciation for snowmobilers who, on the whole, seem to be an accommodating and responsible group. For snowmobile enthusiasts, there are over 3,500 kilometres of trail linking 20 separate snowmobile clubs. For example, the Fundy Trail Snowmobile Club maintains a very scenic set of trails through the hardwood forests in the Cobequid Mountains, over 130 kilometres of which are groomed. The snow in the Cobequids is quite reliable, primarily due to the elevation. For more information check out the Snowmobilers Association of Nova Scotia at www.snowmobilersns.com.

Part III
Around the Province

HALIFAX/DARTMOUTH

For the many visitors who make landfall in Nova Scotia at Stanfield International Airport, chances are their first impressions will be determined by what they see as they make their way into Halifax (www.destinationhalifax.com) by taxi, bus or rental car. After what seems like an overly long and somewhat tedious ride one comes to the rather ordinary-looking suburbs of Dartmouth, but after a few turns suddenly there it is, right in front of you. You see the graceful arch of the Angus L. Macdonald suspension bridge, which connects Dartmouth to Halifax. Rising high over the water and structures below you look down and see a cluster of architecturally pleasing high-rise buildings, some actually with their pilings in the water. Behind them rises a large hill with an impressive fortification festooned with flags and military banners that is the Citadel. Looking toward the harbour mouth you spy a collection of what appear to be older buildings amidst which are the spires of wooden sailing ships and modern yachts. You see ferries, sailboats, container ships and cruise ships intermingling almost nonchalantly. Looking toward Bedford Basin you see another beautiful bridge spanning the harbour, and in between the many cruisers, destroyers, submarines, supply ships and other boats that make up Canada's East Coast fleet. When you look down, the sun fairly glistens off the water and sends shimmering reflections among the glass towers that line the water's edge. It is a wonderful sight. You know you are going to love Halifax.

Somewhat cumbersomely named, the Halifax Regional Municipality encompasses all of what was formerly Halifax County. This area stretches from Hubbards on the South Shore, to Ecum Secum on the Eastern Shore — a distance of over 150 kilometres. This chapter comprises, for the most part, sites and activities of the peninsular city of Halifax, its cross-harbour neighbour Dartmouth, the former town of Bedford and the surrounding areas.

Halifax was founded by the British as a military counterbalance to the great French fortress at Louisbourg. The harbour had long been recognized as one of the best deep-water ports in all of eastern North America, especially because it opens into the expanse of Bedford Basin, where literally hundreds of ships can moor in safety. It is also ice-free year round.

In 1749, Colonel Edward Cornwallis landed with a large number of soldiers and prospective settlers, many of whom were among the dregs of British society. Over the next few years, they laid out a city street grid and commenced building a fortress to guard the harbour. The fortress later developed into the Citadel, one of North America's finest and, ultimately, most successful military installations. Halifax in turn developed into the principal naval centre for the British Empire for over 200 years. The port played a role in the fall of Louisbourg and Quebec, was a strategic part of the British evacuation of New York during the American Revolution and then played a pivotal role in the War of 1812 and the Napoleonic conflict. In the twentieth century, Halifax was the departure point for Allied convoys taking vital troops and supplies to Europe in both world wars and was central to the control of the North Atlantic. The Battle of the Atlantic was planned and fought largely out of Halifax.

Although Halifax has never been the centre of conflict, it has nevertheless paid the price of the fortunes and misfortunes of war. The military establishment has brought prosperity, especially in wartime, and it has left its mark in the many monuments commemorating conflict, including some of the more obscure ones, such as the Northwest Rebellion. This prosperity has had its dark side.

The congregation of sailors, soldiers, privateers, freebooters and all-round scallywags brought murder, mayhem, drunkenness and prostitution. Although Haligonians don't like to admit it, this is as much a part of their past as military pride. Perhaps Halifax's darkest hour came in 1917, when the harbour was the site of the largest man-made, non-nuclear explosion in history. A ship carrying munitions exploded after a collision, and literally flattened much of the city, killing almost 2,000 and wounding many thousands of others in schools, factories, hospitals and homes.

Today, Halifax continues to play a dominant role in Canada's naval defences as home of the Atlantic fleet. At any given time, the city is likely to host large numbers of visiting NATO ships. It has also become a major destination for cruise ships, and there may be up to five at a time in port. Fortunately, the city is big enough and has enough attractions and facilities to easily accommodate these huge influxes of visitors without taking on the frenetic atmosphere of some smaller cruise ports.

Despite, or perhaps because of, its checkered past Halifax is now a very lively and liveable city. As the major regional centre of Atlantic Canada, Halifax offers most of the amenities of larger Canadian cities while preserving the friendliness and sense of community associated with much smaller places. It may seem paradoxical, but Halifax does manage to feel like a big city and a small town at the same time. Many Haligonians, as residents are properly described, live on the peninsula and are able to walk to work in the small core area where most of the government, financial, health and educational institutions are located. The overall population is among the best-educated in North America, largely due to a concentration of universities unmatched by any other Canadian city. Halifax is also the home of one of Canada's premier health centres, the Queen Elizabeth II Health Sciences complex, which provides medical services at no less than a dozen hospitals and other related facilities. For the average tourist, who is probably not that interested in universities and hospitals, there is an abundance of things to see and do, including professional theatre, art galleries, museums, great historical sites and wonderful parks and gardens. However, probably the most enjoyment the tourist will find is in simply ambling around the waterfront, poking into shops in the restored historic districts, exploring the narrow streets looking at examples of Georgian and Victorian architecture or dropping into one of the many fine pubs and restaurants for a bite to eat, perhaps striking up a conversation with the friendly locals or singing along with one of the many good Celtic bands in the city. To do the Halifax area justice, plan to spend at least three days in the area.

Many Haligonians believe the best thing about Dartmouth is the view of Halifax, but this is an injustice to the twin city. Dartmouth has the best lakes, beaches and birding in the metro area, and it has many interesting sites, including several museums, the Shubenacadie Canal project and the Black Cultural Centre.

Ever since its founding in 1750, a year after Halifax, Dartmouth has played second fiddle. While it continues to be a bedroom community for Halifax, as evidenced by recent housing developments in Cole Harbour and eastern Dartmouth, there are signs of change. Dartmouth is home to Burnside, the largest and most successful industrial park in Atlantic Canada, and Dartmouth Crossing, a mammoth retail enterprise. While Dartmouth may not be a tourist destination in and of itself, consider spending a day visiting the sites of downtown Dartmouth followed by a visit to Rainbow Haven Beach for a swim or a walk on some of the fine trails to be found on this side of the harbour. A suggested day trip to sites near Dartmouth is described later in this section.

The traditional rivalry between Halifax and Dartmouth remains despite the amalgamation. Officially, the entire region may be the Halifax Regional Municipality, but only politicians and bureaucrats actually call it that. Everybody else still refers to Halifax, Dartmouth, Bedford, or "the County," depending on where they live.

For further reading on Halifax, try to pick up Thomas Raddall's classic *Warden of the North*, which provides a great history of the city's turbulent past. For a more recent history, *Halifax, the First 250 Years* is an illustrated volume by several respected local academics. Grant MacLean's *Walk Historic Halifax* has seven comprehensive tours that cover the entire city as well as McNab's Island. Anyone visiting Halifax should pick up a copy of *The Coast*, a free weekly newspaper widely available throughout metro. In it you will find a complete rundown of what is going on in the festival, entertainment and local dining scenes. *The Coast* has for years held an annual "Best of" competition whereby locals pick their favourites on a large variety of topics. Keep an eye open for "Coast winner" stickers on attractions, businesses, restaurants and bars if you want to sample Haligonians' top choices.

BEACHES

Crystal Crescent, Sambro

About 16 miles from downtown Halifax, Crystal Crescent is as beautiful a beach as its name implies, noted for clear cold waters and beautiful sand. It has always been a favourite of scuba divers, who look for old bottles and other sea treasures. Getting to Crystal Crescent is a very interesting drive, which follows Herring Cove Road out from the city all the way to the picturesque fishing community of Sambro. From there signs will direct you to the beach road. You can return to Halifax via a more direct route by following the signs for Harrietsfield. Crystal Crescent has a beautiful view of Sambro Island, which features one of Canadian's oldest continuously operated lighthouses. On calm days, sea kayakers use the beach as a launch pad for a visit to this allegedly haunted island. It is also an interesting spot to watch ships, large and small, as they make their way in and out of Halifax Harbour.

Crystal Crescent is a provincial park and its facilities have been improved over the past few years. There are now public washrooms and ample parking.

There is a well-marked trail and boardwalk that will take you from the main beach to other beaches which are usually less crowded. In between the beaches there are plenty of places to sit on the rocks to enjoy a picnic or simply gaze at the sea. The third beach has over the past few years become a favourite gathering spot of local nudists or naturists as they now like to be called. If this makes you uncomfortable you should limit your visit to the first two beaches. Crystal Crescent is also the starting point for the very popular Pennant Point hiking trail.

Rainbow Haven, Cole Harbour

This spacious beach close to downtown Dartmouth has recently been upgraded and has a full range of facilities, including lifeguards and a boardwalk. The kilometre-long strand almost completely crosses the mouth of Cole Harbour. The water is clean, although cold. This beach is a good place for a stop if you decide to take the recommended one-day tour of Dartmouth and surrounding area that is described further in this chapter.

BIRDING

Clarence Stevens, who is well-known to metro birders for his shy smile and boundless enthusiasm when it comes to anything connected with birds, has written *Birding in Metro Halifax*, which is a month-by-month guide to birding in the entire metro area. It is well worth picking up, as it will guide you to good birding spots no matter when you visit.

BOAT TOURS

Murphy's on the Water, Cable Wharf, (902) 420-1015, www.murphysonthewater.com

Whether you want to take a narrated sightseeing tour of the harbour, go on a romantic dinner-and-dance outing, take a day trip to McNabs Island or go for the big catch, Murphy's has a boat for you. In our experience, they run a good ship. The tour of the harbour on the *Harbour Queen* is probably your best bet if your time is limited. It will take you under the bridges, past the naval dockyard, around Point Pleasant and down the Northwest Arm in a narrated journey that lasts a couple of hours. A more recent addition to the fleet is the *Harbour Hopper*, which is a large amphibious craft with massive tires that combines a city tour with a boat tour. After navigating the city streets, it takes to the water and provides a short trip up and down the waterfront. The *Harbour Hopper* is a fun alternative to the more traditional bus and boat tour. For the young ones *Theodore Tugboat*, a real-life version of the children's television character, will be the trip of choice. A two-and-a-half hour tour to Peggy's Cove and back — the only such trip available from Halifax — is also offered. Finally, there is the *Mar II*, a renowned 75-foot tall ship that has circumnavigated the globe twice. If you can't find what you're looking for at Murphy's, you are a confirmed landlubber. Murphy's Web site has a three-minute video that allows you to see each of the various boats and tours.

The Dartmouth Ferry, Ferry Terminal, Upper Water Street/Alderney Drive

This may be the best value in this book. The Halifax/Dartmouth connection is the longest continuously run ferry service in North America. For just over $2, you can ride the ferry that plies the harbour between Halifax and Dartmouth every half hour. On a warm summer day, there is no better place in metro to be than on the open upper deck of the ferry as it passes by ocean-going tankers, giant container ships, submarines — you name it. There is no requirement that you must disembark at each landing, so you can go back and forth all day if you like. The view of the Halifax skyline as you approach from Dartmouth at night is spectacular. The ferry terminal is at the end of George Street right in the heart of the waterfront.

CANOEING

Dartmouth Lakes and the Shubenacadie Canal System

There are probably few people outside of Nova Scotia who realize that for well over a hundred years, Dartmouth has been a centre of canoeing excellence. Known as the City of Lakes, Dartmouth has a number of canoe clubs that have consistently produced Canadian and even world champions. In 2009, the World Canoeing Championships were held in Dartmouth, the largest sporting event ever held in Atlantic Canada. If you would like to get in a little urban paddling, drop into Paddle East Canoe and Kayak, 300 Prince Albert Road, Dartmouth. Situated right on Lake Banook, Paddle East Canoe and Kayak rent both canoes and kayaks. Check them out at www.paddleeast.ca.

If you are up for something a little different, consider paddling some or all of the 100-kilometre Shubenacadie Canal System. The system bisects the province from Dartmouth to the Bay of Fundy and the system takes three or four days to complete. Beginning just outside Dartmouth, it follows the route of the old Shubenacadie Canal, originally opened in 1861 to provide an inland transportation link to Halifax. The canal joins a series of lakes and eventually enters the Shubenacadie River, which may be followed to its mouth on the Bay of Fundy. Most canoeists, wary of the treacherous tides and sandbars near the river's estuary, usually pull out around Milford, where the river becomes tidal. This route combines forest and farmland scenery with stream and open-lake canoeing. Fishing for land-locked salmon, striped and smallmouth bass and trout is good, especially in Grand Lake. Much of the lock system had long fallen into disuse and many short portages were necessary, but a major restoration effort from Dartmouth to Grand Lake has been completed, reducing the number of portages. The entire canal has been designated a National Historic Engineering Site. A series of maps of the entire Shubenacadie Canal system is available through Maps and More. For more detailed information on the history of the canal go to http://shubie.chebucto.org/History2.htm. Refer also to the entry under Shubie Park.

CEMETERIES

The Old Burying Ground, corner of Barrington Street and Spring Garden Road, Halifax

The Old Burying Ground, Halifax's first cemetery dating back to the founding of the city, has been carefully and lovingly restored. The headstones, which have been cleaned and straightened, contain some of the finest examples of gravestone art in the province.

There are some exceptional Masonic stones and a number of very interesting inscriptions. At the entrance to the cemetery, the sandstone arch topped by a lion is Canada's only monument to the Crimean War and the two Haligonians who were killed in service. Although the Old Burying Ground is located on one of the city's busiest corners, once inside its iron gates, you are in a green oasis of tranquility and you will soon forget that the twenty-first century is grinding along a few feet away. If you visit only one cemetery in Nova Scotia, this should be the one. There are a number of informative panels that will greatly enhance a visit to this site. A number of well-known figures are buried here, including General Robert Ross, who was responsible for the burning of Washington during the War of 1812, and Captain Lawrence of the *Chesapeake* who is still remembered for his stirring evocation "Don't give up the ship."

For a list of all those buried in the Old Burying Ground, with details on some of the most noteworthy and photos of some of the best gravestones to visit, see www.angelfire.com/ns/bkeddy/oldburyground.html.

Camp Hill Cemetery, corner of Robie Street and Sackville Street, Halifax

Located to the west of the Public Gardens, Camp Hill Cemetery was opened shortly before the Old Burying Ground reached capacity, and contains the graves of many of the city's early luminaries. Of particular note are the graves of the great reformer Joseph Howe, who many consider to be Nova Scotia's most outstanding citizen; Enos Collins, Halifax's famous privateer banker; and Abraham Gesner, a noted scientist and inventor of kerosene, who effectively saved the northern right whales from extinction when his discovery replaced whale oil for lighting. Also of note is the grave of beer baron Alexander Keith, at which on the anniversary of his birth, a dedicated group of thankful beer drinkers gathers to pay him tribute. Recently, Robert Stanfield, whom many consider our last great premier, was interred at Camp Hill. In addition, there are two Fathers of Confederation and many foreign sailors from the Confederate navy to the Norwegian and Dutch merchant marines.

The *Titanic* Graves

The sinking of the grand ocean liner *Titanic* on its maiden voyage in 1912 is indisputably the most well-known and well-documented marine tragedy in history. Of the over 1,500 who lost their lives, only 328 bodies were recovered, of which 209 were taken to Halifax. There are 150 buried in three cemeteries in Halifax; 121 in Fairview Lawn, 19 in Mount Olivet Catholic Cemetery and 10 in Baron de Hirsch Jewish Cemetery. In 1998, *Titanic* fever gripped the world with the release of James Cameron's movie *Titanic*. While the opening scenes were shot offshore near Halifax, the lasting effect on Halifax has been the heightened interest in visiting the grave sites of these most unfortunate of souls. One of the graves in Fairview Lawn is that of J. Dawson, one of the ship's crew. Although director Cameron denies any connection with the fact that the lead character in the movie is named Jack Dawson, try telling that to the many young women who visit the gravesite annually. A trek to the *Titanic* graves has become a regular day-trip offering by cruise ships that call at Halifax. Fairview Lawn and Mount Olivet are open to the public and have directions and interpretive information on site. Your own visit to the graves will be a more interesting experience if you go there after visiting the Maritime Museum of the Atlantic. The museum offers a 3-D *Titanic* experience and is home to many *Titanic* artifacts. More information on the *Titanic* disaster and the graves can be found at http://titanic.gov.ns.ca.

Also of note in these cemeteries are the graves of many victims of the Halifax Explosion, including entire families and most of the children of Richmond School.

Holy Cross, 1259 South Park Street, Halifax

This was the first Catholic cemetery in Halifax. It contains the grave of John Thompson, Canada's fourth prime minister, who died while visiting Queen Victoria in Windsor Castle shortly after he assumed office. Many believed that Thompson would have been one of Canada's great prime ministers had he not been stricken at a young age. A recently erected plaque identifies this significant gravesite.

Deadman's Island, 24 Pinehaven Drive off Herring Cove Road

Although technically not a cemetery, Deadman's Island does contain the remains of almost two hundred Americans who died during the course of the War of 1812. They are apparently buried in a mass unmarked grave on Deadman's Island. Recently the island was purchased by the city and a plaque erected containing the names of the dead soldiers and sailors. Of particular note are some that were killed during the famous naval engagement between the *Chesapeake* and the *Shannon*, which occurred off the coast of New England. Looking up from the plaque you can see the old Melville Island prison just across the cove where many of these prisoners of war died of disease while being held captive.

CYCLING
Rails to Trails

Halifax is not a particularly bike-friendly city. The roads in the peninsula of Halifax tend to be narrow and there are very few dedicated cycling paths let alone cycling lanes, although that is slowly changing. However the development of Rails to Trails has provided opportunities on both sides of the harbour. One of the best is the trail which runs from suburban Beechville to Hubbards and beyond if you want. The surface varies but in all places it is fine for mountain bikes. Although some portions of the trail are not particularly scenic, many are, particularly the sections through Lewis Lake Provincial Park and portions of the trail that overlook St. Margaret's Bay. You can make a really good one-day biking trip by having someone drop you off at Hubbards and cycle into the city. You will have the prevailing winds at your back most of the way. Another option is to start at the Train Station Bike & Bean, 5401 St. Margarets Bay Road (www.bikeandbean.ca), which is located in the old French Village train station directly on the Lighthouse Route. This relatively new business has become a focal point for cyclists. It is nice to be able to share a coffee or a glass of wine with fellow enthusiasts after a pleasant day of riding. The Bike and Bean also has rentals.

Exercise caution on these trails, which are frequently used by ATV drivers.

GOLF
Granite Springs, Highway 333, Bayside, (902) 852-4653, www.granitespringsgolf.com

This course was carved from the granite hills that rise steeply above the shore around Bayside on Peggy's Cove Road. As the name implies, there is both rock and water.

Although it is built less than a mile from the ocean, it is an inland course and there are no views of the ocean other than from the driving range. The holes are narrow and the greens well trapped. The signature hole, the tenth, features an elevated green sitting atop a huge granite outcrop. The fairway is bisected in a number of places by other granite outcrops. This hole is very close to target golf, a new idea for Nova Scotia.

The clubhouse is without doubt among the finest in Nova Scotia, being constructed entirely of logs with no expense spared. Primarily a daily-fee operation that caters to group outings, Granite Springs welcomes greens fee players in an atmosphere of hospitality and professionalism.

Hartlen Point Forces Golf Club, Eastern Passage, (902) 465-GOLF (4653), www.hartlenpoint.com

This armed forces club holds a commanding position overlooking the eastern entrance to Halifax Harbour. The course is divided into two very different nines. The majority of the holes in the front nine are cut out of the woods surrounding a small cove on the back side of Hartlen Point.

From the regular men's tee, this nine is almost 3,500 yards long. The back nine is much shorter and completely wide open, very similar to a

European seaside course. While it looks easy, the constant wind makes it devilishly difficult. Hartlen Point is not an easy course, but the tremendous views of the entrance to Halifax Harbour and Devils Island, with its picturesque lighthouse and abandoned outbuildings, goes a long way to make up for the punishment this course can exact. Originally built as a military course, it welcomes visiting greens fee players.

Glen Arbour, 40 Clubhouse Lane, Hammonds Plains, (902) 835-4653, www.glenarbour.com

Shortly after it opened, Glen Arbour was being touted as one of the best courses in the province (if not the best) and the accolades are well-deserved. Designed by Graham Cooke, who is also responsible for the exceptional Links at Crowbush Cove on Prince Edward Island, the course meanders 7,000 yards around a series of small lakes set in a pristine mixed-hardwood forest. Many of the holes are extremely demanding, with very long carries from elevated tees over brooks, inlets and marshes. On several holes, massive ancient hemlocks add a touch of grandeur. Developed in conjunction with a real estate development, no expense was spared and it shows. There is a full-service clubhouse with a good restaurant run by friendly and helpful staff. The course is strictly a daily-fee operation, unless you live in the subdivision, and it is expensive by Nova Scotia standards. It hosted the 2005 LPGA Canadian Women's Open, which attests to its stature in Canadian golf. Glen Arbour is a definite "must play" for any serious golfer.

Grandview Golf & Country Club, 431 Crane Hill Road, Dartmouth, (902) 435-3767, www.eaglequestgolf.com.

Grandview is a course which is often overlooked by visitors to the metro area when choosing a good course to play. Located just outside Dartmouth off Highway 7, Grandview is a good challenge for all levels of golfers. The two nines are quite distinct from each other. The front nine is fairly wide open while the holes in the back nine are cut out of the surrounding forest. A ball that is not on the fairway on the back nine is probably lost. The back nine also features several long tight par 4s, particularly number 18. At over 6200 yards from the white tees, Grandview is a real challenge to the average golfer. It has the full facilities that you would expect to find at a semi-private course and offers good value. Recently Grandview became a member of the Eaglequest group of courses.

Private Halifax-area Courses

You can count the number of private courses in Nova Scotia on one hand and three of them are in the Halifax area. If you are a member of a recognized Canadian or American private club, there is a better-than-average chance that you can get on these courses by calling ahead or having your pro arrange the booking.

Ashburn Golf Club (www.ashburngolfclub.com) has two courses, one in Halifax and the other twenty minutes out of town. Old Ashburn, the city course, is a short but tight classic designed by Stanley Thompson with spectacular city views from many holes. The New Ashburn, also referred to as the New Course, is a punishing brute with large fast greens that will challenge even the best. It has played host to the Canadian Amateur Championship. Both courses are well maintained and many of the tee boxes and fairways are complemented by excellent floral displays. Both courses have very large clubhouses with good dining rooms. The New Course has one of the best practice facilities in Eastern Canada.

Oakfield Golf and Country Club (www.oakfield.ca) is located in Grand Lake, thirty minutes outside of Halifax and well worth the short trip. Originally designed by Robbie Robinson in the early 1960's, Oakfield was recently redesigned by Graham Cooke. It plays to par 73 and has a number of holes along the water, including a wonderful par 3 across Fish Lake. Oakfield has played host to the Canadian Women's Amateur and other prestigious tournaments.

Brightwood Golf and Country Club (www.brightwood.ns.ca) is Dartmouth's answer to Halifax' Old Ashburn, a short hilly course with outstanding views of Halifax Harbour. This is Nova Scotia's only course designed by American legends Donald Ross and Willie Park Jr. way back in 1914. Brightwood is known for its friendly members and welcoming attitude so don't hesitate to drop by.

HIKING
Bluff Wilderness Hiking Trails
If you look at a map, you will notice that from the point where Highway 333 and Highway 3 diverge just outside Halifax until they rejoin at Tantallon there is a large inland area with no towns or settlements. This is the Five Bridges Lakes Wilderness Area. Haligonians are just beginning to realize how lucky they are to have a pristine area of this magnitude just outside their city.

Until recently the only way to get into the wilderness area was by some of the old logging and settlement roads that have been in existence for well over a hundred years. However, while these are fine for mountain bikers, the ATV traffic has made most of these old roads unusable for hikers in all but the driest weather. Fortunately, with the recent creation of the Bluff Wilderness hiking trails, there is now another way to access the Five Bridges Lakes Wilderness Area. For an overview of the trail and to obtain maps visit www.wrweo.ca/BluffTrail/index.html.

The Bluffs Trail has four looped trails stacked on one another that lead deep into the heart of the wilderness area. The *Doers' & Dreamers' Travel Guide* describes these trails as being suitable only for experienced hikers, but this is a bit of an overstatement. While it is true that to hike the entire loop system would take more than a day, there are at least two of the loops that make for very enjoyable day hikes. The first is the Pot Lake Trail, which takes about 3 hours to traverse. The second is Indian Hill Loop, which takes the greater part of the day. Either or both of these trails are very worthwhile as they reveal a post-glacial landscape studded with clear lakes and bogs. The trails are moderately strenuous with a fair number of ups and downs and a lot of walking on granite ridges. An interesting feature, particularly on the Indian Hill Trail, is the presence of many inukshuks which have been constructed as trail markers. There is also a very interesting stone creation on the Indian Hill Trail that looks like a prehistoric ruin, presumably built by the trail makers, but who knows?

What is most interesting about these trails is simply the fact that, so close to the city, there is an area where you can get away from any signs of civilization. While it takes about a half an hour to get completely away from the traffic sounds, once you do, there are a number of vistas from which you see nothing but hills, trees and lakes and not a sign of another human being. Most Canadians identify the Canadian wilderness as one of the most distinguishing features of being Canadian and yet few ever actually journey into a wilderness area. While we are not pretending that Five Bridge Lakes is the same as a trip to the interior of the Yukon, it is a worthwhile experience.

The trail head is located on the Beechville-Lakeside-Timberlea Rails to Trails in Timberlea. There is a small sign at 2890 Bay Road indicating the parking area for the trail. Make a right turn onto the Rails to Trails system and then it is about a ten-minute walk to the well-signed trail entrance. To hike this trail you should wear hiking boots and take a map of the trail and compass, along with water and food.

Pennant Point

This is a lovely coastal hike that begins only 30 minutes from Halifax at Crystal Crescent Beach, just past the village of Sambro. You can drive there directly through Harrietsfield or take the picturesque route through Herring Cove on Highway 349. Entering Crystal Crescent Beach road, keep right until you come to the end of the road where there is a large parking lot. From here, a well-marked trail and boardwalk will take you as far as the last beach at Crystal Crescent. The trail begins in earnest here, following the meandering shoreline and occasionally ducking into the woods to avoid some steep or muddy sections. Once past the last beach, it is about a brisk hour's walk to Pennant Point after which the shoreline turns abruptly into Pennant Bay.

This walk is pure Nova Scotia seascape as most people envision it — hard, polished and sometimes blindingly white granite laying down into and meeting the open Atlantic. There are several interesting blow holes which, when the surf is up, can make quite a commotion. Offshore, there are views of lonely Sambro Island with its reputedly haunted lighthouse that dates from the founding of Halifax. Sea birds including gannets, eiders, scoters and osprey are commonly seen. After reaching Pennant Point, it is possible to keep going along the seashore and eventually you will hook up with a trail which will lead you to East Pennant; from there you can follow the road back to the parking lot. If you follow this route, it will take about four hours all told. Unfortunately, those portions of the trail that pass through the woodlands were severely damaged by Hurricane Juan and there are many deadfalls. The most practical course is to return the way you came. The views on the way back are just as exhilarating as those on the way in. This is a beautiful hike at any time of year, but in late June the area is blanketed by thousands of wild iris and orchids, which makes it truly extraordinary.

There can be a fair amount of scrambling over loose rock in portions of this trail so hiking boots are a must.

One word of warning. The last beach at Crystal Crescent is favoured by nudists, as are some of the portions of the trail for the first kilometre or so past the last beach. If this concerns you, you should not forgo the hike, just try to be there early on a weekday morning when it is unlikely anyone else will be around.

Salt Marsh Trail, Bissett Road, Cole Harbour

This is a fairly new trail on the railbed of the old Eastern Shore railway and part of the Trans Canada Trail system. The trail is reached by following Portland Street in Dartmouth until it intersects Bissett Road, about 8 kilometres from downtown Dartmouth. Turn right and look for signs indicating the trail on your left. There are actually two parking lots, with the second one the better choice because you get to the interesting stuff a lot quicker.

What makes this trail interesting is that it virtually bisects Cole Harbour, one of the largest estuarine marshes in the province. After a short trip through the woods, you emerge on a manmade causeway with water on both sides. At certain times of the year, Cole Harbour resonates with the sounds of thousands of Canada geese and other migrating waterfowl, which stop and often overwinter here. In the middle of the causeway, there is a new bridge that will allow you to cross Cole Harbour and eventually reach Lawrencetown, where the trail continues on another old railway causeway. This trail is completely flat, dry and wide, so it's suitable for people of all ages as well as bikes. It is a good example of what Nova Scotians can look forward to as more and more portions of the Trans Canada Trail are completed.

This trail suffered some major damage during Hurricane Juan and it was heartbreaking to see the damage done to the recently constructed bridges, which took such time, energy and money from hundreds of volunteers to complete. Fortunately, restoration work is complete and the trail has returned to its pre-Juan condition.

Cole Harbour Heritage Park, 806 Bissett Road, Cole Harbour

Cole Harbour Heritage Park, one of HRM's newest green spaces, is a provincial park created entirely through the generosity of land donors and community volunteers. The park offers a wide variety of walking or hiking possibilities for all ages, but is especially attractive to families with small children and senior citizens as the trails are short, well maintained and not strenuous. A number of looped trails spread out from the parking lot beside a large red barn, which gives away the fact that these were once farm lands now reverted to overgrown fields, orchards and wood lots. The Panorama

Trail provides an opportunity for an easy stroll to a wonderful vista of Cole Harbour, the only remaining protected tidal estuary in the metro area. Within a short distance, it is possible to experience a number of completely different ecosystems, including a chance to see almost every type of tree native to the province. Altogether, 22.5 kilometres of trail await exploring.

St. Margaret's Bay Rails to Trails

Starting just outside Halifax in the subdivision of Beechville, a series of trails begin that run as far as Hubbards on St. Margaret's Bay. This is one of the many Rails to Trails developments that are occurring throughout the province, many of which will eventually be linked into the Trans Canada Trail including portions of the St. Margaret's Bay trail. Although these trails are always flat, and make for easy walking, there are some portions that are not particularly scenic.

There are, however, several sections of the trail that provide terrific views of St. Margaret's Bay and the offshore islands that lie thereon. One interesting stretch begins at Station Road which is off the Lighthouse Route at Head of St. Margaret's Bay. Turn in at Station Road and park about 100 metres up where the trail crosses this road, then proceed in a southerly direction. You will have Dauphinee's Mountain on your right and interesting views of St. Margaret's Bay on your left. There are several informative plaques along the way that detail the history of fishing, logging and tourism in this area as well as some of the flora and fauna that you might see along the way.

You can follow the trail as long as you wish, although a good point to turn around is the yellow church at Boutiliers Point. There are other portions of this trail that also provide excellent views of the bay, particularly in the Ingramport area.

This trail is also a good place for cross-country skiing in winter.

HISTORIC SITES

Halifax Citadel National Historic Site,
http://www.pc.gc.ca/lhn-nhs/ns/halifax/index.aspx

It has been said many times before, and it can be said again: from the moment you cross the plank bridge over the moat and pass through the arched entrance to the inner courtyard of the Citadel, you feel as if you're stepping back in time. The restoration of the Halifax Citadel had been ongoing for many years but it is now complete. This complex, which has watched over Halifax in one form or another since just after the city's founding in 1749, was one of the jewels of the British Empire. It made Halifax "the warden of the north" and protector of British interests everywhere in North America. Later, it was a staging and communication centre for both world wars. Today, it is a great tourist attraction in which you can easily spend two to three hours.

To best enjoy the Citadel, while planning your trip online take the terrific 3D virtual tour which will whet your appetite for a real visit. Begin your actual tour with the audiovisual presentation *Tides of History*, which sets the background. After that, take a guided tour or explore on your own. There is lots to see, including just about everything a fortress should have — cannons, ramparts, moats and tunnels, drums, bagpipes and marching soldiers. Every day at noon, a gun is ceremonially fired in a tradition that dates back to the nineteenth century. You can visit the Army Museum, which has an excellent display of military paraphernalia and presentations on D-Day, Dieppe and other campaigns in which Canadians played a significant role. Finally, you can stroll around the upper ramparts for a grand view of the city and harbour. As you leave, be sure to walk down to the Town Clock, which is on the east side of Citadel Hill. It was presented to the city by the Duke of Kent, Prince Edward, in 1803, and has come to be Halifax's most recognizable architectural feature. Over the years a number of changes were made to the structure, but by 2005 both the building and the clock face were restored to their original Georgian appearance. There are great views of the Town Clock from lower George Street and the Grand Parade in front of city hall.

The Citadel is Canada's most visited historic park, and no wonder — this is living history.

Province House, 1726 Hollis Street, Halifax, (902) 424-4661, www.gov.ns.ca/legislature

Province House is Canada's oldest legislative building and is generally considered to be one of the best examples of Georgian architecture in Canada. Constructed of sandstone from Wallace, Nova Scotia, it was recently refinished to restore its original appearance. Free guided tours of the interior are given on a regular basis. The grand paintings of various royal figures are impressive, as is the Legislative Library. If you are lucky, you might arrive when the House is in session and have a chance to listen to the rhetoric of the politicians although recent security enhancements do take something away from the overall feel.

On the grounds of Province House you will find a statue of Joseph Howe, Nova Scotia's greatest political figure. There is also yet another one of Halifax's many memorials to foreign wars, in this case the Boer War.

St. Paul's Church, 1747 Argyle Street, Halifax, (902) 429-2240, www.stpaulshalifax.org

This is Canada's oldest Anglican church dating almost from the founding of Halifax. Opened in 1750, it is now a National Historic Site. Based on a plan of a London church by a pupil of Christopher Wren, the timber for the building was pre-cut and shipped from Boston, which was still a British colony at the time. It sits facing Halifax City Hall across the Parade Square where many past and present gatherings for many causes have taken place. The church's interior is well worth viewing and you will note the final resting places of many early Halifax luminaries. There are display cases explaining the many historical events associated with St. Paul's and very fine stained glass. Don't miss viewing the outside windows from Argyle Street, where you will notice a mysterious profile etched in the glass of one of the windows, which dates from the time of the Halifax Explosion. There are any numbers of stories relating as to how it came to be there, none of which can be verified with certainty. The Web site provides a detailed virtual tour.

Pier 21 – Canada's Immigration Museum, 1055 Marginal Road, Halifax, (902) 425-7770, www.pier21.ca

From the exterior of this immense, nondescript, shed-like building, you would hardly guess the important role it has played in millions of Canadian lives. Saved from destruction by a few Nova Scotians interested in preserving the history of this building where 1.6 million immigrants, refugees and war brides first touched Canadian soil, it is now Canada's Immigration Museum. Pier 21 no longer receives immigrants, but it is the last remaining "immigration shed" in the country, and the Canadian equivalent of Ellis Island in New York Harbor. During World War II, over 500,000 troops left for Europe from here. Saved from the wrecking ball and outfitted with a new interior, the building now houses a permanent exhibit which includes a thirty-minute audio-visual presentation *Oceans of Hope*, Immigration Testimonial Stations and a Wall of Honour. There is also a library/research centre which will assist those who trace their ancestry through Pier 21. It also hosts travelling exhibits and provides a venue for live performances. With the transition from simply a National Historic Site to a designated national museum, Pier 21 is receiving the resources necessary to showcase the story of all Canadian immigration. In a very short period of time, what could have been just another pile of rubble has become one of Halifax's top attractions.

Georges Island National Historic Site, Halifax Harbour, www.pc.gc.ca/eng/lhn-nhs/ns/georges/index.aspx

At the time of writing, this small island in the middle of the harbour is not yet open to visitors, but is scheduled for opening in 2010. Finally, the public will get a chance to explore the island's many fortifications on a regular basis, rather than on the one or two days a year it has been accessible in the past. Georges Island was an important part of the Halifax defense complex which included fortifications on all sides of the harbour. One can easily imagine that it would have been nigh on impossible for an enemy ship to avoid the guns embedded inside the island if it attempted to force a passage into the harbour. Perhaps because it has been off limits for so long, Georges Island has become the centre of much speculation as to what really went on there; now we'll finally get to know.

York Redoubt National Historic Site, Purcells Cove Road, www.pc.gc.ca/lhn-nhs/ns/york

York Redoubt is the best surviving example of Halifax's outer ring of fortifications. It sits high above the entrance to the harbour directly across from Fort McNab on McNabs Island. A visit to York Redoubt, which is not as completely restored as the Citadel, is more like going to a park than visiting an historic site, although you will see some of the biggest mounted guns used anywhere in the British Empire.

From the command post there is, of course, a remarkable view of the entrance to the harbour and especially the lighthouse on McNabs Island. A trail leads down to Sleepy Cove, where the fortifications are now off limits due to their deteriorated state, but you can still find places to sit on the rocks where you can watch the huge cargo ships and liners coming and going from the port of Halifax. In the early evening, York Redoubt is usually quiet, with only a few people about, and is an excellent spot for a visit.

MUSEUMS

Maritime Museum of the Atlantic and HMCS *Sackville*, 1675 Lower Water Street, Halifax, (902) 424-7490, www.museum.gov.ns.ca/mma/
The finest of the Nova Scotia provincial museums, the Maritime Museum of the Atlantic documents Nova Scotia's seafaring tradition in a modern, well-designed building at the heart of the city's waterfront. There are three outstanding permanent exhibits that should not be missed. The first is entitled Shipwreck Treasures and has many exhibits showing the history of shipwrecks around Nova Scotia from the 1700s to the present day. There are many salvaged items, which tell interesting and sometimes horrific stories of shipwrecks and their salvagers. The second is the *Titanic* exhibit which details the building, the sinking and the largely unsuccessful rescue missions that followed. As Halifax was the port where those who survived, and those who did not, landed, it played a significant role in the *Titanic* story. There are a number of artifacts from the *Titanic* and its passengers including, believe it or not, one of its famous deck chairs. The most poignant exhibit is dedicated to the Halifax Explosion. A series of photographs and artifacts document the horrendous destruction of this 1917 cataclysm. It is impossible to remain unmoved while viewing this exhibit, which details the consequences to Halifax and its citizens of the world's largest non-nuclear man-made explosion.

The museum has many fine collections including ships' figureheads, anchors, lanterns and navigational instruments, but, unquestionably, the star attractions are the ship models. Everything from kayaks and dories to the grand ocean liners of Halifax's own Samuel Cunard have been reproduced to scale in incredible detail. Many of the museum's models are being restored and new ones created by the Maritime Model Ship Builders Guild, some of whose members you will probably see working at various places throughout the museum. The collection of small craft includes a number of specialized sailing vessels. Equally interesting is the collection of ships' crests, which show ingenuity and craftsmanship. Look for the crest of the *Nonesuch* with its very bellicose rampant beaver.

The museum extends beyond the boundaries of the building to the waterfront where the CSS *Acadia* is moored. The *Acadia* was a hydrographic research vessel that traversed the ocean in scientific endeavour until being retired and restored. Recently, plans were announced to almost quadruple the size of the museum and to incorporate parts of it into waterfront development. It remains to be seen if this will come to pass.

Moored beside the *Acadia* is the HMCS *Sackville*, the last remaining corvette from World War II. While technically not part of the museum, the *Sackville* is most conveniently toured while at the museum. Children love to run up and down the gangways and pretend to fire the now-silent anti-aircraft guns. The *Sackville* is a fitting and very well-restored tribute to thousands of Canadians who served aboard the corvettes in World War II.

For a number of weeks during the summer months Nova Scotia's icon the *Bluenose II* is usually moored between the *Sackville* and the *Acadia*. Until summer 2011, however the *Bluenose II* will be in Lunenburg undergoing renovations. When in port, the *Bluenose II* offers regular tours of the harbour. This is an opportunity that should not be missed.

Nova Scotia Museum of Natural History, 1747 Summer Street, Halifax, (902) 424-7353, www.museum.gov.ns.ca/mnh/

The Museum of Natural History will be one of the highlights of your trip to Halifax if you are traveling with young children. Over the years the museum has made great strides in adding fun things for youngsters to see and do. They will particularly appreciate the live exhibits of Nova Scotia snakes, frogs, salamanders, fish, insects and other creepy crawlies that always excite their interest. They will also enjoy, as will you, the butterfly pavilion, which is a small outdoor exhibit where dozens of exotic butterflies flutter among the flowers.

Most of the Museum outlines the natural history of Nova Scotia from the creation of the continents to the present day. With such a huge time span to cover, it is not surprising that there are many interesting exhibits including an outstanding collection of Mi'kmaq quill work. The collection of Nova Scotia rocks, minerals and particularly fossils is notable as are the model dinosaurs and the Marine gallery, which contains life-size representations of whales, sharks and other giant ocean creatures. There is also an interesting exhibit featuring the natural history of Sable Island with its famous ponies. In addition to the permanent exhibits there are always interesting seasonal or traveling displays. After touring the Museum a visit to the museum shop is an obligatory rite. In the fall of 2009 the museum closed for refurbishment and upon reopening in early 2010 has even more to see and do than before.

Art Gallery of Nova Scotia, 1741 Hollis Street, Halifax, (902) 424-7542, www.artgalleryofnovascotia.ca

Part of the Art Gallery of Nova Scotia is a fine old sandstone edifice that was once the principal post office in Nova Scotia. As you enter, look up and see the statue of Britannia sitting on guard over this area of the city. Although acquisitions by the predecessor Museum of Fine Arts date back as far as 1908, the collection never really got a permanent home and attendant mission until 1988. From a relatively modest start, the gallery has now emerged as one of the premiere small art showcases in Canada.

What is truly outstanding is the collection of folk art. Nova Scotia's best folk artists are represented in a bright and cheerful presentation that should not be missed. Maud Lewis is especially well-represented. As well, keep an eye on the traveling exhibits that regularly stop at the gallery, as many are first class. Tours are available on a regular basis. Also worth visiting is the small gallery shop, which, like many museum and gallery gift stores, contains unusual and interesting items not readily found elsewhere. The gallery's restaurant, Cheapside, is a good place for lunch before or after a visit.

Dartmouth Heritage Museum, (902) 464-2300, www.dartmouthheritagemuseum.ns.ca
The Dartmouth Heritage Museum consists of two historic properties in central Dartmouth. Evergreen House at 26 Newcastle Street was the long-time residence of legendary folklorist Helen Creighton, who collected folklore and ghost stories over a fifty-year period. She was almost single-handedly responsible for preserving hundreds of folk songs, sea shanties and other oral traditions that otherwise would be long forgotten. Her book, *Bluenose Ghosts,* is still a best-seller and will scare the pants off all but the most jaded readers. The house is furnished in the Victorian style of a gentleman's residence. There is a great view of the harbour from the front porch.

The other historic property worth visiting on the Dartmouth side of the harbour is the Quaker House at 57 Ochterloney Street in downtown Dartmouth. Few people know that for a number of years Nantucket whaling crews, who also happened to be Quakers, set up their business in Dartmouth. The Quaker House dates from 1785 and is one of the oldest structures in Dartmouth. It is unique to the area in its Nantucket design. Well-preserved and furnished in appropriate period style, it does merit a visit, although it's only open from June to September.

Both houses can be visited as part of the Dartmouth Heritage Walk which is described later.

Black Cultural Centre for Nova Scotia, 1149 Main Street, Dartmouth, (902) 434-6223 or 1-800-465-0767, www.bccns.com
The Black Cultural Centre is a combination museum/community centre on Dartmouth's east side near the communities of Preston and Cherry Brook, which were settled by blacks very shortly after the founding of Halifax. The centre documents both the contributions and struggles of Nova Scotia's black community as far back as the 1600s in a straightforward manner, including the very interesting story of the Jamaican Maroons and Nova Scotia's connection to the Underground Railway. The Web site has fairly detailed information on the various waves of black migration to Nova Scotia.

OFF THE BEATEN PATH
Herring Cove and Sambro
This is an enjoyable day trip to a couple of traditional fishing villages

only minutes from Halifax, with potential stops at Fleming Park and York Redoubt. The trip can be extended to a full day by hiking the Pennant Point Trail and stopping at beautiful Crystal Crescent Beach.

The route begins at the recently revamped Armdale Rotary. Take the Herring Cove Road exit from the rotary and then immediately bear left at the top of the hill for Purcells Cove Road. This is a pleasant drive through suburban Halifax, which will take you past Fleming Park and then York Redoubt. Near York Redoubt you will pass through an area where forest fires in 2009 destroyed not only many acres of forest, but also a number of upscale homes. Nearing Herring Cove look for one of the few places to park by the ocean from whence you can exit your car and walk for quite a distance over the granite outcroppings. From here, there are terrific views of the entrance to Halifax Harbour. It is also a good spot for viewing sea birds, which congregate in this area.

Next is Herring Cove, a traditional fishing village built on the rocks around a long narrow cove. Turn left on Powers Drive and then right on Shore Road and you will arrive at a parking lot from which you can access the wharf and get an appreciation of this pretty little cove. It's also a very popular spot to fish for mackerel and pollock. From Herring Cove, Highway 349 passes through the small communities of Halibut Bay and Portuguese Cove. In recent years a great number of magnificent homes have been constructed to take full advantage of the sea views in this area. Moving along look for the sign to Chebucto Head and Duncans Cove. A paved road, now sadly deteriorating, leads to an unmanned military communications complex and lighthouse at Chebucto Head. Despite the Private Road sign, the area is open to the public. The parking lot, which sits high above the Atlantic, is a great spot from which to see whales in August and September. You can clamber down the rocks and walk quite a distance in either direction on the smooth granite which marks this coastline.

Duncans Cove is an interesting community of houses clustered around a small sandy cove. There is a tiny five or six car parking area. Walk down Gannet Lane, past the gate until you are almost at what must surely be one of the most architecturally amazing residences in all Nova Scotia. Look for the last telephone pole on the right and follow the path left, not straight, a short distance to tiny Champayne Dam where the path meets the granite shoreline. From here you can follow the path all the way to Ketch Harbour or return the way you came. Along the way there are a number of abandoned coastal fortifications dating from World War II, which are fit for exploring.

From Duncans Cove, the highway leads to the fishing villages of Ketch Harbour and then Sambro, the largest fishing port on this coast. Just past the village, look for the signs to Crystal Crescent Beach, which is also the starting point for the beautiful walk to Pennant Point.

After visiting the beach or taking the hike, you can return to Halifax directly via the paved road to Harrietsfield or retrace your steps to Herring Cove via Highway 349.

Eastern Passage/Cow Bay

Although technically part of the Marine Drive, these two communities are much easier to visit from Halifax than as part of that scenic route, if only because they are part of the Halifax/Dartmouth urban area, with the requisite traffic and occasionally confusing signage. Over the past dozen years, the opportunities for tourists in the area between Dartmouth and the Eastern Shore have greatly increased, with new museums, boardwalks and shopping areas to complement the great beaches, birding and golfing.

To get to the area, follow the signs for Eastern Passage from Dartmouth. Essentially, this tour follows the shore of the eastern side of Halifax Harbour out to its mouth and around to Cow Bay. After passing the Esso refinery, you come to Shearwater, at one time home to Canada's largest naval air installation, but now better known as home to Canada's ill-fated Sea King helicopter fleet, which is at long last being replaced. It is, however, also home to the interesting Shearwater Aviation Museum (www.shearwater-aviationmuseum.ns.ca) where there is a good collection of mostly military planes on display. Next is the Autoport, one of North America's largest import/export sites for cars and trucks. The sight of hundreds, and on occasion thousands, of shiny new BMWs, Mercedes, Porsches and even more exotic cars is impressive. The automobile container vessels themselves are massive and appear ungainly against the low profile of McNabs Island in the background.

Shortly after the Autoport, you come to a 90-degree turn and signage for Marine Drive directing you to Cow Bay. However, continue straight for a very short distance to a parking lot, where you can stop to visit several interesting places. First take a short stroll around the boardwalk that winds its way through a salt marsh to the very narrow passage between the mainland and Lawlor Island. The name "Eastern Passage" refers to this narrow entrance to Halifax Harbour. It was through here that the Confederate raider *Tallahassee* slipped out at night to avoid a Union blockade of the harbour during the American Civil War. Considering that you could throw a stone across the passage from the mainland to Lawlor Island, one can appreciate what a feat of navigation this escape was and why the Union ships ignored blockading this part of the harbour.

At the other end of the boardwalk is Fisherman's Cove, a recent commercial development alongside the working wharves of Eastern Passage. It is intended to replicate a fisherman's village of 100 years ago, but it looks like a lot of other tourist developments, particularly those in Prince Edward Island, which are geared more towards merchandising than historical accuracy. However, there are a number of seafood restaurants worth trying as well as departures for whale watching, deep sea fishing and tours to McNabs Island. Make sure you continue along the boardwalk past the village to the working wharves for a chance to witness some real fishermen (or "fishers" if you prefer) doing things real fishermen do — mending nets, preparing bait, cleaning the catch and drinking beer.

If you like golf or hiking, continue on to Hartlen Point where you can partake of all three, as described elsewhere in the book. Even if you just want to stay in the car, the short drive to the end of the road is worth it for the view of Devils Island and its lighthouse at the mouth of the harbour. From here you must retrace your way to Marine Drive (Route 332) and turn right for Cow Bay.

Nearing Cow Bay you will see the signs for Rainbow Haven Beach, always a pleasant stop. Return towards Halifax on Bissett Road and watch for the parking lot for the Salt Marsh Trail which traverses Cole Harbour. If you still haven't seen and done enough for one day, drop in at the Cole Harbour Heritage Farm (www.coleharbourfarmmuseum.ca) which somewhat incongruously preserves a 1-hectare farm and a number of historic buildings in the midst of modern suburban sprawl. The farm animals are always a hit with the children. From Cole Harbour there are many signs directing you back to Halifax.

There is more than enough to see and do on the Dartmouth side of the harbour.

McNabs Island, www.mcnabsisland.ca

It is hard to believe, but you can find a place with nearly deserted beaches, quiet hiking paths and abandoned forts to explore, all without ever losing sight of the towers of the Halifax skyline. McNabs Island is one of Halifax's best-kept secrets and a recent addition to Nova Scotia's provincial park system.

McNabs is the large island that lies at the mouth of Halifax Harbour. At one time, it had many homes as well as substantial military installations that were part of the Halifax Harbour defence complex. Today, McNabs has a fraction of the daily visitors it had a hundred years ago, when it was an extremely popular spot for day outings by Haligonians. Gone are the amusement parks, tea rooms and bath houses, but McNabs is worth visiting just as much now as it was then. Several hiking trails nearly circumnavigate the island and allow for easy access to most of its attractions. On the Dartmouth side, Wreck Cove is filled with half-submerged barges and sunken vessels. From the ruins of Fort McNab, there is a magnificent view of the entrance to Halifax Harbour. If you are not inclined to wander far from the jetty at the beach, you can amble out to the lighthouse. This will take you along Maughers Beach, also known as Hangman's Beach, where the British navy once hanged deserters and left them for all to see. McNabs is also a delight for birders, as large sections of the island are composed of wetlands that often yield unusual species. It also has the largest concentration of breeding osprey in North America. Sunbathers can lie on the sand beach and watch the ships enter and leave the harbour. All in all, McNabs is well worth a day trip, but you must bring your own food and water.

In September 2003, the eye of Hurricane Juan passed almost over Mcnabs Island and there was extensive damage with trees down everywhere, making the pathways virtually impassable, but all is pretty well back to normal some seven years later. To get up to date information about current and planned activities on McNabs check out the Friends of McNabs Web site listed above. Even more information is found in the society's publication *Discover McNabs Island* which is widely available.

If you don't have your own boat, getting to McNabs requires signing on with a private boat operator who will drop you off and arrange for a pick-up time. Murphy's has regular excursions from the Halifax waterfront or you can take a boat from Fisherman's Cove in Eastern Passage. From the latter it is only a ten-minute run. If you have a kayak, McNabs and its smaller sister island, Lawlor, can easily be reached by launching from the parking lot in Eastern Passage.

PARKS AND GREENSPACE
The Public Gardens, corner of South Park Street and Spring Garden Road, Halifax, www.halifaxpublicgardens.ca
The Public Gardens, in one form or another, have been a part of Halifax since its inception. Started in 1753 as a private garden, the "gardens" as they are called by most Nova Scotians have changed locations several times over the years. The current location dates from about 1841 and has evolved from a place to grow vegetables into a formal Victorian garden. Previous incarnations have seen public skating rinks, tennis courts and boating ponds. For the past 50 years or so, the gardens have been dedicated to horticulture in its most formal presentation. They are well worth a visit at any time of the season when they are open, but most especially in late May and early June, when the tulips are in full bloom.

The vision of the beautiful Victorian bandstand surrounded by thousands and thousands of blooming tulips is a sight not soon forgotten. At other times of the year, rhododendrons and azaleas take over, followed by roses and perennials, then dahlias and gladiolus and, lastly, the autumn splendour of the many specimen trees. There are two exceptional fountains whose trickling waters provide some of the most tranquil spots you'll find in any city. Also worth noting are the exceptional iron-scrolled gates with the crest of the City of Halifax on the southeastern entrance to the gardens.

Children love coming here, not only for the bright colours, but to walk among the many ducks that make the large pond in the park their permanent home. The Public Gardens are indeed public, and perhaps no other place in the city is so appreciated, enjoyed and revered by Haligonians.

Like so many other Halifax public spaces, the gardens were savaged by Hurricane Juan in September 2003. It was unbelievable to see some of the largest and most beautiful trees in the province torn out by their roots and lying like majestic dying giants across the crushed iron fences surrounding the garden. It did not seem possible that things could ever be as they were before but, galvanized into action, the citizens of Halifax took charge and donated massive amounts towards the restoration. Now, some seven years later you would not know that there had ever been such a cataclysmic event unless someone told you. Recently the tea room and public washrooms were completely rebuilt and a third fountain added. If anything, the gardens are more beautiful than ever. Don't miss them.

Point Pleasant Park, Point Pleasant Drive, Halifax, www.pointpleasantpark.ca

Point Pleasant Park is one of Canada's great urban parks and should be included on everyone's list of places to visit in Halifax. The park occupies the tip of the peninsula, where the Northwest Arm meets the harbour proper. For many years, the land was set aside for use by the military as part of the Halifax Harbour fortifications. Technically, the land is still owned by the federal government and leased on an annual basis to the City of Halifax, although it is extremely doubtful if it would ever revert to its former military use.

This 75-hectare park, surrounded on three sides by the ocean was primarily all forest until Hurricane Juan ripped through and devastated the mature pine forest, destroying up to 75% of the trees according to some estimates. There had been considerable controversy surrounding the park management's decision to fell a large number of trees prior to the hurricane to combat the threat of a potential pest; all that seems to have been taken care of by Mother Nature. While it is true that the park looks dramatically different today than it did seven years ago and there are still large portions that are somewhat barren, the reality is that the park's soil was overtaxed and the forest needed regeneration. After the extensive cleanup, the city invited park planners from around the world to submit ideas for a renewed Point Pleasant and in 2007 a comprehensive plan to manage the park for the next fifty years was adopted. It was determined that the best way to ensure the habitat and environmental integrity of the park was to adopt a model based on the use of native Acadian forest species as much as is practicable. A copy of the plan can be viewed on the Web site.

Lest one think that the park is not worth visiting for the time being, keep in mind that the vast majority of things that bring people to the park remain unchanged.

There are still a bewildering number of paths leading to the park's many attractions. Of the two main entrances, first-time visitors should probably choose the one at Point Pleasant Drive; then you can follow the coastal path, a 4.5-kilometre loop. From this path you can see the mouth of the harbour and often large ships coming and going, seals basking on the shoals just offshore, and a number of interesting monuments including the huge anchor of the *Bonaventure*, Canada's last aircraft carrier. The shoreline path is also Halifax's premier jogging route — both the scenery and the cooling breeze compare favourably with the seawall route at Vancouver's Stanley Park. Children love to explore the many fortifications and ruins strewn throughout the park, including the Martello tower, which is open during daylight hours most of the summer. Point Pleasant has something for everyone and on any given day you will find joggers, mountain bikers, dog walkers, picnickers and strolling lovers enjoying the grounds. Of particular note are the many people who drive their cars to the seawall, park and just stare at the ocean. If you have ever wondered whether the lure of the sea is real, just look at the entrancing effect it seems to have on these people. Point Pleasant did suffer a huge blow from Hurricane Juan, but it was in no way a knockout punch.

Sir Sandford Fleming Park, a.k.a. "The Dingle," off Purcells Cove Road, Halifax

In 1908, Sir Sandford Fleming, a Renaissance man of the late nineteenth century and inventor of many useful things, most particularly the world-wide standard time system, donated to the city a large tract on the Northwest Arm facing the Halifax peninsula. Here you will find several miles of pathways, including an interesting walk along the waterfront in both directions from the parking lot. Although it doesn't feel like a public walkway because it passes almost through some backyards, the waterfront area between the Dingle and the Saraguay Club is public. Walking along here provides wonderful views of the North West Arm and the homes of the people fortunate enough to afford to live on it. The centrepiece of the park is the Dingle Tower, guarded by replicas of the famous Trafalgar Square lions. The tower was built to commemorate the 150th anniversary of the attainment of responsible government in Nova Scotia and stands as a lasting reminder that Nova Scotia was the first place in North America to do so. If you're lucky, the tower will be open and you can climb up to take in the view up and down the Northwest Arm. Inside attached to the walls, there are quite a number of provincial, university and other plaques and coats of arms, as well as a portion of the entrance to the home where the great explorer Samuel de Champlain was born in 1567. P.S. We have no idea why the tower is called the Dingle.

Shubie Park, 54 Locks Road, Dartmouth

Centred around the restored Shubenacadie Canal, which was designed to connect Halifax Harbour to the Shubenacadie River and easy access to the Bay of Fundy, Shubie Park has pleasant walks beside this old waterway. The canal was operational for only a few years and became uneconomical in the face of competition from the railways. Large parts of the canal have been dredged and restored for canoeists. The park also has picnic and camping facilities and several small freshwater beaches, as well as playgrounds. The park is located off the Waverley Road; look carefully for the signs, as they aren't too easy to spot.

Sullivan's Pond, Prince Albert Road, Dartmouth

The area's best place to see ducks, geese and swans is Sullivan's Pond, located right in downtown Dartmouth. Youngsters enjoy the action, and birders can be rewarded by an occasional rare visitor amid the teeming mallards and black ducks.

Jerry Lawrence Provincial Park, Highway 3

This small day-use picnic park just outside Halifax is named for a former politician who championed the cause of persons with disabilities. It is designed to be accessible to people with physical disabilities, with a boardwalk around the portion of the lake leading to a dock where fishing is possible. For birders, the park is a good spot for warblers during the breeding season.

Laurie Park and Oakfield Park, Highway 2, Grand Lake
These two provincial parks are located close to each other on Shubenacadie-Grand Lake, one of Nova Scotia's premiere boating and fishing lakes. Laurie Park is very popular with campers as the campsites are located in individually wooded areas along the lakeshore. Breezes off the lake help keep blackfly and mosquito problems to a minimum.

There are boat-launching facilities close to the campground. Shubenacadie-Grand Lake probably contains more species of game fish than any other in the province, including landlocked salmon, striped bass and smallmouth bass. The sheltered coves and remote spots make it ideal for canoeing.

The picnic facilities are adjacent to the campground, also spread out along the shore of the lake. The only drawback to Laurie Park is that swimming facilities, particularly for small children, are minimal. Teenagers and adults may enjoy swimming right off the rocks, but there are no beaches or wading areas for younger children. To those for whom access to a beach is important: go down the road to Oakfield Park, which has one of the finest freshwater beaches in the province. However, if fishing or canoeing is a priority, then Laurie Park is the place to be.

Long Lake Provincial Park, Highway 3, Halifax
This provincial park is located just outside Halifax in an area that is bounded by Highway 3, the Peggy's Cove Road and the Old Sambro Road. It incorporates Long Lake, which at one time was a source for the Halifax water supply, and a large swath of land around it almost as large as peninsular Halifax. It was off-limits for many years and thus preserved from development. The province really didn't seem to know what to do with this site for the longest time, with the result that people just largely did what they wanted. A series of mountain bike trails have become very popular as has off-leash dog walking. The only parking lot for the park is a small one on Highway 3, but there are other entrances in a number of spots. There are walks along both sides of the lake, including one that will take you to the ruins of an old mill on a stream just up from where it enters Long Lake. This is a really nice place in the fall as the park has many varieties of hardwood trees that change colour with the season. At present there are no facilities whatsoever, but that may change as a management plan is currently in the works.

SEA KAYAKING

East Coast Outfitters, 2017 Lower Prospect Road, Lower Prospect, (902) 852-2567, www.eastcoastoutfitters.net
Terence Bay and Prospect Bay are two long narrow bays dotted with many islands that provide some of the most sheltered and interesting sea kayaking in Nova Scotia. East Coast Outfitters provides novices and experts the chance to explore the area by kayak and visit sheltered coves, shipwreck sites and other interesting places that are only accessible by water. There are half-day and full-day tours as well as lessons. Note that Lower Prospect is at the end of the Terence Bay Road and not the nearby Prospect Road.

SPECIAL EVENTS

The Royal Nova Scotia International Tattoo, 1-800-563-1114, www.nstattoo.ca

Contrary to what the name suggests, this is not a gathering of body art aficionados. Neither is it, as some may suggest, a celebration of military might. The Royal Nova Scotia Tattoo is the largest indoor show of its type in the world. It is a tremendous display of pageantry, a tribute to the sacrifices of our forebears, an exhibition of skills by our present defenders and, most particularly, a chance to hear and see some of the best brass and pipe bands in the world. For good measure, throw in a varied assortment of international gymnastic and dance acts, and you have the recipe for an event that no visitor to Nova Scotia should miss.

The show is very popular with children as well as adults and the organizers always involve a large number of local children in the pageantry, singing, dancing and gymnastics. The whole event is a family affair. Annual acts usually include the Gun Run, an exciting and dangerous competition between two naval units that begins and ends with the firing of cannons, the soldiers' race, the navy's very entertaining ladder routines, the United States Marine Corps Band, which also often entertain throughout the city during the week of the Tattoo, and the massed pipes and drums (you've never really heard the bagpipes until you've heard 150 of them playing at once). In the finale, all the bands take to the floor at once, making a spectacle of extraordinary proportions. Odds are that the Tattoo is one event you will remember with fondness for years to come. We consider it one of the absolute best attractions in Nova Scotia.

It runs during the first week of July and attracts visitors from around the world. The best seats sell out early, so if you are planning to visit Nova Scotia during the first week in July, buy tickets online well in advance.

Atlantic Jazz Festival, www.atlanticjazzfestival.ca

By the second week in July, summer is in full swing in Halifax and the days can actually be hot and sultry. For this reason it seems a perfect fit for jazz and blues to combine with Halifax's long summer nights and cool ocean breezes. The Atlantic Jazz Festival generally runs for almost two weeks in mid-July at a number of locations throughout the metro area. The principal locale is the festival tent, which is usually set up at the corner of Spring Garden Road and Queen Street. There are always sprinklings of internationally renowned artists amidst the many local and regional acts that enliven the city for this two-week period. Although most people think of bagpipes and fiddles when they think of Nova Scotian music, you may be surprised at the quality of the jazz and blues that you will hear at the Atlantic Jazz Festival. For jazz and blues lovers it is worth planning your visit to Halifax around this festival.

The Halifax International Busker Festival, www.buskers.ca

In the mid-1980s, Dale Thompson hit upon the idea of bringing together some of the world's best buskers for a festival in downtown Halifax. Now there are busker festivals all over the place, but Halifax is where it all started. In case you don't know, a busker is a street entertainer who plies his or her trade for donations from the public. Every year since, the Busker Festival has brought a new round of jugglers, mimes, gymnasts, fire-eaters and puppeteers. These entertainers are a long way from the average street performers you may be accustomed to thinking of. Many are equal in quality to the acts you might remember from the old Ed Sullivan show, and they are very, very funny. The kids absolutely love them.

Over 40 acts from around the world invade the waterfront and various other nearby performance areas in early August. If you are visiting Halifax at the time, you will inevitably bump into the buskers somewhere in your travels. Buskers seem to bring a happy face to the town, as the zest and energy of these exuberant and fun-loving performers spreads to the crowds. The performers are paid by the voluntary contributions of the audience. At the end of the festival, they all gather in one location for a truly exciting grand finale.

Check the Web site for a video of the previous year's performers and you will get an idea of the quality and variety of these acts.

Atlantic Film Festival, www.atlanticfilm.com

Halifax and the surrounding area has long been one of Canada's top locations for the filming of movies and television shows. Originally, the attraction was the disparity between the American and Canadian dollars, which made it much cheaper to film in Canada than the United States. On many occasions Halifax has masqueraded as Boston or a smaller American city; for example in five Jesse Stone films featuring Tom Selleck. Places such as Chester and Mahone Bay on the south shore substitute for New England towns. The development of the film industry has created a local level of expertise that has spawned a great number of local productions, which run the gamut from the beloved children's character Theodore Tugboat to the irreverent Trailer Park Boys.

The Atlantic Film Festival is a celebration of the best of independent Canadian and international film and other media. There is a definite buzz in the air when the local film celebrities get together with their Canadian and American counterparts in mid-September to screen the latest offerings and party the night away afterward. It is the only opportunity for film buffs not only to see some of their favourite celebs, but also view some excellent, independent films that may never get a box office release. 2010 will mark the 30th anniversary of this increasingly important event.

The Tall Ships, www.tallshipsnovascotia.com

Approximately every three years, Halifax plays host to a gathering of over 40 tall ships in what is regarded as the highlight of the tourist season. A tall ship is a large traditionally rigged vessel which means it has masts and sails. The largest tall ships are often used to train marine and naval recruits and have as many as four masts with dozens of sails. For many people the sight of a large tall ship with all sails set is as fine as it gets.

At one time tall ship gatherings were quite infrequent, but they are so popular and bring so many people into the ports they visit, that there is now a somewhat official cycle of three years. When the ships arrive, usually in late July, they stay for about a week and host social events and some offer on board tours. The waterfront becomes even more hopping than usual, if that's possible. The absolute highlight of the visit is the Parade of Sail when all of the ships put up their sails and put on a parade in the harbour and head out to their next destination. It is a sight worth planning a vacation around. So check the Web site — the tall ships should be around again in 2012.

SPECIAL INTEREST

Casino Nova Scotia, 1983 Upper Water Street, Halifax, www.casinonovascotia.com
A few years ago, some Nova Scotia politicians got the brilliant idea that if they opened a couple of casinos the high rollers would abandon Las Vegas, Monte Carlo and the Bahamas and rush to Nova Scotia to lose their money. Of course that didn't happen. After many years of planning, a stand-alone casino was opened on the waterfront. While losing money is not our idea of fun, the exterior of the Halifax Casino is well designed and fits in very well with the existing waterscape. Undoubtedly, for those who enjoy casinos, it is a welcome addition to Halifax's waterfront. What has been a real success is the casino showroom which brings in some pretty good acts to a small-venue setting.

Discovery Centre, 1593 Barrington Street, Halifax, (902) 492-4422, www.discoverycentre.ns.ca
This small science centre right downtown is aimed primarily at youngsters and contains interactive science and technology exhibits. It has a shop with many fascinating items for sale.

Nova Scotia Centre for Craft and Design, 1061 Marginal Road (902) 492-2522, www.craft-design.ns.ca
This organization, which is dedicated to the teaching and promotion of Nova Scotia artists and artisans, recently relocated to the waterfront in a building beside Pier 21. The Mary E. Black Gallery is the only one in Nova Scotia dedicated to fine crafts. Past exhibits have included a spectacular collection of the work of Nova Scotian wood-furniture makers, the work of theatrical costumers and works by the Metal Arts Guild. Check the Web site for the current and upcoming exhibits. They change six or seven times a year. Admission is free and if you are planning a visit to Pier 21 drop into the gallery for a worthwhile visit.

Alexander Keith's Nova Scotia Brewery, 1496 Lower Water Street, Halifax, 1-877-612-1820, www.keiths.ca
Alexander Keith is a legend in Nova Scotia. In 1820 he started a tradition of fine brewing that remains to this day. The original brewery on the Halifax

waterfront has survived virtually intact, even though principal brewing operations were moved elsewhere years ago, and has reopened as a tourist venture. Guides in period costume will show you how Alexander brewed his beer almost 200 years ago. Along the way you will be regaled with stories and songs and end up at the Stag's Head Tavern, where you can raise a glass of this famous Nova Scotia libation. The whole thing's a lot of fun. No wonder Haligonians made Alexander Keith the mayor. If you find the admission price too steep you can take a virtual tour on the Web site.

A Trip to Peggy's Cove

If there is one place that is synonymous with the rugged beauty of the Nova Scotian coast, it is Peggy's Cove. The famous lighthouse and cove have been featured on countless calendars, jigsaw puzzles, guidebook covers and posters, and in an untold number of paintings. It would be unheard of for a bus tour of Nova Scotia not to visit Peggy's Cove; in fact, dozens of them go there every day of the summer. Such is the fame of Peggy's Cove that visiting celebrities often charter a limousine to take them along winding Highway 333 for a look at the famous lighthouse and cove.

The fact is Peggy's Cove is becoming a victim of its own popularity and at times alarmingly close to a parody of what happens to earth's most beautiful places when they are discovered. Although it is not likely that the tramping feet of the army of tourists who visit the site annually is about to erode away the granite rocks, and while development in the area is strictly controlled, it is difficult to appreciate the beauty of this spot in the company of dozens, or sometimes hundreds, of other people. All around Nova Scotia, there are so many deserted beaches and windswept rocky headlands that it is jarring to suddenly find yourself in a quaint fishing village swarming with throngs of people.

This is not to say that you should even consider bypassing this wondrous spot - there is a very good reason why Peggy's Cove is the quintessential Nova Scotia icon. The trick is to try and time your arrival for one of the less busy times. There are two ways to do this — either visit during the spring or late fall, or visit extremely early in the morning at any time of year. There is no question that the Peggy's Cove area is dramatically affected by light, particularly the early morning rays which, combined with the usual calmness of the early waking hours, imbue the land and sea with a magical tinge. This is the light that makes for once-in-a-lifetime photographs and great paintings. Sunset is also spectacular, but there are sure to be more people around.

It will take about 30-40 minutes to drive straight to Peggy's Cove from Halifax, if you leave for the early light. If you can, try to pick a time during the high tides of a full moon, when the waves are more likely to be large. An alternative to driving out from Halifax is to stay in the area.

Don't make a common mistake and assume that Peggy's Cove is the only place worth visiting along Highway 333. There is more than enough to make for a satisfying day trip from Halifax or to explore from a base along the way. Since most people will be visiting from Halifax, we have set out a circular tour of about 130 kilometres, including a few side trips.

While, obviously, the route can be driven in either direction, the views, particularly of the approach to Peggy's Cove, are better when driven in a counter-clockwise direction from Halifax. Take Highway 103 to Exit 5 and turn towards Tantallon and then follow the signs for Peggy's Cove on Highway 333.

The highway hugs the St. Margaret's Bay coastline through the hamlets of Tantallon, Glen Haven, French Village, Seabright and Glen Margaret. The clear and cold waters of St. Margaret's Bay are dotted with both commercial fishing boats and pleasure craft, and increasingly, huge new homes. Most of the side roads in this area lead to small coves surrounded by cottages and these larger homes. At Hacketts Cove the scenery begins to change from forested hillsides and fields marking the occasional abandoned farm to flatter treeless granite outcrops. The fishing villages of Hacketts Cove and Indian Harbour are every bit as authentic as Peggy's Cove, with a whole lot fewer people around, but, admittedly, a lot less dramatic. Both are excellent examples of small inshore fishing communities.

Before reaching Peggy's Cove, Paul's Point Road and Paddy's Head Road are both worth exploring for the open ocean views visible from their shores. Paddy's Head is a small picturesque fishing community with some extremely good examples of architecture typical of these communities in the 1800s. There is a small lighthouse overlooking an enclosed harbour and great views of the windswept and barren Shut-in Island just offshore.

The first sight of Peggy's Cove and the surrounding barrens is from a ridge called the Whaleback, just outside Indian Harbour. On a clear day the vista is breathtaking. Not only does the small community in the distance with its white church and lighthouse draw the eye, but also the change in the landscape takes one's breath away. Gone are the trees and any traces of civilization other than the village. In its place is barren or lichen covered granite, swept clean of soil by the glaciers that passed through here many years ago. Sitting on top of the granite outcrops, like so many toy blocks cast aside by some petulant child of the gods, are large boulders that were carried along by the glaciers and deposited here. Some of these glacial erratics, as they are called, appear ready to tumble from their perches at the slightest touch. Not without reason have these barrens been compared to a moonscape, although a more accurate comparison is the tundra. The presence of a village clinging to the granite at the ocean's edge in this bleak environment strikes an absurd note at first, but then one is soon drawn into the village itself, the houses, the gardens, the fishing sheds and quays, oblivious to the harsh land and relentless ocean. Not far before the turnoff to the village, you will come across the memorial to those who died in the crash of Swissair Flight 111 in September 1998 at a spot not far offshore. Take the time to stop and walk the short distance to the monument. It will certainly give you pause for reflection. Before you reach the turn off to Peggy's Cove road, keep an eye out for a number of very small parking areas. Each of these have short paths which lead over the granite and around the erratics to the shore, where you'll have a great view of the church and lighthouse without the congestion.

Upon reaching the short road into Peggy's Cove, leave your car in the first parking lot, which is only a couple of hundred yards in, as this area is much better explored on foot than by car, especially if it's crowded, as the roads are very narrow. Here you will find the recently constructed interpretation centre. Drop in and pick up the brochure that explains what you can expect to see not only in the village, but the surrounding area as well. First look for the W. E. deGarthe Memorial, which is just across from the parking lot. For many years this artist maintained a studio right in Peggy's Cove and his paintings of fishermen's lives represented the best in Nova Scotian marine painting. DeGarthe carved into the granite of his backyard a memorial to the fishermen of Peggy's Cove and the travails of the fishing life. This labour of love took much of his time in the latter years of his life. Examples of his paintings are found inside his former home. In the church, if it is open, one can also see two of his murals.

The cove is a tiny inlet just wide enough to allow a small Cape Island fishing boat to turn around. All along its length, small fishing shacks on rickety stilts protrude over the water. Dories, painted in a variety of bright colours, are strung together, their reflections playing off the calmly rippling water. Lobster pots are stacked neatly alongside drying nets, and gulls perch patiently atop weathervanes almost as if they know we expect them to do just that. It's everything you could possibly expect a small fishing enclave to be, and yet it is only the beginning of what this place has to offer.

Just up from the cove you will see the famous white lighthouse with its distinctly greenish light. As you approach, over what is now barren granite that has been polished smooth by eons of waves, you will pass signs warning you of the dangers ahead — giant waves that have washed many to their deaths. Yet, in all likelihood, the ocean won't appear rough — it may even be serene, but there is always a swell that, when it breaks against the rocks that slopes down to the water, produces Peggy's Cove's famous waves. If there has been a tropical storm or hurricane down south, in a few days, massive swells will lead to equally massive waves. Should you be fortunate enough to be here when that happens, usually in the late summer or early fall, it is a sight you will never forget, and you will understand the reason for the warning signs, but please don't be foolish and attempt to go right down to the water's edge.

After clambering over the rocks and photographing the lighthouse up close, drive on for a greater appreciation of this fascinating coastline. About a kilometre and a half past the Peggy's Cove Road, heading towards Halifax, look for another place to turn off on the seaward side of the highway, where you will find a well worn path. Walk down this about half a kilometre to an old concrete foundation, from which there is a commanding view of the coastline — Peggy's Cove off to the right, nothing but barrens and offshore islands to the left. From here, a number of paths branch out, some leading down to the water's edge, others through the barrens. This is another opportunity to get near to some of the glacial erratics, which look much less precariously balanced up close than from afar. The wind always blows here among these fantastic shapes and structures created by the retreating glaciers. Even though you are less than a mile away from the throngs at Peggy's Cove, you are unlikely to see another person. The only sounds will be the gulls mewing overhead, the wind and the surf. You will quickly realize why this area has always held a magical fascination. The reality is that the barrens are anything but barren — they teem with wildflowers, colourful mosses and lichens and many birds. In early summer blue flag, tiny pink dragon's mouth orchids and pitcher plants abound. Later the barrens are carpeted with blueberries and cranberries for the taking. In October it becomes a blaze of red shrubbery. In case you are wondering, the small inlet in this area is called Polly's Cove, presumably Peggy's lesser-known sister.

After Peggy's Cove, the barrens end at West Dover and the forested hillsides reappear. Before leaving them behind there is one more chance to explore on foot. Just past the West Dover sign is a large parking lot for the ball field on the other side of the road. Park here and you will find a number of trails that lead into the barrens, away from the ocean. The farther you go the more amazing the erratics and the higher each granite ridge, providing sweeping vistas in all directions. The area is boggy in places so waterproof hiking boots are in order. Although neither East nor West Dover is particularly attractive, it is worth driving to the end of the West Dover Road for the view of the small fishing communities along the shore of this harbour. You can gain an appreciation of how these communities were linked by boat rather than automobile. While one could go from East to West Dover in a couple of minutes by boat, it takes five times as long to travel from one community to the other by automobile.

Before returning to Halifax, there are two other communities worth visiting, even though they receive a fraction of the visitors that Peggy's Cove does. The first is Prospect. A fine view of the community can be seen from the ridge just before the road descends to sea level. Prospect has no gift shops, galleries or restaurants, although there is a B&B in the most interesting-looking building in the village, a former convent, allegedly haunted. What Prospect does have are rocks, wharves and fishing boats.

The next side road worth exploring leads to Terence Bay. It begins close to the Prospect village turnoff. At Terence Bay, the road divides three ways. Look for the sign to SS *Atlantic* Memorial Park just after St. Paul's church. Here you can see the monument to those who lost their lives in the sinking of the passenger ship SS *Atlantic* just offshore in 1873. Over 500 people lost their lives and 277 of them are interred near the monument in a mass grave. The majority were immigrants hoping for a new life in North America. Sadly, they found death instead. While this site and the monument may sound sombre, in fact the place has a sense of tranquility and beauty. First stop at the small interpretive center to see some of the artifacts salvaged from this famous shipwreck and pick up a map of the short trail to the monument. There are picnic tables, a gazebo and boardwalk which have been well maintained by the residents of Terence Bay. Looking out at the rocks where the *Atlantic* foundered over 100 years ago, one cannot help but think of the sacrifices and hardships endured by our ancestors to create the "good life" most of us enjoy today. For more information on the sinking of the *Atlantic* visit www.ssatlantic.com.

Returning to the fork in the road, drive now to Lower Prospect. This community was the home of renowned folk artist, the late Joe Norris. His former lawn is still adorned with examples of his work, including an excellent representation of the fishing wharf and cemetery, which you will have just passed, and a number of folk art totem poles. The gaiety of this presentation will drive away any lingering thoughts of the fate of those from the doomed *Atlantic*. Drive to the end of this road to find an interesting collection of fishing shacks around a small harbour.

From where the Terence Bay road rejoins Highway 333, there is little of interest before reaching Halifax.

Peggy's Cove loop has always had a great concentration of craft stores, souvenir shops and galleries. At one time, the majority of them were pretty kitschy. However, over the past number of years, the quality has improved greatly, although you can still certainly find junk if you want it.

At the beginning of this sub-chapter, we suggested staying in the Peggy's Cove area to be able to take advantage of the times when the summer crowds are not there. There are now quite a number of reliable B&Bs in the area. Also worth serious consideration is the Oceanstone Inn and Cottages (866-823-2160, www.oceanstone.ns.ca) which is a truly exceptional recent development near Indian Harbour just minutes from Peggy's Cove. There are rooms at the inn or a choice of 5 cottages in a secluded and beautiful location right on the water. An added bonus is the excellent Rhubarb Grill restaurant, which is easily the best place to dine in the area (www.rhubarbgrill.com) (902) 402-3163.

THEATRE

Neptune Theatre, corner of Sackville and Argyle Streets, Box Office 1-800-565-7345, or buy online at www.neptunetheatre.com
Founded in the early 1960s, Neptune has become the premiere showcase for theatre in Atlantic Canada. A series of renowned artistic directors, including the great John Neville, have succeeded in attracting the best in Canadian and international talent to the stage, where a combination of classic dramas, musicals and original productions highlight a season that runs from September to June. In the summer, the stage is often taken over by repertory or travelling national productions.

For almost 35 years, Neptune struggled with an inadequate facility whose saving grace was the actual stage, and many who played it praised it for its acoustics and well-trod warmth. In 1997 Neptune was reborn — an entirely new facility built on the original site, incorporating the old stage. The new facility has proven to be a great success and the future of theatrical productions in Halifax has been secured.

Shakespeare by the Sea, Point Pleasant Park, (902) 422-0295, www.shakespearebythesea.ca
In 1994 a different theatrical experience came to Halifax that imitated the Shakespeare-in-the-Park seen in other cities, such as London and Vancouver. Set in Point Pleasant Park, Shakespeare by the Sea has made use of the ocean, the forest and abandoned forts as backdrops. Productions of some of the Bard's best-known works in totally natural surroundings have proven to be a great hit, not only with fans who go specifically for the plays, but also with people who just happen by the plays as they are strolling through the park on a romantic walk. Imagine coming on a scene straight out of the forest of Arden or stumbling on Hamlet declaiming his soliloquy from the walls of Elsinor — well, actually, Fort Ogilvie. It's great fun!

The Shakespeare by the Sea troupe generally puts on three or more productions each year, which run five or six evenings a week in July and August. Check the Web site for what's playing.

WALKING TOURS

With its narrow streets and small downtown area, Halifax is easiest to visit on foot. There are a number of options for walking tours. *Walk Historic Halifax* by Grant MacLean details seven tours in Halifax, with an emphasis on the events of the past.

The Waterfront

Unquestionably, Halifax's prime attraction is the waterfront, which has become much more accessible to the public over the past decade. You can now walk all the way from the cruise ship terminal and Pier 21 to the casino, passing a number of interesting sights along the way. Gateway Park marks the beginning of the boardwalk and fittingly here you will see a statue of Samuel Cunard, one of Halifax' most illustrious sons. Nearby is the site of the new farmer's market, designed to be environmentally self-sufficient. Heading north toward the bridges next is award-winning Bishop's Landing, which has several fine restaurants and exclusive shops. Across the street are Brewery Market and the old Keith's Brewery tour. Continuing on leads one to the Maritime Museum of the Atlantic, which has outdoor displays in addition to what is inside; a children's playground, which is designed in the shape of a ship, and the CSS *Acadia* and HMCS *Sackville*, both open for touring.

Following this is Cable Wharf where there are more shops and the embarkation point for a wide variety of water excursions. Passing the Law Courts and the Halifax-Dartmouth Ferry Terminal leads into Historic Properties, a group of important buildings that were saved from the wrecking ball at the eleventh hour and served as the catalyst for the entire waterfront redevelopment. Here are high-quality shops catering to the tourist market along with restaurants and pubs. Walking on leads to the waterfront Marriott Hotel and the award winning Purdy's Wharf Towers complex that uses sea water to run the air conditioning systems. The boardwalk then ends at the casino. There are a number of interpretive displays at various points on the waterfront, explaining the different types of ships you might see in the harbour, common marine and bird life and other interesting facts relating to the waterfront. Works of art on the waterfront include "The Sailor," dedicated to Canada's merchant mariners, and "The Wave," a somewhat controversial work that looks better from afar than close up. As if this were not enough, in summer the waterfront is always alive with buskers, bands and other entertainment that are sure to keep you amused. The waterfront is really the heartbeat of Halifax and should not be missed. You don't really need a map, but the annual Halifax guide, which you can obtain in a number of places along the waterfront, gives a list of points of interest.

Historic Halifax

There are a number of walking tours available of Halifax's prime historic sites, which include Province House, the Art Gallery, the Old Burying Ground and St. Paul's Church. The annual Halifax publication, available at any of the tourism bureaus, sets out a route that will take you past these sites and more.

Public Gardens to Point Pleasant Park

This is a very pleasant way to spend a morning, an afternoon or an entire day. Start the tour in the Public Gardens, exiting at the corner of South Park Street and Spring Garden Road. Next cross to Victoria Park and follow it to University. From here you can walk down South Park Street/ Young Avenue to the entrance of Point Pleasant Park, a distance of about half a mile. On the way, you will pass some of Halifax's finest homes and the Church of Our Lady of Sorrows, which was built in one day by a determined group of 2,000 men. Enter the park at the fountain and follow a clockwise direction around the park to the Tower Road parking lot. This will take at least an hour and much probably longer if you stop to enjoy the many diversions the park offers. From the parking lot it is a straight shot down Tower Road back to the Public Gardens. There are a number of interpretive panels along this route explaining the many varieties of architecture found in the Tower Road area.

North End Halifax and the Hydrostone, www.hydrostonemarket.ca

After the Halifax Explosion in 1917, most of North End Halifax lay in ruins. Because large parts of it were rebuilt using a compressed stone material called hydrostone, this area has become known as the Hydrostone area and, today, is one of Halifax's more interesting neighbourhoods.

You can park in the area of Young and Gottingen Streets and tour the Hydrostone, which runs north from there. Most of the streets are boulevards and most houses preserve the unique appearance a Hydrostone building. Be sure to check out the small interpretive display across from the Hydrostone market on Young for a more detailed history of the area. During the course of your walk, you will pass by Fort Needham, a large hill that overlooks the harbour, where there is an impressive monument to the explosion. To really appreciate this tour, you might want to first see the display on the explosion at the Maritime Museum of the Atlantic. Don't fail to check out the interesting shops in the Hydrostone Market.

Northwest Arm

From the parking lot at Fleming Park, a long-established public footpath meanders along the shoreline of the Northwest Arm in both directions. You can't travel far heading toward the top of the arm, but in the opposite direction the path goes for about two kilometres, as far as the Saraguay Club. Along the way you pass a number of very interesting old and new waterfront properties and are treated to some wonderful views of Halifax mansions that can only be seen from the water. At the Saraguay Club, you can either retrace your steps or make your way to Purcells Cove Road. Follow the road toward Halifax until you reach the Frog Pond, an extension of Fleming Park.

Here, you will find an interesting path that takes you along the shores of this small lake and eventually back to the parking lot.

Dartmouth Heritage Walk

A pleasant afternoon can be spent strolling along the waterfront and down the leafy streets of Dartmouth. If you are not staying in Dartmouth, start this tour by taking the ferry to Alderney Landing and exploring the waterfront followed by visits to the Quaker House, the gardens at the Dartmouth Commons, several early cemeteries, the terminus of the Shubenacadie Canal and Sullivan's Pond. The annual city visitors guide has a suggested walking route for Dartmouth.

WILDERNESS AREAS

Terence Bay Wilderness Area

The idea of a wilderness area within the boundaries of a city might seem a bit of a stretch, but at over 11,000 acres the Terence Bay Wilderness area provides real opportunities to get away from the crowds. Despite its proximity to some major roads, it's not that easy to find a way into the area. The best place to enter and experience the granite outcrops that are the hallmark of this wilderness area is in West Pennant. Right beside #11 Bar Harbour Road there is a path that leads directly into the wilderness area. It is about two kilometres to the boundary on what is really an old road. Entering the wilderness area the trail climbs gradually up to the top of a series of open granite ridges. Follow the trail to the left at each fork and you will shortly be at Hospital Hill. The view out to the ocean from here is simply breathtaking and worth the trek on its own. It is possible to make your way down to the small lakes you will see below, but bushwacking will be required.

The Terence Bay Wilderness Area can also be enjoyed from the water. There are launching points for a sea kayak at various points in the Terence Bay area.

WHERE TO SHOP

Halifax has a number of distinct shopping areas offering the best selection of high-quality goods east of Quebec City. If you are simply looking for the lowest prices on everyday goods, your best bet is probably either Bayers Lake Park (www.bayerslakepark.com) off Highway 102 just outside Halifax or the newest large development Dartmouth Crossing (www.dartmouthcrossing. com) at the junction of Highways 111 and 118. Here, you'll find such behemoths as Wal-Mart, Staples and Costco, as well as Chapters bookstores and a number of discount suppliers. However, if you want to sample the best of Nova Scotia shopping, you'll have to park the car and strike out on foot.

Pavillion 22

If you are one of the over 200,000 visitors who come to Halifax annually by cruise ship, your first chance to shop will be at Pavillion 22 where a number of high quality artisans and retailers have set up shop specifically to cater to cruise passengers. The merchandise offered here is well above the usual standards found at some cruise ship terminals.

Historic Properties, Upper Water Street, Halifax, www.historicproperties.ca

Anyone who visits the waterfront will inevitably pass through the Historic Properties, a collection of restored shops and warehouses that house a variety of retailers. While the shops primarily cater to the tourists, the products they offer are high-quality and the atmosphere is unbeatable. For those who want to wait while their better half shops, there are several good pubs and restaurants on the premises.

Granville Mall, Granville Street, Halifax

Basically an extension of the Historic Properties, Granville Mall surrounds Halifax's only pedestrian mall. The buildings here are made of stone and brick, instead of wood, but retain the same ambience as the waterfront stores. A good collection of pubs doesn't hurt either.

Brewery Market, Lower Water Street, Halifax

This complex was once Keith's Brewery. It's a short walk along the waterfront from Historic Properties, and the cruise ship pier. Every Saturday, it hosts the Halifax Farmers' Market (until summer 2010).

Shed 20, Marginal Road, Halifax

The Seaport Farmers' Market will move here in summer 2010. The hours will expand to being open 6 days a week, and the goal is to have a near-zero carbon footprint.

Bishop's Landing, Lower Water Street, Halifax, www.bishopslanding.com

This recent development, just down from the Brewery Market, is located amid the tasteful Bishop's Landing condominium and apartment development.

Here you will find very nice shops, including the excellent wine shop Bishop's Cellar, and pleasant eateries, including Bish restaurant.

Spring Garden Road, www.springgardenroad.com
This is the busiest street east of Montreal and the commercial lifeblood of the inner city. Several upscale shopping arcades share the area with local retail favourites Mills and Dugger's. With many of Canada's well-known retail chains located here, you can buy just about anything in the Spring Garden Road area. The area also features by far the largest selection of restaurants in town, particularly cafés and bistros.

ANTIQUES
Urban Cottage, 1819 Granville Street, (902) 423-3010
This is a unique consignment store just up from the waterfront that offers a wide range of merchandise at some surprisingly low prices; that's because if something doesn't sell the price is lowered every two weeks until it does.

John Daly Antiques, Hydrostone Market, 5525 Young Street, (902) 476-3883
The Hydrostone Market has a great collection of little shops to poke around in and this antique shop is one of the most interesting. And no, the owner it is not **the** John Daly.

Agricola Street
Over the past decade or so a small area of Agricola Street between North and Young has become known for its collection of antique shops and used furniture stores. There is an amazing variety of stuff to be found and many Haligonians like to while away a Saturday afternoon looking for bargains.

ARTS AND CRAFTS
Attica Furnishings, 1566 Barrington Street, (902) 423-2557, www.attica.ca
Attica features what it calls "clean and contemporary… home furnishings," which, when translated, we think means quality artsy things for the home. Owners Christopher Joyce and Suzanne Saul feature their own work as well as those of other top Canadian craftspeople. While, as a tourist, you might not be looking to buy things for the home, this is still a fun store to browse.

Fireworks Gallery, 1569 Barrington Street, 1-800-720-GEMS, www.fireworksgallery.com
This store features an extensive collection of quality jewellery made by Nova Scotian silver, pewter and goldsmiths, along with the work of other Canadian jewellers. The store also sells handcrafted decorative glass such as perfume bottles, paperweights, plates, small sculptures and an interesting estate jewellery collection.

Nova Scotia Art Gallery Shop, 1723 Hollis Street, (902) 424-7542, www.artgalleryofnovascotia.ca
The shop is very small but is an excellent source of Nova Scotia folk art and other "handmades," along with the usual art gallery shop fare. Prints and original paintings by Nova Scotia artists are available for sale across the foyer. Ask for the assistance of the friendly and helpful sales staff to view the work and provide some history on the artists.

Jennifer's of Nova Scotia, 5635 Spring Garden Road, (902) 425-3119, www.jennifers.ns.ca
Excellent Nova Scotian crafts are offered at this well-known business. Originally opened in a building in Shad Bay on the Peggy's Cove loop that was designed especially for selling crafts, Jennifer's was among the first stores in Nova Scotia to feature only quality Nova Scotian crafts. It was a great success and has been imitated by many others since. Don't pass up the chance to browse in this Spring Garden location.

GALLERIES
Zwicker's Gallery, 5415 Doyle Street, (902) 423-7662, www.zwickersgallery.ca
Just off Spring Garden Road, this is one of Nova Scotia's oldest and best art galleries, run by artists who know and appreciate the works they sell. In addition to contemporary paintings you'll find a good selection of earlier works, folk art and First Nations material. They also have a very large selection of antique maps, particularly Canadian ones.

Anna Leonowens Gallery, 1891 Granville Street, (902) 494-8223, www.nscad.ns.ca
Anna Leonowens became famous as the woman who tutored the King of Siam's family. Immortalized in the musical *The King and I* and the movie *Anna and the King*, Leonowens lived in Halifax for some years and was one of the founders of the first art college in Halifax. This gallery, which honours her name, is a showcase for the works of the faculty and students at the Nova Scotia College of Art and Design, located in the Granville Street area. The college is one of the premier places in North America to study art and some seldom-taught crafts, which goes a long way to explain why Nova Scotia is such a great place to buy art and crafts.

WOMEN'S CLOTHING
Mills Brothers, 5486 Spring Garden Road, (902) 429-6111, www.millsbrothers.com
This Halifax institution has undergone a major facelift in the last few years and is now probably the choice for Halifax fashionistas. Mills always has interesting window displays.

Foreign Affair, 1705 Barrington Street, (902) 429-1407, and 5639 Spring Garden Road, (902) 423-6676, www.foreignaffair.ca

There are two locations for this upscale women's clothing emporium where the clothes are pricey, but chic.

The Unicorn, Bishops Landing, 1477 Lower Water Street, (902) 423-4308
A long-established purveyor of fine women's clothing with a terrific sign.

MEN'S CLOTHING
Dugger's Quality Men's Wear, 5476 Spring Garden Road, (902) 425-2525, www.duggersfashion.com
As the name suggests Dugger's sells top-quality men's clothing. It is a favourite with visiting sports celebrities, many of whom know Dugger McNeil, a local sports legend. The store is now run by his affable son Ross, who is one of the province's top golfers, as you will probably gather from the golf paraphernalia throughout the store. Ross will be glad to show you the latest in Hugo Boss and other lines, which he carries. Dugger's is right next door to Mills, so if his and her shopping is on the agenda these stores are good places to start.

Colwell Brothers, Barrington Place (enter through the Delta Barrington), (902) 420-1222, www.colwellbrothers.com
Colwell's offers good solid conservative clothing for men. As Halifax's oldest clothier, it has an established clientele of local businessmen. Lawyers and judges buy their shirts and tabs here.

SHOES
Winsby's, 5504 Spring Garden Road, (902) 423-7324 www.winsbys.com
Winsby's is a long-established and reputable shoe retailer carrying many notable brands of women and men's shoes, but specializing in Rockport footwear.

Kick Ass Shoes (KAS), 5475 Spring Garden Road, (902) 444-7527.
The name says it all. You are either a Winsby's type of person or a KAS type. They are across the street from each other so it's easy to find out which.

BOOKSTORES
Since the last edition, a couple of Halifax's iconic bookstores have closed their doors, victims of the combination of the chain retailers and Amazon, but there are still a number of places for browsing in downtown Halifax.

The Bookmark, 5686 Spring Garden Road, (902) 423-0419, www.bookmarkpei.com
The Bookmark is a smaller store with a nice intimate feel and a very knowledgeable staff.

Maps and More, Summit Place, 1601 Lower Water Street, (902)-422-7106, www.maps-and-ducks.com
This is a travel related bookstore near the waterfont that has a great selection of travel guides and maps.

Woozles, 1533 Birmingham Street, (902) 423-7626, www.woozles.com.
If you are traveling with children or want to bring something back for them, this well known shop in the Spring Garden Road area is the place to do it.

USED BOOKS
Schooner Books, 5378 Inglis Street, (902) 423-8419, www.schoonerbooks.com
This long established bookstore in the south end carries a very large selection of second hand and rare books. Schooner regularly produces a catalogue of rare books, with an emphasis on Maritime Provinces material. You can now shop online, but nothing beats poking around in person.

J. W. Doull, Bookseller, 1684 Barrington Street, (902) 429-1652, www.doullbooks.com
Located in a restored bank building, this store is the ultimate in organized chaos with books literally everywhere. There are many little nooks and crannies to explore and against all odds, the proprietor John Doull seems to know exactly where every title resides.

Back Pages, 1526 Queen Street, (902) 423-4750
Back Pages, just off Spring Garden Road is not as large as Schooner or Doull's, but it still has a good selection, including the occasional rarity.

CRYSTAL
Nova Scotian Crystal, 5080 George Street, across from the ferry terminal, (902) 492-0416, www.novascotiancrystal.com
When Dennis Ryan, first the leader of the very popular Irish folk group Ryan's Fancy and then a successful stockbroker, announced his plans to establish Canada's first crystal factory, there were more than a few sceptics. After all, there was no source of fine silica closer than Europe and no trained glassblowers to be found outside Ireland. No problem for Dennis — import the sand and the glassblowers, set up in the historic Fisherman's Market building and get on with business, which is exactly what he did. This small-scale operation has been around for over a decade. It started with Waterford craftspeople who trained Nova Scotians. Perhaps because it produces quality hand-blown crystal at a fraction of Waterford prices, Nova Scotian Crystal has survived while Waterford has been forced into bankruptcy. Even if you are not buying, it's well worth a visit just to watch this ancient craft in practice. A full line of products can be viewed and purchased on the Web site.

ACCOMMODATIONS

Halifax is one of the most popular destinations for conventions in Canada, particularly in summer, so that advance accommodation reservations are a must. With plans to double the capacity of the convention space, hotel rooms could become a scarce commodity.

Halifax Marriott Harbourfront Hotel, 1919 Upper Water Street, (902) 421-1700, www.marriott.com

This is the only hotel in Halifax that is actually right on the waterfront and the award winning design architecturally complements adjacent Historic Properties. The Marriott is about as convenient as it gets for exploring the waterfront and downtown Halifax. Although not the most inexpensive place to stay, most people are satisfied with their stay at this full service hotel. When booking make sure to ask for a waterfront room – the view is worth the extra price.

Delta Barrington, 1875 Barrington Street, (902) 429-7410 or 1-888-890-3222, www.deltahotels.com

This comfortable hotel is part of an award winning restoration just up from the waterfront. From the Granville Street side, you wouldn't know this building houses a hotel. The original stone facades on Granville Street were carefully removed and replaced, stone by stone, when this hotel was constructed. The Delta Barrington has comfortable rooms and provides first-class accommodation. However, lower rooms overlooking the Granville Street mall with its taverns and shops can be a little noisy, so ask for an upper room.

Delta Halifax, 1990 Barrington Street, (902) 425-6700 or 1-888-890-3222, www.deltahotels.com

This sister hotel to the Delta Barrington is part of the Scotia Square complex that, while not architecturally stunning, is very centrally located and connected to the downtown pedway system that links four major hotels to two shopping centres, the convention centre, the Halifax Metro Centre and the casino. Compared to the other three major hotels in the downtown area, the Delta Halifax is slightly further removed from Halifax nightlife, which makes it more reliably peaceful in comparison to some rooms in the others.

The Prince George Hotel, George Street, across from the Metro Centre, (902) 425-1986 or 1-800-565-1567, www.princegeorgehotel.com

The Prince George, a bit up the hill from the waterfront, is the fourth of the big downtown hotels that are interconnected by the pedway system. It is probably the most luxurious and a favourite with visiting entertainers and celebrities. The Prince George has long been noted for the quality of its restaurant, Gio.

Cambridge Suites, 1583 Brunswick Street, (902) 420-0555 or 1-800-565-1263, www.cambridgesuiteshalifax.com
This recently renovated all-suite hotel with large rooms and kitchenettes is especially suitable for families who want to stay in downtown Halifax for a reasonable price. It is located in the uptown area, close to the Spring Garden Road attractions and the Citadel.

Westin Nova Scotian, 1181 Hollis Street, (902) 421-1000, www.thewestinnovascotian.com
The Westin is the latest international chain to manage what was originally the Hotel Nova Scotian, one of the flagship hotels in the once prestigious CN chain. Located adjacent to the railway station, this large edifice has been completely renovated and many of the rooms enlarged. The extension of the waterfront boardwalk to Gateway Park, a stone's throw from the Westin, has definitely improved its convenience. As Halifax's most southerly hotel, it is closest to the cruise ship terminal and Pier 21. The area around the Westin has a surprisingly diverse and largely undiscovered restaurant scene.

Four Points by Sheraton Halifax, 1496 Hollis Street, (902) 423-4444, www.starwoodhotels.com
This newer hotel is designed for the business traveller, but its convenient location makes it fine for tourists as well. It is within equal walking distance of the Spring Garden Road shopping district, the downtown business district and the historic waterfront area. Rooms feature all the things necessary to conduct business. The lobby has a very interesting collection of drawings of architecturally significant buildings that once graced Halifax.

Marriott Courtyard Halifax, 5120 Salter Street, (902) 428-1900, www.marriott.com
This is Halifax's newest hotel and for your money one of the best values in the city. It has a great location next to the Brewery Market and while not on the waterfront, many of the rooms have an excellent view of it. On the 8th floor the open air Harbourview Terrace is available to guests who want to bring their own wine and watch the harbour lights – trés romantique. The lobby and common areas are enhanced by numerous displays of artifacts that were unearthed during the excavation of the foundation. Attached to the hotel are the two very good Cut restaurants.

The Halliburton House Inn, 5184 Morris Street, (902) 420-0658, or 1-888-512-3344, www.thehalliburton.com
For a city that has so many well-preserved private homes from the Georgian through Victorian periods, Halifax has a surprisingly small number of inns or boutique hotels. The Halliburton is one of the best of these. A collection of three adjoining older heritage properties that have been carefully and meticulously restored, The Halliburton is within convenient walking distance of most of Halifax's major attractions. Luxury accommodation

with full facilities and free parking. The Halliburton also hosts Stories, a much under appreciated restaurant.

Lord Nelson Hotel, 1515 South Park Street, (902) 423-6331 or 1-800-565-2020, www.lordnelsonhotel.com

The Lord Nelson, along with the Westin, is one of the two grand dames of Halifax's hotel scene. Its 243 rooms and suites are conveniently located across the street from the Public Gardens, around the corner from Spring Garden Road's shopping and restaurant district and within easy walking distance of the downtown business district and the Citadel. It is also the most conveniently located for Dalhousie and Saint Mary's universities and the Queen Elizabeth II Health Sciences Centre network. The Lord Nelson first opened its doors to the travelling public in 1928. Whether hosting a lavish formal dinner honouring Princess Elizabeth and Prince Phillip, the infamous millionaire Howard Hughes, or the wedding-night celebrations of over 4,000 Nova Scotian couples, the Lord Nelson has been the venue for many memorable events. The hotel recently underwent major renovations, an overhaul of its fundamentally Victorian features to give it more of a contemporary look and feel. Ask for a room overlooking the Public Gardens.

Park Place Ramada Renaissance, 240 Brownlow Avenue, Dartmouth, 1-800-561-3733, www.ramadans.com

This is the principal hotel for travellers with business at Burnside Industrial Park, but it has two reasons to recommend it to the tourist. First, it has most of the amenities of the big Halifax hotels at considerably less expense, and second, children love the giant indoor waterslide. It is a clean, fairly new motor hotel run by a reputable chain.

DINING

In the last few editions of this book we were effusive about the number and quality of restaurants in the metro area. From what had been a culinary wasteland only a couple of decades ago had arisen a seemingly unending supply of brilliant young chefs with great ideas of new and exciting ways to cook and serve our abundant variety of local produce. Halifax became a magnet for chefs such as the Food Network's Michael Smith, who first plied his trade in a small inn in Prince Edward Island.

By the time the last edition went to print it was clear that Halifax had the best restaurant scene of any small Canadian city; better in fact than many larger cities. Alas, things could not continue as they had; there were simply too many good restaurants to be sustainable in a city this size, even with an upsurge in cruise ship arrivals. With the economic downturn in 2009, the number of restaurant closures far exceeded what would normally be the case. Just because a restaurant was good was not enough to ensure survival. We are sad to report that some of Halifax's best restaurants that were in this book for many years have now closed for good. Others are on life support, hoping that less competition and a smaller menu will save them; only time will tell.

So does this mean that Halifax has returned to its moribund restaurant ways of the not so distant past? Absolutely not. Perhaps in a case of survival of the fittest, the restaurants that continue to do well usually offer either great value for the money or cuisine that is worth paying for, even in a recession. There still remains a great variety of restaurants within a broad price range.

There is every reason to eat well while you visit Halifax, no matter what your budget.

As almost all restaurants now have their menus online, there is no reason to go into great detail about what's available, but we do recommend some favourite choices.

LONG-TIME FAVOURITES

These are restaurants that have proven their worth over the years and maintain uniformly high standards. Although some may be in the more expensive category, compared to Halifax's other dining choices, we believe you always get your money's worth.

da Maurizio, 1496 Lower Water Street (Brewery Market), Halifax, (902) 423-0859, www.damaurizio.ca

Chef Maurizio Bertossi was among the first of the many great chefs to open his own establishment in town and he set a standard of quality and, above all, consistency that blazed the trail for others. After preparing Northern Italian haute cuisine in very pleasant surroundings at the Brewery Market for over twenty years, in 2007 he decided to concentrate on his other restaurants and sold to Andrew King. Andrew tutored under Maurizio for ten years before stepping in as executive chef and the transition has gone very smoothly. Everything from the appetizers through the pastas and entrées to the desserts is generally terrific. For many people, the real attraction of da Maurizio is the pastas. There is usually a choice of about a dozen that are served in appetizer portions.

All of the entrées are good, but the veal especially so. If you have room for dessert, you will find many delicious choices.

Da Maurizio's has an extensive wine list, and some high end wines, but there are plenty of reasonably priced wines as well. This is a popular place for groups, probably because of the mix-and-matching that goes on in trying the various pastas and appetizers. The service is professional, courteous and unobtrusive. Perhaps most importantly, da Maurizio has established a reputation for reliability, and we feel perhaps more confident in recommending this restaurant than any other in this book for that very reason.

Fid Resto, 1569 Dresden Row (The Courtyard), Halifax, (902) 422-9162, www.fidresto.ca

Monica Bauché, proprietor, and chef/proprietor Dennis Johnston delivered their Franco/Asian fusion with flair for over a decade before deciding to get a little more casual. The completely reshaped menu still looks first and foremost to local ingredients, with reduced prices. The decor in the small dining room is now more funky than before. The menu is sparse compared to most restaurants, but changes with regularity. An eclectic blending of ingredients and cultural foods is the hallmark of dishes offered at Fid. When the results of his labours are placed before you, however, it is clear the chef is concentrating on perfection in whatever he has undertaken and also having fun. How else do you explain an appetizer called "The Mayhem" or a main course of "Angry Clams"? For dessert, the moelleux au chocolate, a rich mound of cake that oozes beautiful warm chocolate sauce from within when forked, is worth mentioning and thankfully still on the new menu. The wine list has been chosen with a view of matching the unusual cuisine. Fid is one restaurant that we can guarantee will deliver dishes that you have not seen or tasted elsewhere, because most of them have been invented right here by Dennis Johnston.

Bish World Cuisine, 1475 Lower Water Street (Bishop's Landing), Halifax, (902) 425-7993, www.bish.ca

Bish is one of a trio of restaurants operated by Maurizio and Stephanie Bertossi, who established Halifax's perennial favourite da Maurizio, and it's where you'll find chef Bertossi practising his craft. Located in Bishop's Landing, the harbourfront trendy residential development, Bish caters to the upscale crowd and does not disappoint. The restaurant is adjacent to the harbour, with floor-to-ceiling windows, a boardwalk and a few passers-by between diners and the water. During the summer months, diners can dine al fresco on the patio. Bish is one of the most stylish restaurants in the city. The clean lines of the contemporary furnishings and accessories, the soft blond-wood panelling, crisp linens, sparkling modern tableware and stunning floral arrangements come together to give a feeling of contemporary elegance and luxury. The food is billed as "world cuisine". It is innovative, but what really makes it work is the use of available fresh ingredients, careful preparation and the obvious attention to detail. The result is a flavourful and satisfying gastronomic experience. The presentation of the food is consistent with the surroundings, artistic and tasteful (no pun intended). The wine list is pricey but extensive. The service is unobtrusive, knowledgeable and thoroughly professional. Now that Maurizio is here many people in Halifax have a new favourite.

Chives Canadian Bistro, 1537 Barrington Street Halifax, (902) 420-9626, www.chives.ca

One of Halifax's most popular restaurants, Chives is located in the renovated Pacific Building, a 1940s Bank of Nova Scotia location originally constructed by the Canadian Pacific Railway Company. The restaurant decor is modern but manages to create a warm atmosphere by incorporating many natural materials — wood, stone and sand. One of the vestiges of the building's history as a bank is a vault now used as a wine cellar, which you can visit if you are having trouble making a selection. For the ultimate private dining experience, inquire about a table in the vault. Chef Craig

Flinn has become very well known for his insistence on using only locally available ingredients and changing the menu completely as the seasons do the same. The five course tasting menu featuring Nova Scotia flavours is a good choice for the entire table.

Some of the recipes for chef Flinn's most requested dishes including his justifiably famous biscuits are on the Web site.

The Press Gang, 5218 Prince Street, Halifax, (902) 423-8816, www.thepressgang.ca

Victor Syperek owns a number of interesting establishments in the Argyle Street area, one of the most happening places in the city. He is an artist by profession and the street sign hanging above the entrance on Prince Street, a large wooden representation of a roving press gang of the type that once terrorized Halifax's waterfront, is one of his works.

The name of the restaurant is a reference to the notorious British practice of enticing naval recruits to His Majesty's service after deviously fogging the judgment of the young (and not so young) men with ample quantities of ale. The consent thus obtained, the press gang would follow to ensure that service was rendered. The Press Gang is in the basement of the 250-year-old Carleton House. The stone walls, wooden beams and catacomb-like rooms transport you to the time when that might have been a concern, at least for the men in the group. Today, it makes for a cozy and slightly conspiratorial atmosphere.

The Press Gang is generally a very good restaurant with an interesting and extensive menu that becomes an excellent restaurant when it comes to seafood. This is probably the best place for oysters and maybe even lobster in town. The daily catch likely will be an interesting fresh fish selection, such as yellow fin tuna or arctic char.

The wine list has something in all price ranges, but is weighted to the expensive category. The service is informal and accommodating, but can seem a bit harried at times. This is a very busy restaurant and you will be aware of that as the evening progresses, when all the tables are filled, the grand piano in the reception area has been put in gear, the bar stools fill and the decibel level in this low-ceilinged facility climbs several notches. All in all, this place makes for a great evening out, especially if you're with a group of four or more.

Onyx, 5680 Spring Garden Road, Halifax, (902)428-5680, www.onyxdining.com

The extremely high standards of modern chic set by Bish and the now departed Seven seem to have inspired long-time local restauranteur Robert Risley to reach even higher. Onyx is one of the newer entries into the Halifax high-end restaurant sweepstakes. A local restaurant expert entitled his review on Onyx "Chic and Sexy" and that says it all. The long narrow room is dominated by a stunning bar made from onyx, which is lit from below. From this bar emanates some of the most delicious pre-dinner drink creations in town. The rest of the décor is in line with the theme set by the bar. Bolsters separate diners seated on a long leather bench. Tables are separated by metallic sheers. Onyx delivers on the food as well, including some dining options not available at other Halifax restaurants. The house specialty is the herb-crusted rack of lamb and it is special. Chef Tahir Salamat was trained largely in the Middle East and Hong Kong and the Asian influence is apparent on many of the offerings. As far as wine goes, suffice it to say that Onyx received the *Wine Spectator* Award of Excellence in its first year of operation. Named as one of Canada's ten best new restaurants in Canada for 2004, Onyx has upped the ante for all the others.

The menu, drink and wine list are all available online, as well as shots of that fabulous bar.

Fiasco, 1463 Brenton Street, Halifax, (902) 429-3499, www.fiascorestaurant.com

This is one of Halifax's smaller and certainly more intimate restaurants, which is chosen mostly by couples out for a romantic evening. Although chef Martin Keyzlar is Czech, the influence at Fiasco is definitely French. What Keyzlar can do with sauces is amazing, and it is these sauces combined with traditional Nova Scotian fare such as salmon, scallops or beef that set his cooking apart and guarantees a taste experience unique in Halifax. Everybody raves about his calamari. The wine list is not extensive, but has quite a number of reasonably priced selections.

Stories, 5184 Morris Street, Halifax (902) 444-4400, www.thehalliburton.com/stories-restaurant

Stories is the Rodney Dangerfield of high-end Halifax restaurants — it doesn't get the respect it deserves. Situated in The Halliburton House Inn, Halifax's top boutique inn, Stories became known for its game dishes of which there is always at least one on the menu. Lately however, it has evolved into a restaurant that places an emphasis on buying local and the menu reflects that — something for everyone, not just carnivores. The wait staff is very knowledgeable and helpful. Stories is not overly pricey and the wine list is probably the most reasonable of any of the high-end restaurants. Don't pass on the signature appetizer, pan-seared rice paper–wrapped scallops. They are unbelievably tasty.

BISTROS

These are restaurants that are generally less expensive than those listed above. They all have one thing in common — great ambience and good food.

Il Mercato, 5650 Spring Garden Road, Halifax, (902) 422-2866, www.il-mercato.ca

This is one of three of the Bertossi family restaurants to be included in this book. With Il Mercato, they are demonstrating that they can still deliver the best, but at moderate prices. Nothing on the main menu costs more than $25, including the grilled shrimp, scallops or rack of lamb. The antipasto is especially good, as are most of the other appetizers. Foccaccio, pizza and pasta dominate this menu. For desserts, you needn't look any further than the homemade gelato, especially the pistachio.

The décor and atmosphere are in keeping with an Italian trattoria — wide open and filled with the conversation of enthusiastic diners. Some people find it a bit too noisy, but for most it is one of the first choices on Spring Garden Road. The wine list is short and reasonably affordable.

Saege, 5883 Spring Garden Road, (902) 429-1882, www.saege.ca
Self-described on the web page as "an inviting neighbourhood bistro," the owners are understating the excellent value of this award winning restaurant. Browse their web site to view the menus, checkout the restaurant photos that profile the restaurant's charming décor, and beautifully presented food. Saege is a welcome addition to the Spring Garden Road restaurant scene.

Economy Shoe Shop Café and Bar, 1661-1663 Argyle Street, Halifax, (902) 423-7463, www.economyshoeshopgroup.ca
The Economy Shoe Shop is not as much a place to eat as an experience. The Shoe, as everyone calls it, is part of Victor Syperek's restaurant and bar group that dominates a block of Argyle Street. It is a collection of bar rooms and restaurants randomly strung together where people seem to wander aimlessly from place to place. Take a look at the Web site and you'll get a better idea.

When Halifax started to become popular with the movers and shakers of the film business, they needed a place to meet, talk and most importantly, be seen, and the Shoe became that place. There is almost always at least one movie or TV show in production at any time of year and this of course means there are almost always movie stars in town. By celebrity word of mouth the Shoe has become well-known throughout the entertainment industry, and when someone thinks they might have a chance to bump into Harrison Ford, Tom Selleck, Sean Penn or any number of other celebs who have been seen here, some regularly, they flock to this place. So do those who want to be mistaken for celebrities and dress and act accordingly. It all makes for one unusual atmosphere.

So what about the food? Frankly we have found both the food and service inconsistent, but have to admit that so many other people rave about it that maybe we're missing something. Anyway, at the Shoe, it's not about the food.

SEAFOOD

Most of the high end restaurants listed above do a very good job on seafood, but in terms of restaurants that bill themselves as seafood emporiums there is only one that we can recommend. As a general rule most of the other seafood places have taken dead aim at the mass tourism market, catering to the thousands who stream off cruise ships, arrive on bus tours or come as part of conventions. There's just something about quality and quantity that don't seem to mix with seafood. In order not to discourage those on limited budgets we have recommended some good fish and chip places as well (see page 120).

McKelvie's, at the corner of Bedford Row and Prince Street, Halifax, (902) 421-6161, www.mckelvies.ca

McKelvie's is the best choice for a wide selection of seafood done just about any way you can imagine. It is housed in a refurbished fire hall, giving a spacious atmosphere for dining just across from the Maritime Museum. Delivering consistent quality for many years, McKelvie's is a favourite place for business lunches. Their crunchy haddock is almost legendary. A reasonably complete wine list, friendly service and fair prices will make you glad you skipped some of the other waterfront possibilities.

STEAKHOUSES

Cut Steakhouse and Urban Grill, 5120 Salter Street (at the corner of Lower Water and Salter Street), Halifax, (902) 429-5120, www.cutsteakhouse.ca

Cut offers two types of dining experiences, the Urban Grill, a casual cosmopolitan dining downstairs, or the more sophisticated menu and surroundings of the Steakhouse upstairs. The Grill is open for lunch and dinner, while the Steakhouse is open only for evening meals. The Grill features smaller courses, suitable for sharing and some amazing burgers. The Steakhouse is an experience in culinary decadence from appetizers to desert. True beef connoisseurs will be very happy with their menu choices — various cuts and selections of wet or dry aged US Prime, Kobe and local beef are all on the menu. Selected in 2008 as one of Canada's best restaurants by *enRoute* magazine, and given a four diamond rating from CAA, we know why.

Ryan Duffy's, 1650 Bedford Row, Halifax, (902) 421-1116, www.ryanduffys.ca

Under new ownership at a different location, Halifax's original premier steak house has updated its décor and improved its offerings, while managing to keep their prices very reasonable. Featuring Alberta AAA beef, and USDA prime select beef for their in house dry-aged cuts, you won't be disappointed. Their lunch offerings that go well beyond steaks are tasty and well prepared. Given the simple but elegant surroundings and the well prepared food, you will be pleasantly surprised when you get the bill. This restaurant offers very good value for money.

The Keg, 1712 Market Street, Halifax, (902) 425-8355, www.kegsteakhouse.com

We wouldn't ordinarily include a chain restaurant in this book, but the Keg is an exception. This is a great place for the under-thirty set who either can't afford to eat at the more upscale places or frankly are just a bit intimidated by them. Unlike almost every other chain we could name, The Keg does have the friendly atmosphere it extols in its television ads. The booths are comfortable and you get a fair meal at a fair price.

ITALIAN

Not overlooking the fact that da Maurizio or Il Mercato are probably at the top of most people's lists, here are some more suggestions.

Ristorante aMano, 1477 Lower Water Street, Bishops Landing, Halifax, (902) 423-6266, www.ristoranteamano.ca

aMano is the Italian term for by hand, a fitting name for the newest addition to the Bertossi Group of restaurants. Everything here, from pastas to pizzas to sauces, is made by hand, authentically Italian and oh so tasty. The salads and gelato are awesome too. Located in the harbour front area of Bishop's Landing, Ristorante aMano offers you a dining experience of a typical neighbourhood trattoria. At the time of writing, nothing on the menu was over $20. It is Alison's favourite quick escape to the food of Italy without having to get on a plane.

Café Chianti, 5165 South Street, Halifax, (902) 423-7471, www.cafechianti.ca

Café Chianti has been around a long time and has a legion of devoted followers who wouldn't go anywhere else for pasta or some of the traditional Italian dishes such as veal parmigiana. Located at the bottom of South Street handy to the Westin, Café Chianti describes itself as Old World. It will re-open in early 2010 after a fire damaged the interior, surely with an updated look and the same great menu. The pastas are strong on the classics such as cannelloni, lasagne and manicotti. For some reason, for at least twenty years Café Chianti has also had a mini specialty in goulash and beef stroganov which are both excellent. For dessert the profiteroles have kept people coming back for decades. Recently the wine cellar was upgraded and there is plenty of selection at fairly reasonable prices.

GREEK

Opa Greek Taverna, 1565 Argyle Street (corner of Blowers and Argyle Streets), Halifax, (902) 492-7999, www.opataverna.com

The interior of Opa looks like something tourists in Greece are used to seeing as a traditional Greek taverna. The atrium area is open and airy, the murals and prints of Greek scenes are predictable, but the proprietors have managed to create an atmosphere of sunny relaxation that is comfortable and a bit playful whether you are on vacation or not. The decor aside, the food is definitely authentic Greek and definitely good. Greek cuisine is known for the quantity and quality of savoury appetizers, of which Opa offers a great number. You could easily make a meal of them and walk away satisfied. However, it is worth hanging in there for the main course. There are no surprises on the very traditional menu, but the food is well-prepared and presents a variety of Greek flavours and textures. The wine list is adequate. This is definitely good value for the dollar.

Estia, 5518 Spring Garden Road, Halifax, (902)-429-8331, www.estiarestaurant.ca

Estia's name comes from the Greek word for "hearth," meaning warmth. Maria and Peter Katsichtis opened Estia in 2009, with the intention of offering traditional Greek cuisine made from their favourite family recipes, along with the warmth of Greek celebrations, which almost all involve family and food. We believe they have succeeded. The Greek food is authentic and includes a variety of meat, seafood, vegetarian and pasta specials that are sure to please. The portions are generous and the wine list, while not extensive, is very reasonable.

TURKISH
Anatolia, 1518 Dresden Row, Halifax, (902) 492-4568
Despite the fact that the Greeks and the Turks have not had much in common, their food sure does. Anatolia is Halifax's first Turkish restaurant and it's very good. Set in an older house just off Spring Garden Road, the bright dining area is covered with Turkish rugs and other items that are tasteful additions to the dining experience. Like Opa, Anatolia offers a very large selection of appetizers, or mezes as they are called in Turkey. You will recognize many as being similar to Greek offerings, including hummus, stuffed vine leaves etc., but there are differences such as avocado prawns. All the main entrées are cooked over an open charcoal brazier visible from the dining area. There are many types of lamb and chicken kebabs, and every one that we have sampled has been great. For $28 there is a set menu that provides a good introduction to the much underrated Turkish cuisine. Anatolia is licensed with a limited selection of wine and beer.

JAPANESE
Dharma Sushi, 1576 Argyle Street, (902) 425-7785,
www.dharmasushi.com
Halifax has gone from having no sushi restaurants not that many years ago to having almost too many. Very popular with the younger crowd, Dharma Sushi is regarded by many as one of the best. Everything is understated in this small restaurant where simple woodblock prints adorn the white walls. Owner Hideki Yamamoto is in residence most nights and together with chef Kitajima, Dharma offers carefully and artfully prepared sushi and other Japanese dishes. The menu includes far more than just sushi, so there should be something to the liking of just about everyone. It is also very reasonable — much more so compared to some of the high end Japanese restaurants in town. If you can't get into Dharma Sushi, another great choice is I Love Sushi at 5220 Blowers Street, (902) 429-6168, which is a stone's throw away.

CHINESE
Cheelin, Brewery Market, 1496 Lower Water Street, Halifax,
(902) 422-2252, www.cheelinrestaurant.com
Halifax has never had a shortage of Chinese restaurants, most with similar menus and décor. Cheelin is different in that it is definitely upscale, sharing space in the Brewery Market with tony da Maurizio, but without upscale prices. The secret to Cheelin is the fact that the chef doesn't just turn out good renditions of Chinese favourites, but innovates using local ingredients

to produce great dishes not offered elsewhere in town. The Hunan haddock is a case in point. As well, Cheelin does not use any MSG. The décor is bright and the service friendly. The fact that Cheelin has been recommended in *Where to Eat in Canada* for twelve straight years says a lot.

THAI
Baan Thai, 5234 Blowers Street, (902) 446-4301, www.baanthai.ca
Halifax's most popular Thai restaurant changed location in 2009, moving from the Spring Garden Road area to the very competitive Argyle Street area. The décor is that of an authentic Bangkok restaurant and some of the staff come from there as well. A very extensive menu features classic Thai dishes including a number of excellent curries. Prices are fair and the service very hospitable.

PIZZA
While Il Mercato offers great pizza, if you're just looking to pick up something really good to take away there are a number of perennial favourites, all of which have their die-hard loyalists. Tomavinos, 5173 South Street, Halifax, (902) 425-7111 or 422-9757 www.tomavinos.ca, located at the bottom of South Street not far from the waterfront, is the most convenient for most visitors. Salvatore's, 5541 Young Street, Halifax, (902) 455-1133 www.salvatorespizza.ca, in the Hydrostone Market, is a little more out of the way but worth the bother, not that visiting the Hydrostone Market is ever a bother. Both places specialize in real Italian thin-crust pizza topped with a variety of usual and unusual ingredients that set them well above the run-of-the-mill fare found at most pizza places. Also deservedly popular is Euro Pizza, 31 St. Margarets Bay Road, (902) 479-7979, which has a great white pizza and as a bonus excellent souvlakis as well.

FISH & CHIPS
One of the side effects of the increasing affluence and sophistication of Halifax diners has been the gradual demise of the neighbourhood fish and chips joint. At one time there were about a dozen of these in the city, mostly in the north end where the legendary Camille's, among others, was located. Now such places are hard to come by, but we're glad to say still very much in existence. When you just feel like biting into a crispy deep-fried piece of cod or haddock, or maybe gorging on fried clams and damn the cholesterol, try one of these spots.

Fries and Co., corner of Chebucto Road and Connolly Street, Halifax, (902) 455-5250
This steady performer has been churning out fish and chips orders by the thousands annually to satisfied customers. A very traditional neighbourhood joint.

John's Lunch, 352 Pleasant Street, Dartmouth, (902) 469-3074, www.johnslunch.com

For many years John's was a rundown-looking little building covered with green vinyl siding not far from the Woodside ferry terminal. Recently it had a face lift, but it's never been the appearance that attracts people to this restaurant. Just about all the seafood here is deep-fried. If you have come this far, however, you will soon realize that if you are going to fool with the fried stuff, this is the place to do it. The staff at John's Lunch has perfected the art of deep-frying to a point very few shops ever come even remotely close to accomplishing. John's Lunch uses fresh clams from Chezzetcook, and they are justly famous. Even a Governor General and her husband have stopped in to sample this fine fare during a visit. All the other seafood items, especially the scallops, are perfectly cooked, in fresh oil, at the right temperature, in a very light batter.

PUBS AND TAVERNS

Haligonians have a venerable tradition of taking meals in pubs and taverns where the dollar often seems to go further. Over the past twenty years the quality of food in the best pubs has risen well above ordinary pub grub. In the evening many of these venues come alive with many of the best local performers. Our favourites, in no particular order, are as follows:

The Old Triangle Irish Alehouse, 5136 Prince Street, Halifax, (902) 492-4900, www.oldtriangle.com

The name of this pub was chosen by the three owners because of the ancient belief that a grouping of three, or triad, would bring good luck. The owners were more famous for their Irish music than hospitality before opening the pub, but have successfully made the transition from touring musicians to purveyors of food, drink and music. The pub occupies three rooms: the Snug, the Pourhouse and Tigh An Cheoil (house of music) and you are promised the three most important ingredients of a memorable occasion no matter where you sit — food for the body, drink for the spirit and music for the soul. The menu, which is available online, offers some authentic Irish selections as well as the usual Canadian pub fare. The food is good, the surroundings cosy, the music and crowd are lively, and the Triangle serves a sufficient variety of beer to earn its title as an alehouse. You can easily pass a comfortable and entertaining evening here. The schedule of performances is also available on the Web site.

Stayner's Wharf Bar & Grill, 5075 George Street, Halifax (next to the Dartmouth Ferry Terminal), (902) 492-1800

There may be many similarities with pub menus in the offerings at Stayner's, but the food served here is good, too good to be called pub grub. It's fresh, simple and appealing, served in a pleasant atmosphere by friendly and attentive wait staff. It is a relaxing and comfortable place for a simple, good meal. The seafood medley is one of our personal favourites and the chowder is a true Maritime one, not overdone with thickeners but a simple flavourful milky broth with lots of seafood bits. The pan-fried haddock is also a good choice, as is the other traditional pub fare from chicken wings and nachos to burgers and melts. It is a little pricier than most pubs, but that is because the food is simply better than most.

The Lower Deck, Historic Properties, Lower Water Street, (902) 425-1501 www.lowerdeck.ca

With its nautical decor and its location in the Privateers' Warehouse at the Historic Properties, the Lower Deck has been a success from the day it opened over 35 years ago. They serve a good lunch and very good beer. The communal tables get rocking when there is entertainment. If you want to have a great night out in Halifax you won't do much better than "the Deck".

Your Father's Moustache, 5686 Spring Garden Road, (902) 423-6766, www.yourfathersmoustache.ca

The Moustache has a very nice open-air deck and a good menu with a reliable kitchen. The daily haddock special is one of the best deals in town, and this is one tavern where they won't overcook the fish. The Pub Club is justifiably famous. The "Stache" also offers very good entertainment. Almost every night there is a band, karaoke or a performance of some kind.

Durty Nelly's, corner of Argyle and Sackville, (902) 406-7640, www.durtynellys.ca

Modeled after a legendary Irish pub, Durty Nelly's is one of the newest and definitely most successful entries in the competitive Halifax bar scene. The selection of Irish quaffs on tap and the look of the place are more than reminiscent of the Auld Sod. The menu was designed to reflect the best of what could be found in Ireland and it does. The fish and chips are really exceptional and when you order hot wings here they are that — really hot.

The Seahorse Tavern, 1665 Argyle Street, (902) 423-7200

The Seahorse is Halifax's oldest tavern, having first opened its doors in the 1940's. It has gone through many phases and today is known for being probably the top spot to catch up and coming local talent. For an alternative to traditional pub music come to the Seahorse, but get there early because it's usually packed.

VEGETARIAN
Satisfaction Feast, 3559 Robie Street (902) 422-3540, www.satisfaction-feast.com

After many, many years in the downtown area, Satisfaction Feast, Halifax's beloved vegetarian restaurant, moved away from the hustle and bustle to the relative tranquility of the north end. This was fitting as the place was started by a follower of the Sri Chinmoy spiritual philosophy. It is one of a number of similar restaurants worldwide. The menu shows heavy Mideastern and Asian influences where of course vegetarian dishes are much more accepted by the general public than they are in good old Halifax. However,

Halifax does have a significant and growing vegetarian population as well as more non-vegetarians who are looking for an alternative to the meat-heavy offerings of traditional restaurants. Satisfaction Feast is where they will find it.

FAMILY DINING
Quinpool Road Area, www.quinpoolroad.ca
Most of our restaurant recommendations are based on the assumption that the reader will be staying at one of the downtown hotels or visiting the city on a cruise ship. However, if you've got wheels and want to eat relatively cheaply with lots of choices, Quinpool Road is the place to do it. Those addicted to fast food will find most of the chains here and the more discerning will find just about any type of food you could possibly desire. The following are just a sample of what is available.

Athens Restaurant, 6273 Quinpool Road (902) 422-1595. A traditional family owned Greek restaurant that has a huge following.

Freeman's Little New York, 6092 Quinpool Road (902) 455-7000. One of Halifax's oldest and most popular pizza places.

Ardmore Tea Room, 6499 Quinpool Road (902) 423-7523. Not really a tea room, but an old fashioned diner that has been around forever.

King of Donair, 6422 Quinpool Road (902) 421-0000. The place to try Halifax's quirky take on the Greek specialty, donairs.

King Wah, 6430 Quinpool Road (902) 423-2587. The best of a number of Chinese restaurants in the area.

Phil's Seafood, 6285 Quinpool Road (902) 431-3474. A real contender for best and most reasonably priced fish and chips in town.

The Chickenburger, 1531 Bedford Highway, Bedford, www.chickenburger.com
When you eat at the Chickenburger, you realize why fast food became so popular in the first place. Since 1940, metro residents have been making the drive along the Bedford Highway to eat at this local landmark. The secret of their success is simplicity. There are no special sauces, secret recipes or other gimmicks, just really good chickenburgers, cheeseburgers and milkshakes. The neon and chrome interior harkens back to the original era of drive-ins in the late 1940s. Worth the drive.

SOMETHING DIFFERENT
The Fireside, 1500 Brunswick Street, Halifax, (902) 423-5995, www.thefireside.ca
The Fireside is essentially a glorified lounge, but it has to be one of the most intimate spots in town for a quiet supper or late-night drink. When the place was renovated, fireplaces were added along with comfy sofas and wingback chairs to curl up in, making for a cozy atmosphere. The menu is fairly straightforward, with an emphasis on hot appetizers, which will warm you up as you sit by the fire. This is a great spot to drop in after Neptune or a movie.

Cheapside Café, 1723 Hollis Street, (902) 424-4494, www.agns.gov.ns.ca

Located in the Art Gallery of Nova Scotia, Cheapside Café is close to the Halifax waterfront and across the street from historic Province House. The menu is innovative and the food is excellent in both presentation and taste. The decor is very bright and cheerful, tending to funky elegance. The staff is upbeat and friendly. It is a very popular spot for lunch or early dinner. The wine list is reasonable and the desserts are exceptional.

Mosaic, 1584 Argyle Street (902) 405-4700, www.mosaicsocialdining.com

Mosaic offers something no other Halifax area restaurant does, or at least not as well — small plates, which are really a local version of tapas. The restaurant encourages groups to sample and share a wide variety of moderately-priced dishes; hence the theme of social dining. It is extremely popular with groups of students and young professionals. The other attraction is the cocktails which are exceptional.

Hydrostone Market, 5531 Young Street (902) 454-2000, www.hydrostonemarket.ca

The Hydrostone area in north end Halifax is one of the most interesting neighbourhoods in the city. Much of the vitality comes from the shops and eateries in the Hydrostone Market, which was built in 1918 after the area was literally flattened by the Halifax Explosion. There are five eateries in the market, any one of which is a good choice. Our personal favourite is Epicurious Morsels, (902) 455-0955, www.epicuriousmorsels.com, at which Chef Jim Hanusiak has been delivering mouth watering soups and entrees for years. This is also a great place for brunch. The Eggs Benedict might be the best in town.

jane's on the common, 2394 Robie Street, (902) 431-5683, www.janesonthecommon.com

Speaking of brunch, jane's is without doubt the place for the large number of fans who wouldn't consider any place else. To state that this restaurant is wildly popular on the weekends would be an understatement. Expect a wait, but hang in there — it's worth it.

LIGHTHOUSE ROUTE
Halifax to Lunenburg

When most people think of Nova Scotia, they conjure up images of lighthouses, lobster traps and fishermen's dories clustered around sheltered coves. These images, while somewhat stereotypical, do suit the Lighthouse Route perfectly. Stretching from Halifax to Yarmouth along the Atlantic coast, the Lighthouse Route traverses Nova Scotia's South Shore. It is one of the oldest settled areas in the province and includes many of Nova Scotia's most interesting towns and communities, in particular Chester, Mahone Bay, Lunenburg, Liverpool and Shelburne. For the most part, it is an area that has enjoyed prosperity because of the sea. Whether it is today's lucrative lobster and scallop fisheries or yesterday's shipbuilding and trade, the sea has contributed substantially; even to some of the more dubious activities such as privateering.

While the Lighthouse Route has many beautiful lighthouses, it also has some of Nova Scotia's finest beaches and wild areas. If one were to explore all the options available on a tour of the Lighthouse Route, it would easily take a week to get from Halifax to Yarmouth. By all means avail yourself of the chance to spend at least a few days on this wonderful coast, as the Lighthouse Route is probably the best serviced of any of Nova Scotia's trails, with fine accommodations, dining and shopping available along the entire way. Technically, the Lighthouse Route begins at Halifax and includes Peggy's Cove, which was included in the Halifax/Dartmouth section of this book, as it is more conveniently toured on a day trip from metro.

For detailed information online visit www.destinationsouthwestnova.com.

From Halifax, you can follow Highway 3 through the suburbs of Lakeside and Timberlea, but there is little of interest to travelling vacationers. The Lighthouse Route is best picked up from Exit 5 off Highway 103. Turn left onto Hammonds Plains Road and follow it until it ends at Highway 3 about 2 kilometres further on. Now bear right and proceed straight through the light and you will find yourself at Head of St. Margaret's Bay from whence a beautiful drive commences, following the winding shoreline of the bay to the community of Hubbards. On a clear day, the more distant islands in the bay almost seem to be mirages floating on top of the water. At Boutiliers Point by the yellow church, take a detour via Island View Drive for a panoramic view of the entire bay from high above the shoreline. This road rejoins the Lighthouse Route a little further on. After passing through Ingramport you will come upon a number of small sandy beaches where you can get out and stretch your legs or go for a swim although the water is usually pretty cold. Queensland is the most popular of these beaches, but Cleveland Beach near Black Point is better for walking.

Next is Hubbards, a pretty little village nestled around a protected cove, which devotees of the former CBC series *Black Harbour* will undoubtedly recognize, as the show was filmed here. Hubbards is also noteworthy for its many fine summer homes and cottages. For the visitor there are some nice places to stay around the cove and a couple of good places to eat, including lobster dinners at the venerable Shore Club.

At the western end of the village, look for the turn to follow the Lighthouse Route around the Aspotogan Peninsula, which separates St. Margaret's Bay from Mahone Bay. If you would like to try your luck fishing, the government wharf at Fox Point is a good place for mackerel and pollock fishing, when they are in season.

Further along, you will come to Northwest Cove and Aspotogan, two of the prettiest authentic fishing villages in all of Nova Scotia, although recent aquaculture developments have residents worried.

At Blandford, the largest community on the peninsula be sure to take the road to New Harbour for an excellent view of East Ironbound Island, as well as Big and Little Tancook. The cliffs of East Ironbound and its picturesque lighthouse are clearly visible from this road. Life on East Ironbound was immortalized in *Rockbound*, a controversial novel by Frank Parker Day. At one time vilified by residents for its honest and grim portrayal of life on the island, the novel is now considered a classic description of life on the edge.

Rejoining Highway 3, it is not far to Chester (www.chesterns.com), the first of a series of classic Nova Scotia towns that punctuate the shore all the way to Yarmouth. Founded in 1759 by New Englanders, Chester has had a long and distinguished history as a summer resort. In place of the fishing boats that are seen in the harbours of most Nova Scotia coastal communities, Chester's Back Harbour is a haven to sailboats and yachts. Many of the summer cottages, particularly those on some of the islands, are really mansions and seem to belong more in coastal Maine than Nova Scotia. Summer in Chester revolves around sailing, golfing, dinner theatre and socializing. The atmosphere is laid-back, for residents and visitors alike. A walk around this historic community is highly recommended, if not to view the splendid architecture and gardens then to explore the many fine shops which offer high-quality clothes and crafts.

Leaving Chester, the Lighthouse Route follows the shores of Mahone Bay to the beautiful town of that name. Along the way, just past the village of Western Shore, you will find the road to mysterious Oak Island. Approaching Mahone Bay, look for the turnoff to Indian Point, where a short drive will take you to this sheltered community amidst the islands of the bay. Retracing your steps, you will have a magnificent view of the three waterfront churches in Mahone Bay (www.mahonebay.com), certainly one of the most photographed scenes in the province.

Founded in 1754 by the same German, Swiss and French Protestants who settled Lunenburg, the town later acquired a large influx of New Englanders. Mahone Bay has always been a prosperous community, first with mills at the head of the bay and later with shipbuilding. Prosperity is readily evident in the many fine homes in the town. Over the past 25 years,

Mahone Bay has become a magnet for artisans attracted by the tranquility and beauty of the community. Do yourself a favour and take the time to stroll around and explore the many interesting shops in this town — chances are you won't even notice the absence of chain stores, fast food restaurants and supermarkets.

The Lighthouse Route follows the shoreline of Mahone Bay as far as Maders Cove and then cuts across to Lunenburg, about 15 kilometres away. A more interesting route to take is the road to Hermans Island and then continue around the shore of Princes Inlet. This road passes a number of beautiful old homes boasting spectacular gardens and unexcelled views of the Mahone Bay islands. To take this alternate route, look for the sign to Maders Cove not far outside Mahone Bay. This route rejoins Highway 3, just past Second Peninsula, several kilometres outside Lunenburg.

Lunenburg (www.explorelunenburg.ca) is one of Nova Scotia's oldest communities and certainly one of the most interesting. Founded in 1753 by the British, it was settled by Protestant farmers from Germany, Switzerland and the Montbeliard region of France on the Swiss border. The intention of the British in settling Lunenburg with Protestants was to counterbalance the Catholic Acadian communities, which had been established in the province for more than 100 years. In fact, there was apparently a small Acadian community at the present site of Lunenburg when the Protestant settlers arrived. What became of these Acadians is unknown. The town was originally laid out in an orderly grid on the side of the hill overlooking its fine harbour. Most of the buildings in the old part of town date from the early 1800s, but some were built much earlier. Lunenburg has an architectural integrity unsurpassed in Nova Scotia, perhaps in all of Canada. In 1991, the entire Old Town section was designated a national historic district by the federal government and in 1995 it was designated a World Heritage Site by UNESCO. There are currently 890 of these sites in the world and tourists come from all over the globe to visit them. The province of Nova Scotia recently acquired a substantial number of historic waterfront buildings from private owners to ensure that the integrity of the historic shoreline will be maintained.

The tourist information centre, located in a lighthouse replica, has a sweeping view from the lookout on the second floor. Nearby, there is a cairn erected by the citizens of France in memory of the French Montbeliard Protestants. The cairn lists many of the original spellings of some of the most common South Shore names, such as Boutilier, Coolen and Dauphinee. In addition to its impressive scenery and architecture, Lunenburg is also known as the home of the *Bluenose*, Canada's most famous sailing ship. Today, Lunenburg is home port to the *Bluenose II*, an exact replica of the original, which can often be seen moored at the Fisheries Museum. Lunenburg makes an excellent base from which to tour the Lighthouse Route, as it has some very good inns, fine restaurants and interesting craft and souvenir shops. It really is the top highlight of many along the Lighthouse Route.

BEACHES

The best beaches on the South Shore are pretty well all located between Lunenburg and Yarmouth, but there are a couple worth mentioning on this section of the Lighthouse Route.

Queensland

This is probably the most popular beach in the Halifax area, just on the Halifax side of Hubbards. At high tide, the beach virtually disappears and becomes too crowded for most people's taste. However, it is supervised with washroom facilities. If you want to avoid the crowds, try Cleveland Beach, a few kilometres closer to Halifax, or Bayswater, on the Blandford Peninsula.

Bayswater Beach

This small and sandy beach is located at the end of the Blandford Peninsula. Unprotected and facing the open ocean, this beach can be cold and foggy, but on a clear warm day it is exceptionally refreshing and usually not crowded. It is also a good picnic stop on a trip around the Blandford peninsula.

BIRDING

The Southwest Nova Tourism Association Web site has an excellent coloured brochure on birding routes along the Lighthouse Route that can be downloaded at http://www.destinationsouthwestnova.com/Birding/2009BirdingNS.pdf

Big Tancook Island

A trip to Tancook Island provides more than the usual rewards for bird-watchers. From the ferry, which leaves from Chester, one can see eiders, cormorants, terns, ospreys and the occasional offshore wanderers such as petrels and shearwaters. There are very few natural predators on the islands, which translates into good wildlife watching. Deer, rabbit and pheasant are all remarkably tame on the island. A flock of wild turkeys has even been introduced, which has, according to some residents, run amok.

CEMETERIES

The Old Burying Ground at Mush-a-Mush

Mush-a-Mush was the First Nations name for the Mahone Bay area. This cemetery, conveniently located just behind the Mahone Bay tourist bureau, contains the graves of the earliest European settlers, who were mostly German. Many of the oldest headstones are inscribed in that language. At the tourist bureau, pick up the pamphlet that describes some of the more interesting markers, and take some time to reflect in this beautiful location at the very head of Mahone Bay.

Hillcrest Cemetery, Lunenburg
For people who enjoy rambling in old graveyards, Hillcrest Cemetery is a great find. It dates from the town's earliest days and contains examples of almost every type of tombstone used throughout the centuries in Nova Scotia. The earliest graves are of German settlers and are carved in old German script. One interesting grave is that of 14-year-old Sophia McLachlan, noticeable because of the wrought iron fence that surrounds it and the cast-iron broken heart that adorns it. The touching story of this young girl is related on a plaque beside the grave. It describes how she died of a broken heart after being falsely accused of stealing $10. Obviously, there was a high premium put on honesty and character in those days.

The Hillcrest Cemetery also contains the graves of many of the founders of Lunenburg and if you have already taken the walking tour, you will find the names of many of the former property owners whose homes you may have visited.

CYCLING
Big Tancook Island
There are numerous potholed roadways and abandoned farm roads throughout Big Tancook Island, making a mountain bike a necessity, but also making for some great riding.

Lunenburg Area
There are a number of small peninsulas served by paved roads around the Lunenburg area that are well worth exploring by bicycle. The absence of heavy traffic and the flat terrain make them particularly suitable for day trips, using Lunenburg as a headquarters.

Bicycles can be rented at the Lunenburg Bike Barn, 579 Blue Rocks Road, Lunenburg, (902) 634-3426, www.bikelunenburg.com, where you will get suggestions as to where to ride. The roads to Blue Rocks, Stonehurst, Second Peninsula and the Riverport Peninsula are particularly rewarding and we strongly recommend that if you are going to do some bike touring while in Nova Scotia, Lunenburg should be near the top of your list.

DIVING
Lunenburg Marine Park
In 1994 the HMCS *Saguenay* was intentionally scuttled to create Atlantic Canada's first marine park. Settling in 11 to 30 metres of water, the sunken destroyer has rapidly become one of the most popular dive sites in Eastern Canada. As expected, the wreck has attracted an amazing variety of marine life, including lobster, cod, pollock and the ominous looking wolf fish. If you are an intermediate or better diver and would like to visit this site, you can make arrangements through one of the dive shops in Halifax.

GOLF
Chester Golf Course, (902) 275-4523, www.chestergolfclub.ca
On a beautiful summer's day, there is probably no nicer place to be in Nova Scotia than on the links at Chester Golf Course. A number of the holes are of the true links style, wending their way along the shores of Chester Harbour. The 18th hole is a great finishing hole, arcing around a saltwater marsh, requiring pinpoint accuracy on the approach shot to the green, which is almost completely surrounded by the marsh. When the wind is up, which it often is, hitting the green can be a challenge for the best golfer. The third hole, a killer uphill par 5 was voted best in the province although we think it should have been voted most likely to cause a club toss. Glorious views of the bay, dotted with islands, sailboats, ferries and fishing vessels, can be seen from over half of the holes on this course. In the distance are the Big and Little Tancook islands and the "cottages" of many of the summer residents of Chester. The course itself is a combination of some older holes, many of which are not difficult, and some newer holes, most of which are very challenging. All in all, Chester Golf Course should be on your must play list.

Bluenose Golf Course, Lunenburg, (902) 634-4260, www.bluenosegolfclub.com
This short nine-hole course runs up, down and over a hill with exquisite views of Lunenburg Harbour. There is usually a breeze from the sea that is welcome, especially if you are hauling your clubs up a couple of the holes that are quite steep. There is only one par five and the course concludes with four very short par fours which make it a good course for scoring. This course is easy on the eyes, wallet and score card; just do not get blocked out by the cannons on the third hole.

Osprey Ridge Golf Club, Bridgewater, (902) 543-6666, www.ospreyridge.ns.ca
This is the newest course on the South Shore. Located just outside Bridgewater, it was built on a combination of farmland and woodland as a daily fee course. Designed by top Canadian golf architect Graham Cooke, who is also responsible for the exceptional Glen Arbour, Osprey Ridge was nominated by *Golf Digest* as one of Canada's top new courses in 1999. As the course has matured, it has become a top attraction for visiting golfers and in 2009 hosted the Nova Scotia Men's Amateur Championship. Despite the fact that it is a championship course by a top designer, green fees are fairly reasonable. There is also a full-service clubhouse and pro shop.

HISTORIC SITES
Lunenburg Academy, www.lunenburg.ednet.ns.ca
It is not too often that schoolhouses are worthy of a visit in their own right, but Lunenburg Academy is the exception. This building, originally constructed in 1894, is the finest surviving example of nineteenth century

academy architecture in Nova Scotia and perhaps Canada. It sits high on a hill overlooking not only Lunenburg but the entire countryside; a genuine landmark that can be seen from miles around. Constructed entirely of wood, with towers, pediments, ornamentation and dozens of windows the academy stands in sharp contrast to most of the grim educational facilities constructed in the twentieth century. The interior woodwork shows a patina from many generations of studious Lunenburgers. Despite being declared a National Historic Site, the academy is still in use as an elementary school. Check at the tourist bureau for open hours.

MUSEUMS

Ross Farm, Route 12, New Ross, (902) 689-2210, www.museum.gov.ns.ca/rfm/

Ross Farm museum is a working farm that replicates life in Nova Scotia about 150 years ago. Located on the site of a 324-hectare grant made to Captain William Ross in 1816, the present farm encompasses 24 hectares and 11 buildings. Ross, along with 172 of his disbanded soldiers and their families, established the settlement of New Ross. This farm was run by the Ross family through five generations until 1970.

During the course of your visit, you will likely see fields being worked by a team of oxen, a blacksmith shoeing horses, and craftspeople working with nineteenth-century tools to make snowshoes, hay rakes and other implements. Ross Farm is especially appealing to children, who love the horse-drawn cart rides, the molasses cookies hot from the oven at the old farm house, and the lambs and other young animals that are always around, especially in the early summer. There is something about the smell of new-mown hay, the sound of horses' hooves or the sight of bread dough rising on a kitchen table that evokes nostalgia for a simpler life, when rewards for hard work were more immediate. Ross Farm is providing a valuable service in keeping alive old crafts, husbandry and agricultural techniques that might be lost in the technological jet stream. While Ross Farm is a bit out the way, the drive from Chester Basin is through pleasant rolling countryside and New Ross is a nice little community well-situated along the Gold River.

Mahone Bay Settlers' Museum, 578 Main Street, Mahone Bay, (902) 624-6263, www.settlersmuseum.ns.ca

This small museum, located in a period house on Main Street in Mahone Bay, is worth a visit especially if you have an interest in the genealogical history of the area. A recently completed permanent exhibit focuses on the 1754 settlement of the "foreign Protestants" as the German and Swiss settlers were known at the time. An excellent map identifies the areas in Europe from whence the settlers came and the areas in Lunenburg County where they came to stay. The Inglis-Quinlan collection of eighteenth and nineteenth-century china is also worth seeing. Some of the items are genuine rarities, including Sunderland Lustre and Chinese export porcelain.

Fisheries Museum of the Atlantic, 68 Bluenose Drive, Lunenburg, (902) 634-4794, www.museum.gov.ns.ca/fma/

One of the flagships of the Nova Scotia Museum complex, the Fisheries Museum focuses on this pivotal aspect of Nova Scotia's economy, from its earliest times to the present day, emphasizing the contribution of the Lunenburg area. Located in restored waterfront warehouses, the museum blends in with the still-active commercial waterfront of Lunenburg Harbour.

A tour of the museum commences with the aquarium, which displays a number of the species native to the North Atlantic. Here, you can see what surely must be the world's largest living lobster in captivity, the only halibut we have ever seen in an aquarium, and other groundfish such as cod and pollock. A touch tank, which always captivates children, displays crabs, starfish, scallops and other sea denizens.

After visiting the aquarium, one should tour the different galleries, each with its own theme: the inshore fishery, the Grand Banks fishery, the role of the schooner *Bluenose*, the rumrunners of the 1920s and 1930s, and many aspects of a fisherman's life. One exhibit, the August Gales, focuses on the loss of six schooners with all hands, off Sable Island in August 1926 and 1927. It provides a sombre reminder of the inherent dangers that fishermen, then and now, face every day that they are at sea. Demonstrations such as ship launchings, net mending, dory building and so on, make this a living museum. For many, the highlight of the museum is a visit aboard the ships permanently moored alongside the wharf, the schooner *Theresa E. Connor* and the modern trawler *Cape Sable*. A tour of the *Theresa E. Connor* will give you a better appreciation of the working side of this famous racing schooner.

Also usually in port is the *Bluenose II*, an exact replica of the famous schooner that is as much a part of Nova Scotia folklore as the word bluenose itself. Built and raced out of Lunenburg in the 1920s and 1930s, the original *Bluenose* never lost a race. An enduring source of pride for all Canadians, the ship has been featured for many, many years on the Canadian dime. The *Bluenose II* was built in 1963 and has sailed countless thousands of miles as Nova Scotia's floating ambassador. Don't miss the opportunity to visit this Canadian icon on your trip to the museum if it is there. As previously stated, *Bluenose II* is undergoing renovations in Lunenburg until summer 2011. A complete tour of the museum and the boats takes about two hours. Although the admission fee is somewhat steep, it is worth every penny. An added bonus, when in port, is the opportunity to get out on the *Bluenose II* for a two hour cruise of Lunenburg harbour. The schedule is posted well in advance and can be found on the *Bluenose II* website, schoonerbluenose.ca, where reservations can be made.

OFF THE BEATEN PATH

Big Tancook Island, www.tancook.ca

First settled over 150 years ago, Big Tancook Island is one of Nova Scotia's undiscovered gems. Lying eight kilometres off the coast of Chester, it is one of three inhabited islands in Mahone Bay. The Tancook Island adventure begins with the ferry trip from Chester, which provides panoramic views of Chester Harbour and the islands in Mahone Bay. This is a passenger ferry only. There is no car-ferry to Tancook except for residents. On the way, there is a possibility of seeing whales, giant bluefin tuna or porpoises, as well as many sea birds. If you're lucky, the ferry will stop at Little Tancook on the way and you will get a glimpse of life on this even smaller island where only a few people still live.

Don't be discouraged by the noise and dust that's kicked up by the locals who meet the ferry. Once you're away from the wharf, you'll realize Tancook Island is a remarkably peaceful place. Birdsong competes with the sound of the ocean, and the air is filled with the scent of juniper, fir and wildflowers. Hectares of abandoned fields are being reclaimed by wild raspberries and strawberries.

The pace is relaxed even by rural Nova Scotia standards. Everyone says hello and there is no sense of urgency to anything. In addition, there is a feeling of genuine remoteness, particularly on the back side of the island, even though Chester is less than 45 minutes away.

If you visit the Web site in advance you can print off a map of the island that lists a number of places to see. You will easily spend the better part of a day exploring the various points of interest, including the rugged cliffs of the south shore, which face the open sea and the sheltered waters of Southeast Cove.

You may want to spend more than a day on Tancook as it puts a spell on you. There is a B&B, a restaurant and craft shop as well as a small museum to explore. Tancook is famous for its sauerkraut and if anyone is selling it when you're there, grab it.

Routes 12 and 14

These two routes both start near Chester and cross the province to Kentville and Windsor respectively. Neither is a designated tourist route, although Route 12 passes through the heart of Nova Scotia's Christmas tree farming country, the Ross Farm Museum and the town of New Ross, which has a lovely location overlooking several lakes and the Gold River.

Near Windsor, Route 14 passes by Mount Martock and some scenic farm country along the upper reaches of the Avon River. Both routes are used primarily for travellers and truckers to cross directly from one coast to the other.

Blue Rocks, Stonehurst and Second Peninsula

The Lunenburg peninsula is home to the picturesque villages of Blue Rocks and North and South Stonehurst. Blue Rocks, where the slate gray and black rocks really do appear blue in certain light, has long been a favourite spot for artists and those searching for that picture-perfect fishing community. Fishing shanties built on small islets, a group of homes at the end of the road not much bigger than doll houses and colourful, well-tended gardens all lend an air of timelessness to Blue Rocks. Make sure to turn right at Herring Rock Road or you will miss the most scenic part of the village.

Several kilometres past Blue Rocks are the communities of Stonehurst South and Stonehurst North, which face each other across a long, narrow inlet. Of the two, Stonehurst South is the more interesting, being very similar in appearance to a Newfoundland outport. There are few trees and many of the buildings cling to the exposed rock. On an overcast or foggy day, with the drone of the fog horns and the ever-present mewing of the gulls overhead, the place can be extremely mournful.

The contrast between the Blue Rocks area and Second Peninsula could not be greater. Where Blue Rocks is rugged, rock-hewn and rough, with the emphasis on the sea, Second Peninsula is green, pastoral and agricultural. On one side, Second Peninsula fronts Mahone Bay. On the other, the road winds between small coves and dairy farms, going no place in particular. This makes it a delightful spot to dawdle around by car or bike.

Riverport Peninsula

The Riverport Peninsula, which juts into the Atlantic between Lunenburg and the mouth of the LaHave River, contains some of the best country architecture in the province with many examples of the Lunenburg style.

Riverport was once the home of many sea captains and the waterfront is lined with several huge mansions erected by these prosperous mariners. Lower Rose Bay has an exceptional collection of period homes around a picturesque cove while the approach to Kingsburg, at the end of the peninsula, reveals a spectacular view of the village against the backdrop of the scenic islands in the distance.

At Feltzen South there are more views, including Lunenburg across the bay and a small fishing fleet in a protected anchorage.

There are a number of roads that penetrate the Riverport Peninsula, most of which are dead-ends. The best advice is simply to get out and explore. There are numerous beaches, including the exceptional Hirtles Beach. As well, there are numerous hiking opportunities, particularly around the mouth of the LaHave. Also not to be missed is the Ovens Natural Park. All in all, the Riverport Peninsula is easily worth a day's exploration, particularly by bike.

PARKS AND GREENSPACE

Graves Island Provincial Park, www.novascotiaparks.ca/parks/gravesisland

A man-made causeway leads to this small island just east of Chester, which is now a very popular campground and picnic area. There are several trails that circle and cross the island. There is also a small beach for swimming or launching a kayak and a good playground. Graves Island Provincial Park always has a cooling ocean breeze on a hot day and is very suitable for family outings. It is also the site of the first geocache in Canada.

The Ovens Natural Park, Riverport peninsula, (902) 766-4621, www.ovenspark.com

The Ovens Natural Park is a well-run private park and campground centred around one of Nova Scotia's most interesting natural phenomena. A hiking path along the top of the coastal cliffs leads to the Ovens, a series of sea caves eroded into the face of the cliffs. Concrete stairwells lead down to several of the caves, including the Cannon and Thunder caves, where the entering waters compress the air, causing thunderous booms. A caution to families - these two caves can be frightening for young children. Balconies overlook the entrances to several other caves in the park. Along the pathway, visitors can enjoy great views of Lunenburg Harbour and Cross Island.

For a really interesting look at the Ovens, take the Zodiac boat tours that are offered on a regular basis. If the weather is cooperative, these small crafts go right into some of the caves. Since the water in this area is extremely clear you can see a long way down. Some of the caves are flecked with iron pyrite (fool's gold), which glistens in certain light. It is no wonder that these caves have figured prominently in local legends.

In the 1800s, the Ovens was the site of a gold rush, and panning for gold on the beach still produces results. A small museum on the site commemorates the gold mining and documents the history of the Ovens. The area is also popular with scuba divers, who like to explore both the geological formations and the wreck of a side-wheeler a short distance from the shore. Recently, a decommissioned destroyer was sunk nearby to create an underwater park.

In late August, the Chapin Brothers' Concert by the Sea is held on the grounds of the Ovens Natural Park. Renowned children's entertainer Tom Chapin and other family members and friends present a blend of children's entertainment and folk songs, many of which were written by their late, great brother, Harry. Most nights will find at least some of the members of this musical family entertaining at the diner or the campground.

The Ovens offers campsites and several very nice cottages. Altogether, there is a lot to do and see at the Ovens. With caves, cliffs and gold, the Ovens is what kids and adults would describe as a "neat place."

Bayport Plant Farm, Route 332, West Rose Bay, (902) 766-4319
From the moment you enter the grounds, it is obvious that this commercial operation is much more a labour of love than simply a commercial nursery. Retired naval captain Dick Steele has long been an innovator in horticultural circles through his introduction of new plant species to the province, particularly azaleas, rhododendrons and alpine plants. The woods around the plant farm are literally being transformed from the typical alders and poplars into luxuriant blooming dogwoods, rhododendrons and other non-native species. A delight to visit at any time of year, but especially in late May and early June, Bayport Plant Farm is one of Nova Scotia's most interesting gardens. If you find something you would like to purchase for your own garden, all the better.

SOMETHING DIFFERENT
The Shore Club, 250 Shore Club Road, Hubbards, (902) 857-9555, www.shoreclub.ca
Hubbards is home to the Shore Club, which bills itself as the last of the great dancehalls. This is truly a Nova Scotia institution that has somehow

survived into an age when driving out into the country for a Saturday night dance is now a rarity anywhere in North America. In summer the Shore Club has regular dances which appeal to people of all ages and you'll definitely feel welcome even if you don't know anyone else there. If you would like to experience a blast from the past, stay in Hubbards, walk to the Shore Club which is an easy walk along Shore Club Road, and dance the night away in the confines of a building that doesn't look like it has changed much in fifty years. As an added bonus the Shore Club is also one of the few places in Nova Scotia that serves traditional lobster suppers. We love it.

SPECIAL EVENTS

Chester Race Week, Chester, www.chesterraceweek.com

Usually around the first week of August, Chester drops any pretence of having a genteel side and succumbs to a madness known as Chester Race Week. Sailors from all over the Maritimes and New England converge on the town for Canada's largest keel boat regatta. However, the racing almost seems to be secondary to the socializing. If you like sailing and all that goes with it, Chester is the place to be in early August.

Classic Boat Festival, Mahone Bay, www.mahonebayclassicboatfestival.org

Recently selected as one of Nova Scotia's best festivals, the Classic Boat Festival is held annually in late July and is the largest event of its type in Canada. A classic boat refers to any boat built before 1965. Homage to the town's shipbuilding past, the harbour is truly a spectacle when filled to capacity with wooden sailing boats of all sizes and shapes. There are numerous events, including workshops demonstrating traditional small craft building techniques. However, without doubt, it is the Parade of Sail that is the star attraction of this festival.

The Great Scarecrow Festival & Antique Fair, Mahone Bay

Mahone Bay is a great town to stroll around at any time of year, but recently the locals have made early October a definite time to visit. Virtually every business and home in the Mahone Bay area decorates their yards and porches with scarecrows of every imaginable shape and size. The scarecrows aren't really scary, but often very funny and some are extremely well done. Kids love them, so scarecrow watching is a great excuse to take the children.

Additional reasons to visit are to view the entries in the pumpkin carving contest or browse the three halls where antique dealers from across the province set up shop.

International Dory Races, Lunenburg

Starting out from a bet made in a bar, the international dory races between teams from Nova Scotia and Gloucester, Massachusetts, have been held since 1916. A dory is a small boat originally designed to be lowered into the waters of the Grand Banks from a schooner and used for long-line fishing by a two man crew. Propelled by oars, the dory was made to hold a lot of fish and not built for speed. Despite their ungainly appearance, it is amazing how fast the rowers can get these boats moving. In addition to the dory races you can watch scallop shucking, fish filleting and lobster boat races.

This is a great time to visit this most quintessential of fishing towns.

Lunenburg Folk Harbour Festival, www.folkharbour.com
This early August festival, which just celebrated its 25th anniversary, features four days of all acoustic singing and dancing on the waterfront, in the Opera House, at the bandstand and on Blockhouse Hill. If you have an interest in traditional music, this is the place to be. The emphasis is on local and regional talent, so the festival always features a large selection of the best Maritime artists. If you are from out of province, you might not recognize all of the names, but we guarantee you'll remember them after seeing them perform.

Nova Scotia Folk Art Festival, (902) 640-2113, www.nsfolkartfestival.com
This is an event that takes place for only one afternoon once a year, but if you have an interest in folk art you won't want to miss it. Lunenburg County is generally recognized as being the centre of the folk art movement in Nova Scotia, and virtually every folk artist in the area makes an appearance at this show. It provides an opportunity not only to buy good folk art, but also to meet the artists in person. Unfortunately, because it is restricted to a half-day, the crowds are immense and it can get pretty hectic so arrive early.

SPECIAL INTEREST
Oak Island
In 1795 three boys exploring a small island in Mahone Bay came across an old block and tackle hanging from an oak tree over a depression in the earth. Oak Island already had a reputation for strangeness with the locals because it was covered with oak trees, which were not native to the area. The boys were familiar with tales of buried pirate gold and were sure that they had stumbled across hidden treasure. The next day they returned with digging tools and began a search for the treasure chests that no doubt were just below the surface.

Two hundred years, millions of dollars and six lives later, the treasure has still not been found and Oak Island has taken its place alongside the pyramids and Stonehenge as one of history's unsolved mysteries. What is known is that the island is apparently interlaced with a series of underground tunnels and pits, all connected somehow to the ocean, so that whenever a pit is excavated to a certain depth, it fills with water. An entire false beach has been unearthed, as well as mysterious runes and other signs that keep people searching. The whole island is one giant engineering booby trap designed to protect something as yet undiscovered. The theory that Oak Island holds pirate treasure has long been discarded by most. It is far too complex to have been built by pirates, who were not known for their engineering skills. Carbon dating indicates that work on the site predates European settlement in the area, so whoever built it came a long way to hide whatever is hidden. Theories abound, including involvement by the Knights Templar with the Holy Grail, Sir Francis Bacon or even aliens. Dozens of books have been written and documentaries made each with some new light to cast on this enduring Nova Scotia enigma. Today, the search for the solution of the Oak Island mystery continues. If you would like to know more about the history of Oak Island, two of the most recent books on the subject are *The Secret Treasure of Oak Island* by D'Arcy O'Connor and *Oak Island Gold* by William S. Crocker.

In the last edition we expressed optimism that the island would finally be open to the public on a regular basis, after being held for many years by two secretive and obsessed treasure seekers who despised each other. The island had, at last, been offered for sale to the province. Alas, the government passed over the purchase and the island was sold to another private consortium. Thus, we can only report that for the time being this wonderful marvel remains off limits for all except for one day a year. By all means, take the short Oak Island Road and drive to the causeway and who knows, maybe you will get a chance to explore the island.

THEATRE
**Chester Playhouse, Chester, (902) 275-3933,
www.chesterplayhouse.ca**
This small facility has been presenting a full schedule of productions from spring through fall for over seventy years. Nothing too serious, the emphasis is on entertainment, particularly for the many summer residents who are used to good theatre back home in Toronto and elsewhere. In the fall, the emphasis switches from theatrical productions to music.

WALKING TOURS
Chester
Chester has recently produced three self-guided walking tours. One covers the sites of Front Harbour and features over thirty points of interest. Another tour features the Old Burying Ground, many of the "Chester Cottages," and the churches. This tour commences at the Lordly Manor which is currently being restored as Chester's local museum and should be fully open for summer 2010. Although it is in pretty rough shape right now, it does have interesting exhibits on Oak Island and the infamous Butterbox Babies episode in Chester's history. This tour concludes at the town library and the Lightfoot Tower from where, if it is open, there is a tremendous panorama of Chester Harbour and the offshore islands. Be sure to inquire in the library. The third tour focuses on the sights of the Back Harbour including many fine homes and a reputedly haunted bridge.

Chester is one of Nova Scotia's real delights and we strongly recommend attempting all or some combination of the walking tours and making a morning or afternoon of your visit to this charming town. A word of warning: you won't realize how hilly Chester is until you walk it; best perhaps to stop along the way at the Fo'c'sle, Chester's venerable tavern, especially if it is a hot day. Copies of the walking tours can be obtained at the tourist bureau located in the old train station on the edge of town.

Mahone Bay

The many interesting shops, beautiful houses and, of course, the three famous waterfront churches make Mahone Bay one of Nova Scotia's most pleasant towns in which to take a stroll. The Settlers' Museum has prepared four suggested walking tours, which can be combined into one long walk to cover the whole town. Brochures for these tours can be downloaded at www.settlersmuseum.ns.ca. Limited numbers of laminated copies to borrow can be picked up at the museum or the tourist bureau.

Lunenburg

Above all, Lunenburg is a walker's delight. The Lunenburg Heritage Advisory Committee has prepared a historic architectural walking tour guide to the town, which anyone who is interested in architecture should pick up from the tourist bureau. This informative guide details the development of Lunenburg architecture and the different styles from the eighteenth to the early twentieth century, including numbered examples of some of the finest buildings in town. While it is true that the streets of Lunenburg are steep in places, a walking tour is the only way to absorb the ambience of this wonderful town. The narrow streets, the overhanging Lunenburg bumps (a form of architecture unique to the community), the well-tended gardens and the many interesting shops are best explored on foot.

Lunenburg has three exceptional churches, all well worth visiting. St. John's Anglican (www.stjohnslunenburg.org), originally built in 1754, is second in age only to St. Paul's in Halifax. Architecturally, both inside and out, it is among the finest churches in Nova Scotia. It is believed that the original frame was imported from Boston. Over the years, the design was altered on a number of occasions, although the architectural style, which has been described as carpenter Gothic, was perfectly suited to the location and the surrounding buildings. The interior, with its extravagant use of polished wood, has warmth not often found in Nova Scotian churches. Tragically, this architectural icon was burned to the ground on Halloween night in 2001 by persons unknown. For the next several years a white plastic covering shrouded the church from view while underneath it the church was being faithfully restored. In 2005, St. John's emerged from its cocoon very much as beautiful as it ever was. Visiting the church now you have to look closely at some of the floorboards and pews to notice the faint charring.

The second interesting church is St. Andrew's Presbyterian, which dates from 1828, although the Presbyterian congregation in Lunenburg dates from the founding of the town and is the oldest in Canada. One of the most interesting features of St. Andrew's is its copper codfish weather vane, which symbolizes not only Christ but the fishing legacy of this town. In Lunenburg, you will also find Zion Evangelical Lutheran Church, the oldest Lutheran church in Canada, dating from 1770. Although the interior is somewhat austere, this church has a collection of early Lutheran memorabilia, including a display of German Bibles.

After visiting the Fisheries Museum, continue walking along the waterfront to the former site of the Smith and Rhuland Shipbuilding Works. These yards produced over 400 wooden ships, including the original *Bluenose* and its successor *Bluenose II*, the replica of the HMS *Bounty* used in the 1960s film, and a number of other famous ships. Along the way, you will pass a site where inshore boats are still made for commercial or private use. Also along the waterfront, you will notice Thomas Walters & Sons Marine Blacksmiths, still an active business, and the Scotia Trawler yachting supply store, which carries everything boaters may need.

Lunenburg is one of the few Nova Scotia towns where you can take a professional guided walk. Contact Lunenburg Town Walking Tours, (902) 634-3848, www.lunenburgwalkingtours.com, where Eric Croft has been entertaining visitors for years.

WHERE TO SHOP

The South Shore is noted for its many fine crafts, antique and tourist-oriented shops. Chester, Mahone Bay and Lunenburg all provide delightful opportunities to poke around looking for handcrafts, folk art, jewellery and many other products, most locally made. In previous editions we had identified some of our favourite places and businesses, however, there are so many very good shops that we simply no longer have the space to list them individually. By all means obtain a map of Chester, Mahone Bay or Lunenburg and you will find a listing of the various galleries and shops. However there is one place that is truly special and must be mentioned because we'd hate for you to miss it. It is Houston North Gallery, 110 Montague Street, Lunenburg, (902) 634-8869, www.houston-north-gallery.ns.ca. This gallery specializes in Inuit and folk art. The Houstons were among the first individuals to recognize the significance of Inuit art. Living in the high Arctic, they befriended and later introduced to the world some of the best-known sculptors and printmakers working today. After leaving the Arctic, they set up a gallery in Lunenburg to display and sell the works of the artists they met. If you are a collector of Inuit art, this is one of the best galleries in Canada.

For folk art, their emphasis is on Nova Scotian artists who have been nationally recognized for their talents, in particular, the paintings of Joe Norris. From time to time there are also samples of the works of such recognized masters as Collins Eisenhauer, Ralph Boutilier, Maud and Everett Lewis and others. Although much of the folk art is humorous and often self-parodying, these are serious artists who have been featured in *Folk Art in Canada*, the definitive work on Canadian folk artists.

You can take a virtual tour of the gallery on the Web site.

ACCOMMODATIONS
**Rosewood Cottages, 187 Shore Club Road, Hubbards,
1-888-265-9950, www.rosewoodonthecove.com**
Hubbards is probably the nicest small community on St. Margaret's Bay
and a good base from which to visit Halifax and the Peggy's Cove loop on
the east side, and Mahone Bay and Lunenburg on the west. There are a
number of good lodging choices in the area, and Rosewood Cottages, in
our opinion, is the best. Victorian-style cottages right on the cove offer all
amenities. There is easy walking to beaches, restaurants and interesting
shops; as well it is a stone's throw from the legendary Shore Club, where
you can dance the night away every weekend in summer.

WESTERN SHORE
**Oak Island Resort and Spa, 36 Treasure Drive, Western Shore,
1-800-565-5075, www.oakislandresortandspa.com**
This property has been around for some time, but in recent years new
owners have poured a lot of money into making it one of Nova Scotia's
foremost resort and convention facilities, and it has worked. The resort has
a splendid location overlooking legendary Oak Island. There are a wide
variety of accommodations including some really nice chalets right on the
shoreline. There are indoor and outdoor pools, tennis, a marina and sea
kayaking so there is no reason to be bored. The restaurant has also been
upgraded and is what one would expect from a full service resort.

MAHONE BAY
In keeping with its small-town image, Mahone Bay has no motels, hotels
or even sizeable inns. Accommodations are almost exclusively B&Bs,
although there are a few cottages available on the outskirts. One of the reasons we aren't recommending anything in this charming town is that every
time we do, it closes or changes hands, which is not unusual for B&Bs.
The most recent Nova Scotia government guide lists some 25 entries for
Mahone Bay, but only about half are actually in town. Most now have Web
sites so if you order a copy of the *Doers' & Dreamers' Travel Guide* you can
make your own decision.

LUNENBURG
No town in Nova Scotia has such a large selection of quality accommodations as Lunenburg. The great number of preserved buildings of
many architectural styles has made this place a natural for inns and
B&Bs. While we do have some favourites we simply have not had the
chance to stay in most of Lunenburg's inns. Our policy is not to include
a place we haven't visited no matter how good the reviews from other
sources, so there are definitely lots of good choices aside from the ones
we recommend.

Boscawen Inn, 150 Cumberland Street, Lunenburg, 1-800-354-5009, www.boscawen.ca
The Boscawen Inn is a restored Victorian mansion on a hill over-looking Lunenburg Harbour in a very quiet area of town. The rooms are all attractively appointed with Victorian furnishings. Some of the rooms on the top floor have a wonderful view of the harbour, as does the terrace. The adjacent McLachlan House is also part of the inn and the rooms here are similar in style to the main inn. Visitors will find the innkeeper and staff both friendly and helpful. A full buffet breakfast is included.

1880 Kaulbach House Historic Inn, 75 Pelham Street, Lunenburg, 1-800-568-8818, www.kaulbachhouse.com
This inn, located in one of Lunenburg's historic buildings (aren't they all), offers good value in what can be a surprisingly pricey town. The six rooms in the inn are all well-appointed and the atmosphere is very friendly. If possible, ask for a room away from Pelham Street, which is fairly busy, although hardly a freeway. A really good full breakfast is included in the price. While enjoying the delicious breakfast, guests often share information and recommendations on places they have visited and things that they have seen.

FAMILY ACCOMMODATIONS IN THE LUNENBURG AREA
Atlantic View Motel & Cottages, 230 Masons Beach Road, (902) 634-4545, www.atlanticview.ca
Topmast Motel, Masons Beach Road, (902) 634-4661, www.topmastmotel.com
Lily Front Motel & Cottages, 693 Masons Beach Road, (902) 634-8085, www.lilyfrontmotel.com
For families, there are three good choices for accommodations, all of which are located just outside of town, each offering something different. The Lily Front, the Topmast and the Atlantic View offer motel-style accommodations with some cottages available. The Topmast offers an excellent view of Lunenburg across the bay, the same view that was once featured on the Canadian $100 bill. The Atlantic View is located just across the road from Masons Beach and has a pool. The Lily Front, located in First South, has a very nice childrens' playground area, pedal boats and row boats, all in a very quiet setting.

The Ovens Natural Park Oceanview Cottages, (902) 766-4621, www.ovenspark.com
Not that far from Lunenburg, The Ovens has several cottages that range from rustic to reasonably new, the newer ones being quite expensive. The Ovens is also attractive to tenters, as it has a number of camp sites right on top of the cliffs overlooking the LaHave Islands. This is a terrific place to camp if you like to be serenaded by the sound of the sea.

DINING
Dauphinee Inn, 167 Shore Club Road, Hubbards, (902) 857-1790,
www.dauphineeinn.com
The best view of Hubbards Cove is from the deck of the Dauphinee Inn. This is a good place to stop for lunch or refreshments, or at dinner one can linger awhile to watch the sailboats coming and going in the cove. The chowder is outstanding. Also of interest are various offerings that you cook yourself on granite rocks heated to incredible temperatures. The rocks are brought to your table along with beef, seafood or chicken, which you place on the rock with tongs. It's a lot of fun and safer than it sounds — kids love it.

The Trellis Café, 22 Main Street, Hubbards, (902) 857-1188,
www.trelliscafe.ca
The Trellis is right on the Lighthouse Route in the pretty village of Hubbards and it advertises itself as a purveyor of "real" food. That translates into a full menu of some traditional and some untraditional dishes, for example, lobster melt. The décor is simple and bright. The Trellis is a very popular breakfast and lunch spot with the locals and tourists alike. It's also open for dinner, when things are generally a little quieter.

Julien's Pastry Shop, 43 Queen Street, Chester, (902) 275-2324,
www.juliens.ca
This small French bakery and sandwich shop makes some of the best pastries found anywhere in Nova Scotia. Didier Julien has become an icon of pastry in the past decade and now has a shop in the Hydrostone Market in Halifax, but this is the original. You owe it to yourself to try something here.

Seaside Shanty, Route 3, Chester Basin, (902) 275-2246,
www.seasideshanty.com
This restaurant is located adjacent to the government wharf in Chester Basin, which may explain why its seafood is so fresh. The one thing you won't find on the menu is fish and chips or anything that comes close to a deep fryer. There are many types of chowder and the drunken mussels are famous. The seafood chowder is just about the best chowder we've tasted in the province. Even a small cup is a meal in itself. For a view to go with your meal, try to get a table on the deck that overlooks the entrance to the bay. This is a very popular spot with the summering Chesterites and many famous names have passed through, including good old Pierre Elliott Trudeau himself.

The Innlet Café, Route 3, Mahone Bay, (902) 624-6363,
www.innletcafe.com
You can't miss The Innlet Café as you approach Mahone Bay from the Halifax side. This has been one of the area's most popular restaurants for thirty years. Always busy, it offers outdoor dining with a view of

the famous three churches, or indoor dining in an award-winning restoration. Informal and unpretentious, the Innlet offers a wide selection of local recipes. Mussel soup, chowder and pea soup are good starters. The Innlet Café is one of the few restaurants we know that offers mackerel. The stir-fries are a house specialty. The Innlet is a good choice for either lunch or dinner as well as a nice place to stop for tea and apple strudel.

LUNENBURG

Lunenburg hosts throngs of tourists in the summer, many arriving on bus tours. Most of them pile into one of the many restaurants lining the waterfront area, all claiming to be experts in seafood. What these places mostly sell are deep fried foods that do not show off what a good chef can do with fresh seafood. There are many good restaurants in Lunenburg, so don't plunk yourself down in the first one you come to. We have three choices that offer completely different dining experiences.

Magnolia's Grill, 128 Montague Street, Lunenburg, (902) 634-3287

Magnolia's Grill is not the type of restaurant you would expect to find in Lunenburg. With its six booths and two small tables, a collection of Elvis memorabilia, humorous salt and pepper shakers and an extremely relaxed, informal attitude, it is quite different from the more staid establishments in town. After prospering for over two decades in the very competitive Lunenburg restaurant scene, Magnolia's has achieved semi-legendary status.

While the menu changes daily, there are always pasta and seafood selections with an emphasis on Cajun and Caribbean cooking. Magnolia's often offers seafood selections that aren't easily available elsewhere, such as cod cheeks.

The Key Lime pie alone is worth the trip, as postcards from Floridians, who should know, attest. The staff is friendly and laid-back, as are most of the clientele. Prices are reasonable. Magnolia's is very popular and very tiny, so try to arrive at off-peak hours or you may find yourselves waiting on the street. Thankfully a patio has been added in recent years that has eased the congestion.

The Knot, 4 Dufferin Street, Lunenburg, (902) 634-3334

The Knot is a tiny pub done up in a nautical manner. There are six semicircular booths, very low ceilings and lots of polished wood. The effect is very much like being below decks on a schooner. Right now, the food at the Knot is as good as you'll find in any pub in the province. The Caesar salad is excellent, the steaks are great for tavern fare, and the fish and chips are fresh. Even if you don't want to eat, this is a friendly little spot to relax and enjoy a few cool beers and maybe strike up a conversation with one of the many locals who frequent the place. There is also an outdoor section for warm days.

Fleur de Sel, 53 Montague Street, Lunenburg, (902) 640-2121, www.fleurdesel.net.home

When Fleur de Sel first opened a few years ago, Chef Martin Ruiz Salvador began offering something completely different in Lunenburg – fine French cuisine. Some questioned whether this would go over with normally frugal Lunenburgers once the tourist season was over. However, from the day it opened, Fleur de Sel has been garnering accolades. People now come from Halifax and further just to sample Chef Salvador's innovative take on seafood or try something different like the sweetbreads. The Sunday brunch is very popular. By Lunenburg standards Fleur de Sel is expensive, but not for the quality of the food being served. This is one of the best small town restaurants in the province.

LIGHTHOUSE ROUTE
Lunenburg to Yarmouth

Just a few kilometres from Lunenburg is the town of Bridgewater, the largest on the South Shore (www.bridgewater.ca).

While Lunenburg's prosperity has always centred on the sea, Bridgewater's economy has looked to the land, in particular farming, lumbering and manufacturing. Today, Bridgewater's stability relies to a large extent on the Michelin Tire factory. This is a solid, prosperous community of hardworking individuals, and it shows. Over the years, fires have levelled many of the downtown buildings, robbing Bridgewater of an architectural integrity similar to Lunenburg. However, a stroll around town will reveal many fine old homes. A visit to the two municipal parks is definitely worthwhile, as is a stop at both of its fine museums.

The next section of the Lighthouse Route from Bridgewater to Mill Village passes through small communities that are largely unchanged from 100 years ago. There are three fine beaches and some excellent scenery, particularly around the LaHave Islands.

On leaving Bridgewater, the Lighthouse Route follows the west bank of the LaHave River as it gradually widens towards its mouth. While passing through the small communities of Pleasantville and Pentz, one can enjoy excellent views of the communities on the eastern side of the river. The white spires of three churches are framed on a background of green hills and fields. To find out if the grass really is greener on the other side, you can take the small ferry across the river at LaHave. It has been in operation for over 175 years.

At Fort Point, a museum and small park commemorate the site of one of the earliest settlements in Canada. In 1632, Isaac DeRazilly, a French nobleman and explorer, established Fort Ste-Marie-de-Grace on this site, which commands the entrance to the LaHave. It was DeRazilly's hope that this area of Nova Scotia would become a permanent French settlement. Several small communities, such as Petite Rivière, did spring up under the protection of the fort. Unfortunately, internecine feuding among the French commanders in Acadia eventually doomed the colony. Most of the colonists left for Port Royal on the Bay of Fundy. Although all traces of the original fort are long gone, the small museum on the site is definitely worth visiting.

At Moshers Point lookoff, there is a sweeping view of the mouth of the LaHave River and the LaHave Islands. Further on, at Dublin Shore, there are a number of houses and a small bridge made almost entirely from beach stones. The government wharf is an excellent spot for mackerel and pollock fishing, and a place to strike up conversation with the locals, who frequent the wharf when the mackerel are running.

The route continues on past Crescent Beach and Rissers Beach before reaching Petite Rivière. This village has fine examples of many of the best-known Nova Scotian architectural styles. Take away the telephone lines and paved roads and there is very little evidence of modern influence. From Petite Rivière, you can take a side trip to Green Bay or continue on through the picturesque communities of Broad Cove and Cherry Hill. Little Harbour Road at Cherry Hill leads to a tiny cove. The Lighthouse Route then follows the shore of Medway Harbour until it turns inland to reunite with Highway 103, which you must follow for a short distance to cross the Medway River.

The next side road takes you to Port Medway, founded by New England settlers in the 1700s. It has many fine houses, but, unfortunately, some of the best examples sit empty and are apparently abandoned. Port Medway Lighthouse Park tells the story of the areas ship building past. The Old Meeting House is refurbished and operated as a museum. It is an example of an unusual style of architecture and found only in a few places in Nova Scotia. An old graveyard overlooking the entrance to the harbour is a peaceful spot to contemplate the vitality this community must have exhibited 200 years ago.

From Port Medway, the road to Long Cove Point leads to a lighthouse overlooking the entrance to Medway Harbour, where there are some magnificent views of the coast in both directions and the islands at the mouth of the harbour. The wooden lighthouse appears to have been the model for the miniature lighthouses that adorn the lawns of many houses in this area.

Next are East and West Berlin, which, unlike their namesake, remain apart and never the twain shall meet. West Berlin wharf is one of the more picturesque on the South Shore, and provides excellent photographic opportunities from the main highway. The road to East Berlin leads to a shingle-and-sand beach and very clear green water. There are only a couple of cottages on the near end of this beach.

At Beach Meadows, the community has installed a picnic and playground facility at the juncture of the beach and the salt marsh meadows for which the community is named. Make sure you stay on the Lighthouse Route, which follows the coast and provides excellent views of Coffin Island, with its prominent lighthouse and abandoned fishing sheds.

Brooklyn, the home of the AbitibiBowater Pulp and Paper Mill, one of the largest employers in the area, is a very attractive and well-kept community with some excellent gardens. It is also the birthplace of country and western legend Hank Snow. As a tribute to Hank, the town has built an extensive playground on the site of his former homestead on Hillside Avenue. While the children play, you can visit the Pioneers' Cemetery across the street before moving on.

Liverpool (www.queens.ca), the county seat of Queens County, was founded in 1759 by New England Planters attracted to its fine harbour. Unlike Halifax and Lunenburg to the east and Shelburne to the west, Liverpool maintained strong ties with the American colonies. In fact, many were fifth and sixth generation descendants of the Mayflower pilgrims. That is, until the outbreak of hostilities in the American Revolution, when despite these ties, Liverpool was not spared the predations of American raiders. As is often the case with friends who fall out, the Queens County men became the bitterest of foes to their former American brethren. From 1776 to 1815, Liverpool was the base of Nova Scotia's privateers. Operating under letters of marque granted by the British crown, ships such as the *Lucy*, the *Rover* and the infamous *Liverpool Packet* mercilessly marauded American ports and shipping. Huge fortunes were amassed — most especially by Enos Collins, who went on to establish the Privateers' Warehouse in Halifax, the showpiece of the Historic Properties.

With the cessation of hostilities, Liverpool settled into a long period of prosperity centred around shipbuilding and lumbering. Today, the nearby AbitibiBowater pulp mill in Brooklyn provides the local economy with stability, although there are worries about its future.

Despite its illustrious history, Liverpool, at first sight, is not an attractive community. The mill and other industrial developments overshadow much of the east side of town, while the main street and downtown area lack a focal point of interest. However, if one explores some of the side streets, a collection of attractive homes and churches in different architectural styles reveals itself. The walking tour is probably the best way to see just what Liverpool has to offer. It really is an underappreciated gem with no less than four museums to explore.

From Liverpool, the Lighthouse Route cuts overland until White Point, where it travels through the summer communities of Hunts Point and Summerville, both of which have very nice beaches and a number of rental cottages right on the water. From Summerville, Highway 3 and Highway 103 join together as far as Sable River. The ocean is visible only occasionally along the way. To appreciate the beauty of this coast, which includes the seaside adjunct of Kejimkujik National Park and the wonderful Carters Beach, you have to get onto the side roads. The Lighthouse Route turns left at Sable River and heads around the Lockeport peninsula. At Louis Head you will find one of the few beaches on this shore that have extensive clam flats and the warmer water that usually goes with them. A sign on the beach indicating the presence of the protected piping plover is really a joke considering the number of dogs running free in the area the last time we were there. For a better appreciation of the Louis Head area, turn to the shore at the Breakwater Road and follow a small path to the end of the road, where access to a second, less despoiled beach is available.

From Louis Head, the Lighthouse Route travels through the small fishing community of Little Harbour and the former shipbuilding centre of Allendale before reaching Lockeport. Along the way, short side trips to Pleasant Point and the tidy community of Osborne are worthwhile for the excellent views of the islands of Lockeport Bay and the town of Lockeport.

Lockeport is a pleasant community located on what would otherwise be an island if it weren't connected to the mainland by Crescent Beach. For many years, beautiful Crescent Beach was featured on the back of the Canadian $50 bill. The town itself has always been a fishing community and of late has been very hard-hit by the closure of two large fish plants. However, the residents have rallied in the face of economic hardships and civic improvements can be seen around town as the community finds ways to compensate for the crisis in the fisheries. For families with small children, the playground at Lockeport is worth a visit in and of itself.

From Lockeport, the Lighthouse Route continues inland until it rejoins Highway 103 briefly at Jordan Falls. At the white Anglican church, turn off 103 to take an alternative route around the shoreline through the communities of Jordan Ferry, Jordan Bay and Sandy Point before reaching Shelburne. Although most of this route is no more interesting than the official Lighthouse Route from Jordan Falls to Shelburne, it is perhaps worthwhile for the spectacular view of the entrance to Jordan Bay, which may be seen from Lower Jordan Bay. The government wharf in this small community is very picturesque, with Demings Island just offshore.

The town of Shelburne (www.shelburnenovascotia.com) owes its existence directly to the American Revolution. In the spring of 1783, 5,000 Loyalists left New York and headed to Nova Scotia to establish a new community. Later in the year, another large wave of refugees followed, making Shelburne North America's first real boom town. By 1785 it claimed to be the largest settlement in British North America and the third or fourth largest on the continent. These new pioneers, many of whom had been members of the wealthy American colonial gentry, found living conditions in Nova Scotia tougher than expected, especially when British food grants stopped in 1787. The surrounding countryside simply could not support the large population and, as a result, many of the Loyalists moved on - to New Brunswick, Ontario or even back to the United States. By the 1820s, the population had dwindled to 300. At the county museum, an early map of Shelburne is on display showing the community as it existed shortly after its founding. You will note that it is many times larger than the town that exists today.

Those hardy souls who did remain in Shelburne have done reasonably well. Shelburne has the world's third-largest natural harbour, although this is not readily apparent unless you drive out to Sandy Point. Shipbuilding, shipping and fishing have been the mainstays for the past 200 years. Shelburne is now a regional centre for the southwest coast and comfortable in its role as a very liveable small town, not the metropolis it once promised to be. The lack of change and development has had a very positive side for Shelburne. The Dock Street area is one of the best-preserved historic districts in Canada and a must-visit destination for every tourist. It has been the site of numerous movie shoots including *The Scarlet Letter* and *Moby Dick*.

Leaving Shelburne, you travel on Highway 103 to the community of Birchtown, founded by black Loyalists, before turning toward Gunning Cove, Roseway and Ingomar, where there is a sizeable and colourful fishing fleet centred around the government wharf. From Ingomar to Clyde River, the road hugs the coastline much of the way providing pristine views of Cape Negro Island and the mouth of the Clyde River.

Coming to Port Clyde, you cross the mouth of the Clyde River and start around another peninsula. At Cape Negro, a dirt road leads to the tiny community of Blanche from where there are views of the entrance to Negro Harbour and several lighthouses. At Port LaTour, the Lighthouse Route turns sharply towards Barrington, while continuing straight leads to Baccaro.

Next is the excellent Sand Hills Beach at Coffinscroft, and then the town of Barrington (www.barringtonmunicipality.com), which is one of the oldest communities on the South Shore. It was founded in 1761 by settlers from Cape Cod and Nantucket Island, who were fed up with the strict Puritanism of Massachusetts. Barrington has a very well-preserved village centre, with no less than five museums. The business centre of this area is Barrington Passage, which is also the gateway to Cape Sable Island.

After Barrington Passage, the highway passes through the fishing communities of Shag Harbour and Woods Harbour, both of which have large facilities where lobsters are stored before being taken to market. Neither of the communities are particularly attractive, but the ocean views from this shore on a clear day are unbeatable. At Shag Harbour, the Chapel Hill Museum is in an old church, which has a tower observatory from where, on a clear day, you can see as far as Seal Island, many miles offshore. It is also the scene of one of North America's most well known UFO incidents. In 1967 many people witnessed a strange glowing object plunge into the ocean not far offshore. What happened next has been a matter of conjecture and controversy ever since. Some claim signs of debris and mysterious sulphurous slicks on the surface were found by fisherman rushing to the site thinking a plane had gone down, however air traffic control claimed that no aircraft was in the vicinity or reported missing. As usual in matters of this type the military was accused of a coverup and hiding the evidence of a crashed flying saucer. The truth will probably never be known, but it is one of the few cases that has been officially classified as an unidentified flying object.

Next, you will arrive at the first of a number of long fingers of land that extend into the open Atlantic from southwest Nova Scotia. Most of these peninsulas are well worth exploring, especially on a bicycle.

The first peninsula is Pubnico (www.pubnico.ca), which at one time had over 20 communities with variations on the Pubnico name. Now there are a mere nine on the map. The Pubnicos mark the beginning of Acadian settlement on the Lighthouse Route. French settlement in this area dates from 1653, although most of the communities were settled by returning Acadians after the expulsion. Driving through East Pubnico, there is a fine view of West Pubnico, with its large church dominating the skyline across the water. West Pubnico has a small Acadian village and a museum. These are worth stopping at if you would like to get a sense of how life was lived by the Acadians from the 1600s onward. While conditions were definitely gruelling back then, they are far less so now. The Pubnicos are among the most prosperous communities in Nova Scotia, and for good reason. This is the centre of the largest and most productive lobster fishery in the world. Take the time to drive out to West Pubnico wharf to observe the goings on

— the fishermen are all friendly, but you might have trouble understanding some of them, as they slip effortlessly from French to English and back, sometimes in one sentence. Most of the colourful new boats that you will notice tied up, side to side, were built right in the community.

From Pubnico, the highway passes through Argyle, whose Baptist church dates back to 1806. Its overgrown cemetery includes graves from as early as 1760. The next community is Ste-Anne-du-Ruisseau, with its magnificent black and white Catholic church that is worth visiting to view its beautiful interior. As is often the case with Acadian communities, the church dominates the skyline for many miles around.

Next is the pretty village of Tusket, which was founded by yet another distinct group of Nova Scotian settlers — the Dutch United Empire Loyalists from New York, who arrived in 1785. Tusket has some very fine old homes and Canada's oldest surviving courthouse (www.argylecourthouse. com) which dates from 1805. The building can be toured during the summer months. It also has genealogical information on the largest Dutch settlement in the province.

From Tusket, the Lighthouse Route passes through Arcadia, where the short Uktobok Trail offers an opportunity to view the Chebogue salt marsh — the largest salt marsh in the province. Not long after Arcadia, you enter the outskirts of Yarmouth, where the Lighthouse Route ends. Yarmouth is described under the Evangeline Trail section.

BEACHES

Without question, the Lighthouse Route between Lunenburg and Yarmouth has the finest collection of beaches not only in Nova Scotia, but probably all of Canada. There are so many that finding a beautiful deserted strand is not that hard. If you are familiar with the throngs who occupy every last inch of space on New England beaches in the summer it's almost hard to believe that not that far away the situation is completely different.

South Shore beaches and the piping plover.

The piping plover is one of the rarest and most threatened of North American shorebirds for the simple reason that it likes the same thing we do — beautiful sandy beaches. It isn't hard to figure out who has won the battle of the beaches, at least up until the last twenty years or so. The piping plover was facing extinction if something wasn't done and lately serious efforts to save this tiny bird have been put in place. Almost all the beaches listed below host at least some piping plover pairs and if you arrive during the breeding season of June and July you may find some areas off-limits. More importantly, even if a beach has no restrictions at this time of year you should keep your dogs leashed or, better yet, leave them behind. Of course if you are a birder, a visit to the South Shore beaches at the right time of year can be very rewarding.

Crescent Beach, Lunenburg County

Crescent Beach forms a natural causeway to the LaHave Islands. As the name implies, it is a 4-kilometre crescent of sand. There are no facilities here, and a limited number of parking spaces. As is usually the case with most beaches in Nova Scotia that have limited facilities, there are often only a few people. Sometimes when the much more popular Rissers Beach down the road is fogged in, the sun is shining at Crescent Beach. It is a favourite with windsurfers.

Rissers Beach, Route 331, Lighthouse Route, www.novascotiaparks.ca/parks/rissers.asp

Rissers Beach Provincial Park is centred around a fine saltwater beach at the outflow of Petite Rivière. There are two campgrounds, one right on the ocean and the other in an open area on the other side of the highway. There are several picnic areas, change rooms, supervised swimming and canteen facilities. A small interpretive centre gives an explanation of the flora and fauna, not only of the beach area but also the tidal estuary that flanks the beach. The boardwalk that crosses the salt marsh is an excellent spot to view migrating shore birds.

The beach is fine sand, in places very dark, dotted with many kinds of shells. This is among the best beaches we know of in Nova Scotia for shell collecting; sand dollars, razor clams, dog winkles, basket shells, astartes, moon shells and many fossilized shells are found here. The interpretive centre on the way out can help you identify your finds.

As with all beaches on the Atlantic coast, the water is clear, but chilly. The best time for swimming is usually late August and early September.

Cherry Hill Beach, Route 331, Lighthouse Route

The wise decision to concentrate all facilities in the area at Rissers Beach has deflected people pressure from other beaches in this area. Cherry Hill Beach is one of the beneficiaries of this policy. This really is one of Nova Scotia's great undiscovered beaches. Suffice it to say that Cherry Hill Beach still supports a small breeding population of piping plovers and is extremely popular with birders. If you are seeking solitude, this is a good place to find it.

Summerville Beach, Route 3, Lighthouse Route

Of all the beaches in Queens County, Summerville is the most accessible. It is literally right off the Lighthouse Route in the community of the same name. This kilometre-and-a-half-long sweep of fine whitish-grey sand, usually lapped by perfectly breaking waves, has been designated a provincial park, so there are good facilities and lots of parking. Nearby is the Quarterdeck Restaurant and a small store for any supplies you might need. With all this going for it, you might expect Summerville to be crowded. It isn't. For one thing, the beach is so big that it would take thousands of people to fill it. Luckily for you, there are so few people and so many good beaches in this area of Nova Scotia that even the best of them are seldom crowded. Like all South Shore beaches, the water is clear and cold.

Carters Beach, Port Mouton

On a coastline noted for its beautiful beaches, Carters Beach stands out supreme. It may just be the best beach in the province and an undiscovered one at that. Turn off the Lighthouse Route at the sign for Southwest Port Mouton. About 5 kilometres later, a sign will lead you to Carters Beach. There is next to no parking and absolutely no facilities.

There are actually three beaches: the first and third are short crescents, the middle beach is a long broad strand. What all three have in common is a very fine sand that glistens gold in the bright sunlight, incredibly clear cold water, an abundance of interesting beachcombing, particularly for sand dollars, and an extensive dune system that blocks an offshore wind.

The second beach can only be reached by fording a small stream that enters Port Mouton Bay between the first and second beaches. At high tide, the water can be waist-deep and numbingly cold; use extreme caution, or follow a trail along the stream that leads to a safer crossing about ten minutes further away. It is worth it to reach the second and third beaches, as odds are they will be almost entirely yours. The third beach ends at dunes that are among the highest in the province and rival those at Cavendish National Park on Prince Edward Island. From the top of these dunes there is an incomparable view back over the beaches and Port Mouton Bay. The trail along the top of the dunes may be followed as far as Southwest Port Mouton if desired.

Right now, Carters Beach is unprotected and undeveloped, but it has been discovered by the ATVers, whose machines are already seriously eroding the dunes. The beauty of this spot is universal and it would be inexcusable if it were destroyed.

Black Point Beach, Little Harbour off Route 3

At Little Harbour, follow the sign to Arnolds. The pavement soon turns to dirt and about 6 kilometres later the road ends. Get out and listen - you will hear a dull roar. Follow the sound and you will arrive at Black Point Beach or Hemeon's, as it is often called locally. This is one of Nova Scotia's great shingle beaches. If you are fortunate enough to be here shortly after a big blow, the waves will be huge and the noise of the swash and backwash of the water through the stones is almost deafening. This is nature at its most awesome and there is not a lot to do other than stare. Unfortunately, a recently constructed home has made getting to the beach a little more difficult, but remember, in Nova Scotia all beaches are public.

Round Bay Beach, Round Bay

Round Bay is a tiny community just off the Lighthouse Route between Roseway and Port Clyde. Turn down Ferry Road and follow it past a cluster of cottages to the beach, which is completely hidden from the main road which might explain its lack of visitors.

The first thing you will notice on exiting your vehicle is the beautiful round flat stones that completely encircle the bay. After crossing the stone barrier, you come to a wonderful white hardpacked, mica-flecked beach. The beach stretches for almost a kilometre to a brook, all the while flanked by the unusual stones and sand dunes behind it. The water is extremely clear and there are views of a number of offshore islands. Round Bay is often deserted and is one of Nova Scotia's great undiscovered wonders.

Sand Hills Beach, Route 309, Lighthouse Route
This is another wonderful Nova Scotia beach recently protected by its designation as a provincial park. From the parking lot, several boardwalks lead to different areas of the beach. Take the one to the right and you will come out to a broad expanse of white sand. At low tide, you can walk out on hard packed sand for hundreds of metres. The shallow water makes this one of the warmer beaches in the area. It is also popular with clam diggers and beachcombers.

BIRDING
Shelburne County
Shelburne County has long been recognized as one of the best places for birding in Nova Scotia. Cape Sable, Bon Portage and Seal Islands are all legendary for the rarities spotted on them, in some cases the only Canadian, or even North American, record of some species. In addition to these exotic locales, Shelburne County has plenty of more accessible sites. Any serious birder should definitely head over the causeway to Cape Sable Island and drive down to the very tip of the island where the appropriately named Hawk Beach offers miles of beach on one side and marsh on the other. Offshore is Cape Sable with its beautiful lighthouse marking the southernmost point in Nova Scotia. Cape Sable is ideally located along migratory routes to regularly produce rarities. In recent years the tens of thousands of brant who frequent the marshes by day and fly to the ocean at dusk have attracted birders from all over the world in March and April.

CEMETERIES
Hammond Street Cemeteries, Shelburne
Shelburne's three original cemeteries are located within a short walking distance of each other on Hammond Street. Buried in these grounds are the forebears of a great many Canadian families. Unfortunately, none of the cemeteries or stones have been particularly well kept, although we have noted some improvements over the past few years.

GOLF
Liverpool Golf Club, White Point, 1-866-683-2485
www.whitepoint.com
This is a great little nine-hole course with a number of holes that play right along the shore, overlooking beautiful White Point Beach. On these holes, it very much has the feel of a links course. There are separate tees for a front and back nine, which make for an interesting second nine. Golf packages are available if you are staying at White Point Beach Resort. This is certainly the best of the nine-hole courses in the province.

River Hills Golf & Country Club, Clyde River, (902) 637-2415, www.riverhillsgolf.ca

Formerly the Shelburne Golf Club, this course expanded to 18 holes a few years ago. The older holes follow the meanderings of the Clyde River close to its entrance to the sea. The river comes into play on a number of holes. Salt marshes teeming with wildlife are a welcome distraction, although you won't think so if you hit your ball into one. One particularly scenic par three is all carry over water, with the river running along the entire right side of the hole. This is a friendly course at which you should be able to score well on the older holes, but the new ones will spell trouble for most. They are long, narrow and generally just mean.

West Pubnico Golf & County Club, just off Highway 103 in West Pubnico, (902) 762-2007, www.pubnicogolf.ca

It's hard to know what to make of a course that has a sign that forbids playing in rubber boots or high heels. The rubber boots are understandable, since most of the members are lobster fishermen. In fact the club's logo ball has a lobster on it, but the high heels? In any event, this is another course that has expanded to 18 in recent years. The old front nine is kind of typical, but the new back nine is very well-designed and maintained, and will provide a challenge for most. Since the lobster fishermen in this area have the summer off, there are some pretty good golfers on this course.

HIKING

Kejimkujik Seaside Adjunct, Port Joli

Kejimkujik National Park has a seaside adjunct of 2,187 hectares located off Highway 103 between Liverpool and Shelburne.

Part of this adjunct is the St. Catherines River Beach trail, which provides an opportunity to see what the South Shore must have been like thousands of years ago, before the intervention of man. To reach the entrance of the trail, turn toward Port Joli off Highway 103 and follow the Parks Canada signs to the parking lot. Leaving the parking lot, the trail wanders through a boreal forest until it divides. If you bear right this will take you around Port Joli. Head to St. Catherines River Beach, a distance of about eight kilometres. For a shorter hike stay left and follow the trail about two kilometres to a spectacular view of St. Catherines River Beach and St. Catherines River Bay. Whether you take the longer or shorter route you will cross tundra-like heath that is alive with song birds and wildflowers. Particularly wet areas of the trail are bridged by wooden platforms. At Harbour Rocks, where the remains of an old homestead are found, it is common to see seals basking offshore, looking around from the water, only their heads bobbing in the surf, like curious mermaids. The trail follows the course of the shore approximately one kilometre to St. Catherines River Beach, which is a broad expanse of crystalline sand flecked with quartz and mica that gleams in the sun. Behind the beach there are large dunes. The beach itself is actually a spit about a kilometre-and-a-half long, which ends just opposite Black Point and the trail that enters the seaside adjunct from

Southwest Port Mouton. From late May through June and early July, this beach is restricted to protect the piping plovers that nest there. Even if the beach is closed, the walk is more than rewarding.

Wear waterproof hiking boots, as the trail is wet and rocky in parts. The hiking itself is easy to moderate, depending upon what direction is taken once the shoreline is reached.

MUSEUMS

Wile Carding Mill, 242 Victoria Road, Bridgewater, (902) 543-8233, www.museum.gov.ns.ca/wcm/

Operational from 1868 to 1968, the Wile Carding Mill is the last remaining example of over 70 such mills that existed in Nova Scotia 100 years ago. Carding is a process whereby wool is stretched in order to be made into yarn or batting. The mill is preserved in very much the same condition as the day it closed. In its heyday, the mill was one of more than a dozen businesses operating on Sandy Brook, including a foundry, carriage works, chair factory and traditional grist mills, all using the stream as a source of energy. Today's bucolic appearance of this stream belies its former prominence as the industrial centre of Bridgewater.

DesBrisay Museum, 130 Jubilee Road, Bridgewater, (902) 543-4033, www.bridgewater.ca/desbrisay-museum/

Like many small-town museums, this one started out as a private collection, in this case, that of Judge DesBrisay, a French Huguenot who resided in Bridgewater during the 1800s. He bequeathed his wealth to the town and in 1967 a museum was built to properly house the collection. It is now located in a spacious centre, laid out in the modern interpretive style favoured by most museum curators. The museum provides exhibits of interest to both adults and children, although there is definitely an emphasis on the past industry and commerce of the Bridgewater area. A portion of the museum is set aside for traveling exhibits. Recently, the museum was the beneficiary of the folk art from the Chris Huntington/Charlotte McGill collection, considered one of the best collections of Nova Scotia folk art ever put together.

The museum is surrounded by the 8.5 hectares of Woodland Gardens, a natural woodland park, which is being developed by the town. There are walking trails surrounding a duck pond, and good places to picnic. Adjacent to the museum is the municipal swimming pool.

Fort Point Museum, 100 Fort Point Road, LaHave, (902) 688-1632, www.fortpointmuseum.com

This museum, which is part of Fort LaHave National Historic Site and is not to be confused with Fort Point in Liverpool, contains a very well laid out history of the life of Isaac de Razilly, both in Canada and elsewhere. De Razilly was one of the truly interesting characters of early colonial Nova Scotia. A wealthy and connected French nobleman who counted Champlain and Richelieu among his business associates, he established what was very similar to a feudal barony at this site in 1632. Over 40 families were brought over from France to establish the settlement. Unfortunately de Razilly quarrelled with other French commanders in Acadia and the settlement eventually fizzled out, with most of the settlers relocated to the Annapolis Valley area. A number of interesting artifacts excavated from the site of the fort are on display. The museum also focuses on the subsequent German settlement in the area in the 1700s. The location is also notable as being the site of Canada's first school. There is much to see other than the museum, including a lighthouse, gardens and a cemetery.

LaHave Islands Museum, 100 LaHave Islands Road, (902) 688-2973, www.lahaveislandsmarinemuseum.ca

The LaHave Islands was once a community spread across the numerous islands that dot the mouth of the LaHave River. The economy was based entirely on the fishery, particularly the inshore ground fishery. As that gradually waned so did LaHave Islands. Today only two islands are inhabited and the economy relies more on summer tourism than the fishery. In order to preserve their past the community has converted a former church into the LaHave Islands Museum. The exhibits have been donated by the islanders and represent their seafaring history very well. The most interesting exhibit is a rosary found by a small girl many years ago in the mouth of a 50-pound codfish. The entrance to the church faces the water, harkening to the times when parishioners arrived for Sunday service by boat. The Web site provides an abundance of material on life on the LaHave islands.

Parkdale-Maplewood Community Museum, Barss Corner Road, (902) 644-2893, parkdale.ednet.ns.ca

There are literally dozens of small community museums throughout rural Nova Scotia and we have visited just about every one. Most of them don't make it into this book because they are, quite frankly, dull, dusty and boring. The ones that do make it usually do so because there is a genuine spirit that animates the exhibits and brings the community alive. It often takes just one person to make the difference between a waste of time and 30 minutes well-spent. With the Parkdale-Maplewood Museum you get the feeling that there are many people who want to make this place work. The museum, which is quite off the beaten path not far from New Germany, features biographies and photos of the people whose creations and possessions make up the exhibits. One exhibit by a local designer of knitting patterns features a very interesting directory for the use of local plants. An amazing spectrum of dyes can be made from materials readily available to those who know the secrets of the various plants and animals in the area. All of this is more interesting than it sounds.

Perkins House and Queens County Museum, 105 Main Street, Liverpool, (902) 354-4058, www.museum.gov.ns.ca/peh

These facilities form one museum complex in a quiet area of town surrounded by large mature hardwoods and some beautiful older homes. Perkins

House was the home of noted Nova Scotian diarist Simeon Perkins, a transplanted Yankee businessman who held many prominent positions in Liverpool in the late eighteenth century. His home has been refurnished in a style consistent with what Perkins would have brought with him to Nova Scotia from his native Connecticut in 1760. The dark interior, low ceilings and broad plank floors predate the much more luxurious homes of the early nineteenth century.

The adjoining Queens County Museum, 109 Main Street (www.queenscountymuseum.com), is an attractive modern building designed to complement the architectural lines of Perkins House and could easily pass as an original outbuilding.

The displays outline the natural and social history of Queens County with an obvious pride of place. Simeon Perkins' original diary, open to the date of your visit, is a highlight. It is interesting to note when reading it that the Nova Scotian weather has not changed much in 200 years. Also available for use is the Thomas Raddall Research Centre, which contains genealogical material on Queens County families.

Sherman Hines Museum of Photography, 219 Main Street, Liverpool, (902) 354-2667, www.shermanhinesphotographymuseum.com

Liverpool Town Hall, an elegant late-Victorian structure, is no longer the site of spirited council meetings, but the home of the Sherman Hines Museum of Photography. Sherman Hines, a native of Liverpool, is one of Canada's pre-eminent photographers. He has produced over 100 books of photographs and won innumerable awards, many of which are on display. His book *Nova Scotia* is probably the best-selling book ever published about this province.

The museum, however, is not centred around Sherman Hines, but rather is a potpourri of photographic equipment and a number of galleries featuring the works of noted Canadian photographers including Yousuf Karsh, William Notman and the ever popular W.R. MacAskill. Exhibits are changed regularly in the main gallery and they often feature some of Sherman's best work, as well as the work of other noted contemporary photographers.

Sherman has donated his extensive collection of photographic equipment, which dates back to the earliest days of photography. This complex is decidedly not a tribute to an artist, but rather a tribute by an artist to his community and province. This relatively new museum is a worthy addition to the Lighthouse Route.

Little School Museum, Lockeport, (902) 656-2850

From this tiny building, where one teacher faced as many as 65 students in all grades, one can see, across the street, the huge modern high school. The contrast is striking. The exhibits are similar to those seen in many small-town museums. Of note are the papers of a local doctor, and especially an autograph book. The penmanship of the entries is beautiful and far beyond what could be expected from students today! An annex building constructed in the same style as the schoolhouse hosts marine exhibits.

Historic Dock Street, Shelburne, www.shelburnenovascotia.com/museums

Shelburne's Dock Street is a collection of public and private buildings that through a combination of planning and good luck have been preserved in close to original condition. The absence of modern intrusion gives the waterfront streetscape an authentic eighteenth-century maritime look; so much so that Disney chose Dock Street to represent a late 1600s New England town for the filming of Hawthorne's *The Scarlet Letter*. Millions of dollars were spent eliminating any traces of modernity and the area is the better for it. Subsequently many other productions have been filmed here including most recently, *Moby Dick*. While some of the 'revisions' such as the spire on the warehouse are not authentic, most of Dock Street is original. Four of the buildings, which have thankfully been returned to their original form, are open to the public. A single-price-admission ticket can be purchased for all the Dock Street attractions which will save over purchasing individual admissions at each place. Dock Street is one of Nova Scotia's must see attractions.

Ross-Thomson House, Shelburne, (902) 875-3219, www.museum.gov.ns.ca/rth

An original general store and residence dating from 1785, the Ross-Thomson House provides a good idea of the types of goods available at that time to the new settlers. The exterior is a fine example of late eighteenth-century New England architecture.

Shelburne County Museum, (902) 875-3219

Located next to the Ross-Thomson House in another fine old Shelburne home, this museum features the history of the county with an emphasis on shipbuilding. An interesting exhibit focuses on Donald MacKay, the Shelburne native who went on to win fame in Boston as the designer of such famous clipper ships as the *Flying Cloud* and the *Sovereign of the Seas*. Also of note is Canada's oldest fire engine — a small contraption used in Shelburne in the late 1700s. When you see it you'll know why so many of these communities burnt down in the eighteenth and nineteenth centuries.

The Dory Shop Museum, Shelburne, (902) 875-3219, www.museums.gov.ns.ca/dory

A dory is a small wooden boat that was used in the Grand Banks fishery for over one hundred years. The dories would be lowered into the water from the deck of a schooner and a two man crew would hand line for cod until the dory was full to the gunwales and then row back to the mothership. Given conditions on the North Atlantic more than a few didn't make it and there was always a need for new dories. The John Williams Dory Shop is the sole survivor of seven dory shops that existed on the waterfront 100 years ago. The museum has examples of several types of dories and how they were built. Unfortunately, master dory builder Sidney Mahaney died in 1993, at age 94, for a while leaving arch-rival Lunenburg as the only place where these venerable craft were still produced on a commercial basis in Nova Scotia. However, dory-making skills are still demonstrated at the Dory Shop and the shop sells replicas of dories and other types of boats associated with the Nova Scotia fishery. These make for very good, authentic Nova Scotia souvenirs.

Muir-Cox Shipyard, Dock Street, Shelburne, (902) 875-3219
The latest addition to the Dock Street complex is this shipyard which operated from the 1820s until 1984 building wooden boats ranging from large barques to small pleasure craft. In 2001 the shipyard started building boats again on a much smaller scale. Today, aside from watching wooden boat construction in progress, you learn much about the shipbuilding history of the area.

Shelburne County Genealogical Society, 168 Water Street, Shelburne (902) 875-4299
The repository of virtually every possible record of the Loyalist migration to Nova Scotia, this facility is a treasure for the many Canadians who trace their ancestry to Loyalist roots. Complete genealogies exist for most of the family names, as well as detailed information on many other immigrants to Nova Scotia, including Shelburne County blacks, Welsh and Irish. The centre should also be of interest to Americans whose families were split up at the time of the revolution. The facility is located in the very handsome Coyle House, one of the finest historical buildings in the Dock Street area.

Barrington Museum Complex, (902) 637-2185, Barrington, www.capesablehistoricalsociety.com
From the parking lot of the tourist bureau in Barrington, you can walk to the four museums that make up the Barrington Museum Complex. The most interesting is the reconstruction of a lighthouse that stood on remote Seal Island for many years. The lantern and operating works are from the original light. This is one of the few chances in Nova Scotia to see the interior of a lighthouse, albeit not a real one. You can climb to the top and view all of Barrington Bay.

Also worth a visit is the Barrington Meeting House (www.museums. gov.ns.ca/omh) the oldest nonconformist church in Canada and one of the oldest buildings in the province. Its stark interior is reminiscent of the New England style seldom found elsewhere in Canada. The Barrington Woolen Mill (www.museum.gov.ns.ca/bwm) sits largely as it did on the day in 1962 when this, the last of Nova Scotia's woolen mills, was closed by its owner. The machines sit silently as if waiting for the workers to return at any moment. Of particular interest to Nova Scotians is a mural that contains the first depiction of the Nova Scotia tartan. When people asked what the tartan symbolized, the makers of the mural advised that it was simply meant to be a representation of Nova Scotia's colours. The predominance of blue was an obvious reference to the sea. People liked the design so much that in the early 1950s it was adopted as the official tartan of Nova Scotia.

The last museum in the complex is the Cape Sable Historical Society, (902) 637-2185, which contains genealogical records for the area and a Military Museum. Beside this building is the oldest cemetery in the region with some very interesting tombstones.

Archelaus Smith Museum, Route 330, Cape Sable Island, (902) 745-3361, www.archelaus.org

This local museum is named for Archelaus Smith, the patriarch of Cape Sable Island. It is definitely worth a visit. Not surprisingly, the focus is on the numerous shipwrecks that have occurred around Cape Sable. Of particular note is a wooden chair, every piece of which comes from a different ship, mostly wrecks, including the *Titanic*, and quite a number that went down off the shores of this island. Also on display are several murals and paintings preserved from various halls on Cape Sable Island, complete collections of items that can be found by beachcombers on Cape Sable Island and an extensive array of souvenir china and glassware featuring Cape Sable Island and Clark's Harbour. We forget that 100 years ago, it would not have been unusual to decorate the parlour with plates and cups that contained pictures of local churches, schools or fire halls. These now make excellent collectibles, and this museum shows the variety that existed even in a small place such as this.

OFF THE BEATEN PATH

LaHave Islands

A large group of islands collectively known as the LaHave Islands is scattered across the mouth of the LaHave River. Only Bush and Bell Islands are connected to the mainland by road via the natural causeway of Crescent Beach. Those fortunate enough to have an opportunity to visit Cape LaHave Island will be rewarded with a large sand beach and solitude. There are no communities of any size on the LaHave Islands today, but the narrow winding roads that crisscross Bush and Bell Islands are well worth exploring. The coastlines of these islands are indented with many small coves and inlets. On a map, these islands look like a jigsaw puzzle. There are a number of fishing stations scattered throughout the islands. The LaHaves are best explored by sea and make a great kayaking destination.

Green Bay

From Petite Rivière, a dead-end road leads to the cottage community of Green Bay, which deserves the very overused sobriquet, charming. The road here really is more of a country lane with the ocean on one side and some very nice cottages with well-tended gardens on the other. The water is clear and usually calm. Unlike many places along the coast where the ocean can seem threatening and aggressive, at Green Bay there is a definite gentleness and tranquility to the water. It may be because a number of rock ledges interrupt the sand beach, forming natural breakwaters, or it may simply be the genteel nature of the buildings that face the sea.

Green Bay and Petite Rivière have long been attractive to artists, including J.E.H. MacDonald, one of the Group of Seven. There remains an active artists' community in the area, and they occasionally display their works in local homes.

The road peters out just past MacLeod's canteen and becomes the trail to Broad Cove.

There are a number of cottages for rent in Green Bay. They are usually booked well in advance; however, it is sometimes worthwhile to check in any event for last-minute cancellations.

Western Head

This short loop starts and ends in Liverpool, and has a number of interesting highlights that make the half-hour or so it takes to drive more than worthwhile. At Western Head, you can drive right up to the lighthouse at the entrance to Liverpool Harbour. Across the way is a picture-perfect lighthouse on Coffin Island. In August, fin whales can often be seen just offshore from the Western Head lighthouse. The drive also passes several boulder beaches and at one point traverses the back of the beach with the ocean on one side and a popular fishing pond on the other. At Moose Harbour, a short side road descends to overlook a traditional fishing wharf, which just may be the most photogenic in the entire province. Finally, there is an opportunity to visit artist Roger Savage's studio, which is just a few miles outside Liverpool on this loop.

Baccaro Point

Instead of turning to Barrington at Port LaTour, continue ahead for a circular tour of Baccaro Point. Shortly after the turn, signs direct you to Fort St. Louis, where a short walk leads to a cairn marking the site of a fort dating from the early 1600s, when Charles de LaTour made a base here. Further on, the road leads to Baccaro Point, where there is an air traffic control installation and a lighthouse offering a beautiful spot for a picnic. Leaving the lighthouse, turn left to follow the shore through West Baccaro and back to Port LaTour to rejoin the Lighthouse Route. On a clear day you can see the light on Cape Sable Island from West Baccaro.

McNutt's Island

This large island sits at the mouth of Shelburne Harbour and at one time was a rather thriving community. Today it has but one lone couple. For years getting to McNutt's was problematic, but recently Shelburne Harbour Boat Tours has provided daily service to and from the large wharf on McNutt's and can drop you off in the morning and pick you up in late afternoon. For details, call (902) 875-4439 or visit www.shelburneharbour-boattours.com. The tour begins at the marina and provides great views of the historic Dock Street area from the water. On the way to McNutt's you pass Sandy Point lighthouse. Once on the island there is lots to see and explore. The two residents, semi-eccentric Americans, have set up some interesting and funny things on the island which we won't describe further so as not to ruin the fun. An old road, perfect for cycling, runs from the wharf down the middle of the island to Cape Roseway lighthouse, the third oldest in Canada. From here there are unparalleled ocean views and the ruins of Fort McNutt where two massive cannons lay discarded — too big to bother moving. In the middle of the island is a stand of yellow birch that is truly enormous including the largest specimen in Nova Scotia. For geocachers there are over a dozen caches to find. A trip to McNutt's is a truly different way to spend a day. Obviously you have to bring your own supplies.

Cape Sable Island, www.capesableisland.com

Cape Sable Island, not to be confused with Sable Island which is 150 kilometres out into the Atlantic off the Eastern Shore, has long been known as one of the graveyards of the Atlantic. It is the extreme southern point of Nova Scotia and marks the location where sailing ships made a turn around Nova Scotia, bearing either for Europe or the American seaboard. Unfortunately, over the centuries, many have not made the turn and the shifting sands of Cape Sable have brought about their demise. Probably the most horrendous wreck was that of the passenger liner *Hungarian*, which went down just offshore with all hands and passengers in 1860.

Cape Sable is also famous as the home of the Cape Island fishing boat, or the Cape Islander as it is universally known, which was first built on these shores. This is the basic inshore fishing boat used by lobstermen and inshore fishermen for the past 100 years in Eastern Canada, and it's seen everywhere in Nova Scotia. Other attractions include the fine museum, the many beaches and the 101-foot-high lighthouse at the cape, which is the tallest in Nova Scotia. It is a great spot to check out by bike or kayak.

Cape Sable is a place of great natural beauty and we would like to be able to make an unqualified recommendation to visit here. Unfortunately, there are some detractions, the most serious of which is the destruction of the dunes at Southside Island Beach by the unlimited use of motorized vehicles. Of late, however, the islanders do seem to be realizing the value of what they have and collective efforts have been made to clean up some eyesores and to concentrate on eco-tourism. If you love birding or walking on deserted beaches, Cape Sable Island is a must.

Surettes Island and The Tuskets

There are almost 400 islands in the group known as the Tuskets, which sit between the Pubnico peninsula and Wedgeport in Lobster Bay. Route 308 travels out to a couple of them and you will probably see 100 more along the way. Surettes and Morris Islands are Acadian fishing communities that can legitimately be called backwaters. If you travel to the end of the highway, which ends at the government wharf at Morris Island, you will see the wide, flat-bottomed boats that are used for seaweed harvesting in this area, and you can see in the distance a number of other islands. Usually, this area is very tranquil and seldom visited. The land and seascapes around the bridges that connect the islands are exceptional. On Surettes Island, just before crossing to Morris Island, look for Tittle Road, which winds through a series of pristine salt marshes and ends at the government wharf at Lower Surettes Island.

Wedgeport Peninsula

The largest of the Yarmouth-area peninsulas is Wedgeport, which sticks out like a trident between the Chebogue River on the Yarmouth side and the Tusket River on the Halifax side. There are three distinct tips to the peninsula, two of which are well worth exploring.

The community of Wedgeport, despite its English name, was founded by Acadians returning from exile in 1767. As you enter the town, look for a commemorative granite obelisk, which has a number of incidents from Acadian history set out in cast-bronze plaques. Also, as you enter Wedgeport, look for Cape Wharf Road. From this short road there is an excellent view of the town, the old wharf and a number of derelict fishing boats lying in the salt marshes. For many years, Wedgeport was home to the International Tuna Competition, which pitted anglers from a number of countries against each other to land these giant fish. On Tuna Wharf Road, in the middle of the village, you can check out the history of tuna fishing, and the competition which attracted such luminaries as Franklin Roosevelt and Ernest Hemingway, by visiting the Wedgeport Sport Tuna Fishing Museum and Interpretive Centre. From the centre there is an interpretive trail that leads to the estuary of the Tusket River. After visiting the town, be sure to drive to the very end of the peninsula, where there is an unobstructed view in all directions.

Backtracking as far as Upper Wedgeport, take Black Point Road to its end, then turn right and travel as far as Melbourne, where a left turn will take you out to Pinkney's Point.

This is the narrowest and by far the prettiest of the three points on the Wedgeport Peninsula. The community sits on an island that is almost completely surrounded by ocean and salt marsh. The paved road travels behind a long breakwater and beach with salt marshes on the other side. As you approach, the view is breathtaking and on a clear day you can see many of the Tusket Islands, including the mysterious Murder Island. At Pinkney's Point there is one of the largest and most active fishing wharves on this shore, with a variety of craft moored at any given time.

During your visit to Pinkney's Point or the Wedgeport Peninsula, you may have noticed an unusual number of medium-sized, orange-coloured dogs with large, bushy curved tails. These are Nova Scotia duck tolling retrievers, the only recognized species of dog to be developed in Nova Scotia. The duck tollers are famous for their ability to attract ducks and geese, preying on the natural curiosity of these creatures. Acting very much like a fox, the dogs will roll, jump around and generally act strangely on the shore. For some reason, this seems to attract waterfowl, who are shot, and then retrieved by these dual-purpose dogs. They make excellent pets and there are a number of breeders in the Yarmouth area.

PARKS AND GREENSPACE

Bridgewater Park System

The town of Bridgewater has always been forward thinking and recently made a commitment to Active Transportation or AT as it is usually called. AT is any method that uses only people power to get around, walking, biking, pushing a stroller etc. The benefits of AT to a community are many-fold including better health, less stress and a cleaner environment. Over the past few years Bridgewater has tried to make better use of its parks and greenspace by making sure they are all connected by a greenway.

Several miles outside Bridgewater on the banks of the LaHave River is Riverview Park. A pathway along the river leads to a series of rapids and falls. In the late spring, when the gaspereau and shad are running, there are often dip netters here competing with hundreds of gulls in a gorge that the migrating fish must successfully navigate. This is a very scenic spot from which to watch this ancient pastime. Recently, the town has added walking paths for a considerable distance along both sides of the river, and you can now cross the river via the old railway bridge on the Centennial Trail.

Fort Point Lighthouse Park, Liverpool

This is a great little park at the end of Liverpool's main thoroughfare. It has an extremely photogenic lighthouse of unusual design, cannons for the kids to climb on and great views of the harbour. The lighthouse contains exhibits detailing the town's long history. This is a good spot to start and end a walking tour of Liverpool.

Port L'Hébert Pocket Wilderness

This is just one of a number of small interpretive trails in southern Nova Scotia built and maintained by Bowater Mersey Pulp and Paper Company. This four kilometre circular route wanders through a hardwood forest to the isolated shore of Port L'Hébert Bay and back again. In late fall, the bay is the gathering ground for huge flocks of Canada geese and brant. The trail is usually well-maintained and suitable for all but the youngest of children, but the last time we were there considerable portions of the boardwalk were flooded. If you do not have the time to take the St. Catherines River beach trail or some of the inland trails at Kejimkujik, this trail is a somewhat adequate substitute.

The Islands Provincial Park, Shelburne

http://www.novascotiaparks.ca/parks/theislands.asp

This small park is just across the harbour from the town of Shelburne and has great views of that historic town. It offers the chance to picnic or camp right on the seashore. The Islands makes for a very pleasant morning or evening walk with the ocean nearby.

SPECIAL EVENTS

South Shore Exhibition, 50 Exhibition Drive, Bridgewater, (902) 543-3341, www.thebigex.com

Almost every county in Nova Scotia has an annual exhibition. The South Shore Exhibition or Big Ex, as it is known locally, is probably the best of these. The highlight is the international ox-pull contest. At one time almost every farm in the South Shore area had a pair of working oxen. The strength of these animals was particularly suited to the hilly and rocky farming areas in the interior of the province. Ox pulls were a natural outgrowth of the competition to have the best pair. While working ox teams are few and far between in Nova Scotia today, many farmers still keep a pair for exhibition pulling purposes. There are ox and horse pulls every day while the Ex is on, along with a host of other events that you would expect to find at any country fair, including the obligatory midway. The arts and crafts display at the Big Ex always has an exceptional selection of quilts and hooked rugs, for which the South Shore area is justly famous. Prize-winning entries are often offered for sale at prices far less than similar items at retail outlets. There are three exhibition rings at the Big Ex, so there is always something going on, whether it is the ox pulls, show jumping or cattle judging. This is a great way to spend the day without spending a lot of money.

Shelburne Whirligig Festival, www.whirligigfestival.com

A whirligig is a thingamabob which has moving parts that are set in motion by the wind. They have no known useful purpose other than to amuse, and that they do, very well; especially in mid-September in Shelburne when some dozens of folk artists display their whirligigs and weathervanes on the historic waterfront. Colourful, witty and above all, inventive, it is well worth the time to drop by and see these ingenious contraptions.

SPECIAL INTEREST

Roger Savage Gallery, 611 Mersey Point Road, Liverpool, (902) 354-5431, www.savagegallery.ca

Long recognized as one of Nova Scotia's premier artists, Roger Savage's watercolours feature the natural landscapes of the South Shore. He is often on hand at his gallery, located in his home just outside Liverpool. His ability to capture light and colour is remarkable, and he offers original watercolours, limited-edition prints and a collection of original drawings. If you want some of the beautiful seascapes you have seen while visiting the South Shore captured on canvas, this is the place to go. The Web site gives a good picture of what Roger can do with a canvas.

Hank Snow Country Music Centre, 148 Bristol Avenue, Liverpool, (902) 354-4675, www.hanksnow.com

Hank Snow was truly a legend in country music. A fixture of the Grand Ole Opry for over 40 years, Hank was inducted into the Country Music Hall of Fame, having recorded over 100 albums that have sold 70 million copies worldwide. His trademark tunes *I'm Movin' On* and *I've Been Everywhere* are known from Kalamazoo to Ecum Secum and all places in between, but what many don't know is that this diminutive country gentleman hailed from Brooklyn, Nova Scotia.

The Liverpool train station, which closed in 1981, has been carefully restored to house the Hank Snow Country Music Centre. Currently in its infancy, the museum contains a number of Snow-related material, including his 1947 Cadillac. There is also a lot of material from other Canadian country music stars as well. There can be no doubt that the tribute to this incredibly successful local hero is well-warranted and overdue. The museum is also the home of the Nova Scotia Country Music Hall of Fame.

Rossignol Cultural Centre, 205 Church Street, Liverpool, (902) 354-3067, www.rossignolculturalcentre.com

When famed photographer and Liverpudlian Sherman Hines learned that the old school he had attended was scheduled to be demolished he stepped in and bought it. In his fifty years of traveling the globe on photographic assignments he had collected, well … a lot of stuff. Well it turns out he had enough stuff to almost completely fill more than a dozen rooms and half of the school grounds. The Rossignol Cultural Centre has got to be one of the most pleasant surprises to come along in Nova Scotia in decades. Despite the rather strange name Sherman's place is about fun. The contrasts between collections could not be more extreme. For example, there is a museum of the outhouse — artifacts collected and donated during the time he was photographing his best-selling outhouses books. It's a hoot. There is a truly outstanding collection of Mi'kmaq artifacts and some great folk art. Kids will love the very realistic dioramas of stuffed animals from around the world including a giraffe — how did he get that inside the school? There is far too much to describe inside. Outside is the cultural village where you'll find everything from a recreation of the Fort Edward blockhouse to a replica of folk artist Maud Lewis' tiny home. As an added bonus you can actually stay in a yurt, wigwam, log cabin or the block house. Last time we were there Sherman allowed some twenty young American girls on a cycling tour stay for free in the giant Mi'kmaq wigwam. It easily accommodated all of them. This place is really something different and provides yet another reason to spend some time in Liverpool.

Black Loyalist Interpretive Centre, Birchtown, Highway 3, 1-888-354-0772, www.blackloyalist.com

Lawrence Hill's novel *The Book of Negroes* (Harper Collins), a fictionalized account of the real-life hardships and travails of the black Loyalists, comes alive in the Black Loyalist Centre. During the American Revolution, the British promised freedom and land to black slaves who left their masters to join the British troops. By 1782, it was becoming apparent to the British that they might lose the war, so they made preparations to transport Loyalists out of the American colonies. About 3,000 freed black veterans were evacuated from New York to Birchtown, southwest from the town of Shelburne between 1783 and 1784. The land was mean and the climate harsh. Without sufficient land or tools to make a living, blacks became a cheap source of labour for neighbouring whites. Disbanded and unemployed British soldiers resented the competition from the meagre wages paid to blacks. North America's first race riot ensued as the soldiers drove the blacks out of town. Here is where history begins for many black Nova Scotians. The beautiful seaside setting of the church and graveyard where no headstones mark the graves, walking past the recreated huts of the first settlers, which could not have provided much comfort from a Nova Scotia winter, over the thin soil of the area, to the interpretative panels in the old school house, provide the setting for contemplation of the indomitable determination necessary to survive their brutal circumstances. It is a fascinating story known to few and well worth the visit. Readers may also be interested to learn more about the original Book of Negroes, essentially a book of lists detailing the appearance, origins and abilities of blacks leaving New York for Nova Scotia. Don't be shy about asking questions of the Centre's guides. They are knowledgeable and very helpful.

Le Village historique acadien, West Pubnico, (902) 762-2530, www.museum.gov.ns.ca/av
Located on the tip of a very scenic 17-acre parcel of land jutting off the Pubnico peninsula, Le Village, as it is usually called, was opened only in 1999. The brainchild of members of the local historical society, it is intended, when finished, to recreate an Acadian village of the nineteenth century. Recently the province added it to the stable of government run and funded museums assuring its success. From the newly constructed Visitor Reception building a path leads to a number of Acadian homes, a blacksmith's shop, a traditional fish store, a boat shop and other attractions. An added bonus is the very photographable lighthouse at the end of the point. In a very short period of time Le Village has become a major tourist destination.

WALKING TOURS
Liverpool
The tour begins at the museum complex and follows a rectangular route around the older parts of town and the more interesting parts of the central area. On the way, there are many examples of early Nova Scotia architecture, including a haunted tavern, the exceptional Trinity Anglican Church and the Greek Revival courthouse. Also along the way are Fort Point, where Champlain dropped anchor in 1604, and several of the earliest town cemeteries. The tour takes a couple of hours to walk and brochures are available at the tourism office. This walking tour is certainly the best way to appreciate all that Liverpool has to offer.

Lockeport
Lockeport is another one of the small South Shore towns that is best explored on foot. Obtain a map of the town from the tourist bureau and

start your walk at South Street, just above Crescent Beach. Look back for a sweeping view of this beautiful beach, then walk the length of South Street, which ends at the quiet Colonel Locke's Beach on the other side of town. Along the way you will pass a number of interesting houses, including Nova Scotia's only heritage-designated streetscape. The Locke family streetscape contains five homes built by various members of the Locke family in a number of contrasting styles. Across the way is a large attractive commercial fishing wharf, which offers fine views back to the Locke family homes. Also worth visiting on the walking tour is Reed's Head Park and the old town cemetery, which has many fine tombstones. The entire tour of Lockeport, including a visit to the playground and museum, should take about half a day.

Shelburne

Shelburne has one of the better walking tour brochures available, with many points of interest, most of which are centred around the historic Dock Street area. You will see numerous examples of fine architecture, including churches, early homes and the waterfront.

ACCOMMODATIONS

Lane's Privateer Inn, 27 Bristol Avenue, Liverpool, 800-794-3332, www.lanesprivateerinn.com

Lane's has a great location near the mouth of the Mersey River facing the town of Liverpool. Although the original property is over 210 years old the place really doesn't feel old or tired. It has a good restaurant, nice little pub and a bookroom, all of which give it a cozy ambience that makes for a relaxing stay. Lane's is a good base from which to explore the numerous attractions in Liverpool, all of which can easily be reached on foot.

White Point Beach Resort, White Point Beach, 1-800-565-5068, www.whitepoint.com

Real estate agents use the words location, location, location to describe what makes a place desirable. White Point Beach Resort may just have the best location in Nova Scotia. Built in 1928, the main lodge and most of the cabins are situated on one of the South Shore's finest sand beaches, with just enough weathered granite at the edges to create the sea spray so typical of this coastline. From almost all of the rooms, the predominant sound is the surf, which breaks as symmetrically on this beach as the waves on a Ron Bolt painting.

The facilities at White Point are among the most complete in the province — an excellent nine-hole golf course, a large indoor pool with hot tub, an outdoor pool, well-maintained tennis courts and a good games room. There's also freshwater swimming, canoeing and paddle boating at a small lake on the property.

The only drawback to White Point is that many of the rooms and the dining room do not live up to the quality of the surroundings. Over the years new units have been added and older ones redone. Make sure you ask for one of these, some of which are cottages almost right on the beach. However, the staff are friendly and try very hard. White Point is very popular with families because of its extensive facilities and perhaps even more popular with newlyweds and lovers because of its unquestionably romantic setting. This is one of the few places we know where a foggy day may be as welcome as a sunny one. Whether it's a warm fire in the cabin, a dip in the hot tub or a quiet drink in the lounge overlooking the open Atlantic, few people are disappointed by White Point. As an added bonus for the little ones, the property is almost overrun with tame rabbits.

Hunts Point Beach Cottages, Hunts Point, (902) 683-2077, www.huntspointbeach.com

If you are looking for an alternative to White Point Beach Resort, staying at either Hunts Point Beach or Summerville Beach is a very pleasant alternative. There are several sets of older cottages right on these beaches. Our favourite is Hunts Point Beach Cottages, mainly because of the outstanding view. To the south is the beach, and to the north a very photogenic wharf and collection of boats and fishing paraphernalia. It's a sure-fire combination for artists and photographers. The cabins are fully equipped for housekeeping and have been recently upgraded. The Seaside Takeout is just down the road and the excellent Quarterdeck Restaurant a little further on.

Summerville Beach Retreat Chalets, Summerville Beach, 1-800-213-5868, www.novascotiachalets.com

If the sound of crashing surf and an element of privacy are high on your list of priorities, these fairly new pine cottages are possibly just what you're looking for. Each cottage is equipped with a gas barbecue, woodstove, full kitchen, DVD, large bathroom and a great deck with a good view of the ocean. While not on the beach, these units are close enough that the soothing sound of the surf is always audible. At the same time, each cottage stands well away from the others, in a pleasant woodsy setting. It's only a minute's walk to Summerville Beach. The stars at night make it one of the most romantic spots in the province. Very reasonable off-season rates. Try to get cottage #1, as it has the best setting.

Quarterdeck Beachside Villas, Summerville Beach, 1-800-565-1119, www.quarterdeck.ns.ca

If being absolutely on the beach, expense be damned, is your top priority, then this is your place. This large condominium-like building with 13 luxury two-bedroom, two-storey villas is a real rarity in Nova Scotia. It was built, amid some justifiable environmental concerns, right on the edge of Summerville Beach. You simply cannot get any closer to the water anywhere else in the province. All you'll see from your second-storey bedroom is wide-open beautiful blue ocean. The units are luxurious and include a fireplace, gas barbecue and microwave oven. The Quarterdeck Grill next door is a more-than-passable restaurant, and you are within easy touring distance of Lunenburg, Liverpool and Shelburne. The only potential drawback, aside from the price, is the proximity of the units, each of which is joined to the other like a townhouse. The price drops dramatically in the off-season, so the late fall is probably the best time to stay here.

Cooper's Inn, 36 Dock Street, Shelburne, 1-800-688-2011, www.thecoopersinn.com

The Cooper's Inn, in the restored 1785 home of blind Loyalist George Gracie, is situated right on historic Dock Street and is the only accommodation permitted in the historic area. The name comes from the barrel-making shop across the street, which is still in operation. The exterior of the inn is one of the finest in this historic town, while the interior reflects the refined austerity common in late eighteenth-century homes. Although it is located right on the street, at night there is virtually no traffic on Dock Street and it is easy to imagine the sound of horses' hooves on the pavement. The real pleasure of the Cooper's Inn is the ease with which one can slip into a sense of the past and imagine what life was like 200 years ago. There is also a small but very enjoyable private garden out back. Each room can be viewed on the Web site.

Roseway River Cottages, 50 Riverview Drive Shelburne, (902) 875-3812, www.rosewayrivercottages.com

These fairly new cottages just outside Shelburne are a great place for families. Well-equipped for housekeeping, the cottages overlook the Roseway River and the owners have done their best to ensure that you enjoy it. There are canoes, a pedal boat and an old-fashioned swimming hole complete with swinging rope, as well as bikes, all included in the price. At night, you can make a fire in the firepit, roast marshmallows, look at the stars and tell scary stories.

DINING

LaHave Bakery, LaHave, (902) 688- 2908

Just past the ferry across the LaHave River, be sure to stop in at LaHave Bakery, located in an old general store and warehouse in the centre of the former shipbuilding community. The bakery specializes in traditional breads made from locally grown and milled grains and uses only traditional ingredients. It is also a good place to pick up a sandwich or have a bowl of homemade soup. The bakery serves as a kind of local drop-in centre and there are always interesting people on hand.

The Seaside, Hunts Point, (902) 683-2618

Another one of the many fine canteens along Nova Scotia's South Shore, the Seaside has long claimed to have the world's best clams. We won't risk getting into hot water by siding for or against the Seaside, but will say the clams are great, as are the fish and chips, which are done in a very light batter and not overcooked. The milkshakes, pies and lobster rolls are also recommended fare.

Quarterdeck Grill, Summerville Beach, (902) 683-2998, www.quarterdeck.ns.ca

The odds are that if you find a seafood restaurant with a location as good as the Quarterdeck's, the owners will rely on this to get them by. This is usually confirmed on entering by the *de rigueur* collection of lobster pots, nets and other fisheries paraphernalia so necessary to these establishments. The Quarterdeck does have some of this, but the kitchen is anything but ordinary. The Quarterdeck is trying very hard to be a serious seafood restaurant and, to a large extent, is succeeding. The menu has a selection of every possible type of Nova Scotia seafood, including planked salmon. The dessert menu is more than perfunctory. The servers are enthusiastic and knowledgeable, and genuinely seem to care about what they are serving. The view from the Quarterdeck would go a long way to make you overlook bad food or service. We congratulate the owners for not coasting on it.

Charlotte Lane Café and Crafts, 13 Charlotte Lane, Shelburne, (902) 875-3314, www.charlottelane.ca

In just a few short years, Kathleen and Roland Glauser have put Shelburne on the dining map, garnering two stars in Ann Hardy's *Where to Eat in Canada*. On any given day, Nova Scotians from Yarmouth, Liverpool and Halifax can be found dining with tourists from around the world. Swiss born and trained, chef Roland creates gourmet fare. While he is behind the scenes working his magic, Kathleen is busy charming their ever-increasing clientele. Each and every guest is welcomed warmly by Kathleen and shown to their table. The service is always friendly and efficient.

The diverse menu offers something for everyone. There are several exceptional salads, notably the tangy spinach and orange salad, which is served with a zesty poppy seed and cider dressing. The entrées include several pasta dishes, including our favourites, Spaghettini Gorgonzola and Garlic Shrimp Linguini. From the land and sea options, the Roast Pork Tenderloin with rosemary and port wine sauce, Baked Chicken Camembert stuffed with asparagus, and Lobster and Scallop Brandy Gratin are excellent choices. We recommend saving room for dessert. Selections change seasonally.

The wine list is limited, but the prices are reasonable compared to many better Nova Scotian restaurants. The overall price of the meal will be very reasonable, especially considering the exceptional quality of the food preparation. It is a place worth visiting.

The restaurant is open May to December. It is closed on Mondays in the peak season and closed on Sundays and Mondays in the shoulder season.

The restaurant also showcases an interesting collection of Nova Scotian pottery, folk art, clothing, and other giftware available for purchase.

Lothar's Café, 149 Water Street, Shelburne, (902) 875-3697, www.lothars-cafe.com

One might be sceptical of a chef who used to cook for the Trailer Park Boys, but not in the case of Lothar Mayer who is serving up great German food in downtown Shelburne. Classic dishes like sauerbraten and schnit-zels are complemented by great seafood, beef and lamb. The scallop cakes are Lothar's own creation. This tiny place doesn't have many tables, but it's worth the wait if necessary.

KEJIMKUJIK SCENIC DRIVE

Kejimkujik Scenic Drive follows Route 8 from Liverpool to Annapolis Royal, crossing the widest part of the Nova Scotia mainland. At the heart is Kejimkujik National Park (http://www.pc.gc.ca/pn-np/ns/kejimkujik/index.aspx) and the Tobeatic Wilderness Area (http://www.gov.ns.ca/nse/protectedareas/wa_tobeatic.asp), which combined amount to the largest protected wild area in the Maritimes. One can literally spend weeks in this area without seeing or hearing anything remotely connected to modern civilization. For canoeists and hikers looking for solitude and adventure this is the place to do it in Nova Scotia. Route 8 provides a shortcut for those who do not have the time to drive the entire Evangeline and Lighthouse trails.

The trail starts in Liverpool and passes through the village of Milton, which straddles both sides of the Mersey River. This is surely one of the most scenic riverside villages in the province. Milton has two parks, one of which has a small dam and a fish ladder near a bridge that connects both sides of the village. Nearby, there is a blacksmith shop that has been restored and operated as a small local museum.

From Milton to Caledonia, a distance of some 40 kilometres, the highway travels through very pleasant pine and mixed hardwood forest, quite unlike much of the shorter, less attractive softwood forests that predominate most of the South Shore. Caledonia is a lumbering and former mining community, which has a small museum devoted to the history of these two activities. The fish hatchery at nearby McGowan Lake is open to visitors. Shortly after Caledonia, you'll find the entrance to Kejimkujik National Park, simply known as Keji.

The beauties of Keji are subtle. It has no soaring mountains — in fact it is one of the flattest areas of the province. It has no roaring cataracts — most of the rapids and small falls in the park are just pretty picnic sites. While there are lakes, the waters are so darkly peat-stained that you can barely see your hand in a foot of water. You won't see grizzly bears or mountain lions — the most exotic animal you might see is the rare Blandings turtle or a small ring-necked snake.

Keji is a place of quiet waters and few roads, with little signs of human activity. It is best explored by canoe rather than on foot or by motor vehicle. Only after you have paddled the grassy meadows of the Mersey or camped on one of Keji's many small islands will you come to understand the beauty and tranquility and appreciate the value that the Mi'kmaq ancestors placed on this area.

Keji is seldom crowded. Apart from a few long weekends, at most times you will find yourself alone on the canoe routes and the hiking trails. For the first-time visitor, plan to spend anywhere from a day to a week, depending on your interests. For a day visit, you should definitely rent a canoe at

Jake's Landing, visit the interpretive centre and hike one of the trails along the river. This will give you a good idea of what's here, should you want to come back for a longer visit and camp on one of the islands or make one of the overnight hikes. Keji is also the entranceway to the Tobeatic Wilderness Area which is an even bigger area of preserved wilderness.

Just past the entrance to Keji is the small community of Maitland Bridge, the traditional guiding and outfitting centre for this area. For the next 32 kilometres, the road passes through more mixed forest and some farmland before reaching Lequille just outside Annapolis Royal. At Lequille there is a reproduction of the first grist mill in North America, built by the first French settlers at Port Royal. The reproduction is actually a power station for Nova Scotia Power. It is a pleasant area for a picnic and well worth a short visit. From Lequille, it is a short drive to the outskirts of Annapolis Royal, a town with many beautiful older homes, marking the end of the Kejimkujik Scenic Drive.

BEACHES
Merrymakedge
Merrymakedge is an exception among the beaches in this book; it is a freshwater beach. Located on Kejimkujik Lake within the national park this is a small sandy beach that has very warm lake water. It's a great spot for a dip if you've just completed a morning of hiking or mountain biking. It has complete facilities and is supervised.

CANOEING
Jake's Landing
Most people agree that the only way to really explore Keji is by canoe, because a large percentage of the park's area is water. From a canoe, you can observe the unique flora and fauna of this park and the Mi'kmaq petroglyphs found in a few locations along the shoreline. Lake Kejimkujik is one of the largest in Nova Scotia and is connected to a number of smaller lakes by streams and portages. As well, the Mersey River traverses Lake Kejimkujik on its way to the Atlantic.

Canoes are available for rent at Jake's Landing, near where the Mersey River enters Lake Kejimkujik. There always seem to be enough canoes for everyone, and there are a number of models to choose from, including several large ones that can accommodate adults and children. If you've never tried canoeing before, or would like your children to try it for the first time, this is a wonderful place to begin. From Jacques Landing, you can paddle up the Mersey River a fair distance. There is virtually no current and the waters are almost always calm.

More experienced canoeists will want to get out on the main lake. Kejimkujik is dotted with islands, some of which have campgrounds on them. At certain times of the year, it's quite possible to have a campground all to yourself.

A word of warning — Keji is a big, shallow lake. It can blow up into whitecaps in a matter of minutes, even on the most apparently calm day.

Always stay close to the shoreline and do not attempt open lake crossings under any conditions.

HIKING

Although this is not primarily a hiker's park, there are numerous interesting hiking trails within Keji. Most of the trails traverse woodlands or old farmlands and because of the flat terrain, you will not find breathtaking views like those in Cape Breton Highlands National Park, but more subtle things like old growth forests, gurgling brooks and rare plants and animals found only in this area of Nova Scotia. Of the trails, the following are among the best.

Hemlocks and Hardwoods Trail

Virgin forest is extremely rare in Nova Scotia or anywhere else in the east. The Hemlocks and Hardwoods Trail preserves an untouched stand of 300-year-old hemlock and white pine interspersed with maple, birch and other hardwoods. Most people who hike this trail are struck by the sheer size of the trees. Few have any idea of just how different the original Acadian mixed forest was from the predominantly softwood forests of today. On a quiet morning, parts of this trail have a definitely cathedral-like solemnity. The hermit thrush acts as nature's organist.

Mill Falls Trail

There are a number of trails that follow sections of the Mersey River. The Mill Falls trail starts behind the interpretive centre just inside the park gates, and offers a pleasant preview of Keji's highlights. It is a short trail that follows a series of short rapids and waterfalls to a picnic area. Swimmers come here to enjoy a dip in the pools at the bottom of the falls.

Mersey River Trail

This is a longer excursion along the banks of the Mersey. Portions of it pass through large grass meadows on the banks of the river. From here you can connect to other trails that will take you as far as Merrymakedge Beach or Jeremy's Bay campground.

Goldmines Trail

This is a favourite trail for children who hope that they'll rediscover the gold that was first found and mined in this area in the 1800s. This is a self-interpretive trail that leads to the old gold workings and helps give an appreciation of how well and completely nature can sometimes recover from the ravages of human activity. The realistic plywood cut-outs of miners and early pioneers can give you quite a start if you come upon them suddenly.

MOUNTAIN BIKING
Jake's Landing

Most people are not surprised that Kejimkujik is a great place to take up canoeing, but few know that it is also a good spot to learn the sport of mountain biking. Not only are there a number of gravel fire roads that are usually closed to vehicular traffic, but some of the hiking trails double as bike paths. You can rent bikes at Jake's Landing and take a 10-kilometre loop that follows the Mersey River to Jeremy's Bay campground and then back to the landing along the beautiful banks of the bay, passing a number of sand beaches along the way. There are enough bridges, boardwalks, roots, rocks, mud and narrow passages between trees to let you know why this sport is so popular, but no steep climbs or descents. For anyone eight years and up, it can be a real rush. The 19-kilometre return route to the fire tower offers a great chance to pass through several old growth forests, including a stand of sugar maple and yellow birch.

PARKS AND GREENSPACE
Pine Grove Park, Milton
The AbitibiBowater Pulp & Paper Company maintains a park in a large stand of white pine on the banks of the Mersey River between Liverpool and Milton. The company has augmented the natural beauty by planting hundreds of rhododendrons and azaleas, many developed at the Kentville Agricultural Station. In the late spring, as these shrubs enter their flowering season, the park is particularly beautiful.

WILDERNESS AREAS
Tobeatic and Shelburne River Wilderness Areas
These two contiguous Wilderness Areas forever preserve over 105,000 hectares of Nova Scotia lands from any type of development or exploitation — the largest such area in the Maritime Provinces. Straddling five counties, the Tobeatic, as the area has been called for as long as anyone can remember, has many points of entry, none of them easy. The most usual way is to start in Kejimkujik National Park by canoe and make a series of portages through to Peskowesk and Peskawa Lakes into the Shelburne River. This will take two days and several portages in excess of a kilometre, so you'll know why there won't be many people around, but it is definitely worth the effort. The Shelburne is a National Heritage River which has been used by First Nations as a major transportation route for thousands of years. A trip down the Shelburne to Lake Rossignol and then up the Mersey back to Lake Kejimkujik is the journey of a lifetime and something all Nova Scotians should attempt at least once. Over a hundred years ago American humourist Albert Bigelow Paine made this route immortal in his classic depiction of roughing it, *The Tent Dwellers*. Things have changed very little in the last century and if you really want a true wilderness experience this is the place to do it. Most of the people who take up the challenge of the Tobeatic do so on their own, but there is one company we know of that does do organized trips to the area. Hinterland Adventures (www.kayak-ingnovascotia.com) offers trips from three to twenty-one days exploring this amazing area.

ACCOMMODATIONS
There are no accommodations within Kejimkujik National Park other

than campgrounds. For those not up to camping, there are several very attractive alternatives nearby.

Whitman Inn, Route 8, Kempt, 1-800-830-3855, www.whitmaninn.com

This is a large rambling turn-of-the-century farmhouse with many of its original modest furnishings, located not far from the entrance to Kejimkujik National Park. Each of the nine rooms has a distinct theme as you can see from the Web site. The inn has an indoor pool, hot tub and sauna, which are very welcome after a day canoeing or hiking. The owners are carrying on the tradition of hands-on innkeepers who quickly make you feel at home in this restful setting. The inn offers home cooked meals and packed lunches to take with you on a hike. The Whitman is a good choice for family vacations.

Milford House, Highway 8, South Milford, 1-877-532-5751 www.milfordhouse.ca

Milford House is the oldest continually operated lodging establishment in Nova Scotia. Dating from the 1860s it is intrinsically linked to the golden age of guiding which lasted up until World War II and saw tourists from all over the globe descend on Milford House as the last bastion of civilization before entering the wilderness on hunting and fishing expeditions that sometimes lasted weeks. It was here that the iconic journey described in *The Tent Dwellers* began and ended and where Dr. Eddie Breck, the somewhat eccentric character described in that book maintained his beloved Buckshaw cottage.

Lest one believe that Milford House's best days are behind, think again. The main lodge has been rebuilt after a disastrous fire, but you would hardly know it from the reams of photographs and other memorabilia on display in the common areas and the dining hall. Accommodations are spread between a number of self-catering cabins on the shores of two small lakes and range from luxurious to fairly plain. Working fireplaces adorn most. For diversion there is canoeing, fishing, swimming, hiking or just relaxing on the porch watching for loons or otters on the lake. Milford House's motto is "Rustic, Rural, Relaxed" and it sure is all three; simply, one of the best places to stay in Nova Scotia.

Mersey River Chalets, Maitland Bridge, 1-877-667-2584, www.merseyriverchalets.ns.ca

Located just outside the entrance to Keji on a bend in the Mersey River, this fairly new establishment features large and small chalets, which are all very well designed and spacious, a lodge and something quite unusual - wigwams, which can sleep up to six.

In summer the Cascades restaurant offers good food and a great view of guess what, a cascading waterfall. There is a boardwalk that passes a number of interesting sites, canoeing, swimming, tennis and many other diversions. The developers of Mersey River Chalets are people with disabilities and they have gone out of their way to create a barrier free experience, something pretty unique in a wild setting like this.

DINING

Both the Whitman Inn and Milford House have creditable restaurants and can provide packed lunches for hikers and canoers.

M&W's Restaurant, Route 8, Kempt, (902) 682-2189

M&W are spouses Marilyn and Wayne. We're not quite sure what Wayne does, but we do know that Marilyn runs a mean little diner. On a route with few restaurants, this is a great spot for breakfast or lunch. It's about as informal as you can get - you help yourself to coffee, soda or beer from the cooler while deciding what to order. Your best bet is to ask Marilyn what she recommends. It could be a hearty sandwich with her homemade bread, fish and chips with her excellent batter, or soup made from scratch. While waiting for your order, you'll be kept amused reading the many sarcastic posters, leafing through the many gardening magazines or checking out the interesting flower garden beside the restaurant.

EVANGELINE TRAIL
Yarmouth to
Annapolis Royal

The Evangeline Trail is named for the heroine of Henry Wadsworth Longfellow's epic poem "Evangeline," which describes the travails of the Acadians and their expulsion from their homelands by the British in 1755. Starting in Yarmouth, the trail begins by traversing the largest area of Acadian settlement in the province until it reaches the beautiful Annapolis Valley, which it follows as far as Windsor. It passes through areas where the history of European settlement and agriculture in Canada began, in particular Port Royal and Annapolis Royal. The "Valley" as most Nova Scotians refer to it, is a prosperous and scenic area of farms and charming towns like Bridgetown and Wolfville. The area is noted for its many inns and fine dining, so one has little difficulty finding first-rate food and drink en route. While the trail keeps to the heart of the valley, the tourist has the choice of an alternate route that explores the sparsely settled Fundy coast.

Yarmouth (www.yarmouthonline.ca) is the largest urban centre in western Nova Scotia and has long been one of Nova Scotia's most important communities. Founded in 1761 by settlers from Massachusetts who came to occupy lands vacated by the expelled Acadians, Yarmouth quickly grew to prominence as a shipping centre. The former Massachusetts natives maintained close ties with Boston which remain to this day. Before the advent of railways and highways, Yarmouth was the gateway to Nova Scotia, as almost all traffic was north-south rather than east-west as it is today.

In the 1800s, when Yarmouth was home to one of the largest sailing fleets in the world, shipping interests made this town very prosperous. The Victorian mansions and the heirlooms they contain are the legacies of these wealthy decades.

Although the shipping industry declined, Yarmouth is still very much a busy port and fishing centre. For the visitor, there is much to explore in the Yarmouth area, including two of the province's best museums, the restored waterfront and one of the better walking tours.

On leaving Yarmouth make sure you visit the Yarmouth light and then follow the signs to Overton and Sandford. The latter is a working fishing community centred around a tiny harbour. To reach the inner harbour, fishing boats have to manoeuvre through a passage not much wider than a one-lane street. This street is crossed by the world's smallest functional drawbridge. It is a favourite spot for photographs.

With its collection of lobster pots, floats, and barrels, the sounds of mewing gulls overhead and the smell of the sea and fish, Sandford Harbour is not quite believable. But it's no Hollywood set — the fishermen here make their living on the sea. From Sandford to Port Maitland, the highway provides good views of Cape St. Mary's in the distance. At Port Maitland, there is a provincial picnic park located on the aptly named Sandy Beach.

On crossing over to Digby County, you enter the District of Clare (www.clarenovascotia.com), the largest Acadian community in the province. For more than 45 kilometres, the Evangeline Trail becomes "the longest main street in Nova Scotia," with 11 Acadian villages strung out along the highway, one blending into the next. The Acadian flag, a yellow star (Stella Maris or star of the sea) emblazoned on the French tri-colour, is in evidence everywhere, testimony to the pride that Acadians take in their identity.

Many of the Acadian settlements along the French Shore were founded after the 1755 expulsion of the Acadians. After their lands were seized by the British, many escaped deportation and moved west along the shore of the Bay of Fundy from the Annapolis Basin. Here, they were allowed to practice their religion and develop their distinctive culture, largely undisturbed by their English-speaking neighbours.

Be sure to visit Mavillette Beach and take a drive out to the tip of Cape St. Mary's, where seals can often be observed basking on the rocks. A hiking path leads from the lighthouse along the coast to Bear Cove. The lighthouse at Cape St. Mary's is a rectangular concrete structure, more functional than scenic; however, there are sweeping views of the coast in both directions.

Just before Meteghan, stop for a few minutes at Smugglers Cove Provincial Park, where a set of stairs takes you down to a beautiful sheltered cove with unusual rock formations. Meteghan is the largest community in the Clare region. It is a busy commercial fishing port with a large inshore fleet visible from the highway.

Université Sainte-Anne (www.usainteanne.ca) is the cultural centre of the Acadian community in this area. It is a French-language institution that specializes in, among other things, the instruction of French to English-speaking civil servants and others who are interested in becoming bilingual. The university also has a free Acadian genealogical service, which is used by persons from all over the world who trace their ancestry to Acadia.

St. Mary's Church, adjoining the university, is well worth a visit. This is the largest wooden church in North America. Despite its impressive size, and the interior with its painted ceiling and pewter stations of the cross, it is not intimidating or overwhelming. The church is an impressive achievement for a community of formerly modest economic resources.

At Grosses Coques (Big Clams) Beach, you can watch clam diggers at work or give it a try yourself. The bar clams that are found in this area are of gargantuan proportions.

The church at St. Bernard took more than 30 years to complete and seats nearly 1,000, which would more than accommodate every man, woman and child in the community, as well as those of the several surrounding communities. The interior of the church is somewhat austere and lacks the warmth of St. Mary's at Church Point.

Shortly after St. Bernard, at the Sissiboo River, there is an abrupt change in the landscape. The next section of this shoreline was populated by Loyalists, in particular the towns of Weymouth (www.weymouthnovascotia.com) and Digby (www.digby.ca).

Weymouth is a well-preserved and pretty village near the mouth of the Sissiboo River. The local historical society maintains genealogical records and information on the first settlers. From Weymouth to Digby, the Evangeline Trail follows St. Mary's Bay until the head of the bay, just outside Digby. At Gilberts Cove, there is a restored lighthouse where one can see views of St. Mary's Bay and Digby Neck. Just outside Digby, the Evangeline Trail and Highway 101 become one. To visit the town you must turn off the highway.

Digby was founded in 1783 by settlers who were brought to these shores by Admiral Digby. The grateful refugees were happy to name the new settlement after him. Since the 1930s, the economy has been inextricably linked to the scallop fishery and today it has the largest scallop fleet in the world. Driving into town and turning onto Water Street, you will immediately be struck by the many brightly coloured scallop draggers tied up at the government wharf. Park anywhere near the waterfront and explore on foot.

Digby and the neighbouring community of Smiths Cove have been popular tourist resorts for over a century. Sheltered beside the calm waters of Annapolis Basin, the area has a very favourable climate and a great variety of plant and bird life. The tourist tradition continues at the Digby Pines, a resort in the grand style, and a number of other inns and motels in the area. Before leaving the Digby area, take the short drive out to Point Prim, where the lighthouse guards the entrance to Digby Gut. From the lighthouse there are fine views of the cliffs on the opposite side of the channel and the uninhabited coastline between Victoria Beach and Delaps Cove. If it is calm, you can walk down to the water's edge and see how the waves boil as they wash over the basalt. Try to be here at sunset to watch the sun drop directly into the bay.

Leaving Digby you have no choice but to follow Highway 101 for a few kilometres to the Smiths Cove turnoff. This is a popular summer resort and has a variety of inns, cabins and campgrounds, all of which have emerged to take advantage of its excellent location facing the unique gap in the mountains known as Digby Gut.

Leaving Smiths Cove you rejoin Highway 101 to cross the mouth of the Bear River. An alternative is to follow the banks of the river up to the pretty town of Bear River. Whichever route you choose, just before the Bear River bridge, there is a look-off with a magnificent view of Digby Gut and the Annapolis Basin.

Crossing Bear River, exit the 101 for the communities of Deep Brook, Cornwallis and Clementsport. Cornwallis was the site of a basic training base for the Canadian Armed Forces which is now the Pearson Peacekeeping

Centre (www.peaceoperations.org). The Centre has trained over 18,000 people from over 150 countries in the skills necessary to be effective peace-keepers and helped secure Canada's reputation as a leader in this field. After the base closed the armed forces sold off many of the former base houses for extremely low prices, which attracted retirees who like the favourable climate.

Clementsport has a number of fine churches, most especially St. Edward's, which sits on a hill overlooking the Annapolis Basin. There is also a small museum and one of the oldest cemeteries in the province.

Annapolis Royal (www.annapolisroyal.com) is the oldest town in Canada. European settlement started in nearby Port Royal in 1605, and shortly thereafter centred around the mouth of the Annapolis River. The French controlled the area for over 100 years, until the English took control in 1710. Since then, Annapolis Royal has been variously a garrison town, a provincial capital and a shipping and transportation centre for Annapolis Valley products. Today, it is a quiet town with a great number of attractions, including the Historic Gardens, the oldest street in Canada, the best collection of Victorian mansions in the province and the Fort Anne National Historic Site. Annapolis Royal has been the scene of numerous North American firsts, and the birthplace of a number of British military notables. It has a collection of fine inns and restaurants, second to none in Atlantic Canada. Perhaps most surprising, despite its long and illustrious past Annapolis Royal hasn't the affected air of some tourist towns. Even at the busiest times of year, you will not be jostled off the sidewalks by throngs of visitors. Whether you are sitting on a bench at the Historic Gardens, looking out over the Acadian dykes, or wandering the grounds of Fort Anne, you can hear the wind whispering through the leaves telling you to slow down, relax and listen for the echoes of the past.

BEACHES
Mavillette Beach, just off Route 1 at Cape St. Mary's
With fine firm sand, this is the nicest and largest beach on the entire Fundy coast. Although the water is sometimes too cold for swimming, the beach is a great spot for picnicking, bird watching and walking while taking in the views of the lighthouse and fishing community at the tip of Cape St. Mary's, which rises from the northern end of the beach. A welcome recent addition is a birdwatching platform and interpretive panels. There are full facilities.

Major Point Beach, Belliveau Cove
You can reach this beach via a path that starts at the parking lot of the Acadian information centre in Belliveau Cove. Major Point Beach is a shingle beach made of wave-worn pebbles that make lovely sounds as the waves wash over them at high tide. From atop the highest point of the beach, both the basilica at Church Point and the church at St. Bernard are visible. Just behind the beach, a small chapel and cairn commemorate the site of the first Acadian cemetery in this area, dating from 1755.

BIRDING
Yarmouth Area Salt Marshes

There are 3,237 hectares of salt marshes in the Yarmouth area, by far the largest area in the province. Birders don't need to be told about the attractions of salt marshes, which provide sustenance to a wide variety of species during the spring and fall migrations. The most accessible sites are the Chebogue marsh, particularly around Arcadia, Pinkney's Point and Surettes Island, all of which can easily be visited on day trips from Yarmouth.

Brier Island

Digby Neck acts as a natural funnel, pulling fall migrants down its length to Brier Island, where they rest up for the long crossing of the Bay of Fundy. There have been more species of birds seen in this little island than anywhere else in Nova Scotia, and almost anywhere in Canada. Rarities are not unusual, including occasional European vagrants. Particularly spectacular is the hawk migration, which brings in great numbers of birds of prey. They are everywhere you look. In the fall Acadia University operates the Brier Island Bird Migration Research Station. A pelagic trip on one of the whale-watching boats can yield three species of shearwater, two types of petrels, jaegers, fulmars and even rarer oceanic wanderers. Brier Island is the one place in Nova Scotia where birders are as common as rock doves. No one asks what a spotting scope is or what it is used for. If you make only one dedicated birding stop in Nova Scotia it should be at Brier Island.

CEMETERIES
Garrison Cemetery, Annapolis Royal

This was the first cemetery in Canada. The oldest Canadian tombstone, that of one Bathiah Douglas dates from 1720, although it is known that Acadian burials took place well before then. Unfortunately for posterity, the Acadians marked their graves with wooden crosses which over time simply rotted away. Actually a part of Fort Anne, the cemetery can be entered across from the Garrison House Inn by way of an unusual turnstile in the wrought-iron fence. There is quite a mixture of headstone types to be found here; the most interesting being the early slate markers.

CYCLING
Back Roads of Yarmouth County

Yarmouth is one of the best bases in the province for cycling. The numerous fingers of land that stretch out from the coast on both sides of Yarmouth provide for a fascinating variety of day trips. Most have paved dead-end roads so there is not much traffic. Among the many possibilities is a ride out to the Yarmouth light followed by a trip to Sandford, returning via Darling Lake or around the Chebogue Peninsula or out to Pinkney's Point and back. Don't overlook the many back roads towards the interior, where you can visit such interesting places as Tusket Falls, Ellenwood Park and Deerfield.

GOLF
Clare Golf and Country Club, 423 P.F. Comeau Road, Comeauville, (902) 769-2124, www.claregolf.ca

The original nine holes were built in 1966 and a second nine opened in 1986. In a relatively short time, this course has become known throughout the province as one of the best, particularly the back nine. The course wends its way over a number of hills and dales with occasional views of St. Mary's Bay. It is always well-maintained, and it has about the longest playing season in Nova Scotia. Golf is very popular along the French Shore and this club regularly produces some of the best golfers in Atlantic Canada. It's not particularly easy to find, but if you follow the signs from Church Point or Comeauville on the Evangeline Trail you will get there.

Digby Pines, Digby, 1-800-667-4637, www.digbypines.ca

This is a resort course designed by the legendary Stanley Thompson, but you don't have to be a guest at the Digby Pines to play here. In the Pro Shop, you may notice a score card from Canadian golf great George Knudson, showing a then course record of 64. If you can get within 25 strokes of that score, you'll be doing well. This is a very hard course. The prevailing winds make it play much longer than the listed yardage of 6,146. The greens are postage stamp size and extremely hard to hold on the fly, but don't let this discourage you. This is a fun course to play and has always attracted notable celebrities, including Babe Ruth and Joe Louis. It's always in good shape and has a number of extremely well-designed holes. The green fees are very reasonable considering the fame of this course.

Annapolis Royal Golf and Country Club, on the Evangeline Trail just outside Annapolis Royal, (902) 532-2064, www.annapolisroyalgolf. com

This very short 18-hole course welcomes visitors and doesn't require advance booking, except on weekends. Most of the original nine holes overlook historic Fort Anne and Annapolis Royal as the course winds through old orchards and farmland. The newer nine, opened in 1993, is largely cut out of the woods and is not yet fully mature, but is improving rapidly. Well worth playing for the tremendous views of the historic town and Granville Ferry, across the river.

HIKING
Brier Island

Brier Island offers numerous hiking opportunities, including a coastal trail linking the two lighthouses on the island. You can pick up a map at the lodge and decide if you want to circle the entire island which can be done in a day or try a shorter route. There are numerous excellent lookoffs, some atop very high cliffs and many spots for observing wildlife. If possible try to get down to the bottom of one of the basalt cliffs where you cannot help but notice the fantastic shapes and forms of the columnar basalt. It's very similar to the more widely known formations at Giant's Causeway in

Northern Ireland. As you approach the cliffs, take great care as the rocks are very slippery. In some places the bottom part of a column has collapsed, leaving the upper part hanging seemingly in impossible defiance of gravity. It takes some courage to stand directly under one of these because your mind tells you that it must come tumbling down. Eventually it will, hopefully not when anyone's underneath. Obviously, this type of exploring is not for the little ones.

The Balancing Rock, Tiverton, Long Island, Digby County

In the first edition, we didn't recommend a hike to the Balancing Rock because of the treacherous state of the trail. However, the trail has been completely upgraded and made much safer. Now this hike is a must for anyone who has an interest in nature's marvels, and who doesn't? The Balancing Rock is a wildly improbable geological formation: a 9-metre pinnacle of rock balanced on a base of not more than a few feet square. It looks as if it should fall over at the slightest touch, and yet it still stands after, probably, thousands of years. The trail itself is about a kilometre or so each way from the Digby Neck highway just outside Tiverton, and there is parking at the trailhead. There is a small museum and tourist bureau nearby, where you can learn more about the fascinating geology of this area.

HISTORIC SITES

Fort Anne National Historic Site, Annapolis Royal, (902) 532-2321, www.pc.gc.ca/fortanne

Fort Anne is one of Canada's most important historic sites. Originally a French fort protecting the settlements of the Annapolis Basin, it was captured on two occasions by the British using New England troops. The second capture in 1710 came only after a protracted siege and a valiant defence. However, when the French flag came down, it was never to fly again over Acadia. The Treaty of Utrecht in 1713 ceded mainland Nova Scotia to the English, the fort was renamed Fort Anne and the community was called Annapolis Royal in honour of the reigning monarch. It was the headquarters of British rule in Nova Scotia until Halifax was founded in 1749.

Fort Anne was abandoned in the 1800s and fell into disrepair. A partial restoration was undertaken in the 1920s and 1930s.

On your visit, you'll find a central display building dating from the restoration period, which contains a number of interesting exhibits. These include a replica of the fort as it existed in its prime, a copy of the original 1621 Charter of Nova Scotia and a large collection of pistols and muskets. Also of note is the four-panel Fort Anne Heritage Tapestry, which depicts the four centuries of European settlement in Annapolis Royal. It was completed by a team of over 100 stitchers, including Queen Elizabeth II. The richness of colour and the texture in these panels has to be seen to be appreciated.

The rest of the fort remains largely as it was in the nineteenth century. The walls and ramparts are grassy knolls on which children love to roll and frolic and play at being soldiers. Gazing out over the Annapolis Basin from Fort Anne, one almost expects to see the masts and sails of the next invading fleet emerge from the mist.

MUSEUMS

Firefighters' Museum of Nova Scotia, 451 Main Street, Yarmouth, (902) 742-5525, www.museum.gov.ns.ca/fm

If there is one museum that children won't find tiresome, it's this one. The award-winning displays of firefighting paraphernalia, and especially the bright red fire engines, always captivate youngsters as well as adults. The children can don firemen's helmets and imagine themselves speeding to a fire, seated high in a 1933 Bickle. There is a large collection of pumpers, wagons and trucks dating back more than 100 years. Equally impressive are the ancillary collections of badges, helmets, shields and toy engines. There is also a large Halifax Fire Company banner displaying a very early representation of the Nova Scotia Coat of Arms. In terms of presentation and completeness, this is one of the finest museums in the province.

Yarmouth County Museum and Archives, 22 Collins Street, Yarmouth, (902) 742-5539, www.yarmouthcountymuseum.ednet.ns.ca

In our opinion, this is an excellent example of a county museum. For centuries, Yarmouth sea captains roamed the globe and brought back not only wealth but many interesting curiosities and souvenirs, quite a few of which have made their way into this collection. Housed in an impressive stone building that was formerly a church, the museum has many interesting items, the most noteworthy of which are the ships' paintings. Most of the vessels depicted were built, owned or wrecked in the Yarmouth area. As well, there are fine collections of Chinese export porcelain, ships' china, and Yarmouth County aboriginal artifacts. There is always something interesting on display from the extensive costume collection. The high quality of most of the items on display attests to the former wealth of this town. The most unusual item is undoubtedly the Runic stone — a mysterious rock slab with markings on it that was found near Yarmouth. Some believe the stone was inscribed by the legendary Viking wanderer, Lief Ericson, while others believe it is a modern fake. One can easily spend an hour or more exploring this extensive collection.

In 1996 the museum was bequeathed the Pelton-Fuller house next door and its contents. It is notable as the summer home of Alfred C. Fuller, the original Fuller Brush man, who was from Nova Scotia. Although he gained fame and fortune in the United States, Fuller and his wife returned to this home for many summers. It now remains largely as Mrs. Fuller left it when she last visited in 1994. Guided tours are given by museum staff during the summer.

Also a part of the museum is the Killam Brothers Shipping Office which is located on the waterfront. The name Killam is synonymous with Yarmouth business, some five generations of the family having amassed a fortune working out of this building. The museum offers guided tours of the shipping office as it was in the mid 1800s.

Art Gallery of Nova Scotia 341 Main Street, Yarmouth, (902) 749-2248 www.artgalleryofnovascotia.ca

This relatively new gallery is a branch of the main gallery in Halifax. It offers a number of permanent and travelling exhibitions throughout the year. It also offers art classes, guided tours and community based events.

O'Dell House Museum, 136 Lower St. George Street, Annapolis Royal, (902) 532-7754
Sinclair Inn Museum, 232 St. George Street, Annapolis Royal, www.annapolisheritagesociety.com

The Annapolis Royal Heritage Society operates these two museums on the town's main street. O'Dell House is a former inn and one time stage coach stop. For a brief time the Nova Scotia Pony Express used it as a base. Today it contains both exhibits and the Genealogical Archives.

Sinclair House is much older, parts of it dating from as early as 1710. It is actually a compilation of three separate buildings, all with different styles that somehow come together in surprising unity, which will hold great interest to students of architecture and building. The first Masonic meeting in Canada was held in the house in 1738. A lot has happened in Sinclair House in the last three hundred years, so it's hardly surprising that a number of residents have decided to stick around — as ghosts.

OFF THE BEATEN PATH
Yarmouth Lighthouse

A visit to the lighthouse should be on everyone's list of things to do in and around the Yarmouth area, particularly in the evening around sunset. From Yarmouth turn left at the Yarmouth Horse, a local landmark, and then turn left again on the road marked Yarmouth Bar. There is a great view of the town from the cairn on the other side of the bay that marks the first launching of a ship built here in the 1700s. The highway then travels over a breakwater lined with lobster pots and fishermen's sheds, winding its way past colourful fishing vessels, over a causeway, even passing a couple of sunken ships along the way. The lighthouse is one of the largest and most photogenic in the province. It houses a small museum with memorabilia from the area. In short, the drive to Cape Forchu, which ends at a lighthouse, has everything that has come to symbolize Nova Scotia and the sea. The sun sets over the water behind the oldest lighthouse in this area, on a site reportedly visited by Vikings a thousand years ago.

Route 340

This road cuts a swath through the forests and fields between Yarmouth and Weymouth, bypassing the French Shore. The first part of the route leaving Yarmouth is often called the Lupine Trail for the wildflowers that carpet the side of the road from late May through June. The middle portion passes through heavily forested country with occasional glimpses of pristine lakes. After Corberrie, you enter farm country, where fox and mink ranching has long been a staple of the local economy. While Route 340 is definitely a pleasant drive, it is no substitute for the coastal Evangeline Trail.

Digby Neck

Looking at your Nova Scotia road map, you will notice a long thin peninsula that extends well out into the Bay of Fundy. This is Digby Neck, though it is more like a finger than a neck. Where each joint should be, there is a passage which must be traversed by ferry, first to Long Island and then to Brier Island. There is enough to see and do on Digby Neck to warrant its own scenic trail designation, which it now has, but to most it will always be off the beaten path.

The route starts off inauspiciously just outside Digby, travelling mostly down the centre of the peninsula rather than along the shore. Centreville and Little River both have fishing wharves worth exploring, but the real beauty of the area starts at Sandy Cove. This tiny tree-lined village has one of the prettiest locations in all of Nova Scotia. A narrow gap in the basalt cliffs opens onto an almost completely circular picture-perfect cove, with a village of white houses and white churches clustered around it. There is a large fishing fleet, much of which sits high and dry on the clam flats at low tide.

On the Fundy side of the village, there is another cove with a sandy beach, where the sunsets over the water are spectacular. It was on this beach that a mysterious figure called Jerome was discovered in the 1800s. This man was apparently abandoned on the beach after having had both his legs surgically amputated. Despite living in a number of communities in the area for a great many years, Jerome couldn't or wouldn't ever reveal who he really was or how he came to be on the beach that day. It is a Nova Scotia mystery that will probably never be solved. You can learn more at www. canadianmysteries.ca/sites/jerome/accueil/indexen.html.

Next is East Ferry and the end of the mainland. As you approach the ferry dock, there is a great view of Petit Passage and the village of Tiverton across the water. A lighthouse guards the entrance to the turbulent strait. For a small price, you get what can be an exciting ferry trip to Long Island. If the tide is changing, the waters in Petit Passage can be whipped into a frenzy, and the current is so strong you might wonder if the small ferry is going to be swept right out into the open ocean. But don't worry, it hasn't happened yet.

Tiverton is a traditional fishing village with a number of buildings sitting on pilings over the water. Along with Westport on Brier Island, it is the centre for whale-watching in the Bay of Fundy. Tiverton also has a small museum-cum-tourist bureau where you can obtain more information about things to do in this area. You will see pictures of what is rapidly becoming the famous Balancing Rock of Long Island and you must take the time to visit it.

The highway on Long Island travels inland from Tiverton to Freeport, 18 kilometres away. There is an interesting trail to the shoreline from a picnic park at Central Grove.

At Freeport, another fishing community, a ferry will get you to Westport on Brier Island, which is the end of the line in more ways than one. With its brightly coloured fishing boats lined up in the water, its weather-beaten fishing shacks and the lighthouse at the mouth of the harbour, Westport is everything you expect a fishing village to be and more. It has that timeless other-worldly quality that island communities often have and it's still virtually unspoiled. It's how some of those small islands such as Monhegan off the coast of Maine must have been before the tourists arrived.

Westport was the home of Joshua Slocum who, from 1895 to 1898, became the first person to sail solo around the world. You will notice that the ferry across Petit Passage to Tiverton is named the *Joshua Slocum*, while the smaller ferry between Freeport and Westport is named for Slocum's boat, the *Spray*.

Westport is only part of what Brier Island has to offer. This is a nature-lover's paradise, and is one of the departure points for the best whale-watching along the entire east coast of North America. For birders, it's the best place in Nova Scotia and maybe all of Canada during the fall migration. The entire island is almost encircled by coastal hiking trails, which also offer mountain-biking opportunities. Rockhounds are drawn to the unusual basalt formations as well as the chance to find agates, jasper and amethyst. For the photographer, there are three lighthouses, including Brier Island light, one of the prettiest in the province.

Brier Island is the type of place you may think you are going to visit for a day and end up staying a week. Luckily, there are a number of good hostelries and restaurants to accommodate you.

Bear River, www.bearriver.ca

This delightful community is often called the Switzerland of Nova Scotia. This may be a bit of an exaggeration, but from the centre of town, where you will find numerous old buildings sitting on pilings over the river, there is a maze of streets that wind up the steep hills surrounding the town on all sides. Exploring these side roads, you'll come across one vista after another of forested hillsides dotted with churches and large older houses. From the bridge in Bear River, the view of the Baptist church, with its rounded cupola peering through the trees, is one example. It is particularly pretty in the fall.

The Tourist Bureau is located inside a large windmill and nearby is a riverfront boardwalk and nice picnic area.

In the nineteenth century, Bear River was a jumping-off point for hunting and fishing trips to the interior, and Bear River guides were famous throughout the northeast. Today, it is known for artists and craftspeople who have settled here in considerable numbers and given the place a very laid-back and relaxed atmosphere.

There are several ways of getting to Bear River. The easiest is to go straight from Smiths Cove rather than crossing the bridge on Highway 101. When leaving Bear River to return to the Evangeline Trail, ask for directions for the Deep Brook road, which will take you back on one of the most scenic side roads in the province.

PARKS AND GREENSPACE

Smugglers Cove Park, Meteghan

Smugglers Cove Park is well worth a visit. A wooden staircase descends a steep bank to a small protected cove with interesting rock formations and a sea cave where, for many generations, smugglers stored their illicit goods before distributing them throughout the province.

Historic Gardens, 441 St. George Street, Annapolis Royal, (902) 532-7018, www.historicgardens.com

This is one of the Evangeline Trail's most popular attractions and from its appearance you would never guess that the Historic Gardens have been in existence only since 1981. A number of mature specimen trees were preserved when the gardens were created to provide shade and a sense of age. There are a variety of gardens centred around various historic themes, including a garden as it would have existed in the early colonial days, a Victorian garden and a knot garden. The rose garden contains specimens dating from medieval times. Perhaps the nicest part of the garden is that which overlooks the small marsh and Acadian dyke. A short trail leads around the marsh with lovely views back to the gardens. There is a very good bakery, as well as a gift shop.

The Historic Gardens is a place of serenity and quiet peace. It has a calming affect on all who visit, so if you are perhaps a bit frazzled and uptight, as vacationers can sometimes get, make sure to include a stop here in your itinerary.

SPECIAL EVENTS

Le Festival Acadien de Clare, Clare Municipality, www.festivalacadiendeclare.ca

Held in early August this is Nova Scotia's largest Acadian festival and Canada's oldest. The many contests and tournaments have a French flair, and the festival is a great opportunity to sample Acadian cuisine and hear some great music. Believe us, the Acadians know how to have a good time and their joie de vive is contagious. The highlight is undoubtedly the *fais dodo en Acadie*, which brings together Cajun musicians from Louisiana to reunite with their Acadian brethren in an evening of song and celebration.

SPECIAL INTEREST

Upper Clements Theme Park, Upper Clements, 1-888-248-4567, www.upperclementsparks.com

When the province of Nova Scotia decided to get into the theme park business a number of years ago, there were quite a few sceptics. The decision to compete with the likes of the Disney Corporation and Busch Gardens, with the taxpayers' money, was not greeted with enthusiasm in too many circles except, perhaps, in the Annapolis Valley. Many wondered why the site was so far from any major centre. After all, only a few people outside Annapolis County had ever heard of Upper Clements.

Unfortunately, at least for the present, it appears that the nay-sayers were correct. The park has not been the viable financial enterprise that the promoters hoped it would be, although it has certainly provided a needed boost to the economy of the immediate area. It is now run by a private company, which is making every effort to keep it open.

The criticism of the park is somewhat unfortunate, as it has undoubtedly affected many Nova Scotians' and Maritimers' attitudes and caused them to stay away. This is a mistake. Although the park is not about to put Disneyland out of business, it is worth a family visit.

Located on a site overlooking the Annapolis Basin, the park is centred around a small lake. As much natural vegetation as possible has been retained by the planners so that the landscape is authentically natural.

There are many familiar attractions such as bumper cars, boats and an attractive carousel, some creative playgrounds and a number of ongoing activities such as face painting and juggling. For adults, there are craft shops featuring the artisans and their work. Clowns, magicians, jugglers, minstrels and other assorted characters wander through the grounds. Folk dancers, square dancers and other acts appear regularly on an outdoor stage.

There are two very interesting rides at the park: the flume, which is a water ride aboard a hollowed out log, and the tree topper, a roller coaster built among the tall trees. Built entirely out of wood, the latter is reminiscent of a turn-of-the-century structure. Although this certainly is not the scariest or longest of roller coasters, its old-fashioned authenticity gives it a special touch.

All in all, Upper Clements Park is an interesting and enjoyable place to take the family.

WALKING TOURS

Yarmouth

Yarmouth's Sea Captains' Homes and Mercantile Heritage brochure is available as a map from the tourist bureau. The highlights of the tour are the many fine nineteenth-century mansions that show several architectural styles, including Empire, Classic Revival, Queen Anne Revival, Gothic Revival and Georgian. Perhaps the most interesting is the former home of Alfred Fuller, the founder of the Fuller Brush Company, which is the ultimate Gothic Revival house. The tour also visits Killam Wharf, where you have a fine view of the busy Yarmouth waterfront. This is a most enjoyable walk and the best way to visit this historical community.

Digby

A fire in 1899 destroyed much of Digby's core area and what's left is not particularly attractive. What makes a walking tour in Digby interesting is the waterfront. You can obtain a pamphlet listing the main sites of Digby from the tourist bureau. Across the harbour, you can enjoy an unimpeded view of the scallop fleet before proceeding through the downtown core and then out onto the wharf, where you might see scallops or fish being unloaded. This is one of the busiest and most colourful wharfs in Nova Scotia. From here, you have a fine view of the town on the one side and the Digby Pines Golf Resort on the other. On the way back to your car, consider going via Queen Street, passing Trinity Church and the Old Courthouse.

Annapolis Royal
All of the attractions in Annapolis Royal can be comfortably visited on foot. When you pick up a copy of the official walking tour at the tourist bureau, you will notice that St. George Street curves in an arc around the waterfront. The best place to park is the Historic Gardens. From here, you can strike out and see the sites, which include beautiful Victorian mansions, some of the oldest wooden houses in Canada, Fort Anne, Garrison Cemetery, the Courthouse and a whipping tree. A boardwalk, a public wharf and a couple of museums are further down on the waterfront. There are also a number of good restaurants and shops to occupy your time. With stops, you will have little trouble filling the better part of a day exploring this historic village.

WHALE-WATCHING
Digby Neck
The warm Gulf Stream water colliding with the cold outflow from the Bay of Fundy, combined with the tremendous tidal influence on the waters in this area, produces some of the most plankton-rich waters in the world. This attracts whales, particularly baleen whales — the largest animals on earth. From the spring to late fall, whale-watching cruises head out into the Bay of Fundy on a daily basis from Tiverton and Westport. Seeing whales is a virtual certainty because of the numbers that congregate in the bay throughout the warmer months. Often seen are humpbacks, fin whales (second in size only to the blue whales) and right whales, the world's rarest whale. Smaller minke and pilot whales, along with several species of porpoises and dolphins, are commonplace. As a bonus, you are bound to see hundreds of pelagic sea birds as well as puffins.

The cruises from Westport are on larger vessels, including the *Cetacean Search*, run by the Brier Island Oceanographic Study Research Group, which has been collecting data on whales for over 25 years. The Tiverton cruises use smaller boats, including Zodiacs, which provide a different type of encounter. Whichever you choose, you can be assured that your odds of getting close to these magnificent creatures are as good as anywhere in eastern North America. Whale-watching off Digby Neck should be one of the highlights of your Nova Scotia vacation.

It's a good idea to make reservations well in advance, especially during the summer months, and some require them at all times. The following is a list of some of the operators: Brier Island Whale and Seabird Cruises, Westport, 1-800-656-3660, www.brierislandwhalewatch.com; Petite Passage Whale Watch, East Ferry, (902) 834-2229, www.ppww.ca (closest to Digby — no ferries to take); Freeport Whale and Seabird Tours, Long Island, 1-866-866-8797; Pirate's Cove Whale Cruises, Tiverton, 1-888-480-0004, www.piratescove.ca; and Ocean Explorations, Tiverton, (902) 839-2417, 1-877-654-2341, www.oceanexplorations.ca (Zodiacs).

ACCOMMODATIONS

The Yarmouth area, despite having an abundance of great Victorian buildings, really doesn't have any great inns that we have visited. There are some good B&Bs and a lot of pretty ordinary hotels and motels. It's too bad because Yarmouth does have a lot to offer.

L'Auberge Au Havre du Capitaine, Highway 1, Meteghan River, (902) 769-2001, www.havreducapitaine.ca

The French Shore has always had a shortage of good accommodations, but the recent improvements at Au Havre du Capitaine have helped remedy the situation. Located in a large old manor house that has a modern addition, the manor is located in the heart of Acadian Nova Scotia and is a good base for exploring the area. The rooms are well-appointed with a combination of antiques and good quality reproductions. The bathrooms are modern and some have Jacuzzis. The atmosphere is very laid-back and informal, much the Acadian way, with a generous dose of genuine hospitality. The dining room is the best for many miles around. Prices are quite reasonable.

Baie Ste-Marie Ocean Front Cottages, New Edinburgh, 1-866-769-0797, www.nsoceanfrontcottages.com

These four-and-a-half-star cottages are among the most beautifully sited in Nova Scotia. Owners Jacques and Anna Doucet picked an ideal spot on a bluff overlooking the mouth the Sissiboo River where it drains into St. Mary's Bay, or Baie Ste-Marie in French. Each cottage has an all-glass front rising to cathedral ceilings so the visitor has a panorama of the Bay and distant Digby neck. The list of amenities in these two-bedroom (one a large loft) cottages is amazing — Jacuzzi, dishwasher, washer, dryer, barbecue, gas fireplace, movies, satellite TV, polished stone floors and countertops and even binoculars to view the extensive bird life on the flats. Designed for longer-term stays, you simply cannot find a better base from which to explore the Acadian/Clare region or lower Annapolis Valley. Since there are only three cottages, you will need to reserve well in advance.

Brier Island Lodge, Westport, 1-800-662-8355, www.brierisland.com

Brier Island Lodge has a spectacular view of Westport and Grand Passage from its location high on a bluff on the northern side of town. Originally a small lodge with a good restaurant, a new wing has been added, which has some of the most comfortable units you'll find anywhere in Nova Scotia.

The view from the second-storey rooms is worth the price alone; the sunrises are especially notable. Several of the rooms have Jacuzzis. You can sit in them and watch the fishing boats go by. While Jacuzzis might seem a bit out of place on Brier Island, your legs take a pounding on those whale-watching cruises. Hiking trails to two lighthouses start right from the back of the property. Brier Island Lodge has the type of informal comfort that may entice you to stay much longer than you planned.

Digby Pines Golf Resort, Digby, 1-877-375-6343, www.digbypines.ca

The Pines is almost certainly Nova Scotia's finest resort. It is situated on a bluff overlooking the Annapolis Basin and the town of Digby, and consists of a large attractive stuccoed main lodge topped with a copper turret surrounded by 31 one- and two-bedroom cottages. Many of the rooms in the main lodge and some of the cottages offer spectacular views of the basin. The cottages are our favourites, especially those located furthest from the main lodge. Each cottage has its own sitting room with a stone fireplace, which the staff lay with kindling and paper each day.

The resort has an abundance of facilities, including its own 18-hole golf course, tennis courts, a large deep swimming pool surrounded by white parched walls that reflect the sun's rays throughout the sunbathing area, somewhat like a Roman bath, a health club with modern facilities, hiking trails, volley ball, croquet, shuffleboard and numerous other activities. Service is friendly and courteous and not in the least intimidating.

The main dining room features a bounteous breakfast buffet and gourmet dinners with an emphasis on Nova Scotia specialties such as salmon, lamb and scallops.

The Pines offers packages for the family, golfers and whale watchers. Whether one is strolling around the beautifully manicured grounds or sitting at the patio bar overlooking the Basin watching the scallop fleet depart for the open seas, this is a beautiful location. The Pines is a great base to use for exploring the many natural and manmade attractions of the lower Annapolis Valley, although it is certainly not inexpensive.

Harbourview Inn, Smiths Cove, 1-877-449-0705, www.theharbourviewinn.com

Unlike many other Nova Scotia hostelries, the Harbourview Inn was built and has always functioned as an inn. Located in a very scenic setting overlooking the Annapolis Basin, it has a variety of rooms and suites. It also has a pool and tennis court. This is a very popular place for touring cyclists. The Web site lets you view all rooms and compare prices.

ANNAPOLIS ROYAL

Annapolis Royal has so many good places to stay for a town of less than a thousand people that it is an embarrassment of riches. It's really too bad that some of them couldn't be teleported to Yarmouth, Sydney or even Halifax. It's really hard to choose between the four choices below.

Queen Anne Inn, 494 St. George Street, Annapolis Royal, 1-877-536-0403, www.queenanneinn.ns.ca
This restored mansion on historic St. George Street is well-furnished with some impressive antiques. The large bedrooms and bathrooms make you feel like you're staying in the mansion that this place once was. There are really gorgeous shots of all the rooms on the Web site. Full breakfast included.

Hillsdale House, 519 St. George Street, 1-877-839-2821, www.hillsdalehouseinn.ca
Right across the street from the Queen Anne and equally well-furnished, Hillsdale House has a wonderful carved fireplace in the dining room. The rooms are quite spacious with large bathrooms. A full breakfast is included in the price. Hillsdale House also has extensive grounds that run down to the river. The Hillsdale House once entertained George V so it can rightfully call itself "fit for a King".

Garrison House Inn, 350 St. George Street, (902) 532-5750, www.garrisonhouse.ca
The oldest of the Annapolis Royal inns and among the smallest, this establishment overlooks Fort Anne. Try to get a room overlooking the cemetery — you might get to see one of the ghosts that are said to walk the grounds at night. The Garrison House is also noted for its excellent dining room.

Bread and Roses, 82 Victoria Street, 1-888-889-0551, www.breadandroses.ns.ca
This differs from the other Annapolis Royal mansions in that it is made of brick. It is a beautifully designed and furnished house with nine guest rooms, all of which you can view on the Web site. It also has a nice garden.

DINING

Austrian Inn, Route 1, Yarmouth, (902) 742-6202
One of only a few German restaurants in Nova Scotia, the Austrian Inn on the outskirts of Yarmouth is worth checking out. The menu, besides offering the expected German and Austrian fare, also has an extensive selection of Nova Scotia seafood dishes. The portions are ample and the service is efficient and pleasant. The wine list is not extensive, but pricewise in keeping with the menu.

Rudder's Seafood Restaurant and Brew Pub, 96 Water Street, Yarmouth, (902) 742-7311, www.ruddersbrewpub.com
Rudder's is designed to blatantly appeal to the tourist market, but it doesn't let that stand in the way of serving pretty good food. The location on the waterfront is the best in town and the micro-brewery is putting out some very fine products.

Capeview Restaurant, Mavillette Beach, (902) 645-2519

The Capeview has a marvellous location overlooking beautiful Mavillette Beach. It has really good rappie pie — crusty, with lots of chicken in it — as well as excellent fish and chips. The fish is usually flounder or haddock done in a very light batter. This is a good lunch stop.

Chez Christophe, 2665 Highway 1, Grosses Coques (902) 837- 5817, www.chezchristophe.ca

You would never guess that in this modest white farmhouse you will find the best Acadian cooking in the province. Paul Comeau opened this place in 1996 just to serve the small local community, but it didn't take long for word of his amazing prowess with traditional Acadian dishes to spread. The atmosphere is not that much different than dropping into someone's home; in fact it was known as Chez Christophe for Paul's grandfather long before it was a restaurant. If you're lucky there may well be some Acadian music on tap to make this a truly memorable experience.

Brier Island Lodge, Westport, 1-800-662-8355, www.brierisland.com

The view from one of the four solarium tables at the Brier Island Lodge is about the best of any restaurant in the province. Chances are the seafood you order was caught by one of the fishing boats you can see from your table. The cooking is no letdown either, particularly the fresh fish. Try whatever is freshly caught and it will be prepared to perfection, definitely not overcooked. Also, well worth trying are the fishcakes or the smoked fish dinner. This is the only place we have ever seen periwinkles on the menu. The vegetables and desserts are a bit of an afterthought.

The Annapolis Room, Digby Pines Golf Resort, Digby, 1-800-667-4637, www.digbypines.ca

Over the years the Pines' principal dining room has had its ups and downs, but under new management this seems to be an up period. The Annapolis Room offers gourmet dining in a grand dining room befitting a resort of this calibre. Appetizers of solomon gundy, homemade paté and Nova Scotia smoked salmon are exquisite. The main courses feature salmon, lamb, scallops and other traditional Nova Scotia fare, as well as a sampling of poultry, pork and beef dishes. The desserts range from simple sorbets to some amazing creations with chocolate. All the courses are presented in an eye-appealing manner on attractive china. The service, mostly by summer students, is friendly and attentive, although could perhaps be more knowledgeable. The wine list is extensive by Nova Scotia standards and has a fair amount of variety. As one might expect, it is expensive. The Pines offers an excellent breakfast buffet which, along with the traditional fare of eggs Benedict, fresh fruit, cereals, etc., sometimes includes such unusual items as smoked fish cakes and finnan haddie.

Boardwalk Café, 40 Water Street, Digby, (902) 245-5497, www.boardwalkcafe.netfirms.com
Overlooking Digby Harbour and the Boardwalk, this down-home kitchen offers Digby's famous scallops as fresh as you will find anywhere. Flash-fried, tender and succulent, these are the best scallops that we have eaten in Digby or just about anywhere. The proprietor specializes in home cooking and baking, making this a great spot for lunch or dinner overlooking Digby's picturesque wharf and scallop fleet.

Garrison House, 350 George Street, Annapolis Royal, (902) 532-5750, www.garrisonhouse.ca
The dining room of the Garrison House Inn is spread through three small rooms, each of which offers an intimate place to dine. Chef Pat Redgrave places his emphasis on fresh local ingredients and the results are apparent on the diner's plate. Fish, pasta and pizza are the mainstays, accompanied by a great variety of vegetables. A recent dinner included beet greens, two types of garden tomatoes, green and yellow beans, cauliflower, broccoli and zucchini as accompaniments! The grilled flounder is as good as this simple dish can be. The desserts aren't disappointing, particularly the pies, which have flaky, tasty crusts, so often lacking in restaurant offerings. There is an extensive wine list featuring plenty of Nova Scotia selections. Prices are pleasantly moderate for the quality of the food and the presentation.

EVANGELINE TRAIL
Annapolis Royal to Halifax

From Annapolis Royal to Halifax, the Evangeline Trail traverses the Annapolis Valley, site of Canada's earliest farming communities. The landscape is decidedly pastoral and peaceful as Route 1 follows the course of the Annapolis River, winding its way between the North and South mountains. These "mountains" are really extended ridges that run the length of the valley from the mouth of the river at Annapolis Royal to Grand Pré, just past Wolfville. Between them, there is some of the richest agricultural land in Canada, where fruit, vegetable, dairy and grain farms make this the breadbasket of Nova Scotia.

Leaving Annapolis Royal, you cross the mouth of the Annapolis River via a causeway on which the Annapolis Tidal Generating Station is located, one of only three in the world. The visitors' centre explains how the tides are harnessed to produce electricity, and identifies possible future sites for development of a much larger tidal project. Recently, Nova Scotia embarked on a program permitting private enterprises to try to demonstrate that generating power on a massive scale from the tides of the Bay of Fundy could be feasible. If you have an interest in alternate energy sources it is definitely worth a stop.

Just past the causeway, make the short detour to the Habitation, the actual site of the first European settlement in this area in 1605. Along the way, you'll pass through Granville Ferry, which, like neighbouring Annapolis Royal, has many elegant old homes, plus a great view of Fort Anne and the Annapolis Royal waterfront across the river. After visiting the Habitation, you have the choice of a coastal detour to Victoria Beach, or directly rejoining the Evangeline Trail.

Near the mouth of the Annapolis River the route passes some of the oldest farms in Canada. Although little trace of the original Acadian homesteads remains, the dykes that hold back the sea and the river are a lasting legacy from the first settlers. The churches and large homes in the area date from the arrival of the New England Planters in the late 1700s. At Granville Centre, look for an unusual octagonal barn. Also keep an eye open for oxen, which are still occasionally used in the fields here. Bridgetown (www.town.bridgetown.ns.ca) is the quintessential Annapolis Valley town with its tree-lined streets, well-tended gardens, beautiful homes and elegant churches. It also has a riverfront park where you can fish for striped bass and shad, or launch a canoe. The commercial area on Queen Street contains a number of fine brick buildings. The Cyprus Walk booklet will take you past all the major attractions, including the James House Museum and Tea Room, which is over 160 years old.

Continuing on Route 1, you will soon come to Middleton (www.discovermiddleton.ca), which calls itself the "Heart of the Valley." Sites to look for include the old Trinity Church, which dates from 1791, one of three operational water clocks in North America and the MacDonald Museum, located in an old red brick school. Riverside Park offers a chance to walk along the banks of the Annapolis River or picnic under the shade of some fine old maples.

From Middleton to Kentville, the Evangeline Trail passes through an area of prosperous farms and tidy villages. Roadside farm markets offer a veritable cornucopia of produce, especially in August and September. Near Berwick (www.town.berwick.ns.ca), you will begin to notice apple and pear orchards - the most famous products of the Annapolis Valley. At Kingston there is a turnoff for CFB Greenwood, one of Canada's largest air bases. Low-flying Aurora surveillance trackers are a common sight in this area. As you approach Kentville (www.town.kentville.ns.ca), the landscape becomes quite urbanized with industrial and residential areas. Although the drive is pleasant, there is not much reason for stopping until reaching the town, the largest urban centre between Yarmouth and Halifax.

Kentville was named for Queen Victoria's father, the Duke of Kent, who was a visitor here in the early 1800s. A walking tour will give you a good sense of the town's highlights. Also of interest are the grounds of the Agricultural Station and the 7 kilometre Rails to Trails which runs from one end of town to the other.

From here, after passing through the shopping centres of New Minas and the pastoral community of Greenwich, it is a short distance to Wolfville (www.wolfville.ca).

As the home of Acadia University (www.acadiau.ca), Wolfville, like many university towns, combines an air of refinement and sophistication with vitality and perhaps an overlay of zaniness. The melding of education and the laid-back atmosphere of a small town has worked well for this community.

Founded by New England Planters who moved into the rich agricultural lands that had been cleared and developed by the Acadians 150 years earlier, Wolfville has always been a prosperous town. This is evident in its many fine homes, gardens and tree-lined streets. It also has the good fortune of having one of the best climates in the province, being free of the chilling influence of the Atlantic. Wolfville is an excellent base from which to tour the Annapolis Valley and explore the many interesting sites along the Fundy coast. It has an abundant supply of inns and some very high calibre restaurants. There is no better time to visit the Wolfville area than late September and early October, when the harvest is at its peak and the days are clear and warm. It is truly a season of "mists and mellow fruitfulness."

Just a few miles east of Wolfville is Grand Pré, famous worldwide as the site of the deportation of the Acadians by the British in 1755. After visiting Grand Pré National Historic Site, return to the Evangeline Trail, but do not follow it. Instead, cross the road and drive up the hill to the beautiful Covenanters' Church. This was one of the first churches built by the Planters. Its clean symmetrical lines and tall spire make it one of the prettiest churches in all of Canada.

Returning again to the crossroads, you will see a large house on a hill to your right. This was the boyhood home of Robert Borden, Canada's Prime Minister from 1911 through World War I. He was the third Nova Scotian to occupy that post and perhaps its most notable. Continuing on the Evangeline Trail, you must travel on Highway 101 to cross the mouth of the Gaspereau River. On the other side, be sure to turn off to Avonport to continue on the scenic route. You will soon arrive at Hantsport (www.hantsportnovascotia.com), a small tree-lined village that once was the major port for this entire area. A visit to the Marine Room in Churchill House, the town's museum, will provide surprising details of the magnitude of the ventures carried on from this small town. Large ships still call at Hantsport to pick up lumber, gypsum and produce. Heading out of town, look for the monument to William Hall, the first black person as well as the first Canadian to receive the Victoria Cross. He was a native of Hantsport and his heroics during the Indian mutiny earned him this prestigious honour.

From Hantsport, the Evangeline Trail winds by farms and orchards until crossing the Avon River, where you enter the old town of Windsor (www.townofwindsor.ns.ca). Originally called Piziquid, Windsor later became an important British outpost with the establishment of Fort Edward. It was to Windsor that instructions to expel the Acadians were sent by Governor Lawrence in Halifax, and much of the planning and direction for that expulsion was done there. Today, all that remains of the fort is the blockhouse, which is worth a visit, if only for the fine views from the top of the hill.

Up until recent years, Windsor had a long and prosperous history as a shipping and later a textile manufacturing community. It is the site of Canada's oldest private school, King's-Edgehill School (www.kes.ns.ca). As well, it has a viable claim to be the home of the great Canadian sport of hockey. Long before players took to the ice in Kingston, Ontario, and other places that also claim the birthright, British officers were playing a version of the game on the ponds around Fort Edward. The town was also the home of William Chandler Haliburton, Nova Scotia's famous author, creator of Sam Slick. Haliburton's home is now a museum and definitely worth a visit. Also, be sure not to miss Shand House. Finally, as if that wasn't enough, check out the giant pumpkins at Howard Dill's farm just outside town.

From Windsor, the traveller has two choices — either continue to Halifax via the Evangeline Trail or pick up the Glooscap Trail and explore the Fundy shoreline. If you are going to Halifax, the major feature en route is the Uniacke Estate Museum Park in Mount Uniacke. After stopping here, it is easier to reach Halifax by way of Highway 101 rather than continuing on Route 1, which passes through suburbs and strip malls.

BEACHES
Scots Bay, Route 358, King's County
True beaches are extremely rare along the Fundy coast, so Scots Bay is an

exception. A long arc of gravel and sandstone, too cold for swimming, this is a great beach for explorers. Rockhounds will want to look for the agates that are quite common here - look in the small streams that cross the beach for plain-looking stones that show their true colours when wet. The children will want to check out the mudflats and tidal pools that are exposed at low tide. Driftwood aficionados can do well here, as Cape Split extends like an arm across the mouth of the Minas Basin, capturing whatever flotsam heads that way. All told, this beach is a nice surprise and a good place to cool off if you've taken the long hike to Cape Split and back.

Evangeline Beach, Grand Pré

Evangeline Beach is really two beaches. At high tide, the shore is gravelly and the water cold, muddy and uninviting. At low tide, the water's edge has receded in some places by almost a half-mile. To get to the water, you have to walk through the mud, which squishes between your toes like putty. Once you get over the initial squeamishness, it's fun. When the tide turns, it comes in at a pace that is almost as fast as you can walk. On a warm day, the mud flats heat up the water so that by the time the tide is all the way in, you are covered in mud and silt, and everything you have on is stained red, but you will have enjoyed the Bay of Fundy at its warmest. All in all, it's not your ordinary day at the beach.

BIRDING

Robie Tufts Nature Centre, Wolfville,
www.wolfville.ca/robie-tufts-nature-centre

The Tufts Nature Centre is a tribute to Nova Scotia's foremost ornithologist, author of the definitive *Birds of Nova Scotia*, and former Wolfville resident, Robie Tufts (1884–1982). This is a living interpretive centre at the site of a large chimney stack where chimney swifts have made their home. Every summer evening at dusk, the birds create an aerobatic spectacle as they funnel their way into the chimney for their nightly roosting spots. Like whale-watching, it is something you have to see to appreciate. It is just another one of nature's spectacles. Birders can observe a similar phenomenon in Middleton, where the chimney at the old high school has an even larger swift colony.

Evangeline Beach, Grand Pré

Every August, hundreds of thousands of sandpipers and other shorebirds descend on the mud flats of the upper reaches of the Bay of Fundy to fatten up before making the long migration south. There is no better spot to observe the fall migration of these birds than Evangeline Beach, not far from Grand Pré. The best time to observe them is at the mid-point between high and low tides, when there is a sufficient area of the mud flats exposed to make the birds easy to find, but not so much that they become lost in the miles of open mud flats. If you've never experienced the thrill of seeing 20,000 birds on the wing, swooping and soaring almost as if they were one, then you should visit Evangeline Beach. By far the majority of the birds are peeps — the smallest types of sandpiper — but there are also thousands of semipalmated plovers, black-bellied plovers, ruddy turnstones, sanderlings and others. There is also a good chance to see peregrine falcons, which capitalize on the abundance of available prey.

On the way to Evangeline Beach, you pass through the dyke lands of Grand Pré, where marsh harriers, red-tailed hawks and other birds of prey are common.

CANOEING
Annapolis River
A one- or two-day excursion without portages along Canada's oldest settled waterway makes for a very relaxing trip. It is not difficult to evoke images of the Acadians as one paddles alongside their ancient dykes on this usually tranquil river. There is good fishing for shad, striped bass and trout. There are many places to put in or take out. The Annapolis County Web site is an excellent resource for planning a trip on the Annapolis River, as it contains detailed descriptions of the river and what you might expect to see and experience.

CEMETERIES
The Old Burying Ground, Main Street, Wolfville, http://ees.acadiau.ca/content/fieldtrips/ft10.htm
Wolfville has one of the best-preserved pioneer cemeteries in the province. Many of the New England Planters who took over Acadian lands are buried here, including the town's founder, Elijah DeWolfe. The stones feature a number of very good and well-preserved examples of the work of the anonymous Horton carver, including many angel heads. The burying ground has a directory to the grave sites to assist those looking for specific names or wanting to trace family roots.

CYCLING
Wolfville Area
This area is one of the most popular cycling destinations in the province. There are hundreds of miles of paved roads that criss-cross the Annapolis Valley between Annapolis Royal and Wolfville. With its many fine inns and restaurants, Wolfville is a great base for day trips to Grand Pré, Cape Split and other destinations on the Fundy coast. Several tour companies offer guided and self-guided tours of the Valley.

GOLF
Eden Golf Club, Route 201, Paradise, (902) 665-2319, www.edengolf.ca
With a name like Eden in a place called Paradise, you would expect to shoot a great score here and you just might. This is one of the prettiest and best-maintained courses in the province. The soil is fertile and well-drained, making for a green course that is easy on the eyes and relaxing to play. It is also a very friendly course that is happy to accept visiting green fees.

Paragon Golf Club, Evangeline Trail, Kingston, 1-877-414-2554, www.paragongolf.ca
One of Nova Scotia's lesser-known 18-hole layouts, Paragon deserves more publicity. It is a full-length course set amid pine trees in the central Annapolis Valley. The sandy soil ensures good drainage and the course is always in good condition, being among the first courses in the province to open in the spring. Most of the holes are straightforward, but some on the back nine, which lies in a small pine valley, are exceptional and may remind seasoned golfers of the sand country courses in North Carolina.

Berwick Heights Golf Club, Route 221, King's County, 1-902-847-9000, www.berwickheightsgolf.com
This is the Annapolis Valley's newest 18-hole layout located not far from Berwick, Apple Capital of Canada. Nestled not far from the flanks of North Mountain the course has many of the fine views and pastoral landscapes that make Annapolis Valley golf a unique experience. Approaching the large clubhouse you can be excused for thinking that this is a wide open course, but first looks are deceiving. While there are a number of holes that have little trouble, most are cut from the mixed hardwood forests that are a feature of the valley. Although only 6065 yards from the whites, this is a tough course. Most of the par fours are tight and the greens, subtly crowned in many cases, are difficult to hold. The starting four holes are especially challenging, including the 193 yard fourth which requires a long straight uphill shot over a ravine to a well trapped green. Generally not crowded and very reasonably priced, Berwick Heights Golf Club is a good addition to the already-excellent Annapolis Valley golf experience.

Eagle Crest Golf Course, Centreville, (902) 679-3033, www.eaglecrestgolfcourse.com
This is one of the province's newest courses, the front nine designed and built by a farmer on his own land in 1994, the back nine on acquired land in 1999. While the front is relatively flat and wide open, the back nine winds its way up and over a series of hills and dales dotted with a number of ball-hungry ponds. The scenery on this nine is very pleasant. This is a daily-fee operation that is quite reasonably priced and much easier to get on than other busy Annapolis Valley courses.

Ken-Wo Golf Course, New Minas, (902) 681-5388, www.ken-wo.com
Ken-Wo lies halfway between Kentville and Wolfville, hence its name. One of the valley's premier courses, Ken-Wo first opened in 1921 and has the look of a stately, mature course. It starts off relatively easy and gets progressively harder. The last five holes are among the toughest finishing holes in the province. Ken-Wo is a very popular course which has played host to a number of national and provincial championships. It is pretty well mandatory that you book a tee time in advance. The Web site has hole-by-hole pictures of the course.

Avon Valley Golf Club, Falmouth, (902) 798-2673,
www.avonvalleygolf.com
Set in the rolling farmland just outside Windsor, Avon Valley has a pastoral setting, winding its way through orchards, fields and working farms. The 18-hole layout is not particularly difficult and is well-suited to the bump and run game. The course is usually in very good condition, particularly in the late spring, when some of the Halifax area courses are still soggy and plagued by black flies. It's not so easy to find, so you should probably ask for directions in Windsor.

HIKING

Delaps Cove Wilderness Trails, www.annapoliscounty.ns.ca/
recreation/parksandtrails/delapscove.html
These trails provide a unique opportunity to hike the basalt shores and cliffs of the Bay of Fundy. To find the trails, follow the highway map towards Delaps Cove on the Fundy side of the North Mountain. Just after the sign for Delaps Cove, when the highway veers sharply right, keep straight onto a dirt road and follow it for 2 kilometres to the parking lot.

There are two circular trails joined by another trail — something like a barbell. Most people hike the first loop, the Bohaker Trail. This starts out in the woods and makes its way quickly to the rocky shore, where it follows the coast. The trail gets progressively higher until it reaches a small driftwood-choked cove. A tiny stream tumbles over the edge of the basalt, forming ribbon-like falls. You can make your way down to the cove via a natural set of basalt stairs, or you can stand on the lip at the top of the falls. From here, the trail follows the stream a short distance before returning in a loop to the parking lot. After visiting the falls, you can continue for 2 kilometres to Charlie's Trail, which leads to a series of look-offs. The extra effort is worth it if the bay is not foggy.

If you hike only the Bohaker loop, you can do it in a half hour, but allow double that to explore. The trails are well-marked and maintained. There was once a thriving community in this area, but you would not know it now as the forests have completely reclaimed the farmlands.

Kentville Ravine, Atlantic Food and Horticulture Research Centre
While a visit to the agricultural centre is always worthwhile when the rhododendrons and azaleas are in bloom, many aren't aware that almost any time of year is a great time to hike the Kentville Ravine trail that starts at the centre. There are signs indicating the trailhead in the parking lot. The trail begins by making a steep descent down a ravine to a clear stream that meanders between some massive old growth hemlocks. In a matter of minutes one is transported from the busy roadways of Kings County to almost complete silence. Rays of sunlight break though the curtain created by the limbs of the hemlocks and tiny waterfalls cascade over moss covered rock. It's simply hard to believe a place this tranquil and foreign can exist so close to a major town. The trail follows the stream, crossing it several times and eventually climbs up very high as the ravine becomes a chasm. From

here you must retrace your steps back to the centre. Not surprisingly, this trail is very popular with those who have discovered it.

Wolfville Dykes

The town of Wolfville is flanked on its seaward side by a series of dykes, originally built by the Acadians over 300 years ago. Easily accessible almost from the heart of the town, these are great places to walk or bike, providing an opportunity to get into the country at a moment's notice. From the elevation of the dykes, there are fine views of the cliffs of Blomidon and the smaller bluffs along the Cornwallis River, as well as the spires and cupolas of Acadia University looking towards the town. When the tide is out, it is certainly not difficult to see why Wolfville was originally named Mud Creek. Harriers and other hawks are almost always present, patrolling the meadows on the one side and the salt marsh on the other. Shore birds frequent the mud flats in the spring and fall. The dykes can be reached from a laneway across from Randall House Museum or at the end of Gaspereau Avenue extension.

The Pools, just outside Wolfville

A delightful short hike to a series of small waterfalls and pools on the Gaspereau River, only minutes from Wolfville. There are a couple of ways to get to the trailhead, but the most scenic is from White Rock. Take White Rock Road off the Evangeline Trail at Greenwich, just across from the old high school. Follow this road several kilometres to the small community of White Rock and continue straight for almost a kilometre. Just past a bridge, you will see a small parking lot where the trail begins. The trail leads to a metal foot bridge over the Gaspereau River and then on to Hell's Gate generating station. It continues a short distance beyond the station, along the small road that bears to the left, following the course of the Gaspereau River just over a kilometre to the first of a series of small waterfalls with pools at their base. All told there are five pools by most people's reckoning, although what's a pool and what's not can be the subject of debate.

This hike is particularly enjoyable on a hot summer day, as the pools are a great spot for a dip. The woods are alive with many species of warblers that nest in the area and a goodly number of wildflowers. One note of caution: as the trail moves from one pool to another, it becomes very steep and narrow, and in some places it is quite scary. Needless to say, it is not for small children.

Cape Split, Scots Bay

This is one of Nova Scotia's most popular hiking trails, despite its length of almost eight kilometres each way. The trail starts at the end of the road just past Scots Bay and eventually leads to the open meadows on the cliffs high above the end of Cape Split. The trail is fairly well marked, but you must make a decision once you come to the end of the fence. Turning left will take on the difficult shore route which follows the coastline mostly along the cliff tops. This is the more interesting route, but it can be challenging and scary for those with a fear of heights. Going right will take you on a moderate trail that goes mostly down the spine of Cape Split through second-generation forests where deer are frequently seen. As you near the end of either trail you will pass very close to sheer drops of hundreds of metres — you must be very careful. More than one careless hiker has paid very dearly.

At the tip of Cape Split you will emerge onto grass meadows that offer breathtaking views of the Bay of Fundy. The incessant howling wind reveals the true source of the word Blomidon — blow-me-down. At the very tip, you can look down at the split rock formation that gives the cape its name. In the spring and early summer, sea birds nest on the stack. If the tide is right, you can make your way down to the shore, but this is not advisable as it is easy to get trapped by the changing tide. We are glad to write that the province has recently acquired Cape Split and eventually it will be a provincial park. Hopefully this will lead to an upgrading of the trail in a manner similar to Cape Chignecto.

Uniacke Estate Museum Park Trails, Mount Uniacke

The Uniacke Estate contains over 2,500 acres of land surrounding a grand country home. Over the past number of years, the province has laid out seven walking trails that begin at the parking lot of the estate museum. One very gentle trail suitable for people of all ages is the Lake Martha/ Drumland Field loop. This trail follows the shoreline of Lake Martha for about one kilometre before returning via the Drumlin trail which rises gradually from the shores of the lake. At the top, the forest is cleared and there is a field from which the view of the Uniacke mansion is exceptional. The vegetation is such that you can only see the old house and not any of the modern surroundings such as the parking lot. It is very easy to imagine yourself transported back 200 years in time and viewing the property much as Uniacke must have done way back then. This is simply one of the best views in the province. The trails that lead away from the lake follow the course of the old highway and return through a wetland and barren area. This loop will take substantially more time and effort. Some of these trails are particularly suitable for cross-country skiing as well.

HISTORIC SITES

Port Royal National Historic Site, Port Royal, (902) 532-2898, www.pc.gc.ca/lhn-nhs/ns/portroyal/index.aspx

This replica of the first successful attempt at permanent settlement in Canada, established by Champlain and DeMonts in 1605, is located on the protected inland waters of the Annapolis Basin.

Befriending the local Mi'kmaq, the French set up what was to become the most significant venture in the early history of European settlement in North America - the fur trade. Exchanging European goods for furs, the French soon had a great business going with the First Nations until the English got wind of it. In 1613, an expedition led by Samuel Argall destroyed the Habitation. Although the buildings were destroyed, the colony was not, and it was from this site that Acadian settlement expanded, first to the mouth of the Annapolis River at present-day Annapolis Royal, and up the banks of that river throughout the fertile Annapolis Valley. The Argall raid did set off a bloody war of colonial supremacy between France and England that lasted off and on for 150 years, until 1763, when France finally withdrew from what is now Canadian soil.

The list of North American firsts at Port Royal would fill two pages of this book, but perhaps the most interesting was the Order of Good Cheer. This was really a social club designed to help fill the long hours of the Canadian winter. Each member of the settlement was responsible for entertaining and feeding the others for one night each month. One man, Marc Lescarbot, wrote the first play performed in North America, while others sang or told stories.

When you tour the Habitation, and in particular the common room with its large fireplace and tables set with pewter awaiting the next meal, you can feel the camaraderie of those early days and almost hear the walls ringing with the sound of laughter and toasts to the king. During your visit, you'll also see the trading room, where the skins of beaver, wolf, bear, otter and seal were stored, the apothecary's, where Louis Hebert practised the first European medicine in Canada and the chapel where confessions were heard and the first native peoples north of Florida converted to Christianity. Despite its small size, in the short time of its existence the Habitation had a tremendous impact on the history of North America and its institutions and is one of Canada's most important historical sites.

Grand Pré National Historic Site, Grand Pré, (902) 542-3631, www.pc.gc.ca/eng/lhn-nhs/ns/grandpre/index.aspx

The Grand Pré National Historic Site is a commemoration of the 1755 deportation of the Acadians. The village that stood near here is said to be the first community that was destroyed by the deportation order. Buildings were razed and families intentionally split up and herded into sailing vessels. The true story of the event is reconstructed in the new interpretive centre which was opened in 2003. However, it is the church which is the centrepiece of the park. This beautifully tranquil spot with fine landscaped gardens and a long row of ancient willows by a small pond gives visitors a place to contemplate the terrible suffering that the deportation inflicted on the Acadian families. Standing in front of the church is the famous statue of Evangeline, the hero of Longfellow's poetic fictional account of these events. If you look at the statue from one side, you see a young vibrant woman. If you look at it from the other side, you see the aged and world-weary Evangeline who found Gabriel on his deathbed. A photograph of the statue of Evangeline with the beautiful stone church in the background is one of the most familiar images of Nova Scotia's cultural heritage. Grand Pré is another of the "must sees" on any visit to Nova Scotia.

Fort Edward National Historic Site, Windsor, (902) 798-4706,
www.pc.gc.ca/lhn-nhs/ns/edward/index.aspx
This historic site on a hill right in the town of Windsor contains a block-house built in 1750 which makes it the oldest in Canada. It is a miracle that this entirely wooden structure has survived intact for over 250 years. The blockhouse is open to explore with many interpretive panels inside and on the grounds. There are great views of the surrounding countryside.

MUSEUMS
North Hills Museum, 5065 Granville Road, Granville Ferry,
(902) 532-2168, www.museum.gov.ns.ca/nhm/
For most visitors headed to the Habitation at Port Royal, this little museum is a pleasant surprise. It is housed in a restored saltbox that dates from the middle 1700s. The furnishings are the personal collection of Robert Pat-terson, a retired Ontario banker and antiques dealer, who restored the house in a manner to best display his extensive collection. The quality is uniformly high and contains a lot of furniture, glass and silver, as well as some paint-ings and sculpture. Patterson bequeathed the house and its contents to the province on his death in 1974. North Hills is a superb example of period restoration and demonstrates just how liveable these old houses can still be.

MacDonald Museum, 21 School Street, Middleton, (902) 825-6116,
www.macdonaldmuseum.ca
In 1903 Middleton was chosen by tobacco magnate William MacDonald as the site for an experimental consolidated school, the first of its kind in Canada. This school became the model for hundreds of others that were subsequently built across Canada in the early 1900s, and many Canadians have fond memories of their time spent in the old red brick schools.

The museum preserves one classroom much as it would have looked in the 1940s, but there is much more. Most interesting is the Nova Sco-tia Museum collection of over 150 antique clocks, including some excep-tional tall case clocks and a number of Nova Scotia–made timepieces. The museum also houses a research library for genealogical searches.

Prescott House, 1633 Starrs Point Road, off Route 358,
(902) 542-3984, www.museum.gov.ns.ca/prh/
In the early 1800s Charles Prescott, a gentleman farmer and businessman, built this beautiful country house. He was responsible for the development and introduction of a number of important apple species in Nova Scotia, including the Gravenstein, Nova Scotia's most popular apple. With its fine period antiques and delightful gardens, Prescott House is a good place to make your final stop on a day trip to Cape Split and the upper Minas Basin area.

Haliburton House, 414 Clifton Avenue, Windsor, (902) 798-2915,
www.museum.gov.ns.ca/hh/
This was the home of Thomas Chandler Haliburton, a judge and historian but best known as the author who created Sam Slick — the fast-talking,

opinionated Yankee clock peddler who was constantly bemused by the say-ings and doings of the Nova Scotians. Although his writings are seldom read these days, in his day Haliburton was almost as popular as Charles Dickens and Mark Twain. The number of famous sayings that derive from Sam Slick is truly astonishing. Just a small sample includes "The early bird catches the worm," "Give and take," "Raining cats and dogs," "Barking up the wrong tree," "Facts are stranger than fiction," "Quick as a wink," "Jack of all trades and master of none," "Honesty is the best policy," "I wasn't born yesterday," "Live and let live," "You can't get blood out of stone," "Every dog has its day," "Drink like a fish," and "A stitch in time saves nine." Obviously someone with this type of wit and wisdom deserves to be more widely read.

Clifton, as Haliburton's house is properly called, sits high on a hill at the end of a long winding driveway on the outskirts of Windsor. It is a wonderfully designed home, of no definable architectural style. The house is well-furnished with period antiques.

Shand House, Windsor, (902) 798-8213, www.museum.gov.ns.ca/sh/
This provincial museum in Windsor contrasts quite sharply with Halibur-ton House, the other provincial museum in town. It was built in 1890 by a Windsor businessman in Queen Anne style, with ornate interior wood-work. What is particularly striking and unique about Shand House are the many fine pieces of furniture, including a unique grandfather clock that were crafted in the furniture factory owned by the Shands. The furniture is very similar to the Eastlake Style and every bit as well-made. The home contains all of the amenities one would have expected to find in the per-fectly modern home of the 1890s. The house has a particularly good loca-tion high atop a bluff overlooking the Avon River.

Uniacke Estate Museum Park, Mount Uniacke, (902) 866-0032, www.museum.gov.ns.ca/uemp
If you are coming from Annapolis towards Halifax, you might be museumed out by the time you get to Mount Uniacke. Don't be; Uniacke House, the summer residence of one of Nova Scotia's first attorney generals, is an archi-tectural gem. Built in the neo-classical style in the early 1800s, it occupies a commanding position on the shores of Lake Martha, which was named for Uniacke's wife. The interior is replete with the finest furnishings of any of the Nova Scotia museum properties. It is fortunate that most of Uniacke's original furniture was preserved with the house until its acquisition by the province in 1949. When Uniacke built the house, he was a wealthy and prosperous Halifax figure and was able to buy the finest British and Amer-ican furniture, much of which was purchased directly from George Adams in England and still bears his mark. Also of note in the house is a portrait by John Singleton Copely, as well as two excellent portraits by Robert Feke.

In many other places in this book, you will see comments relating to the rigours of early life in Nova Scotia. Uniacke House is one of the exceptions to the general rule, and provides an example of just how well those few who controlled the reins of power in early Nova Scotia did live.

The extensive grounds feature no less than seven walking trails. Trail guides are available in the house.

OFF THE BEATEN PATH

Victoria Beach

Instead of returning to the Evangeline Trail after visiting Port Royal, consider making a side trip to Victoria Beach. On the way, you will pass through Karsdale, a community with many older homes and the former residence of renowned folk artist Maud Lewis. Overlooking the entrance to Digby Gut, Victoria Beach is a great place to see the powerful Bay of Fundy tides. This is a fishing village with a large wharf, a colourful collection of boats and a small lighthouse.

A cairn marks the former terminus of a short-lived pony express that operated between Halifax and Victoria Beach in the mid-1800s. From Victoria Beach, the news was transported to Saint John by boat and then on to the States. Like its more illustrious American counterpart, the Nova Scotia pony express became obsolete with the development of the telegraph.

Route 201

This is a pleasant alternative to Route 1 through the Annapolis Valley. It runs parallel to the Evangeline Trail from Annapolis Royal to Wilmot, just past Middleton, on the other side of the Annapolis River. It passes by the farms and orchards for which the area is well-known. The roadbed tends to be a bit like a rollercoaster with many small undulations. While the map shows a number of communities on Route 201, none of them really even amounts to a hamlet. This road and its surroundings are as bucolic as it gets.

At Tupperville, there is a small museum in the Old Schoolhouse. In Centrelea, you will pass the scene of the Bloody Creek massacre, where 28 British soldiers were slaughtered by a combined Mi'kmaq and Acadian force in 1757. Although the highway does continue past Wilmot, your best bet is to return to Route 1, as there is little of scenic value past this point.

The Fundy Coast

From Digby Gut to Blomidon, a ridge of volcanic basalt known as the North Mountain separates the Annapolis Valley from the Bay of Fundy. Even though it is only 17 kilometres or so from the heart of the valley to the shore, it might as well be a hundred miles away, given the difference in climate between the two areas. On any given day in the valley, it might be a sweltering 30° C, but on the shore it won't be much more than 20° C.

While the Annapolis Valley has thrived on agriculture, the small communities of the Fundy Shore have eked out a living from the fishery.

Following the Fundy Shore is a fascinating alternative to the Evangeline Trail. For one thing, you'll see a lot of folk art adorning the yards and cottages along the way. You'll come across a number of tiny harbours where at low tide the fishing boats will be high and dry and quite photogenic.

The beaches, while not for swimming, are great spots to collect driftwood, which seems to accumulate more in the Bay of Fundy than anywhere else in the province. You can begin your tour of the Fundy coast at Parkers Cove, crossing North Mountain on a side road that begins not far from Annapolis Royal. If you want, you can backtrack to the end of the road at Delaps Cove, where the highway ends and a good hiking trail begins. From Parkers Cove, the paved highway follows the shore through a number of small fishing communities. The shoreline is quite regular here and the ocean is usually in view. Most of these communities have interesting wharves and several have lighthouses overlooking the harbour. From Port Lorne you have to zigzag inland and back a number of times on paved roads. Keep a good eye on the map and the road signs — it can be confusing.

The difficulty in reaching these remaining coastal villages is more than offset by their beauty and the sense of isolation. Don't expect lodging or gas, although there are a couple of stores and takeouts.

Near Port George, the highway runs right along the bay for a considerable distance and you can plainly see the unusual basalt rock formations that make up much of this coast. There is a small picnic park where you can stop to explore the shore.

Next is Margaretsville, the largest community on this shore. It has a lighthouse and government wharf.

Morden is a tidy little cottage community. A stone cross on the beach marks the site where a group of Acadians from the Port Royal area spent the winter attempting to avoid the deportation order of 1755. There are picnic tables and access to the beach nearby. This is one of the best picnic sites along the entire coast.

After Morden, the villages of Harbourville and Canada Creek are both worth finding your way to. Lastly, be sure to visit Halls Harbour, which is the prettiest of all the Fundy coastal villages. A small stream enters the bay through a chasm in the cliffs. The cove, the wharf and surrounding houses make up a scene that you will surely photograph. If you have time to make only one side trip to the Fundy Shore, Halls Harbour is the place to go. It also has one of Nova Scotia's few lobster pounds where boiled lobster is available right on the wharf.

Blomidon and Cape Split
This is one of the most enjoyable of all the day trips in this book, offering something for everyone — hiking, rockhounding, beachcombing and birding, all through some of Nova Scotia's most historic and scenic areas. If you plan to take in even half of the suggested activities you will have a full day.

Start the trip by turning at Greenwich toward Port Williams (www. portwilliams.com), just west of Wolfville. Port Williams is a lovely little village on the banks of the Cornwallis River, with a number of fine old homes and churches and a couple of good antique stores. Not far past the village you'll come to a crossroads where the beautiful St. George Church, dating from 1760, presides over a quiet rural setting. The cemetery contains the graves of many early Planters, including Prescotts, Gesners and Bordens, all of whom played important roles in the history of the province.

Continuing on past apple orchards and 200-year-old farmsteads, you soon arrive at Canning (www.canningnovascotia.ca). Formerly called Apple Tree Landing, this was once a major port for the export of apples. A small park on the far side of the village marks the site of the former shipyards. Canning is no longer a port, but it remains one of the prettiest communities in Nova Scotia, featuring a main street canopied by tall trees. Turn left at the Borden Monument towards The Lookoff. Route 358 soon ascends the North Mountain, from the top of which there is a spectacular view of the patchwork of orchards, fields and woodlands of the Annapolis Valley.

Leaving The Lookoff, Route 358 continues on to another impressive sight on the other side of North Mountain — the curving arc of Scots Bay melding into the long finger of Cape Split. Descending to this small community, you will feel the cool air of the Bay of Fundy coast. The pavement ends just past Scots Bay, but the trail does not. Here you can continue on foot another 8 kilometres to the very tip of Cape Split on one of Nova Scotia's most popular hiking trails.

Retracing your steps, look for the small unmarked road to Scots Bay beach where agates and other semi-precious stones are commonly found. Continuing to backtrack for about 8 kilometres, look for the left turn marked "Blomidon." A short dirt road will connect you to another paved road. Make a left turn and drive to the Blomidon Provincial Park at the end of this road. You are now at the base of this famous cape, home of the legendary Glooscap and sacred to the Mi'kmaq people. Here again, you can continue on foot on a number of trails that traverse the park, providing spectacular views of the entire Minas Basin from Glooscap's very threshold.

When you begin the return trip in your car, stay on the pavement, which will take you back to Canning and from there to Wolfville or Kentville. Along the way, look for a number of unusual rock formations, including a small arch. You can extend your drive by taking side trips to Medford, Kingsport, Lower Canard and Starrs Point. There are actually three short loops that all return to Route 358. They are great for cyclists and pass through some of the most fertile land in Nova Scotia. A great variety of crops are grown, and U-picks and roadside markets abound. At Starrs Point, you will pass Prescott House before returning to Port Williams.

Gaspereau Valley

This picturesque valley lies about 2 kilometres from the main street of Wolfville, separated by a high ridge from which there are excellent views of the Minas Basin and Blomidon. Take almost any side road heading away from the ocean between Grand Pré and New Minas and you will find the Gaspereau Valley. The tiny Gaspereau River, a favourite of tubers, winds its way from a dam high on the South Mountain to the ocean at Avonport. Along the way, it passes through fields and orchards. The valley is crisscrossed and paralleled by numerous roads, many of which are not well-marked on the map. If you wish to explore, you might end up at Lumsden

Dam, a great little swimming spot, or at a suspension bridge from which a path leads to a lovely area known as The Pools, where the river bubbles gently through a series of small waterfalls into a series of pools. The best thing to do is to ask locally for directions to any of the sites. The large white tower you see near the mouth of the river is a remnant from the days when signals were passed between Halifax and Annapolis via a series of signalling towers.

PARKS AND GREENSPACE

Valleyview Provincial Park, www.novascotiaparks.ca/parks/valleyview.asp

As the name implies, the raison d'être of this provincial park is its tremendous view of the Annapolis Valley from a ridge high on North Mountain just outside Bridgetown. There are both picnic tables and campsites. Even if you don't plan to stay, it's worth the short detour from Bridgetown for the panorama of the valley from the lookoff.

Atlantic Food and Horticultural Research Centre, 32 Main Street, Kentville, (902) 679-5333

On the east side of Kentville, you will find this agricultural research centre, one of 19 in Canada. Despite the boring sounding name there is actually a lot to see here. There are 243 hectares of beautifully landscaped grounds and, for the serious horticulturist, experimental crops and plantings to inspect. On the grounds is Blair House, which details the history of the agricultural station and the many varieties of fruits, berries and ornamental shrubs that were developed here. The agricultural station is particularly glorious in the late spring when thousands of rhododendrons are in bloom, many of which are varieties developed right here. The centre is also the starting point for the beautiful Hemlock Ravine trail.

Blomidon Provincial Park, www.novascotiaparks.ca/parks/blomidon.asp

This is one of Nova Scotia's most interesting provincial parks. It contains Blomidon Mountain, home to the legendary Mi'kmaq demi-god Glooscap. New World North Americans don't have the legacy of ancient gods, mythical heroes and sacred sites that are so much a part of European, Asian and African cultures. However, the native peoples of North America certainly do. Blomidon is a sacred site to them and if you've been brought up on the tales of Glooscap, as most Canadian children have, this place is magical. The park preserves and protects Blomidon and the sense of mystery that goes with it. It can be explored on a series of interconnected trails that start from the parking lot at the entrance to the park. The Joudrey Trail offers a spectacular view from the top of Blomidon across the Bay of Fundy to Five Islands. From up here you'll understand why this was a place fit for the home of a god. The Woodland Trail will return you to the starting point through a beautiful hardwood forest. Plan on making a day of it or, better yet, set up your tent at one of the many campsites.

SPECIAL EVENTS

Apple Blossom Festival, various towns throughout the Annapolis Valley, www.appleblossom.com

This is the granddaddy of all Nova Scotia festivals, fast approaching its 80th year.

Held in late May to early June to coincide with the blooming of the apple trees, this festival features a large parade, many contests and musical events, but the best reason to go is simply to take in the majesty of the valley in full bloom.

The Pumpkin Festival, Windsor, www.worldsbiggestpumpkins.com

If you happen to be in Windsor in early October, be sure to stop in at the Pumpkin Festival. Windsor's Howard Dill is legendary in pumpkin-growing circles as the developer of the Dill Atlantic Giant pumpkin, which set off a frenzy of giant pumpkin–growing around North America. Every October, participants from all over the continent ship their largest pumpkins to Windsor for the weigh-off. We won't pretend that there is a great amount of excitement in watching these behemoth pumpkins being slowly lifted on and off the scales, but having a giant pumpkin photo in your vacation album is something to talk about. The fair is held on the grounds of Hants County Exhibition, the first and longest-running agricultural exhibition in North America. Besides just watching competing pumpkins, there is much to see and do, in particular the pumpkin regatta. Believe it or not, people hollow out giant pumpkins and race them on Lake Piziquid! Have a look at the Web site to see what we mean.

SPECIAL INTEREST

Oaklawn Farm Zoo, follow the signs from Aylesford on the Evangeline Trail, (902) 847-9790, www.oaklawnfarmzoo.ca

Oaklawn Farm is Nova Scotia's only real zoo, an outgrowth of a hobby farm that just kept getting bigger. It has a world-class collection of big cats — especially noteworthy are the jaguars — and a number of gibbons and lemurs. There are a considerable number of farm animals, including a huge herd of pygmy goats that is constantly entertaining to watch. Oaklawn Farm is just about the most informal and relaxed zoo you are ever likely to visit and the size of its collection of animals will surprise you. Needless to say, it is a delight for children and well worth the reasonable admission fee.

K.C. Irving Environmental Centre and Botanical Gardens, Acadia University, Wolfville, (902) 585-5242, kcirvingcentre.acadiau.ca

The children of legendary New Brunswick oil tycoon K. C. Irving and his wife Harriet decided to honour their memories in a most commendable fashion — by donating to Acadia University an exceptional environmental centre and botanical garden. The attraction for the tourist will be the gardens, which cover six acres and feature plants from nine habitats of the Acadia Forest Region. That was the natural forest cover for most of Nova Scotia, but sadly far too much has been clearcut and replaced with plantations of softwoods. The gardens will give visitors and Nova Scotians a chance to appreciate the wealth of habitat to be found in this province.

Windsor Hockey Heritage Centre, 128 Gerrish Street, (902) 798-1800,

A number of Canadian communities claim to be the birthplace of hockey — one is Windsor, which has put forward a very convincing case that a version of the Canadian game was first played on some of the ponds in the Windsor area, especially Long Pond, by British soldiers garrisoned at Fort Edward. The Windsor Hockey Heritage Centre contains a small but interesting collection of mostly local hockey memorabilia. There is an audiovisual presentation prepared a number of years ago that documents Windsor's claim to be the birthplace of hockey. Well worth a short visit. While you are there check out the Mermaid Theatre's puppet collection which is housed next door.

WALKING TOURS

Bridgetown

Bridgetown is one of the valley's prettiest towns and you will want to get out of your car and take a look around. At the tourist bureau, buy a copy of a small booklet that describes what is called the Historic Cyprus Walk and enjoy the sites of this quaint little town.

Kentville

The walking tour of Kentville is a good example of how a self-guided tour with a good pamphlet that explains the local history can make a place much more interesting than you might suspect at first glance. Kentville has a number of interesting attractions, including walking paths along the Cornwallis River, fine Victorian and Georgian homes, a museum in the old courthouse, the architecturally interesting Cornwallis Inn, once a large hotel, and an old cemetery dating from 1774. The complete tour takes two or three hours.

Wolfville

The town of Wolfville has several pamphlets on walking in the area, including the dykes and several parks; however, none is really a walking tour of the town. Wolfville is unmistakably an attractive town and well worth exploring on foot. Park on the university grounds and stroll along the pathways of Acadia University, which has a number of fine old buildings, a small art gallery and the exceptional new K.C. Irving Environmental Centre and Botanical Gardens. From there, walk up either end of Main Street to view the Victorian mansions that flank both entrances to town. Also of interest is the restored shopping area near the old train station.

Hantsport

The town of Hantsport has a fine one-hour walking tour that starts at the tourist bureau near Churchill House, which is well worth visiting, both for its architecture and for its marine memorial room. The tour will take you past a number of fine old sea captains' homes, down to the waterfront, where you can observe the dramatic effects of the Fundy tides and on to the gravesite of William Hall, Canada's first recipient of the Victoria Cross.

Windsor

In the past few years, no town in Nova Scotia has done more to promote itself as a tourist destination than Windsor. There is an excellent walking tour, which takes you to 20 points of interest starting and ending at the waterfront. You can take a long or short version of the hike. The longer version of this walk takes in the grounds of King's-Edgehill School. There is an amazing variety of things to see and learn about in this little town, including several museums and the Birthplace of Hockey exhibit.

WINERIES

The Annapolis and Gaspereau Valleys have seen an explosion of grape growing over the last decade as vintners have come to realize that the nearby slopes and soils of the area have the potential to be among the best terroirs in North America. There are now six wineries in the area that welcome visitors, with more planned. All of them are worth a visit and a complete list can be found at www.winesofnovascotia.ca/index.php.

Domaine de Grand Pré, Route 1, Grand Pré, 1-866-GPWINES, www.grandprewines.ns.ca

This is Nova Scotia's oldest winery and certainly among the most interesting to visit. It has the feel and look of Europe which is not surprising since the owners are Swiss. From the moment you walk up from the parking lot you will notice that no money has been spared in making this an impressive operation. There is a lot to do. You can wander through the finely landscaped grounds and grapevines, have a meal at the award winning Le Caveau restaurant, take a guided tour and of course sample the product, which includes the excellent Stutz cider. One thing that definitely will impress you is the cobblestone walkway into which grapevine patterns are intertwined. If you are staying in the Wolfville area try to have lunch or dinner here.

ACCOMMODATIONS

All of our recommendations for where to stay in this part of Nova Scotia are in Wolfville. There is a reason for this. Wolfville is by far the most interesting place to stay on this section of the Evangeline Trail. Not only does it have the best collection of inns, restaurants and shops, but it is central to many other activities such as hiking, cycling, birding and golf.

Victoria's Historic Inn, 600 Main Street, Wolfville, 1-800-556-5744, www.victoriashistoricinn.com

For many years this place seemed like an aging dowager compared to Betsey Harwood's Tattingstone Inn, which is almost next door. However, about a decade ago, the dowager visited the fountain of youth. The inn was redone inside and out, and restored to its Victorian elegance. Now it is perhaps the finest Victorian home in Nova Scotia. Not only were the inn's gingerbread exterior, beautiful stained glass, and elaborate wall mouldings restored, but the inn was modernized without losing any of its romantic charm. There are a great variety of rooms, all of which are nice, and some of which are truly special. The Cottage Room features a lovely white metal and brass queen-sized bed, which complements the white wicker and white hand-painted furniture. The bathroom is larger than many rooms in which we've stayed in our travels. Off the bedroom, there is a wonderful tiny enclosed balcony, almost like a loveseat, tucked away in the eaves of the house. The restoration of Victoria's was obviously an expensive undertaking, as the pricing of the accommodations reflects, but if you are interested in romance in a quality setting where no details have been left unattended, it is well worth it. The Web site lets you view each room with attendant price so you know exactly what you're getting.

The Blomidon Inn, 127 Main Street, Wolfville, 1-800-565-2291, www.blomidon.ns.ca

Located in the former home of shipowner Captain Burgess, this is one of Nova Scotia's longest-running and most successful inns. Dark wood predominates in the original portion of the house. The entrance and the stairs are particularly striking. Over the years, there have been a number of additions made. There are 29 rooms with a considerable amount of variety. The best are very good, but a number of others must be rated as average. The Web site sets out four categories of rooms which are priced accordingly. The Blomidon has two other things going for it; an excellent restaurant and very beautiful grounds. It's one of the most popular spots for weddings and honeymooners in the province.

Tattingstone Inn, 620 Main Street, Wolfville, 1-800-565-7696, www.tattingstone.ns.ca

This is unquestionably one of Nova Scotia's best small hostelries. This Victorian home has been refurbished with a combination of antiques and modern reproductions, as well as an impressive art collection. The entire inn is clean, airy and upbeat — none of the mustiness here that seems to linger about some other establishments. Most of the bedrooms are equipped with four-poster beds and feature very large marble-tiled bathrooms, usually associated with larger hotels. Along with the main house, there is a smaller carriage house and honeymoon suite located in Toad Hall. The inn also has a swimming pool and tennis court, not usually found at Nova Scotia inns. To be fair, we have heard some complaints recently, but have not noticed anything amiss in our visits. Rooms with rates can be individually viewed on the Web site.

Gingerbread House Inn, 8 Robie Tufts Drive, Wolfville,
1-888-542-1458, www.gingerbreadhouse.ca
This eclectic collection of quite different rooms is located just off Main Street behind Victoria's Inn. The name refers not to the fact that it looks like the witches' house in Hansel and Gretel, but rather the Victorian gingerbread pattern that adorns much of the exterior of the rambling premises. Whether it is original or faux doesn't matter — some people think it's garish while most think it adds a distinctive touch. Have a look at the Web site and decide for yourself.

The Gingerbread House offers many amenities not found in other Wolfville inns, including hot tubs (not Jacuzzis) in many rooms. Believe us they are very welcome after a day of hiking, biking or golf. Many rooms also have private outdoor patios or decks from which you can enjoy the well kept gardens. The reception area doubles as both the breakfast nook, from which hearty breakfasts are served and as an art gallery, which contains many fine and representational works of Nova Scotia's coastline by Daniel Richards, a very gifted artist. You just might be tempted to take one home.

The owners of the Gingerbread House offer a wide variety of accommodation at varying prices. You will almost certainly find something to suit your personal taste and budget.

DINING

Halls Harbour Lobster Pound, Halls Harbour, (902) 679-5299,
www.hallsharbourlobster.ns.ca
The Halls Harbour lobster pound is one of the very few places in Nova Scotia where you can buy fresh cooked lobster and eat it on a picnic table overlooking the wharf. While this is an extremely popular pastime in Maine, it has never really caught on in Nova Scotia. Halls Harbour pound is the exception. Some people think that the only way to eat lobster is fresh, almost right off the boat — you'll have your chance to find out by eating here.

The Port Pub, 980 Terry's Creek Road, Port Williams,
(902) 542-5555 www.theportpub.com
The Port characterizes itself as a gastropub which means it has better food than that found in your regular pub, and it sure does. Located in a brand new airy building on the banks of the Cornwallis River The Port is unusual in that it is a cooperative owned by over 40 shareholders. As much as possible the restaurant serves produce from the local area, which is not a problem as Port Williams is near the centre of Nova Scotia's most diverse agricultural region. The fine fare on the menu is complemented by the libations created on site at the Sea Level Brewery. The Port has really caught on and for good reason. It's a great place to eat and drink.

The Blomidon Inn, 127 Main Street, Wolfville, (902) 542-2291,
www.blomidon.ns.ca
The Blomidon Inn has two dining rooms. If at all possible, try to ensure that you are seated in the library, a very cozy room with four or five tables

and a cheery fireplace. The other dining room is larger and more formal. The menu for both is the same.

The Blomidon has an extensive menu with something for everyone with the emphasis on seasonal produce. The Laceby family is synonymous with gourmet cooking in Nova Scotia. Recently, the Blomidon has gotten very serious about its wine list, and it now has one of the most extensive selections of wines in the province, at fair prices. As a bonus, the menu contains matching wine recommendations which can be purchased by the glass. This has helped the Blomidon win the prestigious *Wine Spectator* Award of Excellence. The Wolfville restaurant scene is extremely competitive and the Blomidon is determined to keep the respected position it has held for many years, through innovation and consistency.

Acton's Grill and Café, 406 Main Street, Wolfville, (902) 542-7525, www.actons.ca

Acton's was founded by the owners of the very successful Fenton's Restaurant in Toronto. The Wolfville venture is equally successful, although obviously on a smaller scale. The service is impeccable and the cooking usually flawless. Wolfville restaurants have the highest uniform standards in the province, so to attract the dedicated following that Acton's has is a real indication of its strengths. The menu is varied and offers a wide variety of Nova Scotia specialties, often done in new and intriguing ways. The atmosphere is somewhat formal, but definitely not stiff - there are always a few Acadia students splurging. If you really want to treat yourself, stay in Wolfville a week and try all the good restaurants.

Tempest World Cuisine, 117 Front Street, Wolfville, 1-866-542-0588, www.tempest.ca

Tempest chef Michael Howell is the new kid on the Wolfville restaurant scene and boy, is he making an entrance. This restaurant has got everybody talking and the reviews from coast to coast are overwhelmingly positive. In a very short time Howell has become a celebrity chef with his own cookbook and frequent media appearances. All you have to do is look at the menu and you will know that you're in for something special. World cuisine is the right description — there's Thai, Malaysian, Spanish, Mexican, Greek and other ethnic influences evident in most offerings. Chef Howell does not disappoint on delivery — the food looks and tastes fabulous. The surroundings are chic, the wines appropriate and the atmosphere terrific. As a real plus there is a variety of tapas available from 8:30 onward on weekends. Just check out the menu on the Web site and see if you can resist booking a reservation.

Le Caveau Restaurant, Domaine de Grand Pré Winery, Grand Pré, (902) 542-7177, www.grandprewines.ns.ca

Unquestionably, one of the main reasons to visit Domaine de Grand Pré Winery is a chance to have a dinner at Le Caveau restaurant or lunch at the Pergola which are the two dining choices offered by the winery. Le Caveau is in a very stylish building constructed solely for the purpose of housing the restaurant. The interior features white walls with blond wooden paneling, a wooden beamed roof and ceramic tile floor which creates a decidedly Northern European atmosphere. You could be in Switzerland, Germany or Denmark. The menu is definitely Swiss-oriented with the emphasis on game and beef. It's also the only place we know in Nova Scotia that offers Lobster Thermidor. Wines are of course those offered by Domaine de Grand Pré. Service is semi-formal and unobtrusive, just like the Swiss. Le Caveau offers yet another great choice in the Wolfville area, in fact in 2009 it won the Restaurant of the Year award from the Taste of Nova Scotia organization. If you visit the winery at lunch time try something at the outdoor Pergola which offers some of the main menu items as well as quiche and sometimes fondue.

GLOOSCAP TRAIL
Windsor to Truro

The Glooscap Trail (www.glooscaptrail.com) is a V-shaped route that explores the upper regions of the Bay of Fundy. It is named for the legendary demi-god Glooscap whom the First Nations believed lived in this area. Many of the unique landforms in the upper Bay of Fundy are associated with stories of Glooscap. There is little doubt that there is something magical about the Bay of Fundy region. It has the world's highest tides, which create a number of unusual phenomena including tidal bores, whirlpools, and rivers and bays that become high and dry twice a day. The region is also widely known for its fossils and native gemstones, such as amethyst, garnet, jasper and agates, all of which can be readily found by enterprising rockhounders. Recently the Bay of Fundy was selected as Canada's entry in the world wide competition to find the seven natural wonders of the world. Have a look at www.fundyfun.com for more on what's in store for you in the Bay of Fundy area.

In terms of scenery, the region around Parrsboro has cliffs, mountains and unusual rock formations that rival the Cabot Trail for beauty. Yet the Glooscap Trail is nowhere near as well-known or visited as most of the other Nova Scotia trails. It is definitely worth taking the time to explore if you're looking for an off-the-beaten path experience, particularly with the development of Cape Chignecto Provincial Park, which makes some of the remotest parts of Nova Scotia accessible.

Much of the Glooscap Trail doubles as the Fundy Shore Ecotour (www.fundyshoreecotour.ns.ca), which highlights the natural beauty of this coastline. Whenever you come across a signed Ecotour attraction, you won't go wrong checking it out. A number of interpretive centres have been established along the route and at some of these you can get a copy of the Fundy Shore Eco-Guide, which describes the more than two dozen eco-sites along the upper Bay of Fundy. If you can't find a copy, it's okay; most sites are described in this book.

The Glooscap Trail begins at Windsor, passing a number of elegant Victorian mansions and several early cemeteries on the way out of town on Route 1. On the hill to your right, look for King's-Edgehill School, Canada's oldest private school. It was also the site of Canada's first university, King's College, which later moved to Halifax. Also down this side road you will find Howard Dill's farm where this esteemed gentleman, captured in a wooden sculpture on Windsor's main street, first developed the Dill Atlantic Giant pumpkins which are now grown throughout the world. If you are passing through in late summer or fall, drop in and you will see a truly giant pumpkin patch. Farmer Dill's property is also the site of Long Pond, where Canada's national pastime, hockey, is said to have originated. Turn left at the beginning of Route 14 and follow it through an area known for its gypsum mines. In the tree-lined village of Brooklyn, make a sharp left at the War Memorial and after about one kilometre turn left again at the high school. From here it is reasonably clear sailing on Route 215 as far as Maitland.

The first views of Minas Basin, with its high tides and sandstone cliffs, are seen shortly after Summerville, where the wide mouth of the Avon River empties into the Bay of Fundy. From here on, the red and blue waters of the bay are in sight almost constantly, as the Glooscap Trail passes through several farming communities.

At Cheverie, there is a picnic area right beside the water, which comes within 15 metres of the road at a high tide. At low tide you can walk along the beach here. A little further on, take Shipyard Road to the shore, where there is a beautiful view back to Cheverie with its white-steepled church sitting atop the red cliffs.

At Bramber, Ocean Beach Road leads to a gravel beach flanked on both sides by cliffs. This area is very popular with striped bass fishermen.

Further on is Walton, a community that was the host to barite and silver mining operations for many years. Large concrete silos are all that's left of the loading facilities at which large ocean freighters once docked. Be sure to take Weir Road out to the small lighthouse, one of few on this shore. It sits at the mouth of the Walton River where a short path leads to a look-off. The view from here is magnificent, and a harbinger of things to come further along the Glooscap Trail. This is also a great spot to note the effects of the tides, which rise 12 metres here every 12 hours.

Just past Minasville, turn left for Burntcoat Head and follow the paved road around to Noel. Many places claim to have the world's highest tides, but most impartial observers identify the Burntcoat area as the actual record holder. An interpretive park at the site where the Burntcoat Head lighthouse has been rebuilt explains the phenomenon of the Fundy tides.

Noel, a small town with a lovely location at the head of Noel Bay, is protected from the ocean by 300-year-old Acadian dykes. From here to Maitland there are many fine views of the bay as the Glooscap Trail winds its way through some excellent farm country.

Anthony Provincial Park at Lower Selma provides picnicking near the shore and a wharf from which you can clearly see Salter Head, the last major landmark on this part of the trail. This is about the only feasible place to swim anywhere along this shore.

Next is the historic town of Maitland (www.maitlandns.com), located at the mouth of the Shubenacadie River, which at this point is nearly a kilometre wide. Many communities along the Minas Basin were known for shipbuilding, but perhaps none were as famous as Maitland. It was here that the *William D Lawrence* was launched in 1874, the largest wooden ship ever built in Canada. Maitland was home to a number of prosperous ship owners, and while nothing really remains of the shipbuilding sites, the homes have survived. In 1995 Maitland was designated Nova Scotia's first Heritage Conservation District because of the large number of well-preserved historic homes. The Lawrence House Museum allows you to tour the interior of one of these buildings, and learn more about the fascinating history of this area.

From Maitland, the Glooscap Trail turns inland following the course of the Shubenacadie to the bridge at South Maitland. Make sure you stop at the small parking lot and walk the short distance out to the remains of the old railway bridge, where there is a lookoff. At South Maitland you have a choice — either cross the river and follow Route 236 into Truro, or keep on going to the town of Shubenacadie and proceed to Truro from there. If you are interested in seeing either the tidal bore or the Wildlife Park, the latter is the preferable route. If you are interested in getting back to the sea as quickly as possible, take the bridge.

Continuing from South Maitland, the Glooscap Trail follows a relatively uninteresting route into Shubenacadie, passing the entrance to Tidal Bore Park on the way. Shubenacadie is a busy and prosperous community, and is one of the centres of the Mi'kmaq in mainland Nova Scotia. There are a number of Mi'kmaq craft outlets between here and Truro.

From Shubenacadie, the Glooscap Trail turns north to Stewiacke (www. stewiacke.net), which bills itself as halfway between the equator and the north pole. This gives you an idea of just how big Canada really is. From here the Amazon is just as close as the north pole, which is just beyond the last Canadian Arctic island. Between Shubenacadie and Stewiacke, you will pass the entrance to the Wildlife Park, a must visit if you have young children.

Stewiacke is the centre of one of the province's most productive farming areas. The rolling hills that surround the town are dotted with the silos and barns.

From Stewiacke, you can proceed directly on Route 2 to Truro, through the farming towns of Brookfield and Hilden, or turn left towards Princeport and follow a longer scenic route that parallels the Shubenacadie River and then Cobequid Bay. The Caddell Falls lookoff, a great place to see bald eagles, is on this route. A small portion of the latter route is unpaved, and if you do take it, be sure to turn left where the unpaved road ends. This will take you to Route 236 and on to Truro through the intriguingly named Old Barns.

Truro (www.truro.ca) is known as the "Hub of Nova Scotia," not only for its central location, but also because of its many activities. It was originally the Acadian settlement of Cobequid, but after the Acadian deportation New Englanders resettled here. The Truro area has long been associated with agriculture, and since the 1800s has been home to the Nova Scotia Agricultural College (www.nsac.ca). Notable industries include the Stanfield's textile firm.

Truro is a stable and prosperous community, which is readily apparent from the many elegant Victorian and brick buildings scattered throughout town. The sister community of Bible Hill is home to the annual Nova Scotia Exhibition and the Truro Raceway, where sulky racers take the post several days a week. As you approach the centre of Truro you will notice an increasing number of tree sculptures which are a recent addition to the town's points of interest. Truro is worth a stop, particularly to visit its impressive Victoria Park or to take a walking tour among the fine buildings and tree sculptures.

BIRDING
The Lower Shubenacadie River

This is one of eastern North America's premier sites for bald eagles. Anyone driving the Glooscap Trail in this area will almost certainly see at least one of the many eagles that frequent the river. You can increase your chances by visiting either Tidal Bore Park or the Caddell Falls lookoff. If by chance you are around in the winter, you might see a congregation of up to 100 eagles when the tomcod spawn on top of the ice floes. This is indeed an unforgettable sight.

GOLF
Truro Golf Course, Golf Street, Truro, (902) 895-2508, www.trurogolfclub.com

This is a relatively flat and fairly wide open 18-hole layout right in the town of Truro. The course is usually in good shape and fun to play, although it is often quite windy. It is one of the oldest clubs in the province, dating back to 1906. In 1997 the club was host to the Canadian Senior Amateur Championship.

MUSEUMS
Lawrence House Museum, Maitland, (902) 261-2628, www.museum.gov.ns.ca/lh/

This handsome house was the home and office of William D. Lawrence, one of Canada's great shipbuilders. From this building he drew up the plans for Canada's biggest wooden sailing ship, the *William D Lawrence*, or "the Great Ship" as it was called in these parts. More than 4,000 people flocked to the small town of Maitland to see the launching of a ship that was more than twice the size of the usual ocean-going vessels of the time. Over the next eight years, it turned a handsome profit for its owner on a number of worldwide voyages.

The majority of the furnishings in the house are original. Of particular interest is a collection of ship paintings representing the *William D Lawrence* and other vessels built in Maitland during its heyday. The house has an unusual spiral central staircase and a covered walkway to the privies. This museum is a fitting tribute to a man with big ideas and real vision.

Colchester Historical Museum, 29 Young Street, Truro, (902) 895-6284, www.genealogynet.com/resident/colchester/home.htm

This is the county museum for Colchester and is housed on two floors in an attractive older brick building, typical of many found in the town. The first floor is dedicated to travelling exhibits, which usually are very informative, and worth seeing. For example, during the 2004–2005 season an excellent display of the Acadian culture and history in Colchester County was on display and more recently the story of the 100,000 British

Home Children who were sent to Canada between 1869 and 1930. The second floor contains the Colchester County archives, including an extensive collection of family genealogies. This will be of interest to those with Colchester County roots. One of the most interesting permanent items on display is a very large needlework tapestry displaying the history of Truro. It is truly an exceptional work which on its own makes the trip to the museum worthwhile.

OFF THE BEATEN PATH
Newport Landing
This finger of land sticks out between the confluence of the St. Croix and Avon Rivers, on the one side, and the Kennetcook and Avon on the other side. As the name implies, it was the site of a landing by New England Planters, who took over the nearby lands of expelled Acadians. The drive around Newport Landing is nearly circular, winding up and down through some of Nova Scotia's most pastoral country. The roadway is lined with many fine Lombardy poplars and other specimen trees, and with distant views of church spires in Windsor. At Avondale, a wharf has been constructed at the site of the original landing and there is a small museum that tells the story of the area and the legacy of ship building. From Avondale there is a panoramic view up and down the Avon River, including a fine view of Windsor, with Mount Martock in the background. The beach, such as it is, is known for fossils.

Along the way, you will pass the Old Stone House, which is alleged to have been built circa 1699. This would make it the only surviving Acadian structure in the province. It is alleged to be a French mission, but some historians disagree as to the accuracy of these claims. Near Newport Landing there are several beautiful captains' mansions, which attest to the former prosperity of this community. This detour is well worth the half-hour that it takes.

Routes 236 and 14
A quick glance at the map will show that Hants County is traversed by a couple of routes other than the Glooscap Trail. If for any reason you are in a hurry and can't afford the time to travel the shoreline route, we would recommend Route 236. The first part of this route, which starts just past Brooklyn, travels through the communities of Stanley, Mosherville and Clarksville before arriving at Kennetcook. For most of the way it follows the banks of the Kennetcook River through farming country. From there, Route 236 passes mostly through woodlands until rejoining the Glooscap Trail just past Maitland.

The alternative is Route 14, which is the most direct route across Hants County. This road is much more heavily travelled than Route 236, particularly by large trucks. The surface is not good and there is little of interest along the way.

Stewiacke River Valley
The valley of the Stewiacke River runs east along Route 289, providing an

alternate route to Pictou County and Cape Breton from the busy Trans-Canada Highway. It passes through a number of quiet agricultural communities and uncut forests. Much of the way it parallels the river. Although there is a small museum at Upper Stewiacke, there is not a lot of reason for stopping along the way; the route is more of a pleasure simply for the drive through some pretty countryside.

PARKS AND GREENSPACE
Smiley's Provincial Park, just off Route 14, 10 kilometres from Windsor, www.novascotiaparks.ca/parks/smileys.asp
Follow the signs from Highway 14 at Brooklyn to find this small park, which is typical of the many interesting places that can be discovered by exploring inland Hants County. A small trout stream meanders over gravel bars in the shade of elms and maples. There is an old-fashioned swimming hole under a bridge just past the parking area. This is a great spot for a swim and a picnic. There are also a lot of caves in Hants County, although their locations are kept fairly secret to protect the bats that inhabit them. Smiley's might be a good place to ask the locals. If you do go to a cave don't ever do it alone and make sure someone else knows where you went.

Tidal Bore Park, off Route 215, 1-800-565-RAFT, www.tidalboreraftingpark.com
This is a private park on the banks of the Shubenacadie River just off the Glooscap Trail at Admiral Rock. From an observation area that overhangs the river, one of Nova Scotia's great natural phenomena, a tidal bore, can be observed. Anyone who spends any time near the head of the Bay of Fundy will run across the term "tidal bore" again and again. What is a tidal bore? Essentially it is a rush of water brought in by the incoming tides that is forced upriver, against the current and over the naturally outflowing water. The force of the tide is caused by the funnel shape of the Bay of Fundy, which is wide at its mouth and narrows down along its entire length. The tides that rise and fall are gradually constricted near the head of the bay so that they are squeezed up into the rivers that flow into the bay at this end.
   Given the obvious play on words and the occasional disappointed expectation of visitors who have been led to expect an onrushing tidal wave by over-enthusiastic Chambers of Commerce, it is easy to be facetious or dismissive of this phenomenon. A visit to Tidal Bore Park, which we believe is the best place anywhere to observe this event, should change most opinions about whether a tidal bore really is boring. For a small admission fee, visitors are directed down a set of very steep stairs to an observation deck that overlooks extensive mud flats on an area of the Shubenacadie River not far from where it drains into the Bay of Fundy. The times for the tidal bore are published annually in brochures distributed by the park to most information outlets in the area and on the Web site. Try to time your arrival at least 10 minutes before the bore is due, to give yourself time to get down to the platform and to allow for the slight deviancy in times when the bore does occur. It is amazing that the prognosticators can be as

accurate as they are, many months in advance, as to exactly when the tidal bore will arrive.

When you get to the observation platform, you will see a small calm channel winding between extensive mudflats. Next you will hear a rushing sound that is accompanied by a wind, picking up out of nowhere. The tidal bore, which is really a wave up to two metres high, passes by and the waters begin to rapidly cover the mudflats. At this point you will be asking yourself - is that it? Wait a few minutes until the mudflats are covered and suddenly the waters of the river start to boil and turn into foaming rapids. What you're seeing is the friction created by one body of water being forced upriver, while a second one underneath it goes downriver through the force of gravity. The calm little stream you saw minutes ago is now a full-blown, raging river. It is easy to understand why the Mi'kmaq believed that this entire area of the province was the home of gods. You will have a new appreciation of the forces of nature after seeing a tidal bore and its aftermath at the Tidal Bore Park. For the truly adventuresome, and you will observe them from the observation deck, there is an opportunity to traverse the bore and the rapids by boat. This experience is described further on. The park also offers a swimming pool, accommodations in log cabins, and many other amenities.

Stewiacke River Park, www.colchester.ca/stewiacke-river-park
Eight kilometres outside Stewiacke, this municipal park offers camping, picnicking, hiking, fishing and swimming along the banks of the Stewiacke. If you noticed the muddy colour of the river at the town of Stewiacke, you will be surprised as you near this park that the waters are now crystal clear. The influence of the tides ends just outside town. This pleasant park, set among a large grove of hemlock, is particularly popular with fishermen as, at various times of year, salmon, trout, striped bass and shad can all be caught. There is a lovely little loop trail that follows the shore of the river and passes through some lovely forest.

Victoria Park, Brunswick Street and Park Road, Truro
www.colchester.ca/victoria-park
Victoria Park, on the edge of town, occupies over 400 acres of land which contains a great deal of varied topography. It's probably fair to say that with the recent damage to Point Pleasant Park in Halifax, this is the best municipal park in Nova Scotia. Primarily wooded, Victoria Park is laced with walking trails that lead to many interesting features, most particularly Joe Howe Falls and Waddell Falls, which both tumble over Lepper Brook as it traverses the park. Also not to be missed is the trail to the Wood Street lookoff, where there are great views of Cobequid Basin. For families with small children, the picnic sites, playgrounds, new swimming pool and wishing well offer a great variety of things to do.

SPECIAL INTEREST
Shubenacadie Wildlife Park, Route 2, near Shubenacadie, (902) 758-2010, www.wildlifepark.gov.ns.ca

This is the best of Nova Scotia's wildlife parks and the one that attracts by far the most visitors. On display you will see virtually every animal that can be found within the province and a few that cannot. Of particular note is the moose, which is seldom seen in zoos, and the Sable Island horses — a unique domestic breed that has evolved from horses abandoned on that remote Nova Scotia island in the seventeenth century. Among the predators there are wolves, cougar, black bear, lynx, bobcat and the elusive fisher to name a few, along with many species of their prey. This is one of the most popular destinations in the Province for young children who will get a chance to feed deer, ducks and geese and wonder at the colours of the handsome peacocks and other exotic birds.

In 2006 Ducks Unlimited opened the Greenwing Legacy Interpretive Centre on the grounds adjacent to the wildlife park. This is a really excellent place for children, and adults for that matter, to learn the value of our wetlands. It is very much hands on and uses simple techniques to explain complicated processes. The Microeye is a device that magnifies onto a large monitor the goings on in a bowl of water filled with tiny denizens from the wetlands nearby. It will fascinate children of all ages. After visiting the centre, be sure to take a stroll on the boardwalk which you can stretch to a 1.5 kilometre walk to St. Andrews marsh or simply observe the wildlife in the ponds just out the back door.

Glooscap Heritage Centre, 65 Treaty Trail, Truro, (902) 843-3496, www.glooscapheritagecentre.com

You can't miss the Glooscap Heritage Centre — the giant statue of Glooscap is visible for a mile or more from the Trans Canada Highway, just outside Truro. For the aboriginal first nations of Nova Scotia Glooscap is a sacred figure, a legendary demi-god who was responsible for many of the myths and traditions that are a key part of the Mi'kmaq heritage. So it is no surprise that this aboriginal centre bears his name. The Millbrook first nation has done very well in attracting businesses to the Power Centre which is situated on Millbrook land. With the commercial success of the centre assured, the band decided to create a heritage centre which would both celebrate the Mi'kmaq and at the same time explain to non-natives why maintaining their traditions is so important to them. They have done a very good job. The first things you notice on entering the centre are the very striking cast aluminum representations of petroglyphs that adorn the walls. These depictions are based upon actual petroglyphs found in Kejimkujik National Park that are rapidly deteriorating in their natural settings. Six interpretive cases contain exquisite examples of quillwork, beadwork, basketry and traditional clothing as well as some ancient artifacts. An 18 minute multimedia presentation describes the history of the Mi'kmaq people and pulls no punches in detailing the many abuses these people have suffered at the hands of others. While it might make some uncomfortable, for most it provides a wake up call to centuries of neglect and malfeasance.

For children, the highlight of the visit will undoubtedly be a chance to have their picture taken at the feet of Glooscap who stands proudly in an outdoor area that is reachable only by going through the centre. After seeing the exhibits a visit to the gift shop is definitely in order as it contains some excellent aboriginal artwork and jewellery.

Tidal Bore Rafting

Tidal bore rafting is Nova Scotia's version of white water rafting. See Tidal Bore Park for a description of a tidal bore and how it creates the rapids.

At the Tidal Bore Park not far from Shubenacadie, you will board Zodiacs, which each hold six to eight people. The boat catches and rides the onrushing tidal bore, which signals the beginning of the river's transformation. After the bore passes, a series of eddies and whirlpools develop, at which point you can shoot the rapids that now envelop large portions of the river. For most people, this is the highlight of the trip. Usually about seven to eight passes through the rapids are made. Once the rapids die down with the rising tide, the rest of the trip is spent exploring upriver as far as the junction with the Stewiacke River. You'll probably see bald eagles in their nests, land on a sandbar and watch it disappear beneath your feet as the tide rushes in and travel up a small tributary where ships were once built. By the time you return, the river might be as calm as glass, with no hint that it undergoes a Jekyll and Hyde-like transformation every few hours.

Whether it's the quiet anticipation of the arrival of the bore, the rush of excitement the first time the Zodiac crashes headlong into a giant wave or the majesty of the bald eagles slowly taking flight from one of the many perches along the river, there is little doubt that this will be one of the highlights of your trip to Nova Scotia. This is a ride in Mother Nature's theme park. Do it!

A few hints. No matter what, you're going to get good and wet, so have an extra set of clothes and footwear on hand. Leave your watch, keys and wallet at the information office. Only waterproof cameras are safe. The rafting is very popular, especially around the highest tides, so reserve as early as you can. There are now a number of operators offering river rafting. They include Shubenacadie Tidal Bore Rafting at 1-800-565-RAFT, www.tidalboreraftingpark.com, which is based at Tidal Bore Park. Shubenacadie River Runners, 1-800-856-5061, www.tidalborerafting.com, is based in Maitland and offers a longer trip, following the progress of the tide as it fills the river. It passes many beautiful spots along the way. Shubenacadie River Adventure Tours, 1-888-878-8687, www.shubie.com, is in South Maitland and offers mud-sliding as an interesting sideline.

Stanfield Factory Outlet, 11 Logan Street, Truro, (902) 895-5406, www.stanfields.com

For many years Stanfield's has been synonymous not only with underwear, but Truro as well. This is a genuine factory outlet located right in the Stanfield Textile Plant, where you can purchase seconds and other products manufactured on the premises.

WALKING TOURS
Truro
There are a number of options for walking tours in Truro. The Truro Heritage Advisory Committee has put out two architectural walking tours that feature detailed commentary on the most architecturally significant buildings in the town. These booklets are available for $2 each at the Truro Tourist Bureau. These walks will be of particular interest to architecture buffs, as Truro has a large number of well-preserved buildings and an amazing number of architectural styles. Also available at the Truro Tourist Bureau is a free guide to the Truro Tree Sculptures. When Dutch elm disease destroyed many of Truro's stately elms, the town made the most of it by commissioning a number of artists to carve the base of the dead trees into representations of many of Truro's most prominent residents and historical figures. You cannot help but notice these as you pass through town. Following the guided tour will take you to 39 of the sculptures and along the way you will also pass most of the other important sites in town. It is a very interesting and educational way to spend an hour or two.

ACCOMODATIONS
Baile Langan Log Cottages, 11533 Hwy 215, Urbania, (877) 562-3304, www.bailelanganlogcottages.ca
These relatively new log cabins overlook the Shubenacadie River in an area not far from where most of the river rafting tours start. The cabins are completely equipped with everything required for a self-sufficient stay. The property is large and there are hiking trails alongside the river with very good birding opportunities. Children will enjoy seeing the red deer that are raised on the property. All in all, this is a very quiet and scenic location from which to base yourself in this area which is under-served by good accommodations.

Best Western Glengarry, 150 Willow Street, Truro, 800-567-4276, www.bwglengarry.com
With the closure of the John Stanfield Inn there really is no distinctive place to stay in the Truro area. There are plenty of motels, but only one, the Best Western Glengarry, could be classified as anything but ordinary. The Glengarry has plenty of facilities including indoor and outdoor pools, free internet and a passable dining room. It's very popular with both business groups and families. We have always found the Best Western chain to be reliable anywhere in Atlantic Canada.

DINING
The Glooscap Trail is probably the most problematic in Nova Scotia when it comes to finding a good meal. Not only are there not a lot of good places to eat, there aren't a lot of places to eat, period. We can only assume that the people who live in this area must love their own cooking, because they surely are not out spending money in restaurants.

Walton Pub, 39 Shore Road, Walton, (902) 528-2670
This is an unprepossessing little place to stop for lunch almost midway between Windsor and Truro. Good pub fare at decent prices. The fish and chips are always reliable.

Murphy's Fish and Chips, 88 The Esplanade, Truro, (902) 895-1275
Usually in restaurant circles the words "family restaurant" are synonymous with bland and uninspired. This is not so in the case of Murphy's, which has made its reputation on seafood, particularly the fish and chips that many rate the best in the province if not Canada. The clams and chips are way good as well. Owner Gerrard Anderson came up with a secret recipe that produces a lovely light and crispy batter. The portions here are generous and the prices reasonable and, oh yes, there is the customary marine bric-a-brac that allows it to retain the "family restaurant" designation without compromising the quality of its food. Very popular so there might be a wait.

GLOOSCAP TRAIL

Truro to Amherst

From Truro, the Glooscap Trail takes a westerly direction following the shoreline of the Fundy coast all the way to Amherst at the New Brunswick border, passing through some of the most unique and interesting seascapes in eastern North America. The area is world-famous for its fossils and many varieties of collectable mineral specimens, drawing scientists and collectors for over 100 years.

After visiting Truro, the quickest way to get back to the Fundy Shore is to take Highway 104 to the exit for Highway 2 at Glenholme and then follow the signs for Parrsboro. An alternate route that avoids this busy stretch of the Trans-Canada Highway is described under Off the Beaten Path.

The first place of interest is Great Village, a community of well-maintained, architecturally interesting homes and outstanding gardens. The imposing St. James United Church carries these words over the entranceway, "Built 1845, Burned 1882, Built 1883." The rebuilt roof resembles the inverted keel of a ship, not surprisingly since the same people who built the church were also shipbuilders. Inside the church is a room dedicated to Great Village's marine past.

If the church is locked, the key may be obtained across the street at the General Store, an operating business in a heritage property. The store contains an interesting display of items from its early years.

Great Village is also noted as the home of Pulitzer Prize-winning author Elizabeth Bishop. Although not as widely known in Canada as she deserves to be, Bishop's descriptions of life in a country village are well-known to New Englanders. To her fans, various parts of Great Village will be readily recognizable from her writings.

Passing through Highland Village and Portaupique, a former Acadian community, the trail reaches Bass River, so named for the striped bass that are still regularly caught in most of the rivers emptying into the Bay of Fundy from Great Village to Parrsboro.

Bass River has given its name to the famous style of chair, first manufactured here in the 1800s. Several furniture manufacturers have come and gone — all lost to fire. The last, the Dominion Chair Company, was located across the street from the general store where the town's museum now sits. Sadly, the chairs are no longer made in Bass River although they are still produced under the Bass River name — in Ontario. An open-air interpretive centre documents not only the history of furniture making, but many other aspects of this once-thriving community. Also of note is the beautiful Veteran's Memorial Park which features a recreation of World War I trenches on one side and a perennial garden on the other. The granite monuments list the names of all who served from the Bass River area in the great conflicts of the last 100 years right up to Afghanistan.

Just outside Bass River, a road heads toward the ocean and the intriguingly named Saints Rest. The road ends at a lighthouse and gravel beach overlooking the mouth of the Bass River. This is a good spot to try fishing for striped bass.

At Economy, the land starts to rise sharply from the coast and from here the coastline is extremely rugged and beautiful with eroded rock formations such as flower pots, arches and stacks. In Central Economy, the last remaining World War II coastal watchtower in Nova Scotia has been moved from its original location directly on the beach, where it was very quickly deteriorating, to form part of an interpretive centre for this interesting area. You can climb the steep stairs of the tower for a view of the vast mud flats of Economy. Downstairs you can get information on the many really good hiking opportunities in the nearby Cobequid Mountains and along the coast.

Turn left at Jacob's Lane in Central Economy for access to some of the largest tidal mud flats in the province. As the tide recedes, it seems to go out forever, exposing miles of ocean floor that are often teeming with clams just under the surface. If you don't actually go out and dig clams yourself, make sure you try some before you leave the area.

The cemetery at Economy dates from 1783 and contains some remarkably well preserved headstones interspersed with modern ones.

Just before the Glooscap Trail climbs Economy Mountain, look for Soley Cove Road to the left. Not far down this road, Ellis Parker Lane leads down to the shoreline from where, at low tide, you can walk all the way to Five Islands marvelling at the amazing colours and shapes of the rocks and sediments as well as numerous waterfalls. Near the end of the road a geological formation known as a flower pot sits in the middle of a small cove completely surrounded by sandstone cliffs. Access to the beach and the island at low tide is possible if you're prepared to scramble down a fairly steep embankment. Great views of the Economy shore can be seen through a hole in the sandstone not far from where you'll end up after descending.

From Lower Economy, the Glooscap Trail climbs Economy Mountain and descends into Five Islands. At the top, there is a spring where travellers have been stopping for as long as the road has existed. This is a great spot for pictures. There is a panorama of the valley below and the Cobequid Mountains in the distance. From Lower Five Islands the trail cuts inland through Moose Brook before reaching the shore again.

The communities of Five Islands and Lower Five Islands are dominated by the islands located just offshore. Like most of the other prominent landmarks in this area, legend ascribes their creation to Glooscap, who in a fit of anger at Beaver threw a handful of sods at him, which became the islands. Beaver's crime had been to build a dam across Minas Basin. Glooscap was apparently no happier with this than present-day environmentalists are with the prospect of a major tidal power project in the bay. The islands, as close to shore as they are have been fascinating people for centuries. Tales of buried pirate treasure and ghosts don't seem out of place here. Moose Island, the largest of the five, has been the site of many treasure hunts. If you look carefully, you will notice a sea arch on Long Island, the third in the chain. Visits to the islands can be arranged with local fishermen or through organized kayak outfitters. On one day a year, when conditions are absolutely perfect, a crazy race called Not Since Moses takes place as runners dash around the Five Islands, often through knee deep mud, before being engulfed by the incoming tide. It's a piece of lunacy that could only occur in a place where islands are not necessarily always islands.

Next is Parrsboro (www.town.parrsboro.ns.ca), the largest town on the Fundy Shore between Amherst and Truro. As such, it is the centre of the fossil and rockhounding activities that are integral to this area. From either direction that you approach Parrsboro on the Glooscap Trail, the highway makes a sharp turn just by the town hall offices. If you follow this turn and keep on going, you will miss the best of what Parrsboro has to offer. The tourist information office is located right beside the town hall.

The main street of Parrsboro is not particularly attractive, but things pick up considerably as you approach the waterfront. This is a former ship-building and wood exporting port located at the head of a tidal river. The entrance to the harbour is very picturesque — a breakwater capped with a scenic lighthouse on one side and the town's wharf with a collection of fishing boats on the other. At low tide, the fishing boats will be high and dry and apparently stranded in the mud of the river bottom. It is hard to believe that within a few hours the tide will rise sufficiently to permit them to sail out of the harbour with ease. The effect is even more striking should there be a small freighter in the harbour.

The attractions of Parrsboro, which include the Ship's Company Theatre, the Fundy Geological Museum, Ottawa House and a number of very scenic drives, are spread out and thus there is no walking tour for this community. The tourist information office is located in the Fundy Geological Museum. Beside the town hall is a giant figure of Glooscap, the area's most famous denizen.

Just north of Parrsboro, the Glooscap Trail splits into two routes. We strongly recommend the route that follows the shore toward Advocate Harbour, then to Amherst. However, if you are pressed for time, the other route, which follows Highway 2 inland through Springhill (www.town. springhill.ns.ca), is a much shorter route to Amherst and also has some attraction. This portion of the trail travels through the heart of Nova Scotia's blueberry country. Many of the pastures and fields have been converted to growing this valuable crop. In the fall, the colours of the reddening blueberry fields and the surrounding maple trees create a beautiful drive through the small communities of Southampton and Mapleton to Springhill. The Wild Blueberry Harvest Festival (www.wildblueberryfest. com) takes place each August throughout the entire blueberry growing areas of Central Nova Scotia and celebrates the fact that Nova Scotia is the largest producer of wild blueberries in the world.

To continue on the more scenic alternative, turn left onto Route 209 just outside Parrsboro. The sea is not visible again until Diligent River, about 15 kilometres away, named over 200 years ago by the visiting governor, who was impressed by the hardworking residents. Next are Fox River and Port Greville, both of which have many fine old homes set on the wide expanse of Greville Bay. At Port Greville you will find a lookoff that allows you to appreciate the symmetrical beauty of this bay. Just outside the village is the Age of Sail Heritage Centre, which celebrates the shipbuilding legacy of the area.

For the next 30 kilometres, the Glooscap Trail winds through, over and above some of the most spectacular coastal scenery anywhere in the world. On a clear day, there are splendid views of Cape Split and Blomidon across the bay and Cape d'Or up the coast.

At Spencers Island, take the road to Spencers Beach, where there is a cairn marking the legend of the famous mystery ship *Mary Celeste,* which was built here. More details on her fate are available at www.maryceleste.net. Also on the beach are a picturesque lighthouse and an unobstructed view of Spencers Island just offshore. From the beach you can see as far down the coast as Cape Sharp just outside Parrsboro.

The road now cuts across the base of Cape d'Or. Spectacular ocean views return at Advocate Harbour; from there you can see an unbroken line of cliffs all the way to the tip of Cape Chignecto. Offshore is the often fog-shrouded Ile Haute, a place of legend and mystery. Advocate has a beautiful harbour, which is almost completely protected by a natural sandbar. Not far from here is the entrance to Cape Chignecto Provincial Park, which encompasses 4,050 hectares of some of the wildest and most dramatic scenery in Eastern Canada. In 2009, a second interpretive centre was opened at Eatonville, creating access to some of the most famous coastal formations on this shoreline, including the Three Sisters.

From Advocate to Joggins there is a long stretch with very little to see as the highway travels well inland with glimpses of the ocean only at Sand River and Shulie. Apple River, a lumbering centre, is the only village for almost 90 kilometres.

Civilization returns at the former coal-mining towns of Joggins and River Hebert. Joggins is famous for its fossil cliffs, and in 2008 received recognition by designation as a World Heritage Site by UNESCO. A new interpretive centre has greatly increased the enjoyment of a visit to this area. From River Hebert, the trail passes through the farming communities of Maccan and Nappan, where there is a federal experimental farm. If your timing is good, there are places from which to see a tidal bore at River Hebert and Maccan, as well as excellent birding opportunities in the wildlife preserves just outside Amherst. The Glooscap Trail ends at Amherst, far too soon for all but the most jaded of travellers.

BEACHES
Port Greville Beach
From the head of Minas Basin until Parrsboro, the shoreline is dominated by sandstone and mud flats. This makes for great scenery and good clam digging, but very muddy beachcombing. At Greville Bay this

changes dramatically. This semicircular bay stretches from Fox Point to Cape D'Or and most of it is rimmed by a virtually uninterrupted beach, broken only by the occasional stream or small headland. The beach is firm and gravelly with many interesting types of rocks to be found. It is primarily a walking and beachcombing strand due to the relative frigidity of the Fundy waters. If you look closely, there's lots of good driftwood and interesting shells. The beach can be accessed at a number of spots including Port Greville. At Ward's Brook, you can drive right to the beach and probably have it to yourself.

Advocate Beach
This beach forms an almost complete barrier to the entrance of Advocate Harbour. It is considered one of Nova Scotia's best beaches for driftwood and you'll immediately see why the moment you step on its pebbly surface. The easiest way to reach the beach is from West Advocate near the entrance to Chignecto Park.

BIRDING
McElmon's Pond
This is part of the Debert Wildlife Management Area not far from Highway 2 just outside Truro. Developed by the province in conjunction with Ducks Unlimited, the pond, really a small lake, is home to the only breeding population of American widgeons (bald pate) in Nova Scotia. Additionally, blue and green-winged teals and black ducks breed here. In the spring and fall, many more species of waterfowl pass through the park. A series of hiking trails provides access to the more remote sections of the park. A permit, which can be obtained at the Department of Natural Resources office, may be required during the breeding season.

Chignecto National Wildlife Area
This national wildlife area lies just to the west of Amherst. The Amherst Point Migratory Bird Sanctuary, which is one part of the reserve, is a series of impoundments created for waterfowl. It has a hiking trail and a number of viewing points along the road which skirt a section of the sanctuary. The reserve also includes the John Lusby Salt Marsh, which borders Cumberland Basin. Access to this portion of the reserve is more difficult. Chignecto is known for its large variety of waterfowl, both breeding and migratory. Many species that do not breed elsewhere in Nova Scotia, such as the pintail and widgeon, may be viewed here, along with other Nova Scotia rarities such as the moorhen, shoveler and the beautiful black tern.

In addition to Chignecto, the nearby Minudie area is a good spot for migratory waterfowl and sandpipers.

GOLF
Parrsboro Golf Course, Greenhill Road, east of Parrsboro, (902) 254-2733, www.parrsboro.com/golf.htm
This may not be the most challenging nine-hole course in Nova Scotia, but

it is probably the most scenic. In fact, the views of the Bay of Fundy cliffs and the entrance to Parrsboro Harbour are so compelling that they actually do affect your concentration. This is a friendly course worth playing for the scenery alone, although you will probably be pleasantly surprised at your score.

HIKING
Economy Falls, Escarpment and Devil's Bend Trails
These three trails along with the very challenging Kenomee Canyon trail are all part of the Kenomee Trail system which has become a major hiking attraction in the Economy area.

The once-dramatic 27-metre Economy Falls are now less spectacular after a substantial collapse a few years ago, but still definitely worth a visit. The three trails can be combined to make for a full day of hiking. The directions to the trailheads are very well marked. Before starting you can buy a map of the trail system and others nearby at the Cobequid Interpretive Centre in Economy. Turning up the River Philip Road in Central Economy watch for a look-off about a kilometre up, which provides an amazing panorama of the Minas Basin below. An interpretive sign explains the geologic features, including Burntcoat Head and Cape Split. Continue on this increasingly rough road, which passes through some pretty blueberry fields and some ugly clearcuts. The first trail reached is Devil's Bend, which follows the course of the Economy River for 7 kilometres up to the falls. About a third of the way up, a series of look-offs begins, from which you can get great views of the valley and the Cobequid Mountains. This hike is strenuous, and if you have to retrace your steps back to the trailhead, it will consume the better part of a day. If possible, bring two cars and park one at the upper parking area close to the falls.

From the upper parking area it is a short walk to a set of steps that leads down to the base of the falls. Here you can clearly see where the rock has shifted. This area is great for swimming, picnicking and general exploring. To reach the top of the falls, climb the steps to a junction that leads to a lookoff. Perhaps due to the changes in 1997, it is difficult to get a good look from here, but with a little poking about you can get closer to the action. Be careful, however; you don't want to engineer your own collapse.

In 2002, a bridge was constructed across the river just above the falls. It leads on to the Escarpment Trail, which takes a steep path up the opposite side of the river and, after passing the junction of the Kenomee Canyon Wilderness Trail, wends its way through a light dappled hardwood forest to a ford in the river about 1.5 kilometres below the falls. All in all, it is a pleasant way to extend the short trip from the upper parking lot to the falls into a good hike. Be forewarned, however: unless the river is very low, you will have to wade across it on some very slippery rocks. On your return down River Philip Road, you will be rewarded with a breathtaking vista of the Minas Basin stretching from Economy Point to Economy Mountain.

Five Islands Provincial Park

Until a few years ago the Red Head Trail, which skirted the edges of the cliffs to some of the most fabulous look offs in the province, was the gem of Five Islands Park. Unfortunately, the combination of erosion and budgetary restraints has spelled the demise of this great trail. If you want great views from above, Chignecto Park is now the place to do that. However, Five Islands is by no means a lost cause. At low tide it is great fun to walk the exposed ocean bed out to the rock formation called the Old Wife or even all the way to Moose Island. This is an especially magical walk in the early morning as the rising sun projects its rays over the water, sand and rock to create an ever changing display of colours. Don't forget your camera or the fact that the tide comes in very fast. Wear rubber boots if possible.

Wards Falls Hiking Trail

Look for a sign on a dirt road approximately 9 kilometres from the junction of Highways 209 and 2. It is a short drive down this dirt road to the parking area. The trail is a delightful 3.5-kilometre trek that crosses and recrosses a small brook until it arrives at the falls. Wards Falls is not spectacular — about what you might expect from such a small stream. A secure ladder has been erected, which allows access to a gorge at the top of the falls. In places, the gorge is not much more than a metre wide and probably about 30 metres deep.

Even without the falls, this is a very pleasant walk. There are a great variety of ferns, mushrooms and wildflowers and usually the only sounds are the bubbling brook and the birds. It is not unusual to scare up a blue heron, which looks like a ghost as it courses between the trees and underbrush. The Wards Falls Trail is usually dry and it is well marked and maintained.

Cape Chignecto Provincial Park,
www.novascotiaparks.ca/parks/capechignecto.asp

Cape Chignecto Provincial Park offers an extensive variety of coastal and wilderness hiking and walking trails that will inspire all, whether seasoned hikers or casual day trippers. At the Red Rocks trail head right by the Visitor Centre, visitors can choose from eight different trails or walks ranging from a 15 minute stroll to the beach, to the challenging 51-kilometre long Cape Chignecto Coastal Trail. Other less challenging options include the Christie Viewpoint Trail and the moderately challenging five kilometre Fundy Ridge Trail. Experienced hikers may want to try the more challenging trails: McGahey Brook Canyon Trail – 9 kilometres; Mill Brook Canyon Trail – 12 kilometres; or Refugee Cove – 24 kilometres.

While all the trails feature spectacular views and many allow access to the shore, the trail to Refugee Cove is probably the most representative of the best that the park has to offer. Refugee Cove lies about 4.5 kilometres up the coast from the interpretive centre, but according to the official trail maps you cannot reach the cove via the shoreline — instead, you must take a 12-kilometre inland trail and return the same way. This inland trail crosses through some beautiful maple forests and has a number of spectacular viewing points from the cliffs, which in places are hundreds of feet high. The trail rises over several high hills and then descends down valleys on one of the most strenuous treks in Nova Scotia.

An alternative to completing this hike all on the inland trail is to hike to Refugee Cove along the beach and return on the inland trail. Park literature advises that the beach hike is not possible, and for good reason. Don't attempt the beach trek unless you have a guide who can precisely time the low tide to ensure you can safely wade around headlands that are otherwise a complete sea-wall barrier. The tides of the Bay of Fundy are treacherous and the danger should be respected by all. The beach trek is an awesome experience if you are fortunate enough to find a guide. Majestic cliffs rising out of the sea to heights of 152 metres flank you most of the way. In some places the geological strata of the earth are revealed — its layers, folds and changes in colour and texture. Waterfalls cascade from cliff faces, sea arches and caves are there to explore, and photographic opportunities abound.

Arriving via the official trail, Refugee Cove is one of the few areas along this coast where there is a break in the cliffs and a chance to get down to sea level to view the awesome cliffs from below or explore the caves and arches that are found nearby. It was named for a group of Acadians who fled here in an attempt to avoid deportation back in 1755. It's hard to believe that anyone could survive a winter in this environment. If you do manage to reach Refugee Cove by way of the beach, you will definitely have to return via the overland route, because the tide will have risen.

In 2009 the Three Sisters Interpretive Centre opened, allowing access to an area of the park that previously could take days to reach. While it's a long drive down a dirt road to get there, the destination is worth the effort. From the interpretation centre, which is totally run on renewable energy as there is no electrical grid for 20 kilometres, trails lead in two directions. One heads toward the legendary Three Sisters rock formation at the site of what was once the thriving community of Eatonville. This trail has four lookoffs and is simply stupendous. The other trail is a loop to Squally Point which has two lookoffs and a unique raised beach created by glacial activity some 40 metres above sea level. Plan to spend a full day in the Eatonville area.

We simply cannot say enough about the beauty of the Chignecto Park area and, in particular, the places where you can get down to the shore to appreciate the amazing geological and geomorphic diversity.

Wentworth Valley Trails
There are a number of trails all centred around the Wentworth Hostel, which lies about 4 kilometres off Highway 4, just past the entrance to Ski Wentworth if you're coming from Truro or Halifax. Follow the signs for the hostel - the trails start not far from it. Originally built mostly for cross-country skiing, most of the trails are worthwhile for hikers as well — especially one that leads to a spectacular look-off over the valley. This trail

is mostly uphill for about 2 kilometres through the hardwoods that the Wentworth Valley is famous for. There are quite a number of junctions, but at last visit the way to the look-off was fairly well posted. If possible, try to obtain a map from the hostel. The look-off itself is a bare granite outcropping that is definitely not for those with a fear of heights. However, the view from here over the valley, particularly in the fall, is awesome.

Amherst Point
This medium-length circular walk starts about 3.2 kilometres southwest of Amherst. Simply follow Victoria Street out of town to the Amherst Point Migratory Bird Sanctuary. In the parking lot there is a map of the trail and a list of some of the species of birds you might see at any given time. Follow the trail clockwise through abandoned orchards and many varieties of hardwoods to the shores of the small marshy lake. From here the trail circles the lake, crossing a number of small inlets by way of boardwalks. This is a very tranquil place and you'll almost certainly hear and see loons as well as bald eagles, muskrat and often deer, in addition to many species of waterfowl. If you're staying in Amherst, do yourself a favour and come out here first thing in the morning. You'll be glad you did.

KAYAKING
The upper portion of the Bay of Fundy is rapidly becoming recognized as one of the premier sea kayaking destinations anywhere. The towering cliffs and amazing landforms, including arches, stacks and flowerpots combined with legendary mariner's landmarks such as Cape Split and Cape D'Or, make this area irresistible to kayakers. There is no question that travelling the Bay of Fundy area by small craft gives a perspective and understanding of the area that simply cannot be achieved solely from land. The incredible tidal forces that have created the seascapes that attract kayakers in the first place are also a potential great danger. Tidal rips, whirlpools and other hazards that might have confounded Ulysses are not uncommon, so it goes without saying that unless you are an extremely advanced kayaker, this coast should only be attempted in a group with an experienced guide. Most of Nova Scotia's top kayaking outfitters and many national and international tour companies now offer trips to this region, however, Nova Shores Adventures (1-866-638-4118, www.novashores.com) is based right at Advocate Harbour and probably has the most experience in this area.

MUSEUMS
Fundy Geological Museum, 162 Two Islands Road, Parrsboro, 1-866-856-DINO, museum.gov.ns.ca/fgm
In 1984 the Parrsboro area was the site of one of the world's largest finds of early dinosaur fossils. The Fundy Geological Museum which backs on Parrsboro's picturesque harbour was designed to showcase Nova Scotia's incredible fossil record and its geology. Most people, especially kids, will be attracted by the dinosaur bones and recreations of some of the earliest of these creatures. Others will be amazed at the

collection of Nova Scotia minerals and gems, in colours and shapes one doesn't usually associate with, well, "rocks". Many can be found in the immediate area. This museum should be a mandatory stop for anyone who has come to the area looking for rock specimens or fossils.

Ottawa House by the Sea, 1155 Whitehall Road, Parrsboro, (902) 254-2376, www.ottawahouse.org

Ottawa House, the sole surviving building of the original Parrsboro town site, is one of the oldest buildings in the province. It has a splendid location adjacent to the causeway that leads to Partridge Island. On a clear day, the red cliffs of Blomidon on the other side of the Minas Basin appear not too distant at this point. Original portions of the house date back to 1775, although in later years it was considerably expanded by Sir Charles Tupper, Canada's sixth Prime Minister, who used it as a summer home for over 30 years. After the Tupper family sold it, it was used as a hotel for a considerable portion of the twentieth century. For many years the building sat neglected and was in dire need of repair. We are glad to report that in the last five years considerable restoration work has taken place and it is now open seasonally as a community museum.

The beautiful location and historic connections are reason enough to take the short trip from Parrsboro, but there is another. At the end of the beach, just behind a lone cottage that sits at the base of Partridge Island, a short trail begins which will take you up and over the island to the other side where a smallish lookout tower awaits you. The views from here on a clear day are awesome. A large map helps you identify Blomidon, Cape Split and Cape Sharp. It also has a list of important events that have happened within eye sight of the lookout. While the initial climb is steep, the effort is more than rewarding.

Age of Sail Heritage Centre, Port Greville, (902) 348-2030, www.ageofsailmuseum.ca

To commemorate the shipbuilding legacy of this coast, the residents of the area moved an old church and remodelled it into a small museum. There are a number of audiovisual and panel displays that document the history of shipbuilding along this shore. The centre overlooks a small tidal stream. It also has a unique entranceway — a capstan, which you push in order to gain entry.

Amos "King" Seaman School Museum, Minudie, (902) 251-2394

This small museum is dedicated to the remarkable life of the Grindstone King, Amos Seaman. The museum documents his rise from a young lad of eight who moved to this former Acadian settlement and rose to become the richest man in the province, with business interests in many things, especially grindstones. This building and the two churches that flank it were built by Seaman and are about all that's left of this once-prosperous community. The museum is worth a visit, not necessarily for the exhibits but for the story of the man behind them.

Springhill Miners' Museum, 145 Black River Road, Springhill, (902) 597-8614

Springhill, unfortunately, is a byword for disaster for anyone whose memory goes back to the 1950s. A horrendous explosion in 1956 killed 39 miners and the 1958 "bump" killed 75 more. However, what most people will remember is being riveted to the radio or TV screen waiting for the latest report on the fate of the miners trapped underground. After what seemed like an eternity and against all odds, over a week after the bump over a dozen miners were rescued. The attempts to save them became the first international televised media frenzy and the rescued miners enjoyed a brief period of celebrity.

While the museum is not located on the site of the No. 2 Colliery where 1958 tragedy occurred it does tell the story of that and other events. The museum offers a tour of the Syndicate Mine, the last operating coal mine in Springhill, which finally closed in 1970. Underground tours were conducted by former coal miners, some of whom worked the pits in 1956 and 1958 and recalled vividly the tragedies during those years, but there are not many former coal miners left. Still the guides are very knowledgeable and relate the story of Springhill very well. Not for the claustrophobic, the tour winds down an old slope to original coal workings. You or your kids can grab a pick and get a sample from the mine walls. Hard hats, rubber boots and slickers must be worn for the underground portion of the tour — always a popular family photograph. While in the mine, you will get a chance to find out what dark really is when the lights are turned out. This is an interesting and informative tour.

OFF THE BEATEN PATH
Onslow, Debert and Londonderry

As an alternative to the Trans-Canada Highway from Truro to Glenholme and Highway 2 to Great Village, this mostly inland route may appeal to the industrial history enthusiast. Certainly the portion from Londonderry to Great Village will appeal to those who like quiet country backroads.

Leaving Truro, take the first exit to Onslow and turn left to follow the shore through this prosperous pastoral farming community. Nearby, a cairn marks the site of the Isconish portage, a major link in the eighteenth-century route connecting the Acadian communities of the Annapolis Valley with those in Île-Saint-Jean (Prince Edward Island) and the Fortress of Louisbourg.

At McElmon's Road, turn right and follow it past McElmon's Pond Wildlife Sanctuary to Debert, which was once the site of a major military air base that specialized in training pilots during World War II. There is a small museum commemorating those heady days (www.debertmilitary-museum.org). When the base was drastically down-sized, the community converted much of the land into an air industrial park. Debert is still a major training centre for commercial and private pilots, as well as a base for recreational flyers. A centre for glider flying, it is not uncommon to see the graceful, long-winged craft soaring overhead. Debert is also the site of one of the oldest Paleo-Indian sites in North America, dating back almost 11,000 years.

From Debert, follow the highway to Londonderry, about 17 kilometres. Over 100 years ago, this was one of Nova Scotia's busiest industrial centres. There were several large steel mills employing over 2,000 people. This development was made possible by easy access to coal in nearby Cumberland and Pictou counties, combined with the iron ore deposits of Londonderry. However, the iron ore has run out, the mills are gone and the community is a mere fraction of its former self. In a small memorial park on a hill overlooking the town, there are several mementos of the past, including a map depicting the layout in its prosperous days. Looking at where former steel mills, churches, schools and homes once stood, one now sees mostly trees and forests. It is a good reminder of the impermanence of man's works.

Approaching Londonderry you will have passed a road for Great Village. You can either return this way or continue through secluded, often canopied roads that will eventually take you to either Portaupique or Bass River, depending on which way you chose. Make sure you have a map or GPS.

Cobequid Mountains

Many of the back roads, paved and unpaved, that ascend the Cobequid Mountains (really hills), from Great Village to Five Islands, are worth exploring. Narrow winding roads, in places canopied with mature hardwoods, link one small farming community to another. In some instances, the communities exist now in name only — names not to be forgotten, such as Pizzlewig, which once existed up the New Briton Road. In many areas, the back roads traverse blueberry fields, which have increasingly taken over from traditional farming and lumbering land uses. Occasional glimpses of Minas Basin remind you that you are never far from the ocean. The area teems with wildlife and offers one of the best opportunities to see moose or bear in Nova Scotia.

Two Islands Road, Parrsboro

This is a trip not to be missed. Continue past the golf course until the pavement ends on Two Islands Road. About a mile further on is a small parking lot with a trail leading down the cliffs to the beach opposite The Brothers, two offshore islands. Once on the beach, you are very close to Wasson Bluffs, the scene of one of North America's largest fossil finds. The beach also has some of the best rockhounding to be found anywhere. As if this weren't enough, the views of The Brothers and, further down, Five Islands, are spectacular. The contrast of the blue waters and red sandstone cliffs, especially at sunset or sunrise when the colours change with the sun's elevation, is magical. This is, quite simply, a place of extraordinary natural beauty and one can well understand why the first inhabitants believed this area to be populated by gods. Best of all, even in midsummer, you are likely to have this place to yourself.

Resist the temptation to walk out to the closer of the two islands, which can be reached at low tide. The tide, when it turns, comes in incredibly fast and it is easy to get stranded.

The Road to Black Rock

After visiting Ottawa House and the beach at Partridge Island, take a drive to Black Rock, a community that is not on the official Nova Scotia highway map. On leaving Ottawa House, turn left and drive to the end of the road, about 15 kilometres. There you will find a long gravel beach strewn with driftwood. Across the water, seemingly very close, is the coast from Blomidon to Cape Split. As the tide changes from ingoing to outgoing, or vice versa, the current rushes like an immense river between the two shores.

In 2009, just off Black Rock, a sub-sea turbine of about six stories in height was anchored on the sea floor. It remains about forty feet below the surface of the ocean even at low tide. It is an "in stream tidal" turbine which generates electricity from the water current created when tides rise and fall. This is the first deployment of a device of this size in North America. If it survives the harsh environment of the Bay of Fundy and does not have a deleterious effect on the environment, you can anticipate there will be more of these put in place. This is cutting edge technology funded by the provincial and federal governments, the local utility and technology innovators. Unfortunately (or fortunately), there is nothing to look at from the beach, but it is interesting to know that the huge energy potential of the Bay of Fundy may be harnessed yet. We wonder if Glooscap would approve.

The community of Black Rock is a mere shell of its former self, as evidenced by the graveyard that dates from 1790. A memorial lists more family names buried there than houses currently existing in the entire community.

Returning to Parrsboro, you will be rewarded with more great views, particularly of Partridge Island.

Cape d'Or

On the Parrsboro side of Advocate, look for a sign to Cape d'Or. The road turns to gravel and climbs up and over the large mountain in front of you. Coming down the other side, look for a small road to the left. Park here and walk down to secluded Horseshoe Cove, which is framed by a line of cave-studded cliffs on one side and the forest on the other. This beautiful spot once hosted a bustling mining community. All that remains is a few cottages and usually a lot of sea birds seeking shelter in the calm waters of the cove.

After Horseshoe Cove the road continues on to Cape d'Or, a famous landmark first described by Champlain in the early 1600s. The weather here is extremely variable. Sometimes the wind howls with a ferocity that's hard to believe, while at others it's as calm as can be. Only a few years ago the road was barely passable and this place was rarely visited. In recent years it has become one of the primary destinations on the Glooscap Trail. Park your car and find out why.

First visit the observation deck from where, on a clear day, you can see as close to forever as possible in this part of the world. Down below is the lighthouse and former keeper's house, now converted to a restaurant and B&B. Next take the very short loop trail that starts behind the small lighthouse in the parking lot. This will take you to look-offs where you can view the infamous Dory rip, which, at the change of tides, roars past the cape like a raging river somehow transported to an ocean setting. Then follow the path leading down to the lighthouse and enjoy this rugged headland. The power of the sea as it meets the sheer basalt cliffs is overwhelming and intimidating — words cannot do it justice.

The cliffs at Cape d'Or are steep and the grass grows right up to the edges, obscuring them. Although recent fencing is effective, don't allow young children or dogs to wander free. Second, there is a fog horn on Cape d'Or, which can go off without warning. It is so loud, it's frightening and will, at the very least, scare the hell out of you. However, on clear days it's usually silent. Despite these small concerns, this is a highly recommended side trip.

Minudie

The Minudie Peninsula is a finger of land extending between River Hebert and Cumberland Basin. Although you may be coming from Joggins, we recommend that you begin this loop in River Hebert and follow a counterclockwise direction.

The highway follows the course of the river to an interpretive display that explains the history of this area. If you stop there, note the large specimen trees in the field to your left. This is where Amos Seaman's mansion stood until the 1970s. Today, there is no sign of either the house or the railways, wharves and quarries for which this area was famous.

Just past the interpretation centre is the "King" Seaman Museum from which there is a beautiful view back over the fields, forests and rivers. Past the museum the road turns to dirt for a while, but pavement reappears just outside Joggins. The tip of this peninsula has been called Elysian Fields since Acadian times and is a delightful spot to hike, birdwatch or just muse.

Springhill, www.town.springhill.ns.ca

The name "Springhill" rings with tragedy. In both 1956 and 1958 this small town became the centre of worldwide attention when coal mine disasters took the lives of over 100 men. Others were rescued after spending almost nine days trapped just over 3 kilometres below ground. All over North America radios were tuned in to hourly reports of the progress of the rescuers. An earlier disaster in 1891 had claimed 125 lives, including over a dozen boys. The 1958 disaster was the last straw and the major mines were closed, never to reopen. A smaller operation, the Syndicate Mine, operated until 1970. It is now the Springhill Miners' Museum.

Despite the loss of over 1,500 mining jobs when the mines closed, the town has survived. Today, Springhill hosts the province's largest correctional facility, as well as a number of light industries. Like most former coal-mining towns, Springhill would not win any civic beauty awards, but it does have two very popular tourist attractions — the Anne Murray Centre and the Miners' Museum, both of which are well worth visiting.

The Wentworth Valley

In early editions, we didn't include the Wentworth Valley for the simple reason that the Trans-Canada Highway ran smack through the middle of it, creating a stretch that was known as Death Valley by the locals because there were so many accidents on this narrow winding road. A new highway has been open for some time and the Trans-Canada no longer follows this route, so this very scenic place has reclaimed the tranquility it once had. This area is best visited in the fall when the Cobequid Hills are ablaze with colour and the air is at its clearest. If possible, park your car and take a hike on one of the many trails that start not far from Nova Scotia's largest ski hill. This is an area known for its sugar maples, which helps explain the extraordinary fall colours. If you're pressed for time, take Highway 4, which is faster and still scenic, though it is not in the same league as either the Glooscap Trail or Northumberland Shore.

PARKS AND GREENSPACE

Thomas' Cove Coastal Preserve,
www.colchester.ca/thomas-cove-coastal-reserve

Look for a Fundy Shore Ecotour sign as you approach Central Economy and follow the dirt road about 4 kilometres to a parking area overlooking a small semi-circular cove. Recently set aside for public use by the generosity of local landowner Harry MacLellan, Thomas' Cove is an almost completely enclosed tidal estuary. Depending on the state of the tide, you can either walk along the sandy shoreline or explore the tidal flats. There are two 4-kilometre trails that loop around each side of the cove. The Economy Trail provides some great views of the geographic features that make this area so interesting. This trail follows the shoreline around Economy Point to Economy Bay with its tremendous mud flats, before returning inland to the parking area. Note that the trail is atop the scarp and not along the shoreline; however, you can stay on the ocean side well past the first headland at Thomas' Cove. The sandstone formations here are pitted with naturally formed holes that look like some deranged giant took an auger to them. You will notice a spot to get back up to the trail, but be wary of the tide and be prepared to get a bit muddy to get this far.

Five Islands Provincial Park,
www.parks.gov.ns.ca/parks/fiveislands.asp

Located on the side of Economy Mountain, facing Five Islands, there is a 445-hectare provincial park that offers camping, hiking and picnicking in a dramatic surrounding. The hiking trails in the park accent both scenery and the natural features of the area, although the dramatic Red Head trail is now closed. The picnic park abuts the rocky beach at Five Islands. At high tide swimming is possible, but the cold temperatures and tidal currents make it inadvisable. Stick to rockhounding and beachcombing.

Cape Chignecto Provincial Park, www.capechignecto.net

This is Nova Scotia's newest and, at 4,050 hectares, largest provincial park. The park was established to preserve one of the wildest and most remote areas of Nova Scotia's coastline. Within its bounds are old-growth forests, abundant wildlife and utterly fantastic cliffscapes. As new trails and campsites are completed, people are getting the chance to experience a true wilderness adventure. It is possible to follow a triangular route that traverses the entire coast of the park, returning to the start via a combination of old lumber roads that once connected to the abandoned community of Eatonville and deep valley trails. Circumnavigation of Cape Chignecto is considered, by most, to be Nova Scotia's most challenging outdoor adventure. It will take at least three days, and up to a week to do it leisurely. The hiking is, in places, extremely strenuous and those afraid of heights may be intimidated by the portions of the trail that are in some places hundreds of feet above the shoreline, with nothing but air in between.

The park also provides phenomenal opportunities for sea kayakers. Several of the most secluded coves and beaches are reserved for sea kayaking campsites.

At the entrance to the park there is an interpretive centre with very helpful and enthusiastic staff who will make suggestions as to how you can maximize your enjoyment of this wonderful place. Lest this description sound too daunting for some, there are several shorter day hikes including one very short one to Red Rocks that is suitable even for families with young children. Trust us; if you've come this far up the Glooscap Trail, you don't want to miss this place. The recently opened Three Sisters Interpretive Centre in the Eatonville section of the park has made access to some of the remotest parts of the park possible.

ROCKHOUNDING AND FOSSILS

Wasson Bluffs

Wasson Bluffs is a protected area on Two Islands Road outside Parrsboro. The beach below the bluffs can be reached by a short trail from a small parking area, which is marked by an interpretive sign noting this as the place where the world's oldest dinosaur fossils have been discovered. While we're not advocating unauthorized fossil digs, it is also an area of outstanding rockhounding. Turn right at the beach and follow it to the base of the cliffs, where you'll find rocks interspersed with a great variety of crystals. Jasper and agates are relatively easy to find. Not far on is a natural arch.

Cape d'Or

Cape d'Or was named by Samuel Champlain for the glittering nuggets that were discovered near the cape. What Champlain believed to be gold was really pure copper in its native or nugget form, which can still be found in the area.

Joggins Fossil Cliffs, www.jogginsfossilcliffs.net
First brought to public attention by the renowned geologist Charles Lyell over a hundred years ago, the fossil cliffs of Joggins represent the most outstanding example of Carboniferous fossils on earth. Just outside the tiny former coal mining town of Joggins, sandstone cliffs, up to 50 metres high, are interlaced with bands of coal and other fossil-bearing strata. Most of the fossils date from the age before dinosaurs when this part of Nova Scotia was a humid and hot tropical forest. Trilobites, insects and amphibians, as well as petrified trees and ferns from the Age of Coal, are plentiful. Recently, there was a very important find of a creature believed to be a link between amphibians and the first reptiles. The outstanding quality of the Joggins Fossil Cliffs was recognized in 2008 when the cliffs where designated as Nova Scotia's second UNESCO World Heritage Site and only the 15th in Canada. To help gain a better understanding of the cliffs a beautiful interpretation centre was opened that year and many of the best fossils from the Don Reid collection permanently put on display. There are many dioramas and other interpretive displays that will enhance a visit to the cliffs.

After visiting the centre, the cliffs are reached through a set of stairs just behind the back entrance. Serious enthusiasts will want to take a guided tour which lasts up to two hours and will guarantee finding and learning more about the fossils than a self guided tour. However, even on your own, at Joggins the fossils are very easy to find. At a minimum, you can certainly expect to find some fossilized plants. At one time people were allowed to keep what they found, but now all fossils must be left as found.

Even if fossils don't excite you, this location on the upper reaches of the Bay of Fundy will. There are magnificent views across the bay to New Brunswick, waterfalls coming out of the cliffs and many shorebirds. The Joggins Fossil Cliffs is a must on any visitor's list of attractions and a place to which all Nova Scotians need to make a pilgrimage. After all, not many places can claim a heritage going back over 300 million years.

SPECIAL EVENTS
Nova Scotia Gem & Mineral Show, Parrsboro,
www.museum.gov.ns.ca/fgm/mineralgem/show.html
Parrsboro is host to one of Nova Scotia's most unique annual festivals — formerly the Rockhound Round-Up, now the more staid-sounding Gem & Mineral Show — which takes place for a week early in August each year. This is a specialized type of gathering that has tremendous appeal to rockhounds and fossil enthusiasts who gather in great numbers to discuss, trade, sell, and exchange information about their favourite hobby.

SPECIAL INTEREST
Joy Laking Gallery, Portaupique, 1-800-565-5899,
www.joylakinggallery.com
This studio/gallery in the artist's home is set on the edge of a tidal marsh, surrounded by pleasant gardens. Joy Laking specializes in watercolours,

particularly of flowers commonly found in Nova Scotia gardens and in the wild. Her serigraphs feature brightly coloured rural and small town scenes and are very popular. As this is both a studio and a gallery, work in progress is on display. If she is there, Laking will be happy to explain to you the complicated and time-consuming effort that goes into the production of one of her serigraphs. Joy Laking's work can also be seen at the Art Gallery of Nova Scotia and other galleries throughout Canada.

Parrsboro Rock and Mineral Shop, 349 Whitehall Road, Parrsboro, (902) 254-2981

Eldon George is the dean of Nova Scotia fossil collectors and rockhounds. He is responsible for many of the most important finds in the Parrsboro area, including the world's smallest dinosaur footprints and the largest footprints of a crocodilian ever found. These and other fossil and rock specimens from Eldon's collection are on view at his shop on the outskirts of Parrsboro. Admission to the museum, which takes up a portion of the shop, is free. On sale are fossil and rock samples, not only from Nova Scotia but around the world. If you want to purchase something from the Parrsboro area, be sure to enquire whether it is a locally found stone or fossil. An inexpensive grab bag chock full of fossils, coloured rocks, quartz crystals and shells makes a great gift for a child. Open May until the end of October.

Anne Murray Centre, 36 Main Street, Springhill, (902) 597-8614, www.annemurraycentre.com

For over 35 years Anne Murray has been one of Canada's best-known singers. She has racked up more gold and platinum albums, Grammy awards and country music awards than any other Canadian and just about anyone else for that matter. To her credit, Anne has always acknowledged her Nova Scotia roots and Springhill upbringing. Her father was a well-known doctor who worked tirelessly during the mine disasters in the 1950s.

The Anne Murray Centre was opened in 1989 as a tribute to her achievements. Within the centre, Anne's life is documented from her earliest report cards (she was an A student), through her brief career as a teacher, to her emergence as a star of international stature. The presentation is a chronological sequence of audiovisuals and memorabilia, much donated by the star herself. When you visit the Anne Murray Centre, you will realize Anne's wholesome image as a small town girl with few pretensions is genuine and no stage act. You will also realize why her worldwide legion of fans makes this one of Nova Scotia's top tourist attractions.

Heritage Models, River Hebert, (902) 251-2666

Heritage Models, the labour of Reginald "Bud" Johnston, is one of the finest displays of folk art anywhere in the province. Many years ago, Bud started making one-twelfth scale models of well-known buildings and industries in the River Hebert area. His attention to detail and imaginative use of materials combine to give the works that extra something that turns hobby work into real art. People have been coming for years to view the models that at one time were in his front yard. Luckily for all of us, the models are now housed in a permanent home where they are protected from the elements. All told, there are just over 20 models, including the local theatre, the curling rink, the general store and a wonderful representation of an early country fair. The museum represents one man's tribute to his community and its past. You won't regret taking the time to stop and see these works of art.

As an added bonus, a small park has been created beside the centre on the banks of River Hebert. If your timing is good, you'll have a chance to observe one of the best tidal bores in the region.

THEATRE
Ship's Company Theatre, Lower Main Street, Parrsboro,
1-800-565-SHOW, www.shipscompany.com
The Ship's Company Theatre was unique in that up until 2004 it was located in the shell of the *Kipawo*, a vessel that once regularly plied the waters between Kingsport, Parrsboro and Wolfville. A large canvas which covered most of the boat gave a naturally eerie light to the stage. That has changed now with the opening of the new theatre, which still incorporates the shell of the *Kipawo*. The Ship's Company Theatre has been a success for over 20 years, presenting many original plays and works, most with an emphasis on Atlantic Canada. The new theatre will allow for an expanded playbill. Even if you don't have time to see a play during your visit to Parrsboro, drop in and have a look at this most unusual theatre.

WILDERNESS AREAS
Economy River Wilderness Area,
www.gov.ns.ca/nse/protectedareas/wa_economyriver.asp
The Cobequid Mountains and attendant geological Cobequid Fault make for some of the most dramatic scenery in Nova Scotia. The numerous rivers that drain into the Bay of Fundy cleave the hills with deep narrow gorges and canyons that make for numerous waterfalls and rapids. The steepness of these valley walls has protected them from exploitation and today much of our remaining old growth forest is found in places like this. The Economy River Wilderness Area is one of the best examples in the Cobequids and the only one with a developed trail system.

The Kenomee Canyon Trail is an 18 kilometre loop through this protected area, and will take between 8 to 10 hours to complete. It is intended for use by experienced hikers only. The trail takes you along the Economy River gorge and includes steep ascents and requires fording of rivers and streams. Camping is allowed on this trail so long as you obtain a permit and only at designated sites at Chain Lake Stream, Murphy Brook, and Newton Lake. Permits are available at Cobequid Interpretive Centre in Economy. Campfires not permitted for ecological reasons.

However, if you are up to it, this is a great experience. Most of the trees are sugar maple or birch which are gorgeous in the fall. The trail passes nearby several small lakes and several waterfalls. This is definitely one of Nova Scotia's most challenging and rewarding trails.

ACCOMMODATIONS

Four Seasons Retreat, 320 Cove Road, Upper Economy, 1-888-373-0339, www.fourseasonsretreat.ns.ca

The Four Seasons Retreat is a five-minute drive off the highway on the bluffs overlooking the flats at Economy Beach. This is a series of one, two and three bedroom cottages that are extremely well built and contain all the necessary amenities for a daily or weekly stay. The cottages are well-separated and you have a feeling of privacy. Each contains a modern Franklin-type fireplace (it gets cool here at night, even in the middle of July). There is a pool and hot tub, rarities in this area.

One of the main attractions of the Four Seasons is that you can do as little or as much as you want. For our money, it is the best and most relaxing place to stay on this entire shore. For activities, you can try clam digging, which is very popular in this area, or visit a traditional First Nations weir, which has been constructed a short stroll from the cottages. There are a number of trails, and you can walk as far as Economy Point and back. A small beach at one end of the property is popular with striped-bass fishermen.

There are few restaurants or grocery stores in the area, so you should come prepared.

Riverview Cottages, 3575 Eastern Avenue, Parrsboro, 1-877-254-2388, www.riverviewcottages.ca

It is hard to know what to make of a place that seems surprised that you would want to stay a second night. The owners apparently are used to people moving on because there are no televisions, telephones, swimming pool or vending machines. These are old-fashioned cabins built between the 1930s and the 1950s that remind us of what vacations were like when we were younger. The cabins are clean and plainly furnished in a mixture of styles; some are minuscule. The cabins back on the Aboiteau, a lake created years ago by the impoundment of the Farrell River at the entrance to Parrsboro Harbour. The owners have canoes and rowboats available, free of charge, with which you can travel right into the heart of Parrsboro or go the other way, up the quiet waters of the Farrell River.

What else is there to do? Sit and listen to the bull frogs court, read a book, tell ghost stories to your children. These are the types of cabins that will make the stories believable. Not for those who need modern conveniences. The new Web site gives you a chance to see each cabin.

The Maple Inn, 2358 Western Avenue, Parrsboro, 1-877-627-5346, www.mapleinn.ca

There are next to no inns along the entire Glooscap Trail, so it's especially gratifying to have The Maple Inn back in business after being closed for a couple of years. A location right in the middle of town allows you to walk to many of Parrsboro's attractions. The inn itself combines two century-old houses that have been completely renovated. There is one large suite for families and a number of smaller rooms. A full breakfast is included in the price.

Driftwood Park Retreat, West Advocate, (902) 392-2008, www.driftwoodparkretreat.com

If you've come to this area to explore Cape Chignecto Park, this is definitely the place to stay. There are five cottages located just beyond the high-tide line of Advocate Beach only about a kilometre and a half from the entrance to the park. Each of the two-bedroom cottages are two stories with the bedrooms downstairs and the kitchen and living room upstairs. Propane fireplaces, hardwood floors and a well-equipped kitchen make for a comfortable stay. There are decks overlooking nothing but ocean and cliffs. The beachcombing begins a few feet from the cottage. As Cape Chignecto Park has become increasingly popular, so have these units, so advance reservations are a must.

DINING

Masstown Market, Highway 2, Masstown, 1-866-273-0614, www.masstownmarket.com

The Glooscap Trail from Truro to Amherst has few good spots to eat, but lots of good spots to picnic, so it's almost mandatory to stop into the Masstown Market to load up on supplies. Opened in 1969 with only two employees, it now employs over 80. Masstown Market attracts customers from all over the Maritimes who value super fresh, locally grown produce over the blander offerings of most large chains who buy in bulk. In addition to the great produce the market offers the best selection of cheeses and processed meats outside Halifax, with the emphasis always on locally made products. However, first and foremost the customers love the baked products. Come to the Masstown Market and discover what a doughnut should taste like. Oh, and the date cookies are to die for.

That Dutchman's Farm, Upper Economy, (902) 647-2751, www.thatdutchmansfarm.com

The Dutchman is a cheese maker who has built himself a traditional Dutch farm high on a hill overlooking the waters of the Bay of Fundy. His flavoured Gouda cheeses have been popular at Nova Scotia markets for years. A restaurant is located next to the cheese-making facility and has a deck from which there is a splendid view of the water below. While waiting for a sandwich or afternoon tea, children love to poke around looking at the chickens, rabbits, calves and sheep. You can buy some of the cheese or baked goods offered for sale. This place has a different kind of atmosphere and is definitely a different kind of place. The menu is simple and can be reviewed from the café link on the Web site.

NORTHUMBERLAND SHORE
Amherst to Pictou

The Northumberland Shore Route (www.northumberlandshore.com), for a long time known as the Sunrise Trail, begins at the Nova Scotia–New Brunswick border and follows the shoreline of the Northumberland Strait around to the Strait of Canso. It is unquestionably the scenic route to Cape Breton, but its beauty is understated. It is more pastoral than the granite rock coastline of the South Shore where the open North Atlantic crashes onto the shore. Prince Edward Island is north across the Northumberland Strait and almost always visible from any vantage point along the coast and on hilltops along the Sunrise Trail. The waters of the Strait are calmer, more sheltered than those along the Atlantic Coast, and the tides, while significant compared to most areas of the world, are modest compared to those on the Glooscap Trail. The Northumberland Shore does however have a more dramatic side. The "little Cabot Trail" offers a taste of what is to come in Cape Breton. But mostly on this shore, the land and the sea are at peace. Perhaps a just as acceptable name for this part of Nova Scotia's coast could be the Sunset Trail, as the sun appears to sink into the ocean as it sets along many parts of this route.

The Northumberland Shore has excellent birding, a number of very good golf courses, miles of good cycling and by far the warmest water of any of Nova Scotia's shorelines. It also has a number of historic towns, most especially Pictou, the site of Scottish migration to Nova Scotia. Although you could easily drive the entire trail in one day, to appreciate the beauty of this area, two to three days are recommended.

Amherst (www.town.amherst.ns.ca) is the first town inside the borders of Nova Scotia. Its turrets and spires are clearly visible across the Tantramar marshes, which you traverse shortly after entering Nova Scotia from New Brunswick. The name is apparently derived from a Mi'kmaq word referring to the din of waterfowl once heard on this vast marshland. Although it is not a prime tourist destination, the town of Amherst has an architectural integrity that makes it appealing. Most of the larger buildings in the downtown core, including the Court House, churches, post office and police station, were all constructed in the late 1800s using local red sandstone. Take particular note of the First Baptist Church. A brochure detailing the history of some of the more interesting buildings is available at the tourist bureau.

Amherst is also known for having produced no less than four Fathers of Confederation, as you will note by their faces carved on an old elm at the entrance to town. One of them, Sir Charles Tupper, was Prime Minister of Canada in 1896. His former pharmacy still operates in a building he constructed in 1889. Grove Cottage, home of another Father of Confederation, R.B. Dickey, is now home of the Cumberland County Museum, which contains a display of the county's industrial history. The area was once well-known for its diverse and active economy, including mining and manufacturing.

The Northumberland Shore route leaves Amherst on Highway 6 via East Victoria Street, which is lined with a number of fine Victorian mansions, including one exceptional example of sandstone architecture. Just outside of town, take the alternate route via Route 366, which crosses rolling farmland along the New Brunswick border until it reaches Tidnish, the first community on the Northumberland Strait. From here it follows the coast around to the Strait of Canso, a distance of 260 kilometres. At Tidnish there is a very interesting interpretive display that commemorates the Chignecto Ship Railway. This was a short-lived attempt to build a railway across the Isthmus of Chignecto, the narrow neck of land that joins Nova Scotia to New Brunswick. The idea was to put small ships on a railway that would transport them from the Bay of Fundy to Northumberland Strait or vice versa, and thus save several days' sailing. Despite a concerted effort by a great number of labourers, the venture failed. From Tidnish, a walking trail follows the old railbed over a beautiful stone arch and a swinging suspension bridge to Tidnish Dock Provincial Park, which was the terminus of the railway.

Not far from Tidnish, Amherst Shore Provincial Park offers a quiet spot to picnic and swim. From the campground, one can follow a path to the mouth of the river and a serene beach.

On this section of the trail, cottage development sometimes obscures the view of the ocean. The most picturesque areas are the river mouths, such as the Shinimicas River and River Philip. The tidal flats are home to a host of wildlife, particularly at low tide, and are usually accessible near the fishing wharfs.

Pugwash (www.pugwashvillage.com) is one of the prettiest towns on the entire Northumberland Shore. You will note that the street signs are in both English and Gaelic in recognition of the community's Scottish heritage. At the tourist bureau, located in a brick railway station, you can get free samples of the rock salt crystals that are mined just across the bay.

For many years, Pugwash was the host to an annual international conference of scholars and business people started up by the late American industrialist, Cyrus Eaton (www.pugwashgroup.ca). The thinkers were lodged in a beautiful setting at the mouth of Pugwash Harbour. Eaton believed that the beauty of the spot would produce clarity of thought, and he was right, for in 1995 the Pugwash Group was awarded the Nobel Peace Prize.

From Pugwash you can continue to Wallace in one of two ways — directly on an inland route or by following the coastline through Gulf Shore and Fox Harbour. Both routes are scenic and it is hard to choose between them.

Wallace (www.wallacebythesea.ca) is known for its quarried stone, which was used in the construction of Canada's Parliament buildings and the Nova Scotia legislature in Halifax. It has a small museum just outside of town and some nice walking trails at the nearby bird sanctuary. From here, the trail continues to the base of the Malagash Peninsula, the site of the first salt mines in Canada, long since closed. You have a choice of cutting across the peninsula or taking the longer route around the perimeter. While the road on the north side is not particularly scenic, the south side more than makes up for it with its unimpeded views of Malagash Bay and the countryside. Rejoining Highway 6, you pass the Tim Hortons Children's Camp, established for disadvantaged children by the Joyce family, who started up Canada's ubiquitous coffee chain and hail from nearby Tatamagouche.

Tatamagouche (www.tatamagouche.com) is one of Nova Scotia's oldest communities, being well known to the Mi'kmaq for thousands of years. The Acadians settled here in the early 1700s and were followed by Montbeliard Swiss and French Protestants after the Acadian deportation in 1755. These newcomers were, like their fellow countrymen who settled the South Shore of Nova Scotia, culturally akin to German Protestants. As a result, there are German restaurants in the area and an Oktoberfest, which is one of Nova Scotia's best autumn events.

Tatamagouche was a prosperous shipbuilding centre in the 1800s and today is a busy town with a number of distinctive homes, the new Creamery Square development, which hosts a number of museums, and several restaurants and inns. It also has one of the oldest remaining railway stations in Canada which is open to visitors. Recently Tatamagouche was put on the national map by the CBC program *The Week the Women Went.*

River John (www.riverjohn.com), the next town, also has older homes and a pretty setting where the river runs into the Northumberland Strait. Just past the town, a paved side road leads to Cape John where, at the government wharf, one can enjoy a panoramic view of Tatamagouche Bay and tiny Amet Island in the distance.

After crossing the base of Cape John, the trail continues through Seafoam to the fishing community of Toney River, which has a wharf usually lined with colourful lobster boats. Not far from here, look for the turnoff to Caribou and the ferry to Prince Edward Island. Take this turn and follow the highway around the shoreline to the entrance of Pictou Harbour and eventually the town of Pictou (www.townofpictou.ca).

In 1773 the ship *Hector* landed here with 189 Scottish immigrants, the vanguard of a huge influx of settlers that was to significantly shape the future of "New Scotland" — Nova Scotia. From Pictou, the Scots spread around the Northumberland shore and eventually populated most of Cape Breton.

The new arrivals had a definite idea of what a proper house should be built of — good Scottish granite. Despite the abundance of local materials, they imported granite from home. The result is a Scottish-looking town with a North American name.

Pictou had a long period of prosperity from shipbuilding activities before beginning a gentle decline that saw most of the industry in the area centre around the coal mines on the other side of the harbour. Today, Pictou offers a wide variety of experiences for visitors. From the waterfront's Hector Heritage Quay to the deCoste Centre's live entertainment, there is a lot to do and see, including museums, shops and galleries. If you stay at one of the inns or B&Bs, you can use Pictou as a base to enjoy the warm beaches, play the golf courses and explore the surrounding countryside.

BEACHES
Northumberland Strait Beaches
Finding a good beach on this stretch of the Sunrise Trail is not as easy as you might expect. There are many beautiful beaches along this shore. While they make for lovely scenery at a distance, many are not accessible to the public because they are surrounded by private land rendering them inaccessible except by sea, and then only to the high water mark. Other more accessible beaches are lined with cottages and their potentially leaky septic systems don't do much for us. For this reason we have not been effusive in our praise for many Northumberland Strait beaches, particularly those which are surrounded by cottage developments, such as Heather and Cameron Beaches, near Pugwash, which are popular destination for locals despite the cottages. There are however a number of beaches worth visiting.

The province has done what it can to protect a number of smaller beaches in the area, including Northport, Fox Harbour and Gulf Shore. All of them have three things in common — red sand, warm water and a gentle drop-off from the shore. Sandstone does, however, make for murky water and sometimes a muddy bottom, so don't expect the clear blue waters of the South Shore or Cape Breton.

The most popular beach in this stretch is Rushtons, located on the Brule shore. It has much the same characteristics as the other protected beaches, but is much larger. Combined with the fact that it has a full range of facilities, in high summer it attracts a considerable number of people, and on weekends it is simply too crowded for us. Nearer to Pictou you will find Waterside Beach and Caribou Island, both of which offer good swimming and are generally not too crowded. Caribou also has the added benefit of some very good shelling at its far end. You should be able to find slipper shells, scallops and moon snail shells. With any luck you may also find the rare angel wing.

BIRDING
Wallace Bay National Wildlife Area
Ducks Unlimited and the Canadian Wildlife Service have preserved a large marsh at the head of Wallace Bay. A 5-kilometre trail cuts through a portion of the reserve on a raised dyke, offering great birding, especially during migration. In the summer, you can expect to see or hear sora, pied-billed grebe, black ducks, bittern and plenty of red-winged blackbirds. The dyke, which is canopied with young birch, is a haven for yellow warblers and yellowthroat.

The entire Wallace area is a birding hot spot. At or near the mouth of the Wallace River or any of the other rivers in the area, you can expect to see belted kingfishers, herons and migrating shore birds. Inland is a great area for birds of prey, especially marsh harriers, kestrels and bald eagles.

CANOEING
La Planche River
Starting almost in the town of Amherst, the canoeist can follow this stream into the heart of the Tantramar Marshes, where the bird life is spectacular. This is one route that must be travelled both ways, as there is no take-out point in the marsh. It's suitable for one day in and one day out.

CEMETERIES
The Old Burying Ground, Amherst
East of Amherst on Route 206, there is an unusually large pioneer cemetery dating from 1790. The site is interesting not only for the many styles of inscription on the headstones, but the presence of a large number of early black settlers buried in one identified segment of the cemetery. Sadly, almost all the stones are marked only by initials, with no other method of identification, not even dates.

Salem Pioneer Cemetery, River John
There are a number of pioneer cemeteries along this coast, all of which are worth visiting. Perhaps the best is Salem Pioneer Cemetery, which has some very well-preserved headstones dating from the early 1800s and features a number of styles of headstones. The cemetery backs on a tranquil pond and marsh.

CYCLING
Northumberland Shore Cycling
Almost any spot on the Sunrise Trail between Amherst and Pictou is great for cycling. There are no significant hills, and there are many paved side roads with little traffic and, usually, a cooling breeze off the strait. Particularly recommended is the Wallace area, from whence you can explore the Gulf Shore area in one direction and the Malagash Peninsula in the other.

A recently opened portion of the Trans Canada Trail follows an abandoned railbed through forests and farmland for 110 kilometres from Oxford to Pictou.

GOLF
Amherst Golf and Country Club, John Black Road, Amherst, (902) 667-8730, www.amherstgolfclub.com
This 18-hole course just east of Amherst is one of Nova Scotia's most popular courses, drawing players from both Nova Scotia and New Brunswick. The layout starts out with the hardest hole in the course — a long par five on which you must place your drive just so. If you pass this test, there are 17 more to come. This is a deceptively long and challenging course, which is always in very good condition and is a pleasure to play.

Northumberland Links, Gulf Shore Road, near Pugwash,
1-800-882-9661, www.northumberlandlinks.com
The provincial government put a lot of money into developing this course,
which was to be a part of a resort that was never built. It is a championship
layout designed by Cornish and Robinson, who also designed the New
Ashburn course in Halifax. It is fairly long, and downright nasty in high
winds, which are not unusual. The greens are large and at times among
the fastest in the province. There are a number of excellent holes that play
right along the Northumberland Strait, including a par three that features
a sunken boat at the back of the green. Talk about a seaside course!

Northumberland is unquestionably a "must play" for any serious golf
vacationer, but it is being discovered by golfers everywhere, so make sure
you have a reserved tee time. By the way, the large modern house visible
from the fifth hole belongs to Anne Murray. She's an ardent golfer and is
often seen playing the course.

Fox Harb'r Resort, 1337 Fox Harbour Road, 866-257-1801,
www.foxharbr.com
Ron Joyce is the founder of Canada's famous coffee and donut chain,
Tim Hortons. Not long after joining forces with the late Dave Thomas of
Wendy's, Joyce stepped down from the day-to-day operations and decided
to spend some of his kazillions of dollars on a golf resort near his home
town of Tatamagouche. The result is the *ne plus ultra* of Atlantic golf resorts,
designed by Canada's most noted modern golf architect, Graham Cooke.
The course features a number of exceptional oceanfront holes on the back
nine, although truth be told, the front nine is not that interesting. There
are up to seven sets of tees on each hole, so any golfer should be able to find
a course length suitable to their game. The conditions are immaculate from
tee to green. As you play your round, you'll pass Joyce's personal residence,
as well as a marina blasted right out of the sandstone, a lighthouse and a
private airstrip. The club house and rental condos are similar in size and
amenities to the best resort facilities. In every sense of the word, this is a
deluxe operation which has hosted the likes of Tiger Woods, Bill Clinton
and Greg Norman. In order to play here you must be a guest of a member.

HIKING
Caribou/Munroes Island Provincial Park,
www.novascotiaparks.ca/parks/caribou.asp
This provincial park, just outside Pictou, is a stone's throw from the ferry
to Prince Edward Island. It preserves one of the few accessible undeveloped
areas along the Northumberland Strait. At one time it was an island, but
Mother Nature was kind enough to connect it with the mainland by way
of a sand spit, which is Caribou Beach. The hike is really a ramble along
the continuation of Caribou Beach for about 3 kilometres to the end of the
island, directly opposite the ferry terminal. For such a big vessel, the ferry
passes amazingly close to the tip of the island. Along the way, you will pass
a sand beach excellent for swimming, see many unusual types of sedimentary

rocks, find many shells, hear the squawks of nesting blue herons and enjoy the cooling breeze from the strait. This is a good hike for small children, as it's flat and there are plenty of things to keep them entertained. The Nature Conservancy is to be congratulated for spearheading the drive to acquire and preserve this special place.

MUSEUMS

Cumberland County Museum, 150 Church Street, Amherst, (902) 667-2561, www.cumberlandcountymuseum.com

Housed in Grove Cottage, the former home of R. B. Dickey, one of Amherst's four Fathers of Confederation, this is a very good regional museum. It particularly excels at demonstrating the numerous products that were once manufactured in Amherst — everything from pianos to automobiles to lifesavers. It also has a small art gallery, research library and archives.

Creamery Square Heritage Centre, 39 Creamery Road, Tatamagouche, (902) 657-3500, www.creamerysquare.ca

Up until 2009 Tatamagouche's heritage was spread throughout five separate locations. In a wise decision the townsfolk decided to build one complex to house them all. The new heritage centre now contains an excellent display of First Nations, Acadian and European artifacts that mostly came from the old Sunrise Trail Museum. The most important display is unquestionably the fossils that were previously housed in the Brule Fossil Centre. Believe it or not, almost three hundred million years ago in the Permian era, Nova Scotia's land mass was actually located near the equator. At that time, beside a riverbank in an early coniferous forest, creatures such as the dimetredon, seymouria and varanops were laying down footprints in mud-prints that have survived to this day. In 1994, erosion revealed the existence of layer upon layer of fossilized tracts, conifer branches and even giant dragonfly wings. With the help of the National Geographic Society, the tracts were removed and preserved before they were eroded away.

The most interesting exhibit for many will be that focusing on the life and legend of giantess Anna Swan, a native of the area who was famous in her time. She weighed 18 pounds at birth and by age 15 was over 7 feet tall. She married another giant and between them produced the largest baby ever born at 24 pounds, although sadly, it did not live. Anna's story is both enlightening and touching. Also in the centre is a creamery museum. Tatamagouche was famous for its dairy products for many years and the archives for the area. Instead of having five little sites that visitors could easily overlook, Tatamagouche has put them together to make this one of the best regional museums in the province.

The Balmoral Grist Mill, 660 Matheson Brook Road, Balmoral Mills, (902) 657-3016, museum.gov.ns.ca/bgm

Located in an idyllic setting on Matheson Brook, the red ochre mill at Balmoral looks like it belongs on a jigsaw puzzle box or a calendar. The mill is operational and processes oatmeal, whole wheat flour and buckwheat. As you tour the mill and learn how the gristmill process works, you cannot help but notice the wonderful aroma. The only thing missing is a water-wheel, and that is because the Balmoral Mill operated on turbines, which lay in the water below the building. Today, the milling machinery is run by electricity, but in all other respects it is totally authentic.

At the gift shop, you can purchase samples of the grain produced at the mill.

Sutherland Steam Mill, Denmark, (902) 657-3365, www.museum.gov.ns.ca/ssm/

Located in Denmark several kilometres off the Northumberland Shore route on Route 326, this mill was built by Alexander Sutherland in the late 1800s, primarily to ensure a supply of lumber for his carriage-making business. Over the years, the Sutherland family expanded the business to manufacture a large variety of wood products including doors, windows and "gingerbread" house-trim. The mill ceased commercial operations in 1958, but reopened in the 1970s after being restored for operation as a museum.

The mill operates on steam power generated by a huge boiler. There is a fascinating array of gears, pulleys, belts and other doohickeys that are testaments to the ingenuity of rural entrepreneurs who had to design almost everything from scratch. It is amazing how many machines can be operated from one drive shaft. The boiler is always fired and the attendants will put the mill in operation for you if you ask — all by pulling one lever. Amid the whir and whirl of the belts, the buzzing of the saws and the rising of the steam, you might feel you've been transported back to the nineteenth century.

Both Sutherland Steam Mill and Balmoral Grist Mill, which are only a few miles apart, are well worth visiting for glimpses of the industries that have gone the way of the horse-drawn plough. One point of note regarding Sutherland, you must keep a close eye on very young children because of the moving machinery.

Hector National Exhibit Centre and McCulloch House, 86 Old Haliburton Road, Pictou, (902) 485-4563, www.mccullochcentre.ca

The Hector National Exhibit Centre is primarily a genealogical research centre for those who trace their ancestry to the Highland Scots who populated Nova Scotia. The main exhibit hall is gaily decorated with the tartans of various clans whose members made the historic voyage on the *Hector*. Just inside the entrance is a tall case clock made by a local clockmaker, Geddes.

This brick and stone house was the home of the Rev. Thomas McCulloch, who immigrated to Nova Scotia from Scotland in early 1803. He is an outstanding figure in Nova Scotia's history. A Presbyterian minister, an educator and a political reformer, McCulloch left a lasting legacy in Nova Scotia. He championed the cause of free access to a liberal and nonsectarian education for all — a view that was not at all popular in contemporary circles. In 1816 he founded the Pictou Academy, a tribute to his beliefs and thereby began a tradition of excellence in Pictou County education that continues to this day. The academy was known for the number of scholars it produced who went on to great careers in science, medicine and law. McCulloch eventually moved to Halifax to become the first president of Dalhousie University in 1838. You will learn that McCulloch had a wide variety of interests, which are reflected in the items displayed in his home. Of particular note is the John J. Audubon print, a gift from the naturalist and painter, who was a friend of McCulloch's and visited him here in 1833. Also of note are two painted fireplaces and many examples of fine woodwork found throughout the house.

Northumberland Fisheries Museum, 71 Front Street, Pictou, (902) 485-4972, www.northumberlandfisheriesmuseum.com
This small museum, primarily located in a very attractive brick train station, has recently been renovated. There are now three sites that include a lobster hatchery and a lighthouse museum on the waterfront, as well as the train station site that has thousands of artifacts documenting the history of fishing on the Northumberland Strait.

OFF THE BEATEN PATH
Malagash Peninsula
If you are enjoying the pastoral tranquility of the Sunrise Trail, you can prolong your enjoyment by circling the Malagash Peninsula, which extends like a finger into the Northumberland Strait between Wallace and Tatamagouche. Once the site of flourishing salt mines, it is now home to Nova Scotia's most successful winery, Jost Vineyards, which is certainly worth a visit. On the loop, you can stop at a small museum which tells the somewhat less than exciting story of salt mining. You definitely should stop at the day park at Blue Sea Corner Beach, where there is a mile-long sandstone beach unobstructed by the cottages that line so many of the other beaches along the Sunrise Trail.

PARKS AND GREENSPACE
Amherst Shore Provincial Park,
www.novascotiaparks.ca/parks/amherst.asp
This provincial park offers one of the few opportunities to camp at a public facility along the Northumberland Shore. There is a pleasant walk to a warm water and great beachcombing at low tide.

Fox Harbour Provincial Park, near Wallace
Wallace Harbour is one of the most picturesque areas on the Sunrise Trail, free of much of the cottage development on other parts of the coast. The drive to Fox Harbour Provincial Park from Wallace Bay passes alongside the shore with excellent views of the town across the water. The park is located in a very tranquil spot overlooking the entrance to the harbour. At

high tide, this is a good spot for swimming, and, in fact, it is called "warm waters" by the locals. At low tide, it is great for beachcombing and birding.

SPECIAL EVENTS

Gathering of the Clans, Pugwash,
www.pugwashvillage.com/gathering.html
Go to Pugwash in the first week of July and you'll find one of the largest and best-attended of Nova Scotia's many highland festivals.

Oktoberfest, Tatamagouche, (902) 657-3030, www.nsoktoberfest.ca
Tatamagouche has a large population of German descendants and every September (yes, September) they put on the biggest Oktoberfest east of Ontario. It's very strange to drive for miles and meet very few passing cars or see any real signs of life and then seek out the rink in Tatamagouche. Upon entering, you suddenly realize where all the people are — here, by the hundreds. The Oktoberfest isn't just about drinking beer, although there's plenty of that to be had, in umpteen varieties. There's also a seemingly endless supply of great food. The oom-pah-pah bands, often imported from such exotic places as Kitchener, Canada's German capital, play constantly and ensure that everybody gets up for a dance or two. You won't find too many people who don't have a good time at the Oktoberfest, including visitors from out of town, who are treated as honoured guests.

SPECIAL INTEREST

Seagull Pewter, 9926 Durham Street, Pugwash, 1-888-955-5551
Established more than 25 years ago as a small business, Seagull Pewter has become an international success in the art of pewtersmithing. Today, it is the largest employer in the Pugwash area, creating products that are shipped around the world. The pewter shop has nine rooms featuring works manufactured at the adjacent pewter works. Also on display are complementary local and imported handcrafts, gifts and clothes. Don't miss the sale room where discontinued lines are featured at reduced prices. Even if you don't buy anything, it is a pleasure to see how art and craftsmanship are combined to produce so many attractive and collectible pieces, including tableware, picture frames, mirrors, clocks, wine glasses and much more. If you are looking for a genuine souvenir of Nova Scotia, this is one of the best places in the province to shop.

Wild Blueberry & Maple Centre, 105 Lower Main Street, Oxford, (902) 447-2908, www.town.oxford.ns.ca/visit/wbmc.htm
The pretty village of Oxford doesn't get many tourists despite lying just off the Trans-Canada Highway. Over 40 years ago Oxford Frozen Foods set up a blueberry processing plant in the town and it's now the largest in the world. The centre interprets the history of wild blueberry growing and maple sap harvesting that have long been staples of Cumberland County agriculture. There are various blueberry and maple products for sale.

Considering the wonderful anti-oxidant and other properties now known to be associated with blueberries it might be wise to buy some.

Jost Vineyards, off Route 6 Malagash, 1-800-565-4567, www.jostwine.com

The Jost winery, on the Malagash Peninsula, has been in operation for quite a number of years and has succeeded where, up until recently, other small Nova Scotia wineries have failed. The Wine Shop and Delicatessen, located in a large modern building, offers free tasting. The shop sells all Jost wines, including some that are available only at this outlet. Tours of the wine-making operation are offered once a day, when you will learn some of the secrets that have brought the Jost winery a number of international awards. You may be surprised to learn that Nova Scotia produces some of the best ice wine in the world and Jost consistently wins recognition for its annual production of this rare and expensive wine delicacy.

Hector Heritage Quay, 33 Caladh Avenue, Pictou, (902) 485-4371, www.townofpictou.ca/hector_heritage_quay.html

To the hundreds of thousands of Canadians who trace their ancestry to Scotland, the arrival of the *Hector* in Pictou in 1773 was the equivalent of the landing of the *Mayflower* in New England 150 years earlier. Like the Puritans, the Scots were fleeing persecution and dispossession back home. Their traditions were forbidden in Scotland, so it was with great joy that the *Hector*'s passengers were piped to shore in this new land with new opportunities. The Hector Heritage Quay describes in a series of excellent wall panels the events leading up to the exodus of so many Highland Scots in the late eighteenth and early nineteenth centuries. With the help of some good dioramas, you get a sense of what that arduous voyage must have been like, and the hopes and fears of the brave travellers.

The exhibit is contained in a spacious three-storey post-and-beam building, the largest in Canada of this type. At the conclusion of the exhibits, you come upon a replica of the *Hector*, launched in 2000 after a seemingly endless period of construction. Blacksmiths and carpenters are producing authentic materials for the shipbuilders on-site.

The Hector Heritage Quay is a must for those of Scottish descent.

Grohmann Knives, 116 Water Street, Pictou, 1-877-7KNIVES, www.grohmannknives.com

This family establishment on Pictou's main street has been producing superior knives for many years. The factory store offers a huge variety of knives and scissors, including kitchen knives, hunting and fishing knives and jackknives. They offer good buys on seconds. Tours are available to groups of four or more.

WALKING TOURS
Amherst, www.creda.net/~dars/hwt/
The historic walking tour of downtown Amherst includes 17 sites of interest.

It features most of the sandstone buildings along Victoria Street, including the old Customs House, the Court House and the beautiful Amherst Baptist Church. Also of note is Bob's Barber Shop on Church Street, which operates much as it would have done in the early 1900s. The walk may be extended east along Route 6 to include a number of large Victorian houses. Copies of the tour may be obtained at the tourist bureau.

Pictou, www.parl.ns.ca/pictoutour/index.htm
For many years Pictou had no official walking tour, but that has been remedied and now there is a map, a brochure and a virtual tour of 26 highlights in the town, including most of the noteworthy stone houses built in the early 1800s.

Also not to be missed is the Jitney Trail, which starts at the Heritage Quay and follows the shoreline for 3 kilometres. The first half is flat and paved so it's suitable for almost everyone. You'll be rewarded with some great views of Pictou, and along the way you will pass the former summer home of Donald Smith, a.k.a. Lord Strathcona, who was the driving force behind the Canadian trans-continental railway. There's good birding both waterside and in the many wild brambles and fruit trees that line the trail.

ACCOMMODATIONS
Amherst Shore Country Inn, 5091 Route 366, Lorneville,
(902) 661-4800 or 1-800-661-ASCI, www.ascinn.ns.ca.
A few kilometres from Amherst, on a property that runs down to the Northumberland Strait, sits the Amherst Shore Country Inn. You can stay in the inn itself or in one of a number of newer chalets. The latter are deliciously luxurious with Jacuzzis, extra large beds and decks from which you can watch the sun go down over the Northumberland Strait. There is also one cottage right on the water. Most people come here for the wonderful cooking of the Laceby family, who also operate the Blomidon Inn in Wolfville, or to relax in a quiet country setting. You can walk for miles along the shore, swim in the warm waters of the Northumberland Strait or use the inn as a base for touring the area. We have no hesitation in recommending the Amherst Shore Country Inn, as have hundreds of others whose comments are contained in a number of albums on display in the parlour.

Scottish Pines Log Cottages, 2979 Gulf Shore Road, Gulf Shore,
(902) 243-3366, www.holidayjunction.com/scottishpines
These ten deluxe oceanfront log cottages on the Gulf Shore, between Wallace and Pugwash, are very well built and equipped, including microwaves, gas barbecues, coffeemakers and other personal touches, such as quilts on the beds. There isn't much to do on-site, other than enjoy the terrific view or walk on the beach. However, Northumberland Links is only 8 kilometres away, as are the many natural attractions of the Wallace Bay area. Without doubt, this is the best place to stay on the Sunrise Trail between the Amherst Shore Country Inn and Pictou Lodge.

Pictou Lodge Resort, 172 Lodge Road, Braeshore, 1-800-495-6343, www.pictoulodge.com

Built of logs in the 1920s, Pictou Lodge looks more like a traditional western resort than a Maritime one. Despite an illustrious past as a Canadian National Railways resort, with guests such as Clark Gable, Randolph Scott and Queen Juliana of the Netherlands, the lodge struggled to find its identity until new owners took the time and money to make this place a real jewel on the Northumberland Strait. The central lodge has an impressive floor to ceiling double fireplace and large open dining hall, both original to the building. The Rotunda breakfast and lunch area is newer and has impressive views of the Northumberland Strait. Nearby the main lodge are some very large original cabins and a number of smaller motel-like more recent additions. The most desirable accommodation is unquestionably the three and two bedroom units in the executive chalets, sited on the banks of a large pond and also overlooking the Northumberland Strait. Nothing was spared in the construction and furnishing of these suites - fireplaces, fully equipped kitchens, private balconies, barbecues — check out the Web site video for a first hand look at the chalets. Whatever your choice of accommodation, however, don't forget to ask for a room with an ocean view.

Pictou Lodge is six miles from the town of Pictou, handy to the PEI Ferry and is on the shore of the Northumberland Strait, well off the highway. It is ideal for those seeking tranquility and the beautiful scenery. The recreational diversions offered on site include a swimming pool, nature trails, basketball/volleyball courts, bicycles and kayaks, a mini driving range, a putting green and other outdoor game facilities, or you can just walk or swim on the long beach just outside the front door. The lodge also offers fine dining, including very hearty breakfasts. The new owners have done a bang-up job of making this a destination resort and we think the executive chalets are the nicest accommodation in Nova Scotia right now.

Stonehame Lodge & Chalets, 310 Fitzpatrick Mountain Road, Scotsburn, 1-877-646-3468, www.stonehamechalets.com

The well-appointed log chalets and main lodge rooms of Stonehame provide for a very good alternative to seashore accommodations, particularly in the fall. Located as they are, high on a hill that overlooks both Pictou Harbour on one side and the forests and farms of Pictou County on the other, the views are spectacular. If you are planning to use Stonehame as a base, the chalets are to be preferred to the lodge rooms. The chalets have woodstoves, handmade quilts, fully equipped kitchens, and propane barbecues; some have a whirlpool bath, and are closer to the pool. While a continental breakfast is available, there is no restaurant on site or in the immediate neighbourhood, so taking a room in the lodge means you will have to travel to get dinner. The property is located in a very rural part of Pictou County and the proprietors have taken full advantage of the natural beauty of the area. Walking trails lace through the surrounding woodlands and fields and make for great cross-country ski trails in winter.

**The Consulate Inn, 157 Water Street, Pictou, 800-424-8283,
www.consulateinn.com**
After touring Pictou you might get a hankering to stay in one of the original stone houses that make the town so unique.

The Consulate Inn is the place to do it. It is located right on the waterfront with direct access to the Jitney Trail. The rooms are furnished with antiques and can be viewed on line. An alternate choice is the annex, which has newer and quite spacious rooms. The Consulate, which in former times was just that, is a good base for exploring the town.

DINING
**Amherst Shore Country Inn, Lorneville, (902) 661-4800,
www.ascinn.ns.ca**
Donna Laceby is a chef extraordinaire with a sterling reputation, but after many years in the business she decided to turns things over to her son Rob and his wife Mary. Thankfully, it looks like Rob has inherited his mother's cooking prowess. Dinner begins at 7:30 each evening, by reservation only. The menu is a four-course *prix fixe* for which you can select your entrée and dessert at the time of making reservations. Each evening features two of Donna's prize-winning recipes. The emphasis is on traditional Nova Scotia dishes such as salmon and lamb. The pace of the meal is leisurely and the service is friendly and unobtrusive. The view of Northumberland Strait from the dining room is tremendous, and if you are lucky, you will get to see one of the North Shore's beautiful sunsets while you are dining. The wine list has improved recently and there is a wide selection in all price ranges. A meal at the Amherst Shore Country Inn is one of the best dining experiences Nova Scotia has to offer.

**Pictou Lodge 172 Lodge Road, Braeshore,1-800-495-6343,
www.pictoulodge.com**
The new owners have not only put a lot of money into building new facilities, but are out to restore Pictou Lodge's reputation as a place of fine dining. We think they are succeeding. Exceeding Taste of Nova Scotia's guideline of 60 per cent local ingredients, the menu is a cornucopia of seafood, lamb, poultry and vegetables, all local. The Northumberland crab cakes, made from native rock crab, give Chesapeake Bay a run for its money. The dining room at the lodge has always had great ambience and now the food matches it. Oh, and by the way, for you true Scotsmen, they have haggis on the menu.

**Sugar Moon Farm, Alex MacDonald Road, Earltown,
1-866-81-MAPLE, www.sugarmoon.ca**
Nova Scotia is one of only a dozen or so provinces and states that make products from the sugar maple, most notably maple syrup and maple sugar. The sap begins to run in early spring and on a warm, sunny April day (yes they do exist), there is no better place to be than Sugar Moon Farm. While it is fairly remote, the farm has placed good signage in all directions, so

there is no excuse for not finding it.

Sugar Moon Farm is not only a working sugar maple farm, but also a place that goes out of its way to showcase the many ways that maple products can be incorporated into a meal. While there is a small interpretive display and a hiking trail that leads to the original sugar shack amidst the maples, what really draws people here in great numbers is the chance to chow down at the cook house on pancakes with fresh maple syrup. Maple baked beans and local sausage are a close second. For beverages, how about a maple tonic or sugar moon coffee?

The rustic setting of the farm has caught the attention of some of Canada's best known chefs and on a fairly regular basis full course, completely original menus are offered for a select few. If you are interested, check out the Web site and get yourself on the email list to be notified of these culinary happenings. You won't regret it.

NORTHUMBERLAND SHORE
Pictou to the Canso Causeway

Leaving Pictou, the Northumberland Shore route crosses Pictou Harbour via a causeway from which you will notice a colony of cormorants nesting on the pilings of a ruined pier that parallels the causeway. Stay on Highway 106 after crossing the Pictou Causeway until it ends at Highway 104 and then head towards New Glasgow. The other side of the harbour contrasts sharply with Pictou. The towns of New Glasgow (www.newglasgow.ca), Trenton (www.town.trenton.ns.ca), Stellarton (www.stellarton.ca) and Westville (www.westville.ca) make up what is collectively known as industrial Pictou County. Shortly after the coal mines opened in the nineteenth century, the area began to become industrialized. It was here, in Trenton, that Atlantic Canada's first railway was laid out and Canada's first steel mill was started. Trenton Glassworks operated until World War I, producing Nova Scotia glassware that is highly sought-after by collectors. Today, the area retains its industrial prominence by manufacturing tires and paper products, among other things. As with most industrial areas, attractive scenery is not abundant in these communities, although New Glasgow does have a very fine collection of Victorian homes in the Temperance Street area and an interesting short walk along the riverfront. The Museum of Industry is definitely worth a visit. From New Glasgow, turn east and rejoin the Northumberland Shore route at Exit 27, or 27A if you wish to stop at Melmerby Beach.

Merigomish Harbour is one of Nova Scotia's most sheltered waterways, with many tiny coves, tidal marshes and beaches that host an abundance of wildlife. Kayakers and canoeists are just discovering the potential. A great place to explore the harbour is from the wharf at the end of Big Island, where watercraft of all types can be launched.

A small interpretive display in Knoydart commemorates three highlanders who made their way to this area after the Battle of Culloden. A short trail leads to a cairn erected on the shore.

Just before Arisaig, the trail rises to follow a ridge offering a view across the strait to Prince Edward Island. Approaching Arisaig, you will see a wharf with fishing boats below. Continuing on to Malignant Cove, named not because of some sinister happening but for a British man-of-war of that name which foundered here, you will find the start of a short loop around Cape George, which is known locally as the "mini Cabot Trail." The comparison with Cape Breton's scenic route may be a bit of an exaggeration; however, a visit to the lighthouse on top of Cape George is a must. Turn at Lighthouse Road and follow the dirt track about one kilometre to the edifice hundreds of metres above the water. From here, the highlands of Cape Breton are clearly visible. There are a number of trails that will take you down to the shoreline.

The route from Cape George to Antigonish is one of the best sections of the Sunrise Trail. Just past Cape George there is a striking view of a line of cliffs, which head off into the distance towards Antigonish, with Ballantynes Cove directly below. Ballantynes Cove hosts a large fishing fleet, particularly tuna boats. A small interpretive centre explains the history of this fishery in the St. Georges Bay area. At Cribbons Point, there is a fine view of all of St. Georges Bay. Next are Crystal Cliffs, named for the whitish appearance given off by the gypsum content. The phenomenon is best observed from the other side of Antigonish Harbour. Shortly past Crystal Cliffs, the entrance to Antigonish Harbour comes into view. This passage into the harbour lies between two beaches that almost touch. While this effectively limits Antigonish as a port, it has created a shallow harbour that is a haven for wildlife.

Antigonish (www.townofantigonish.ca) is home to St. Francis Xavier University (www.stfx.ca), which was founded in Arichat, Cape Breton, and later relocated here. Shortly after crossing the Antigonish County line, you will have noticed that the Presbyterian churches of Pictou County have given way to Roman Catholic churches. This is because the majority of the Scots who immigrated to this area came from the highlands, a predominantly Catholic area. They settled next to the Presbyterian Scots, who had spread out from the Pictou Harbour area. Antigonish is the shire town and the impressive St. Ninian's Cathedral is the spiritual centre for their descendants. The campus of St. Francis Xavier is mostly modern and does not hold a lot of architectural interest. In the library, you may view the Hall of the Clans, dedicated to the various Scottish families who settled this area. "X," as it is known to its graduates, is the centre of the Antigonish movement and the Coady Institute, both of which have played a significant role in the development of co-operatives and self-help movements in Third World countries. For the most part, the town of Antigonish is a regional centre, not a tourist town. The National Philatelic Centre will be of interest to stamp collectors.

If you travel directly on the Trans-Canada Highway from Antigonish, you can be in Aulds Cove, and at the end of the Northumberland Shore route, within a half-hour. However, in doing so, you will miss two of the nicest beaches in Nova Scotia. The scenic route is not easy to follow in this area, as it crosses and joins up with the Trans-Canada Highway a number of times. From Exit 36, you can stay on the trail until Aulds Cove.

From Antigonish, the Northumberland Shore route passes through the Acadian communities of Pomquet, Tracadie, where the very picturesque St. Peter's Church overlooks the harbour, and Havre Boucher. At Bayfield, off Exit 36, there is a view of the wharf from the entrance to Bayfield

Provincial Park. Here, there is a supervised beach and swimming, but it doesn't compare with Pomquet or Dunns Beach. Our favourite route between Havre Boucher and Aulds Cove is not via Highway 4, but by the Trans-Canada Highway. This is because just past Havre Boucher the highway climbs for a spectacular last view of the Northumberland Shore and all of St. Georges Bay as far back as Cape George. At Aulds Cove, the Northumberland Shore route ends, and from here you can either continue your adventure in Cape Breton or take the Marine Drive along the Atlantic coast back towards Halifax.

BEACHES

Melmerby Beach, Exit 27A off Highway 104, www.melmerby.ca
Melmerby, or the Merb as it is known locally, is one of Nova Scotia's most popular beaches and for good reason. It is a two kilometre stretch of sandy beach with clear waters on both sides. On one side there is open ocean swimming, and on the other, sheltered harbour swimming. These are among the warmest waters in Nova Scotia, particularly in late summer. The beach has full facilities and portions are supervised by lifeguards. This is a very popular spot for windsurfers, as well as sunbathers and swimmers. Take a look at the Web site for some gorgeous pictures.

Big Island, Merigomish
The three kilometre natural causeway that connects Big Island to the mainland forms a beautiful sandy beach for most of its length. The strait waters are warm and from the beach there are distant views of the Antigonish Highlands. The best access is at the end of the beach furthest from the mainland. There are no facilities here and fewer people.

Dunns Beach/Monk's Head
Take the paved road to Southside Antigonish Harbour off Highway 104 and follow it until it ends. It becomes a dirt road for the last kilometre. Park and walk over the dunes to the beach. The first thing that will strike you is the view — Cape Breton on your right and Crystal Cliffs and Cribbons Point on your left, with the lighthouse atop Cape George barely visible in the distance. Straight ahead is nothing but clear blue water. Dunns Beach has miles of sand and warm water. You can walk to one end at the entrance to Antigonish Harbour and see Mahoneys Beach only a stone's throw away across the water, but nearly 30 kilometres by land. Or you can walk the other way to Monks Head and eventually all the way to Pomquet Beach. Maybe you'll stay right where you are and enjoy the view. Chances are you'll have it all to yourself.

Pomquet Beach
You can reach this beach from the crossroads after visiting Dunns Beach or directly via Exit 35 through Pomquet. This beach is similar to Dunns, but with full facilities including lifeguards, an interpretive display and a boardwalk to protect the dunes. Obviously, this brings more people as well,

but not that many. This is a very long beach and it's easy to find a quiet spot of your own. Pomquet Beach is one of a very few where piping plover numbers are increasing.

BIRDING
Big Island, Merigomish
Just past Merigomish, look for the sign to Big Island, which is connected to the mainland by a long causeway. The inner side of this causeway and the tidal marshes near the small wharf at the end of the island are among the best places in Nova Scotia to see great blue herons in large numbers. There are rookeries here and, up until late fall, you will almost certainly see a large number of these magnificent birds. Big Island itself is a pastoral vision of green fields and red soil which is seldom visited.

Cribbons Point, directly off the Northumberland Shore route
From the wharf, a small colony of guillemots may be seen nesting on the cliffs only a few hundred metres from the fishing boats. It is very unusual to see sea birds nesting this close to human activity.

Antigonish Wildlife Management Area, www.gov.ns.ca/natr/wildlife/sanctuaries/pdfs/antigonish.pdf
A short distance out of Antigonish on Route 377, look for a sign to Antigonish Landing. Follow this road until you pass the meat plant. Soon the road ends and a gravel track suitable for walking or biking starts. Park at the gate and walk in either direction along this path that parallels the marshes and estuary of Antigonish Harbour. You will see plenty of waterfowl, blue herons and a variety of sparrows, as well as the possibility of rarities during the spring and fall migrations. Antigonish Landing is a very pleasant and untaxing birding experience. The trail follows the harbour all the way into Antigonish, so you can access it directly from town if you like.

CEMETERIES
Pictou County Artisans
If you are a dedicated cemetery visitor then Pictou County offers a rare treat. For one reason or another the nineteenth century produced a number of exceptionally gifted stone cutters in the Pictou area. Their works and where to see them have been documented by Clyde MacDonald in *Artisans in Stone of Pictou County*. It makes for a fascinating journey to seek out cemeteries in tiny communities around Pictou County to see these works, including the famous Woman in Stone at Garden of Eden cemetery.

GOLF
Abercrombie Golf Club, 79 Abercrombie Loop, Exit 24 off Route 104, (902) 755-4653, www.abercrombiegolf.com
This 18-hole course just outside New Glasgow is a challenge, with tight fairways, a lot of up and down holes, wicked rough, but very puttable greens. If you get hungry, you can just pluck an apple from one of the trees

that grow on the course. The course has just completed a major overhaul of some holes and is now in tip-top shape. This course is one of the most underrated in the province.

Antigonish Golf Course, Cloverville Street, (902) 863-2228, www.antigonishgolfclub.ns.ca
This is one of Nova Scotia's least-known 18 hole courses. At 6,600 yards from the back tees, this is a good test of golf skill. The course is seldom crowded on weekdays and there is a good chance of getting on just by driving up.

MUSEUMS

Nova Scotia Museum of Industry, 147 North Foord Street, Stellarton, (902) 755-5425, www.museum.gov.ns.ca/moi
This relatively new museum was built to house Nova Scotia's collection of industrial artifacts. Although the complex almost fell victim to budget cuts, it opened first on a limited basis and then full-time. Size-wise, it is actually the largest museum in Atlantic Canada, and you'll immediately see why once you enter. The Samson, Canada's first locomotive and one of the world's oldest, has been restored and looks great. Train buffs will enjoy a number of other early locomotives also on display. Nova Scotians can be justifiably proud of the three automobiles exhibited — all were manufactured in Nova Scotia, including one of the present-day Volvos that were, until recently, assembled in Halifax. For antique lovers, there is a collection of Nova Scotia glass that was manufactured at nearby Trenton. It is very much sought-after by collectors, particularly the goblets.

Anyone who has toured other Nova Scotia museums, particularly Sutherland Steam Mill, Cumberland County Museum and Ross Farm, cannot help but be struck by the number of products that were manufactured in Nova Scotia up until the turn of the century. There has always been a lingering debate among Nova Scotians as to whether Confederation and the high-tariff policy that followed were responsible for the death of Nova Scotia industry or if it was simply an inevitable occurrence. Whoever is right, the Museum of Industry is a fitting tribute to Nova Scotia's industrial past.

OFF THE BEATEN PATH
Back Roads of Pictou County
The roads that radiate from Pictou Harbour follow the course of the numerous rivers that empty into the ocean. Several are excellent for a quiet drive in the country. Route 347 passes through MacPhersons Mills, a bucolic setting on Sutherlands River, with a partially restored mill. A shaded country lane, which starts beside the mill, follows the course of the bubbling stream. The mill pond is an excellent spot for a dip.

Also of interest is River Road, which follows the course of the East River as it winds through dairy farm country south of New Glasgow.

Route 374 passes through Eureka, an interesting hamlet spread on both sides of the East River. Not far away is Hopewell, another small village, which has an historic suspension footbridge across the river. Ask locally for directions.

From Alma, another paved road makes a loop around a finger of land between the West and Middle Rivers. At Loch Broom, there is a replica of the first church in the area, which in its peaceful setting could easily double as the church in the wildwood.

Routes 7 and 316

From either side of Antigonish, two roads cut across country to the Atlantic coast. Both are among the most pleasant of Nova Scotia's many cross-provincial routes and are worth driving for the sake of the inland beauty, not just to get from one coast to the other. Highway 7 runs from Antigonish to Sherbrooke, skirting the shores of Lochaber Lake, where you are almost certain to see and hear loons. At Melrose, the highway picks up the St. Mary's River, a great salmon stream, and follows it to the sea at Sherbrooke.

Route 316 starts at South River, just east of Antigonish, and runs through to Isaacs Harbour on Marine Drive. It passes through rolling farmland and then by a number of attractive lakes. At St. Andrews, a pretty stone church with a copper spire is visible for miles around from its perch on a hill. At Frasers Mills, there is a fish hatchery for touring. Further on, one finds Goshen, a hamlet set among farms and lakes.

PARKS AND GREENSPACE
Greenhill Lookoff Provincial Park

From the top of Greenhill, located a short drive from the junction of Highway 106 and 104, there is an excellent view of the fields and forests of Pictou County. This is a very popular spot for picnics, and a place to relax on a hot summer's day.

ROCKHOUNDING
Arisaig Fossil Cliffs

An area of low shale cliffs just outside Arisaig offers one of the province's top fossil-hunting areas. The wafer-thin layers of shale are extremely crumbly and even if you don't find any fossils, it's fun picking apart the shale. To get to the cliffs, park at the government wharf and walk along the beach towards Pictou for about one kilometre. Access can also be had from Arisaig Picnic Park, but the trail is quite wet in places.

SPECIAL EVENTS
The Highland Games, Antigonish, (902) 863-4275, www.antigonishhighlandgames.ca

Every July, Antigonish is host to one of Nova Scotia's most popular annual events, the Highland Games. Held since 1863, the festival features traditional Scottish sports such as tossing the caber, as well as Highland dancing and plenty of piping. The gaily coloured costumes and the sounds of the massed bands make this one of Nova Scotia's most enjoyable festivals.

SPECIAL INTEREST
The Crombie House, Abercrombie, just outside New Glasgow, (902) 755-4440, extension 26
The Sobeys have become one of Nova Scotia's real success stories. Chances are, if you've made it as far as New Glasgow, you have passed any number of their grocery stores, which dominate the market in Atlantic Canada. The Crombie was the home of Frank Sobey, patriarch of the clan and an avid collector of Canadian art. Every Wednesday in summer, the Crombie is open for guided tours of the Sobey Art Foundation's collection of paintings. The Group of Seven and Cornelius Krieghoff figure prominently, along with lesser-known artists. You will definitely be surprised at the quality and diversity of this collection, which for many years was a pretty well-kept secret in the area.

Lyghtesome Gallery, 166 Main Street, Antigonish, (902) 863-5804, www.lyghtesome.ns.ca
The Lyghtesome showcases an excellent collection of some better-known Maritime artists. Original fine artwork from printmakers and watercolourists, as well as a selection of Celtic engravings, make this a very interesting stop.

ACCOMMODATIONS
Antigonish Victorian Inn, 149 Main Street, Antigonish, 1-800-706-5558, www.antigonishvictorianinn.ca
At long last there is a quality place to stay in Antigonish that isn't just another motel. The name says it all — it's a finely restored Victorian home right in the middle of town. The furnishings are a combination of antiques and modern amenities which give the place a cosy feel. It's a short walk to just about everywhere in town, including the Antigonish Landing walking trail. With this place and Gabrieau's Restaurant, it's now a pleasure to spend a night in Antigonish.

The Cove Motel, off Highway 104, Aulds Cove, (902) 747-2700, www.covemotel.com
There is a dearth of accommodations on the water between Pictou and Aulds Cove. The Cove Motel is located on its own small point of land, well off the busy Trans-Canada Highway. There are both motel units and our preference — small well-appointed cabins. There is also a wharf from which you can fish or take out a canoe or paddle boat. The dining room overlooking the Strait of Canso is lined with pictures of successful tuna fishing expeditions for which St. Georges Bay is noted. This is a pleasant exception to the run-of-the-mill motels that predominate this stretch of the coast.

DINING
The Bistro, 216 Archimedes St., New Glasgow, (902) 752-4988, www.thebistronewglasgow.com
New Glasgow fianlly has a good restaurant, in fact a very good restaurant.

Listed in Ann Hardy's *Where to Eat in Canada,* for the first time in 2003/04, and making more recent editions as well, Chef Robert Vinton is setting a culinary standard never before achieved in Pictou County. The Bistro may aptly be described, in our opinion, as one of the better restaurants in the province. Chef Vinton arrived in New Glasgow from Calgary, and he began to practice his craft in this small restaurant with splendid results. An upbeat mood is set on entering the building which was once a storefront pharmacy — as you are immediately struck by the high copper-clad ceiling and bright orange stucco walls, decorated with lively reproductions dominated by a large copy of Van Gogh's *The Café on Place du Forum, Arles, At Night.* The menu is small, changes with the season, but the offerings are all very tempting, and there are nightly specials as well. Vinton is a master of layering flavours and providing that something extra in the culinary experience that tantalizes the palate and the eye. Whether it is the warm spinach salad with Roma tomato, artichoke, red onion and Kalamata olives, the duck spring rolls, Tuscany mussels, the roast rack of lamb with balsamic onion compote and red wine butter, or peppercorn-crusted salmon with Pernod tarragon cream, you will be more than pleased with your choice. Save room if you can for desert. From the simple to wildly decadent, the sweets are creatively prepared and delicious too. The wine list is small but adequate and reasonably priced by Nova Scotia standards. Service is friendly, attentive, but professional, and better than in many restaurants in more urban centres.

Gabrieau's Bistro, 350 Main Street, Antigonish, (902) 863-1925, www.gabrieaus.com

At one time Wolfville was the only university town in Nova Scotia that had an interesting restaurant scene. That changed when chef Mark Gabrieau opened the restaurant bearing his name in Antigonish about ten years ago. Located in a old house on Main Street, there are a number of small, plainly decorated rooms that give a touch of intimacy. The menu is extensive with a larger-than-usual emphasis on vegetarian dishes. Chef Mark offers more interesting salads than any other restaurant in the province. The appetizers are uniformly mouth-watering; most of them are exciting variations of what can be some of the more pedestrian offerings such as calamari, shrimp cocktail, etc. The entrées cover the gamut from pastas, seafood and chicken to steak and lamb. Everything that we have tried here has been excellent. Desserts change daily. The wine list is extensive but pricey. However, this is offset by the quite reasonable price of the food. Service is professional and courteous and frankly a pleasant surprise. Gabrieau's makes spending a night in Antigonish a very enjoyable experience.

The Sunshine on Main Café, 332 Main Street, Antigonish, (902) 863-5381

If you are just passing through Antigonish, the Sunshine is a very good place to stop for lunch. The chowder is good, as are the sandwiches and salads. There is also a great selection of coffees and espressos. Prices are quite reasonable.

CEILIDH TRAIL

The Ceilidh Trail is one of the shorter scenic trails in the province. It follows Highway 19 starting at the Canso Causeway, and goes up the west side of Cape Breton to join the Cabot Trail at Margaree Harbour. A ceilidh is a Scottish celebration of song and dance and, appropriately, this trail passes through an area of almost exclusively Scottish settlement dating from the 1770s. Scottish traditions are still strong in communities such as Mabou, Judique and Port Hood.

The first 25 kilometres of the route from Port Hastings to Port Hood are not particularly interesting; although the Strait of Canso and the Gulf of St. Lawrence are in sight most of the time, the coastline here is flat and regular. As you drive through Port Hood (www.porthood.ca) you will see Port Hood Island offshore. Although there are a number of houses visible on the island, there are now only two permanent residents. Readers familiar with Alistair MacLeod's novel *No Great Mischief* may recognize the landscape as the inspiration for his writing. At the north end of town, take Colindale Road instead of the main highway and you will be rewarded with some fantastic views of Mabou Harbour with its sandy beach and spectacular line of cliffs. This partial dirt road rejoins the Ceilidh Trail just outside Mabou.

Situated at the head of a narrow harbour, Mabou (www.mabou.ca) is an active community that distinguishes itself by the amount of Gaelic in evidence on shop signs and in store windows. Just before crossing the bridge, look for the shrine to Our Lady of Sorrows and its small chapel on a hill. On the other side of the bridge, take a short side trip to the mouth of the harbour and enjoy the landscape. The government wharf has a small fishing fleet and a lighthouse. From here you can also see Mabou Beach. Returning to the Ceilidh Trail, you will pass the Glenora Distillery on the way to the former coal mining town of Inverness (www.inverness.ednet.ns.ca), the largest town on the trail. It has a fine swimming beach. Just north of Inverness, you can take a scenic diversion to Broad Cove on a mostly unpaved and rather rugged road that climbs high above the gulf and provides sweeping views of the cliffs and windswept Margaree Island, just offshore. Rejoining the trail near Dunvegan, you have a choice of travelling inland to Margaree Forks or continuing along the coastal route to Chimney Corner. Both are quite scenic. From Chimney Corner to the end of the Ceilidh Trail at Margaree Harbour there are a number of fine ocean vistas.

BEACHES
Port Hood Beach, Port Hood
This supervised beach just south of Port Hood has wonderful sand and some of the warmest water in Nova Scotia. Add to this the views of Port Hood Island, and you have a winning combination for an excellent family beach.

West Mabou Beach, off Colindale Road
At one time this was a wild and often deserted beach that was easy to see

but hard to get to. It is now a Provincial Park which has brought easier access and the development of some very nice walking trails in addition to the fantastic beach. There is a small interpretive display and picnic facilities. From Port Hood, take Colindale Road, or from Mabou, the West Mabou Road. Soon you will see a long sandy beach backed by an extensive dune system, which protects Mabou Harbour. Even with the upgrades the beach will almost certainly not have many visitors. At West Mabou you can commune freely with the eagles that call this area home.

Inverness Beach, Inverness
Inverness Beach is a huge swath of sand that parallels the village of the same name. An extensive boardwalk system makes for a pleasant walk. The water is quite warm compared to many other beaches further south.

HIKING
Cape Mabou Highlands
One of the most significant developments in Nova Scotia hiking over the past decade has been the admirable contribution by the Cape Mabou Trail Club. The Cape Mabou Highlands was once home to many small farming communities of which nary a trace remains today other than the occasional rock wall or rock pile, usually come upon unexpectedly in deep woods. Today, the hiker finds steep wooded hillsides with softwoods giving way to mature hardwood forests at higher elevations. Along the shoreline, slopes climb dramatically to heights of 300 metres or more. Standing on top of one of the many look-offs you will be hard pressed to find any signs of modern civilization in any direction, other than fishing boats, looking tiny as toys, far below on the Northumberland Strait.

By the year 2000, the hiking club had developed 14 well-marked trails that showcase the ecological uniqueness of the Mabou Highlands in a manner unmatched outside of the national parks. It is easily possible to spend a week hiking in this area, especially if you link up with the Sight Point Trail, which extends further along the coast toward Inverness. The first thing you will need is the excellent map of the trails, which can be purchased at a number of places in town including the general store. Although the trails are well marked, there are so many of them that it is easy to get confused without the map. Buy it!

There are several trailheads accessible by car. The most convenient and easiest to find is at the end of Mabou Post Road, which starts about 10 kilometres down the Mabou Coal Mines Road, which is a right turn off Mabou Harbour Road. From this trailhead you can follow a 16-kilometre loop trail by combining several intersecting trails. The most dramatic is MacKinnon's Brook, which rises 153 metres above crashing surf. The stunning views more than offset the steepness. This trail is definitely not for small children or those with a fear of heights, but anyone else with determination shouldn't have a problem. It is not as dangerous as some other guides suggest, but it does warrant respect and preparation. Other trails lead to some spectacular inland lookoffs that are among the highest sheer drops in Nova Scotia.

If you are going to hike these trails, you will need plenty of water, good footwear, warm clothing for the higher elevations and the map. If you take along these necessities and a sense of adventure, you will be rewarded with some of the best hiking to be found anywhere in Canada and chances are you'll see next to nobody for most of the day.

Mabou Rail Trail
Many sections of the Trans Canada Trail follow abandoned railbeds. Some of these trails are, frankly, quite boring — after all, the railbeds weren't designed with hikers in mind. You might wonder if the Mabou Rail Trail fits into this category, and perhaps give it a pass because there are so many other great trails in the vicinity. This would be a great mistake. This short stretch that runs between Mabou and Glendyer Station must be one of the most scenic rail trails in Nova Scotia.

The trail can be picked up as it crosses Highway 19 just south of the Duncreigan Inn. For the first while the trail is canopied with leaves and offers only glimpses of water through the trees, but soon you will emerge and be treated to the glorious sight of the Mull River estuarine salt marsh. In the distance, the white spire of Mabou Catholic Church set against the hardwood hills, and possibly reflected on the still waters, provides a scene that will make you glad you brought your camera. The trail then follows the salt marsh as it meanders its way inland, surrounded on all sides by as large a variety of trees and shrubs as you can find on any trail in the province. In the autumn there is a plethora of berries, fruits and seed pods, which in turn attract much wildlife. You will almost certainly see bald eagles, as well as many species of waterfowl, shorebirds and songbirds. When you reach the old railway bridge, you are almost at the end and can retrace your steps for a quite different perspective heading back. Walking the Mabou Rail Trail is a great way to start or end the day. The water, the mountains and the village are bathed in a soft light that provides a sense of calm and quietude that makes you feel good about life.

OFF THE BEATEN PATH
Mabou Harbour and Mabou Coal Mines
A very rewarding short drive begins by following the Mabou Harbour Road, which starts at Main Street in Mabou and continues to a dead end near the mouth of the Mabou River. Here there are outstanding views of the extensive dune system that backs West Mabou Beach and the lighthouse nearby. Instead of heading straight back to Mabou, look for Mabou Coal Mines Road and take it to the small wharf that was once the centre of activity for this now all-but-abandoned community. From this road you can reach a number of isolated beaches and photograph coastal vistas of exceptional beauty with very little manmade clutter in the way. This road is also one of the primary access routes to the Mabou Highlands hiking trail system. Returning to Mabou, note the many mailboxes with the name Rankin — the famous singing group of that name hails from this very area.

Lake Ainslie
This is the largest natural freshwater lake in the province. It is a long deep expanse of water surrounded by highlands. Not surprisingly, it reminded the early settlers of a Scottish loch. There are roads completely encircling the lake, yet there are no towns or villages along the shore. This is a pleasant drive through an area of old farms and abandoned settlements. The area is particularly beautiful in the fall when the blaze of mountain colour is reflected on the lake's tranquil surface.

SPECIAL EVENTS
Broad Cove Concert, Broad Cove
This area of Cape Breton has always had a strong musical tradition, and there are probably as many good fiddlers born and trained along this coast as in the rest of the province combined. The Broad Cove Concert is held by the sea on the last Sunday in July in the tiny community of Broad Cove, and is a showcase of Cape Breton talent. If you can't make this concert, try one of the ceilidhs held weekly throughout the summer in Mabou or Inverness.

SPECIAL INTEREST
Celtic Music Interpretive Centre, 5471 Route 19, Judique, (902) 787-2708, www.celticmusicsite.com
This centre is the newest attraction along the Ceilidh Trail and promises to be an important addition to the musical heritage of Cape Breton. Although it has exhibits, it is not so much a place to see things as to hear and do. This place has workshops and musical demonstrations where you can listen to or join in the playing of traditional Cape Breton music. The Buddy MacMaster School of Fiddling will ensure that the great tradition of fiddling continues as dozens of students take up the art every year. The admission price is a bit steep, but if you arrive here while the fiddles are flying you won't begrudge it.

Glenora Distillery, Route 19, Glenville, 1-800-839-0491, www.glenoradistillery.com
With its Scottish settlers and highland hills, Cape Breton has always been the next best thing to Scotland, except for one thing — no whisky. With the establishment of the Glenora Distillery, Canada's only producer of single malt whisky, this problem has been remedied. The distillery is in an attractive traditional-style building at the base of Mount Glenora. Tours and tastings are given regularly and there is a gift shop selling products related to the distillery. There are also fine accommodations and a good restaurant. Glenora has won numerous awards with its whisky; enough apparently to worry the Scotch industry which tried and failed to legally stop them from using the word 'glen' on their products. Talk about going to ridiculous lengths, but you'll definitely want to sample the product to find out why.

ACCOMMODATIONS

Haus Treuburg, 175 Main Street, Port Hood, (902) 787-2116, www.haustreuburg.com

This is a German-Canadian inn on a large waterfront property. There are several plainly furnished rooms in the inn or, probably preferable to most, two-room cottages closer to the water. Cottage 1 has great views of Port Hood Island. The library has an extensive collection of German titles including an amazing number of travel books on Canada. Gourmet dining is available, but should be booked ahead. The owners can arrange boat tours to nearby Port Hood island.

Duncreigan County Inn, 11409 Highway 19, Mabou, 1-800-840-2207, www.duncreigan.ca

The original Duncreigan was an elegant country home overlooking Mabou Harbour, built by a senator for his granddaughter. After a distinguished history the house fell into disrepair and was purchased by Charles and Eleanor Mullendore, who hoped to restore it as an inn. This proved impossible, but didn't deter the Mullendores who rebuilt, incorporating the best features of the original with the modern conveniences many travellers expect. The rooms are spacious and airy with well-designed bathrooms. Some have whirlpools and balconies overlooking the river. Included in the price is a very good continental breakfast with homemade breads and preserves along with lots of fruit and cereal. The Mullendores have managed to walk that fine line between tradition and modernity to create a very good inn in a quiet country setting. Duncreigan makes a great place to use as a base for exploring the Mabou Highlands.

Glenora Inn, 13727 Highway 19, Glenville, 1-800-839-0491, www.glenoradistillery.com

Part of the Glenora Distillery complex, the inn is set amid pleasant surroundings in the countryside between Mabou Harbour and Inverness. The rooms are modern, well-appointed and reasonably priced for Cape Breton. There is a reputable dining room and a very cozy little pub. You can use this as a base to tour the distillery or enjoy the beauty of the Mabou Harbour district and Lake Ainslie. Recently, the owners have added six modern chalets which have a fantastic view of the highlands.

DINING

The Mull Café and Deli, 11630 Highway 19, Mabou, (902) 945-2244, www.duncreigan.ca

For years the owners of the Duncreigan Inn ran a great restaurant right at the inn, but for reasons unknown decided to close it and open The Mull Café. While it certainly doesn't have the ambience or style of the old place it is still pretty good. The menu is very large and ranges from hot dogs to steaks with lots of seafood in between.

The Red Shoe Pub, 11533 Highway 19, Mabou, (902) 945-2996, www.redshoepub.com
This place is owned by the famous singing Rankin family and in a matter of a few years has become one of the places to hear Cape Breton music. There's music every night and the old-fashioned ceilidhs on the weekends. The menu is more upscale than most pubs and the food is good, but it's definitely the music that draws in the big crowds, and for a small place the crowds are big so get here early.

CABOT TRAIL

The Cabot Trail (www.cabottrail.com) has long been recognized as one of the great marine drives in all the world. From sea level at Cheticamp and at Ingonish, the highway rises up, over and along the highest points in Nova Scotia, at times hundreds of metres above the crashing surf below.

Named for explorer John Cabot, who is believed to have landed on this coast in 1497, the trail is a circular route that begins and ends near Baddeck. Although it can be driven in a day, to really enjoy anything more than just the views you need at least three days with stops in the Margaree Valley, Cheticamp and Ingonish. Only then will you have the time to hike the highlands, fish the streams, go whale-watching or golf the legendary Highlands Links at Ingonish. Notwithstanding that the Cabot Trail passes through some wild and sparsely populated areas, it does have a goodly number of excellent accommodations and dining establishments.

One of the great unresolved Nova Scotian debates is whether the Cabot Trail should be travelled in a clockwise or counter-clockwise direction. Both ways have equal merit, so for no particular reason we'll go clockwise. The Cabot Trail is usually considered to start at Baddeck; however, if you've taken the Ceilidh Trail, you can pick it up at Margaree Harbour, with the important proviso that you not miss the Margaree Valley.

The trail leaves the Trans-Canada Highway just south of Baddeck and travels through the small community of Middle River to Lake O'Law, where the trail's beauty is soon apparent. A picnic park beside these small mountain lakes is a nice spot for a short stop. A little further on, the highlands start to rise and the valley walls steepen. You are entering the Margaree Valley (www.margareens.com), famous for its salmon fishing and fall foliage. There are many branches to the Margaree River and each has cut a steep glen through the highlands. Hardwood forests cover the mountains completely and while this is spectacular scenery at any time of year, in late September and early October the foliage in this setting is unsurpassed.

To appreciate the beauty of the Margaree Valley, you should explore some of the more inaccessible glens on the side roads. A trip up to Ross Bridge at Portree will take you by some of the most famous salmon pools, as well as the fish hatchery, which specializes in raising Atlantic salmon. A short side-trip to Philips Mountain is worthwhile for the look-off. The more adventuresome should take a trip on the dirt road up to Big Intervale, where a narrow valley opens up to a remote glen. You will be as deep in the Cape Breton Highlands as the roads will take you.

At Margaree Forks the valley widens and you can travel down either side of the river — both are equally scenic. The Margaree River empties into the Gulf of St. Lawrence at the small fishing village of Margaree Harbour. A short drive to the end of the road on the south side of the harbour will take you to a breakwater, which abuts a small sand beach where you can observe a number of unusual rock formations.

Crossing to the north side of the Margaree, you can take a drive out

Beach Road, which leads to the colourful Margaree Harbour fishing fleet. On the ocean side of the road is a sand and gravel beach, which gives you a view up the coast and a hint of the scenery along this trail.

Driving north from Margaree Harbour, you enter an area of Acadian settlement and pass through the communities of Belle Côte, Terre-Noire, Cap Le Moine, Grand Étang and finally Cheticamp, the largest community on this coast. The Église St. Pierre will be in view for some time. At Cap Le Moine, you can't help but notice Joe's Scarecrow Village, which has over a hundred scarecrows, some of which are pretty creepy.

Cheticamp (www.cheticampns.com) has long been known as a centre for rug hooking, and you should be sure to drop into the Elizabeth LeFort Gallery in the town hall. Mrs. LeFort is acknowledged as the premier artist of her day. Cheticamp is also a centre for whale-watching cruises to the Gulf of St. Lawrence, and the western entrance to Cape Breton Highlands National Park.

Despite Cheticamp's spectacular environs and the many activities in the area, the town itself is quiet and not overrun with great facilities. If you stay in Cheticamp overnight, it is worth taking a drive out to Cheticamp Island, particularly near sunset. Turning toward the island just south of town, take the first dirt road to your right. The road follows the shore and provides great views back to Cheticamp, where the sun glints off the metal roof of the church. Halfway down the island, you'll cross a cattle gate — from here the cattle roam freely and are likely to be in the middle of the road at times, but don't worry, they will move and they love to pose for pictures. The road ends at the lighthouse, which unfortunately is inaccessible because of a chain-link fence.

Just outside Cheticamp, you enter Cape Breton Highlands National Park (www.pc.gc.ca/eng/pn-np/ns/cbreton/index.aspx), one of Canada's oldest national parks, established in 1936. It stretches across the tip of northern Cape Breton from the Gulf of St. Lawrence to the Atlantic. On both ocean sides, the scenery is rugged with cliffs hundreds of metres high plunging abruptly into the sea. In between there is a barren highland plateau containing the highest expanse in Nova Scotia. The habitat here is similar to the Arctic tundra. Moose, rarely seen elsewhere in Nova Scotia, are common here, as are black bears. At the entrance to the park, there is an information centre with exhibits on the various habitats you will see while traversing the park. There is also a good little bookstore, where you might consider picking up David Lawley's book *A Nature and Hiking Guide to Cape Breton's Cabot Trail* to use as a guide for your visit.

Although it's only a 110-kilometre drive from the west gate at Cheticamp to the east gate at Ingonish, fasten your seatbelts. You're in for a rare driving experience and breathtaking views. After entering the park, the highway begins a series of ascents and descents with look-offs at the top. There are many interpretive displays at these look-offs, explaining the geology, ecology and history of the park.

After a number of such look-offs, the highway climbs 500 metres to the top of French Mountain and travels inland along a high plateau. From here, there are several more look-offs, including one above the once-prosperous community of Fishing Cove, now long-deserted and accessible only by a strenuous hike. The Cabot Trail then begins a steep descent via a series of hairpin turns to meet the ocean again at the isolated community of Pleasant Bay, where everyone who isn't a fisherman seems to run a restaurant selling fish.

From Pleasant Bay, the Cabot Trail again cuts inland, however, if you would like to see more of the rugged coast, turn toward Red River and continue on to the rough dirt road until it ends, just past Gambo Abbey, a Buddhist retreat. From here, you can follow a hiking trail into the Pollett's Cove/Aspy Bay Wilderness Area, one of the most remote and truly wild areas in Nova Scotia. Even if you are not interested in hiking, you're bound to be impressed by the view of the solid line of rugged windswept cliffs, which run north from here all the way to Cape St. Lawrence, without the impediment of a highway interrupting the view. However, there is something to be said for views of highways that snake their way up mountains, and as you return to Pleasant Bay, you will see the Cabot Trail doing just that on its way down MacKenzie Mountain to the ocean.

After Pleasant Bay, the Cabot Trail follows the valley through the largest virgin hardwood forest in the Maritimes. A short interpretive trail leads through the forest to the Lone Sheiling, a replica of a Scottish Highland crofter's hut. The highway then climbs over North Mountain, where you will notice that the hardwoods give way to softwoods in the upper regions. The softwoods have been hard hit by an infestation of spruce budworm and there are many dead trees. Descending North Mountain, you enter the Aspy Valley, one of the prettiest interior spots in the park. Here you exit the park briefly, but just before leaving, look for the sign to Beulach Bann Falls, down a dirt side road; it's well worth a visit. While you can re-enter the park a short distance past the village of Cape North, the more interesting route is to follow the shoreline through White Point and rejoin the trail at the picturesque fishing community of Neils Harbour. From here to Ingonish, the Cabot Trail follows the sea closely and, for the time being at least, the mountains disappear and the shoreline becomes more accessible as the number of coastal hiking trails attests. Waterfall lovers should keep an eye open for the sign to Mary Ann Falls, which is also well worth the side-trip down a dirt road. Be forewarned, however, that because these falls are so accessible by car, they are often inundated with fellow nature lovers. At times, the dirt roads to both Mary Ann Falls and Beulach Bann Falls are closed off and accessible only by mountain bikers or hikers.

Next the Cabot Trail enters the resort community of Ingonish (www.ingonish.com), which straddles the park boundary. The part that is in the park tends to be much less commercialized than that which lies outside. Ingonish has everything a great resort community should have — great scenery, beaches, hiking trails, a world-class golf course and a terrific resort, the Keltic Lodge. You can easily base yourself here for a day or a week.

Cape Breton Highlands National Park ends at Ingonish, but the splendour of the Cabot Trail does not. Just outside Ingonish the trail ascends

Cape Smokey, one of the most spectacular rises on the trail. From the top of Cape Smokey, you can see the entirety of northern Cape Breton as far as Point Aconi, Glace Bay and industrial Cape Breton, many, many miles away. Cape Smokey has a day-use park with a great hiking trail.

Once you descend, the scenery is a bit anticlimactic until you reach St. Anns Harbour. Be sure to make the right turn just after Indian Brook or you will end up at the Englishtown Ferry and miss the rugged beauty of St. Anns Bay. The waters of this bay are sheltered between two mountains protected by a bar, which stretches almost completely across the entrance to the harbour. The result is waters that are almost always calm and often reflect a mirror image of the forested hillsides that surround them. There are a number of small picnic parks that take advantage of the natural beauty of this area.

St. Anns is the site of North America's only Gaelic college, where not only the Gaelic language is taught, but the other arts associated with the Scottish heritage are preserved as well.

Just past the college, the Cabot Trail ends at the Trans-Canada Highway, where a wonderful view of St. Anns Bay is framed between Kelly's Mountain and Murray Mountain. From here, it is a short distance to either Sydney or Baddeck on the Trans-Canada Highway.

BEACHES
Aspy Bay
Aspy Bay is almost completely cut off from the sea by two long sand spits. The spits are made of fine hard-packed sand, whitened by the gypsum that is common in this area. These are two of the finest beaches in northern Cape Breton. The north beach can be reached from Cabot Landing Provincial Park and the southern beach from the town of Dingwall. It was on this latter beach that the wreck of the *Auguste* occurred, the history of which is documented in the North Highlands Museum at Cape North. Gold coins and other artifacts still occasionally turn up after a storm. As an added bonus, this Gulf of St. Lawrence water is warmer than the Atlantic and extremely clear. As you travel up the spits toward the harbour entrance, where the two are separated by a distance of only a hundred feet or so, you'll see many migratory birds in spring and fall.

Ingonish Beach, Ingonish
This national park beach has a great setting at the head of South Bay, Ingonish, between Middle Head and Cape Smokey. A sandy shoreline backs onto a beach of smooth pink granite rocks. The ocean water is reasonably warm, but if it's too cold, you can walk to Freshwater Lake, which backs on the other side of the beach. Here, the water is decidedly warmer and calmer. At what other beach can you have your cake and eat it too?

Warren Lake
You might not expect to find one of Nova Scotia's best freshwater beaches in the highlands, but swimming is believing. Warren Lake is about a 3

kilometre-long narrow body of water just north of Ingonish off the road to Mary Ann Falls. A small strand of coarse pink granitic sand fronts the head of the lake. It is ringed by wooded hillsides and no visible signs of civilization, instead of the ubiquitous cottages that surround almost every other freshwater beach. The water is much warmer than the nearby ocean. As an added bonus, there's a good old-fashioned swimming hole just where Warren Brook enters the lake. Washroom facilities and picnic tables are available.

CANOEING

Margaree River, www.chrs.ca/rivers/margaree/margaree_e.htm.
The Margaree–Lake Ainslie River System has been designated as a Canadian Heritage River, one of only two in Nova Scotia. The area is legendary for its Atlantic salmon fishery and attracts anglers from around the world. However, fishing is not the only attraction. There are many places to put in a canoe and paddle down to the mouth at Margaree Harbour. In most places, when the water is high enough, the river, while fast flowing, is really quite gentle. All you need to do really is get in and use the paddles as rudders. The trip down the Southwest Margaree from Lake Ainslie to Margaree Forks takes you through mostly old farm country while the North East Margaree at its upper reaches has some steeper hillsides and better opportunities for viewing fall foliage. On the way down the North East you can stop at a fish hatchery and the Margaree Salmon Museum. If the water is high enough, this trip is particularly breathtaking in the fall when the leaves have turned. Needless to say, the fishing is good.

CYCLING

The Cabot Trail
The Cabot Trail is for many serious road cyclists the ultimate challenge in Eastern Canada. The uphills at Cape Smokey, French Mountain and the Aspy Valley are legendary. The downhills are incredibly exhilarating and dangerous at high speeds. However, for those with the stamina the rewards outweigh the pain of burning thighs and gasping lungs. There are annual organized rides which attract great numbers of cyclists. Check it out at www.atlanticcanadacycling.com/cabottrail

GOLF

The Highlands Links, Cabot Trail, Ingonish Beach, 800-441-1118, www.highlandslinksgolf.com
Stanley Thompson was one of the world's great golf course designers, responsible for many Canadian classics, including Banff Springs, Jasper and the Digby Pines on the Evangeline Trail, but his finest achievement is usually considered to be the Highlands Links at Ingonish. This course has been attracting praise from the day it opened in 1941. Its setting is simply unsurpassed. The view of the highland hills, the Clyburn River and the ocean is breathtaking from every hole, but there is a second and less benign reason for the fame of this course — it's brutally long and difficult. When

you tee off, you can barely see a fire tower high on a ridge, miles and miles away. Most people have no idea that after nine holes, they'll be standing at the foot of the mountain this tower sits on. Unlike conventional courses, the Highlands goes out for nine holes and then back for nine more. There are walks of up to 500 metres between the holes, and for the first 50-plus years of its existence, the course did not allow power carts. Each hole is completely separate from others and with a character and name all its own.

For many years the course suffered from poor maintenance due to government budget cuts, but over the past few years that policy has been rescinded. Millions of dollars have been spent to restore the course to Thompson's original design, adding cart paths and building an extensive irrigation system. The Highlands has been returned to its place of prominence on the Canadian golf scene. After you have played the Highlands and perhaps walked its 11-kilometre length, you will be tired, but regardless of your score, you'll feel that you have been challenged by a course worthy of its fame. No ifs, ands or buts, this is the best course in Atlantic Canada and the number one public course in Canada. In a recent publication *1001 Golf Holes You Must Play Before You Die*, author Jeff Barr selected no less than seven of the Highlands holes for inclusion. That is as many as Pebble Beach and more than the Old Course at St. Andrews and Augusta National. That will give you an idea of the reverence this course inspires in the golf experts.

Perhaps the most pleasant surprise about the Highlands is the extremely reasonable green fees, considering the calibre of the course.

HIKING

Although driving the Cabot Trail gives one a good idea of the splendours of Cape Breton Highlands National Park, you must get off the road to really appreciate the area. One way is to take a few of the dozen good hikes in the park. Here are a few of our favourites.

Salmon Pools

This is a long, dry trail that follows the Cheticamp River as it rises higher and higher into a remote mountain valley. It starts just behind the campground at the Cheticamp entrance to the park and provides a good introduction to the splendours of the highlands. For the first two or three kilometres the trail follows an old woods road canopied by hardwoods. The poetry of Robert Frost will spring to mind as you tramp through the maples and birches. From the first salmon pool on, the trail follows the river as the valley narrows. The river becomes progressively wilder with one gorge after another. The further you go, the better the scenery. You can walk in as far as 7 or 8 kilometres or return when you've had enough. We do recommend going at least as far as the third pool.

Skyline Trail

This hike to a point 400 metres above the Gulf of St. Lawrence offers one of the best opportunities in the park to see a moose close up. The trail starts at an elevation of almost 500 metres and passes through an old burn area, now overgrown with small birch and alders that have been heavily cropped by the moose that frequent this area. After about three-quarters of an hour of hiking, you will come out of the woods on top of a ridge, which overlooks the Cabot Trail hundreds of metres below. The ridge, which falls away on both sides, descends to a point from which there are unparalleled views up and down the coast. You really do feel as if you're on top of the world. The route returns via a loop through more fir trees and highland meadows. This trail is usually wet in spots and the ascent on the return trip can be demanding; however, recent upgrades have included a lot of boardwalks to protect the fragile native plants and keep the feet dry. While most people are thrilled and a little scared at seeing a moose or bear in the wild you must be careful. In 2009 the Skyline Trail was the site of Canada's only known fatal coyote attack, when a young woman, hiking alone, was killed by two unusually aggressive coyotes. A walking stick with a sharp point is a good precaution.

The Coastal Trail

This is the best trail in the park for exploring the shoreline in this area and, when combined with the Jack Pine and Jigging Cove Lake trails, makes for a full day of hiking if you are up to it. You can start the hike at either end of the trail, but our preference is at Halfway Brook because by the time you reach Black Brook Cove at the other end of the trail, you may well be ready for a dip at the beach. The falls at Black Brook are also a very pleasant spot for a picnic. After following the course of Halfway Brook for about 1 kilometre, you reach the open coast and for 5 kilometres scramble over granite outcrops, deserted cobble beaches and driftwood-choked coves. There are ever-changing vistas of the sea as you pass from one headland to the next. There is an abundance of sea life, both offshore and in the tidal pools. Black Brook Cove is a delightful spot where the brook tumbles into the ocean over a series of small falls. Returning, you can either follow the shoreline back or make an interesting loop via the Jack Pine Trail and Jigging Cove Lake, which adds distance to the return trip, but also adds ecological diversity.

Warren Lake Trail

If your preference is a less demanding trail with some length, Warren Lake is perfect. The trail circumnavigates the lake of the same name in 8 kilometres, following the shoreline closely, except at the head of the lake, where it veers away for about a kilometre. Most of the trail is covered with a canopy of maple and birch. There is an interesting suspension bridge over Warren Brook at the south end of the lake. This is an easy and eye-appealing hike on which you will benefit from the breeze off the lake on a hot day. It's also well suited for mountain biking.

Middle Head Trail

This is the most popular trail in the park. It is 2 to 3 kilometres in length to the tip of a small peninsula that juts into the middle of Ingonish Bay. The trail starts behind Keltic Lodge and passes through what used to be an old estate, the remnants of which have all but disappeared. The closer you get to the end, the more beautiful the views and dramatic the scenery. Middle Head is surrounded by cliffs on all sides, so the trail is high above the water, culminating in dramatic sea stacks with active nesting colonies of Arctic terns. The view from the end of the Middle Head Trail is more than worth the effort to get there. Also, despite its popularity, you will have little difficulty finding a secluded rock or boulder to lean against and enjoy the ocean scenery. As there are high cliffs all along this trail, common sense and caution are necessary.

Franey Mountain

The Franey Mountain Trail is among the most strenuous in this book. It is a very steep climb to a high look-off. To get an idea of what the trail will be like, take a short walk up to the Freshwater Lake look-off. If the view from here whets your appetite for more, go to the Franey trailhead; if you feel like this short climb is about to give you a heart attack, try the Freshwater Lake Trail.

The Franey Mountain hike climbs 350 metres in about 3 kilometres. There is not a heck of a lot to see until you reach the summit. Once there, you will find a fire tower. Be sure to look for the small path behind the tower, which leads to a look-off. Once here, we think you will agree that the climb has been worth it. You are up there with the eagles, although they may actually be soaring hundreds of metres below your vantage point. You can see Ingonish Bay, Middle Head, Cape Smokey, Money Point and the Clyburn Valley stretched out below in a sheer drop-off, which may cause vertigo. This really is the type of view that you go on vacation to find. You won't be disappointed.

You can return to your car by retracing your steps down the way you came or by following a gentler descent on an old fire road. If you have children, it's probably more sensible to walk up to the tower via this fire road.

Cape Smokey Hiking Trail

Not all of the best hiking trails in the Cape Breton Highlands are found within the boundaries of the national park. Just south of the park is the Cape Smokey Hiking Trail, which reaches elevations and offers views from the look-offs that equal those within the park. It also provides a very real chance to get a close-up look at a moose, which are plentiful in this area. The trail starts at the picnic grounds located within Cape Smokey Provincial Park, which is at the top of Cape Smokey, just off the Cabot Trail. The park's trail sign lists the return distance as 11 kilometres, but we have seen guides that list it as short as 8 kilometres. Whoever's right, it is a serious hike that calls for waterproof hiking boots for the numerous wet patches. The trail itself is a gradual descent through mostly open terrain to a series of look-offs that are reached by well-marked short side trails. The second look-off is truly awesome, perched as it is hundreds of feet directly above the surf below, something you won't find this dramatically elsewhere on the Cabot Trail. The last look-off at the end of the trail provides a complete panorama of Ingonish Bay, Middle Head and the Clyburn Valley. Pure and simple, one of the great views in all of Cape Breton, but you'll need a wide angle lens to do it justice photographically.

With regard to the moose, the signs of this magnificent beast are everywhere — scat, matted-down sleeping areas right beside the trail and close-cropped young hardwoods. However, be forewarned, these animals are huge. A close-up encounter with a bull moose staring right at you from less than 15 metres away will definitely get your adrenalin flowing. Chances are you won't be thinking of good old Bullwinkle.

North River Falls

Many people believe that the more difficult something is to attain, the more desirable it becomes. This adage certainly applies to the North River Falls trail, which requires at least a six hour time commitment to tackle, and is one of the most arduous treks in the province. Any one who has made the journey to North River Falls will not hesitate to affirm that the effort is more than amply rewarded. At over 100 feet, North River Falls is reputed to be the highest and largest in terms of water volume in Nova Scotia.

The trail is accessed via Oregon Road, which starts just over the North River bridge on the Cabot Trail in the community of North River. Make the short drive to the end of this road and enter the parking area for North River Provincial Park. You will find a large information board with a map of the trail and explanations of various points of interest along the way. Hopefully, there will be some brochures to take with you, but if not, the trail is well marked and only in a few spots is it necessary to look for flagging to find your way. In preparation make sure you have lots of food and water, waterproof hiking boots (definitely not sneakers) and layers of clothing, as the temperature can fluctuate wildly in the highlands. A walking stick is a great help, particularly on the descents. Do not take any small children or people who are not in good physical condition.

From the parking lot the trail soon joins an old woods road which is wide and easy walking for about the first two or three kilometres. There are two bridges which both pass over very pretty tributaries. The second has a series of falls and pools that are a worthwhile destination if you do have small children or are not up for a long hike. Not long after this point the trail meets the river at the site of an abandoned farm. Shortly thereafter you come to the Benches, which marks the uppermost limit for salmon fishing. After this the fun begins in earnest as the trail starts a series of ascents and descents that seem to get progressively higher and more difficult. In places the trail is very narrow with a straight drop on the left side.

Finally, after crossing a small tributary, a dull roar replaces the gentle rushing sound that has been a steady audible companion for the past couple of hours, and almost out of nowhere, there it is. Any number of adjectives could apply — awe inspiring, magnificent, wonderful, but nothing can adequately convey the pure magic of seeing the falls for the first time. A double strand of water plunges over black pre-cambrian rock in a torrent that fairly gleams in the sunlight. In the autumn, the myriad of rustic colours adds to the scene.

The hike does not end at the base of the falls. The trail makes a very steep ascent up the canyon wall opposite the falls for another majestic view from above that reveals the full extent of this cataract and the highlands. Although it is a long journey back, you will not regret having invested the time and energy to get here. If you have come to Nova Scotia for some serious hiking, put this trail near the top of the list. If you are a Nova Scotian, you owe it to yourself to make this trip at least once in your lifetime.

MUSEUMS

Dr. Elizabeth LeFort Gallery & Museum, Les Trois Pignons, 15584 Cabot Trail, Cheticamp, (902) 224-2612, www.troispignons.com

Cheticamp hooked rugs are known throughout Canada for their bright colours, high quality and durability. Elizabeth LeFort is considered by many to be master of this craft. Her rugs are in the Vatican, Buckingham Palace and the White House. On display in this gallery are 20 of her most famous creations, along with the works of others.

The Margaree Salmon Museum, 60 East Big Intervale Road, North East Margaree, (902) 248-2848

This museum is dedicated to one subject — the Atlantic salmon, and, in particular, the fishery on the Margaree. There is a worldwide fraternity of dedicated salmon fishermen who have taken this museum under their wing and have donated a superb collection of flies, rods, paintings, prints and photos. Even if you aren't a fisherman, the colourful and complex flies and the marvellous paintings are more than worth the nominal admission fee.

The North Highlands Museum, Cape North, (902) 383-2579, www.northhighlandsmuseum.ca

This small museum located in a new building documents the history of this part of Cape Breton, with a particular emphasis on farming, the fishery and the gypsum industry, which once prospered in the Dingwall area. Of particular interest is the small exhibit relating to the sinking of the French ship *Auguste* on the shores of Aspy Bay in 1761. On display are a number of artifacts found in 1977, when the shifting sands of Dingwall Beach revealed the buried treasures. The *Auguste* had been carrying many Quebec notables with their wives and children back to France after the fall of Montreal. It was driven aground in a driving snowstorm in 1761. All but seven men died.

OFF THE BEATEN PATH
The Highland Road and Cape Clear

The Highland Road is by far the longest dirt road in Nova Scotia. It traverses the spine of Cape Breton from Middle River just outside Baddeck all the way up to Cape Breton Highlands Park and ends at Wreck Cove on the Cabot Trail. It is part of a huge, largely unknown road system created by forestry giant Stora Enso to exploit the forest resources of Cape Breton. However, it is open to the public and has a couple of real attractions.

At the Wreck Cove end there are a number of large reservoirs created for the hydro project that taps the energy potential of Wreck Cove Brook and other streams that cascade down the highland mountains. These reservoirs have created some very good fishing opportunities.

The other reason to come here is to go to Cape Clear which simply put, is the best inland lookoff in Nova Scotia and it's actually reachable by car. To find your way around what can be a bewildering array of side roads and unmarked turns you must have a map of the Highland Road System. You can buy one from the DNR office in Baddeck. Once you have this head for the well-marked Highland Road entrance at Hunter's Mountain on the Cabot Trail. From here a wide well maintained gravel road climbs gradually through hardwoods until reaching the highlands plateau which is solidly coniferous forest. Once on top it is quite a drive past a lot of clearcuts, but don't be discouraged, you will be rewarded for your patience. Make a left turn at 2nd Forks Brook South Road, which should also have a sign saying Cape Clear. From here the roads start to get problematic, but at most times of year are passable. You'll need to make a few more turns but always follow the most travelled route and eventually you will come to the end of the road and a small parking area. Get out and be prepared to be blown away — literally. The wind almost always howls up here and the temperature will be much lower than in Baddeck.

You will quickly notice paths that lead to a clear area. Follow these, but be careful as you come upon the bare rock top of the cliffs quite suddenly. Once here you are standing over a thousand feet above the confluence of the North East Margaree and 2nd Forks Brook. The view will make you gasp as will the almost sheer drop. There is nothing but highland hills and mountains in sight and no sign that man has ever been here. You are looking into the Margaree and Middle River Wilderness Areas, which due to their steepness and inaccessibility have never been exploited. This is a hard place to find, but once you do you will join only a tiny fraction of people who ever discover this wild and exhilarating place. Return can be made the way you came or by following the Fielding Road down to North East Margaree.

Bay St. Lawrence and Meat Cove
At the village of Cape North, you will see a turnoff for Bay St. Lawrence and Meat Cove, which has long been considered the end of the earth to most Nova Scotians. This is too bad because the drive out to this community is exceptional. About 8 kilometres after the turn, you will find Cabot Landing Provincial Park, where a cairn and bust of John Cabot marks the landfall of the first European since the Vikings to set foot on the Americas after Columbus. From the park, you can walk out to the spit at the entrance to Aspy Bay. Moving on, you come to Bay St. Lawrence, which has a large fishing fleet moored in a sheltered harbour. Overlooking

the community is the large and attractive church of St. Margaret, which replaced an historic church that was destroyed by fire a few years ago. It is definitely worth a short side trip into Bay St. Lawrence to poke around the wharf and harbour entrance.

Not far past Bay St. Lawrence, Cape North, the northernmost point in Nova Scotia, comes into view. You will be hard-pressed to keep your eyes on the winding road with the temptation to look back at Cape North and to look ahead at the slate-coloured cliffs and green fields of Capstick. The pavement ends here and the rugged road climbs higher and higher above the Gulf of St. Lawrence. As you round Black Point, drive slowly, not only because just off the road there is an unguarded drop of hundreds of metres, but because the scenery is positively distracting. Just when you thought you had seen everything there was to see in Cape Breton, you come to Meat Cove, where the scenery is suddenly quite different. Looking down at the tiny little houses clustered around the small cove below, you will be reminded more of Ireland than Canada — not surprisingly either, for the unusually dark rocks that make up this small section of the coast were once linked directly with the Emerald Isle.

Don't expect too much of Meat Cove. The fun is getting there and getting back, although it is the starting point for wilderness hiking on the highlands plateau. This entire scenic excursion will take you about an hour and a half from Cape North village and back, with stops. It's well worth it.

SPECIAL INTEREST

Flora's, Cheticamp, (902) 224-3139, www.floras.com
One of Nova Scotia's largest and most-visited craft shops, Flora's is a regular stop on the bus-tour circuit. Although it can be downright claustrophobic when four or five buses arrive within minutes of each other, the shop is worth visiting for its vast selection of Cheticamp rugs. These are not cheap, but the amount of work that goes into each of them justifies the price. They will last forever.

Gaelic College of Celtic Arts and Crafts, South Gut, St. Anns, (902) 295-3441, www.gaeliccollege.edu
St. Anns is the site of North America's only Gaelic college, where the Gaelic language and the other arts associated with Scottish heritage are preserved. For a small fee, you can tour the grounds and buildings. While the exteriors of the buildings are nothing much, the Great Hall of the Clans is definitely worth a visit. It details the history of the Scottish clan system and traces the history of the Reverend Norman MacLeod, who led a group of St. Anns' settlers on a worldwide odyssey that eventually ended in Wauipu, New Zealand. The college makes a point of maintaining ties between the descendants of the New Zealand settlers and those who remained behind.

If you're Scottish, and even if you are not, for $5 you can buy a history of your clan prepared by the scholars at the college. The gift shop contains numerous Gaelic-related items, including tartans, books in Gaelic and a selection of great Cape Breton traditional music. The Gaelic College is important to Cape Breton, and goes a long way to explain why Cape Bretoners have preserved their heritage so well.

WHALE-WATCHING
Gulf of St. Lawrence
Where the mighty St. Lawrence River empties its massive outflow into the Atlantic, you will find a fertile ground for both whales and whale watchers. Although there are not as many of the really big whales that frequent the Bay of Fundy, what is lacking in size is made up for in numbers. The most commonly seen species is the pilot whale, which often travels in gams (herds) of 20 or more. Also seen are minkes, fin, sei and occasionally humpbacks. Whale-watching boats leave a number of ports along the gulf, including Cheticamp, Dingwall and Ingonish. Most use modified Cape Islander-style fishing boats. An added bonus to any cruise in these waters is the spectacular scenery of the rugged highland cliffs, often studded with sea caves and unusual rock formations. Tales of tragic shipwrecks, buried treasure and other mysterious goings-on are sure to enliven any voyage. Some of the better-known cruises from three different harbours include the following: Whale Cruisers Ltd., Cheticamp, (902) 224-3376, 1-800-813-3376, www.whalecruisers.com; Oshan Whale Cruise, Bay St. Lawrence, 1-877-383-2883, www.oshan.ca; and Fiddlin' Whale Tours, Pleasant Bay, 1-866-688-2424, www.fiddlinwhaletours.com.

ACCOMMODATIONS
The Normaway Inn, 691 Egypt Road, Margaree Valley, 1-800-565-9463, www.normaway.com
The Margaree Valley deserves to be savoured, and there is no better spot to do that than the Normaway. Tucked away on 250 secluded acres, the inn was built in 1928 by descendants of the original settlers from the Isle of Skye. Since 1944, it has been operated by the MacDonald Family, who really know the hospitality business. You enter the property down a long, pine-shaded driveway surrounded by green fields and wooded hills. The inn is a rambling, white and green-trimmed edifice with lots of woodwork and polished hardwood floors. It's cozy and very romantic. There are nine rooms scattered throughout the inn and 19 cabins on the property. Although some of the cabins have wood stoves, and even Jacuzzis, we prefer the comfort of the inn's rooms, each of which has a definite character.

The centrepiece of the Normaway is the common room, with its large stone fireplace and an assortment of books and games. Most nights there will be a fiddler, a piano player or a highland dancer to entertain after dinner. On weekends and special occasions, ceilidhs or barn dances are held in a barn on the property. In fact, it was at one of these gatherings that Ashley MacIsaac first came into public notice. For a modest fee, you can hear some of Cape Breton's best entertainers at a genuine communal gathering. The Normaway has long associations with salmon fishermen, and in August, September and October you're liable to hear a lot of talk about the famous pools of the Margaree and what flies are hot that week.

It's also a great base for hiking.

The dining room at the Normaway is as exceptional as everything else about this place. Come see for yourself why the Normaway has been continuously popular for over 65 years.

Markland Coastal Resort, 802 Dingwall Road, Dingwall, 800-872-6084, www.marklandresort.com

The Markland is a fairly new resort complex in the small community of Dingwall, just north of Cape Breton Highlands National Park. It has a terrific location on a large property overlooking beautiful Aspy Bay, with its miles of deserted beaches. The units are all built of pine and have all the modern conveniences, including very spacious and well-equipped bathrooms. If possible, get a cabin, as the units that adjoin are not well sound-proofed. The Markland also has a decent restaurant, a small swimming pool and easy access to all the wonders of this less-visited area of Cape Breton.

Keltic Lodge and Spa Ingonish Beach, 800-565-0444, www.kelticlodge.com

Keltic Lodge is the grand old dame of the Cabot Trail. Its white gables and red roof are visible for miles around. It is a resort in the old style, offering formal dining and a definite touch of elegance. There is a choice of accommodations — the lodge, the White Birches Inn, which is really a motel, and some excellent cottages. As far as the lodge goes, the rooms vary markedly. Some are large and have excellent views, others are small and face the parking lot. Inquire when booking as to what you are getting.

The Keltic is a place to spend some time. You can tee off at Nova Scotia's top golf course, which is almost right outside the front door. There are spectacular hiking trails that start at the back door.

The Keltic is expensive, but we think that if you snag one of the good rooms you'll be more than happy with your stay at this old resort. There are a number of dining options. The only serious drawback is the utter unpredictability of its main dining room. At times excellent, it is lately more often mediocre. Instead, try the newer Atlantic Restaurant, also on the property, which is less formal and, right now, better.

Glenghorm Beach Resort, 36743 Cabot Trail, Ingonish, 1-800-565-5660, www.capebretonresorts.com/our-resorts/glenghorm

This resort in Ingonish makes a good and much less expensive alternative to the Keltic. It is sited on beautiful North Bay Beach, which has excellent swimming and great rock hounding. The wave-sculpted shapes of sand-embedded granite boulders look almost too perfect to be natural — they look more like Henry Moore sculptures.

The resort has a swimming pool, dining room, lounge, gift shop and both cottage and motel accommodations.

DINING

We continue to be underwhelmed by the lack of good restaurants on what is arguably the province's most important scenic route. Admittedly, there are some local favourites we haven't tried, but overall the dining scene remains bleak.

The Normaway, Margaree Valley, 1-800-565-9463, www.normaway.com

The Normaway offers a *prix fixe* menu with a limited number of alternatives, one of which is usually salmon. The dining room is bright and cheery with light from windows on both sides. There is a good wine list, efficient and competent service and tasty food. Breakfasts here are huge, four-course affairs — you'd have to be a hiker or salmon fisherman to get through it after a four-course meal the night before.

BRAS D'OR LAKES SCENIC DRIVE

The Bras d'Or Lakes Scenic Drive is Nova Scotia's newest tourist route. It wanders around the many arms and inlets of the lakes in a somewhat haphazard fashion, sometimes not easy to follow.

This small inland sea, surrounded by the highlands of Cape Breton on all sides, has long been recognized as among the most beautiful inland waters in the world. It was this scenery that first attracted Alexander Graham Bell to Baddeck in the late 1800s. By following the route described below, you can explore the shores of the Bras d'Or Lakes in a roughly circular route and find out if Bell was right.

For most tourists, the scenic drive begins just outside Whycocomagh where the Trans-Canada Highway first meets the lakes some 40 kilometres from the Canso Causeway. From Whycocomagh the highway follows the shoreline of St. Patricks Channel to the resort town of Baddeck (www. baddeck.com).

For over 100 years, Baddeck has been one of Nova Scotia's top tourist centres. Alexander Graham Bell chose Baddeck as the site of his summer home because of its resemblance to the highlands and lochs of Scotland. Here he conducted many of his most famous experiments, including the invention of the hydrofoil, as well as staging the first airplane flight in the British Empire in 1909. The Alexander Graham Bell Museum on the edge of the town commemorates the great man and his many accomplishments. Today, Baddeck is an attractive village, the sailing centre of the Bras d'Or Lakes, and a central location from which to tour most of Cape Breton. There are a number of inns, restaurants, galleries and shops. The attractive old stone post office and customs house now houses an interpretive centre, which explains the ecology of the region.

From Baddeck the road follows the shore a short distance before merging with the Trans-Canada Highway. This is the only route you can take from here to the other side of Seal Island Bridge. A little further on is the northern terminus of the Cabot Trail, at St. Anns. Not far beyond the Cabot Trail turnoff, you will notice the sign for the Englishtown Ferry, an alternate route to the Cabot Trail. Englishtown was the birthplace of Cape Breton's famous giant, MacAskill, whose exploits are legendary in these parts. There is a small museum with a room displaying artifacts and memorabilia related to the giant. His grave site is just across from the ferry landing and is worth a visit.

Just after the Englishtown turnoff, the highway climbs from sea level to the top of Kellys Mountain, where there are look-offs on both the St. Anns and Big Bras d'Or sides. On a clear day it seems as if you can see forever from up here. After descending the mountain, the highway crosses the aesthetically pleasing Seal Island Bridge to Boularderie Island. To continue along the shores of Bras d'Or Lake, turn right just past the bridge and you can take a leisurely route around the southern tip of the island. This road takes you through cottage country to Ross Ferry, after which it follows the shoreline very closely, offering many opportunities to see Kellys Mountain, Beinn Bhreagh and Baddeck Harbour across the Great Bras d'Or. Follow the road out to Kempt Head for excellent views in all directions, then retrace your steps a few miles as far as Steele's Cross Road and turn right here to cross the island to the St. Andrews Channel side. Here you will pass through an area of large dairy farms before arriving at Grove Point and a small picnic park facing St. Andrews Channel. This is a very pastoral, uncrowded corner of Cape Breton.

Crossing St. Andrews Channel, the Bras d'Or Lakes Scenic Drive turns right and follows the road to Georges River. From here the trail hugs the shore of the lake almost without interruption to Grand Narrows, some 50 kilometres away. At Grand Narrows, you can cross the bridge to Iona or you can continue around Derby Point and back towards Sydney along the shoreline of East Bay. If you follow this latter route, be sure to drive into Grand Narrows and around Derby Point to Pipers Cove and Benacadie and enjoy the great views of the widest part of the Bras d'Or Lakes. Rounding the shore into East Bay, you pass through the community of Eskasoni (www.eskasoni.ca), the largest Mi'kmaq community in Nova Scotia. From here it is mostly cottage lots to the head of the bay where you join Route 4 and head down the other side.

From East Bay the road follows the coastline to the small communities of Ben Eoin and Big Pond. There are pleasant, but not dramatic, views of the waters of East Bay with the green hills of Eskasoni rising in the background. At Irish Cove the highway suddenly rises for a panoramic view of almost the entire Bras d'Or Lake area. There is a look-off and picnic park at the top of the mountain — one of the most photogenic views in Cape Breton.

In Johnstown there is a very picturesque church overlooking the lake, and beside it one can see a shrine to Our Lady of Guadelupe. Soon one arrives at Chapel Island and then St. Peter's, which is described under the Fleur-de-Lis Trail. At St. Peter's, turn right in the centre of town towards Dundee and Roberta. After Roberta, spectacular views of the lakes are around every corner. The drive along West Bay, with the views of Marble Mountain across the bay, is terrific.

At West Bay the highway heads up the other side of the bay for a scenic drive through Lime Hill and Marble Mountain to Malagawatch. Marble Mountain was once a site of a major quarrying operation, the industrial remains of which are very much in evidence around the old workings. There is a lookoff just below the old quarry. From here you can make your way down a very steep climb to the shoreline, which in this area is largely made up of the remnants of crushed marble from the quarry. There are pinks, greens and whites. If you are not satisfied with the view from the look-off, there is a very steep path opposite the look-off which climbs up above the quarry. On a clear day, the view is marvelous, but be extremely careful walking around the old workings. Marble Mountain also has a small museum that details the history of the quarrying operations.

Next is Orangedale, a small village nestled near the head of Denys Basin in a low-lying area of quiet coves and marshes. The village railway station has been preserved as it would have appeared in the 1920s. The local historic society maintains a small museum, and there is also a tearoom. From Orangedale several small unpaved roads lead to the Iona Peninsula. It is a short distance from Orangedale to the Trans-Canada Highway and Whycocomagh, where this tour began.

BEACHES
Frankaleen Beach, Boularderie Island
Take Black Rock Road after taking Exit 14 off Highway 105 for Big Bras d'Or Drive to the end of the road and you will find this lovely sand beach under a line of cliffs and headlands. The Bird Islands are visible off-shore. Although the view is marred by the Point Aconi Power Plant, you won't notice it once you're down on the beach. The beach has a canteen and campground, but is seldom crowded.

BIRDING
Bird Island Boat Tours, (902) 674-2384
Bird Island Boat Tours has been heading out three times daily for over 25 years. A small launch takes you on the 45-minute trip to Nova Scotia's largest colony of breeding seabirds located on two islands. You can expect to see razorbills, guillemots, black-legged kittiwakes, great and double-crested cormorants and everybody's favourite, the puffin. After mid-July, bald eagles are very common. There is also a large colony of grey seals.

Although the boat does not land, it comes within a few feet of the cliffs and shoreline and you will still get close to the birds and seals. The ecological harmony of a seabird colony is truly a marvel to see and something everyone should experience once in their lives. For non-birders the trip is worthwhile for the great scenery — not only around the islands, but of Cape Dauphin with its fairy caves and the numerous lighthouses leading to the entrance of Big Bras d'Or.

GOLF
Bell Bay Golf Club, Baddeck, 1-800-565-3077, www.bellbay.ca
This is one of Nova Scotia's newer championship layouts, having first opened in the fall of 1997. Designed by Tom McBroom, who is also renowned for the Links at Crowbush Cove on Prince Edward Island, this course is built on lands that overlook the shores of Bras d'Or Lake. *Golf Digest* selected it as the best new course in all of Canada for 1998. Despite its newness, the course is in immaculate condition with the fairways among the lushest in Atlantic Canada. The greens are large, fast and true. The last two holes, which take full advantage of a natural gorge, are probably the most memorable. Multiple tee boxes ensure a good, but fair, test for all handicap abilities. The practice facilities are outstanding. The staff is very

friendly and helpful and there's a well-stocked pro shop with a good lounge and restaurant. Although not the cheapest place to play in Cape Breton, this course is all you can ask for in a daily-fee operation.

Dundee Resort and Golf Club, 1-800-565-5660, www.capebretonresorts.com/features/golf/golf-dundee.html
This resort course is one of Nova Scotia's premier 18-hole layouts. It is extremely difficult and strenuous to play, as many holes seem to go straight uphill. Virtually every hole involves a climb or descent and uphill, downhill and sidehill lays are to be expected. Offsetting the difficulty of Dundee is its great beauty. Bras d'Or Lake is visible from almost every hole and is a very pleasant distraction from what can be a frustrating round of golf. However, if you persevere you will find the back nine much easier than the front. This course is nowhere near as crowded as Bell Bay or Highlands Links and much cheaper to play. Make this one of your "must-play" courses in Cape Breton.

HIKING
Salt Mountain Trail, Whycocomagh
For travellers on the Trans-Canada Highway following the Bras d'Or Lakes Scenic Drive, this trail is the first chance to get a good look at Cape Breton's majestic scenery. It starts beside the campground office at Whycocomagh Provincial Park and climbs for 2.5 kilometres through a variety of forest zones and interesting conglomerate rock formations to the top of Salt Mountain. While it is strenuous, the rewards are worth it. From the three lookoffs, one can see Whycocomagh Bay to the south and the Bras d'Or Lakes spread out to the northeast in all their glory.

Uisge Ban Falls
Uisge Ban Falls is among the most accessible of Cape Breton's many beautiful waterfalls. Take Exit 10 from the Trans-Canada Highway and head for Baddeck Bridge. You will notice a steep gorge cut between two fairly significant hills, which is where you are heading. About 15 kilometres along, turn left on North Branch Road and follow it to the picnic park where the trail begins.

The path is well-marked and usually dry. Most of it is through mature hardwoods with plenty of ferns and mosses. It takes about 30 minutes to get to the falls. You will notice the dramatic increase in the height of the walls on either side of the brook as you approach these spectacular falls. You will also see that the view of the first drop is hidden by the rock face of the second falls. Don't try to climb this face. There is a steep and slippery trail that will take you to the top of the second falls. Here, there are two beautiful pools you can swim in or let the water baptize you as it falls from above.

Return via a loop that will take you along the course of the north branch of the Baddeck River, sometimes up to 30 metres above it. Returning by this route takes about an hour. When heading back to Baddeck, you can turn left from the parking lot and return via Baddeck Forks through some lovely back country.

KAYAKING

Kayak Cape Breton, Roberta, (902) 535-3060,
www.kayakcapebreton.com
Kayak Cape Breton is located at Roberta, not far from Dundee Resort. The owners are Germans who sold their successful business and moved to Cape Breton to pursue a dream of living in an unspoiled and beautiful landscape. The waters of the Bras d'Or Lakes are generally much calmer and gentler than the open ocean and have the added benefit of being fog-free — an excellent place to take up the sport of kayaking. Kayak Cape Breton offers not only instruction and kayak rentals, but canoes, bikes and other outdoor equipment as well. There are also a number of well-equipped log cabins for rent.

MUSEUMS

Alexander Graham Bell Museum, Cabot Trail, Baddeck,
(902) 295-2069, www.pc.gc.ca/lhn-nhs/ns/grahambell/index.aspx
The Alexander Graham Bell Museum is part of a national historic site dedicated to Baddeck's most famous resident. The museum is an award-winning design that reflects Bell's interest in aerodynamic structures. It sits on well-manicured grounds that face the Bell estate, across the bay.

Alexander Graham Bell's extraordinary achievements are documented in photographs, audiovisual displays and short films. Of particular interest are the early telephonic devices, the materials relating to early aviation history and the hydrofoils. A visit to the museum concludes at the very impressive Hydrofoil Hall, which contains a full-scale replica of the HD-4, the fastest boat in the world at the time when Bell constructed it in Baddeck. After a visit to the Bell Museum, you'll definitely leave with an appreciation that Alexander Graham Bell was noteworthy for many accomplishments, not only the invention of the telephone.

Highland Village, Iona, (902) 725-2272, www.museum.gov.ns.ca/hv
Highland Village is a collection of about 10 buildings that represent the 200 years of Scottish settlement in Cape Breton. From a highland turf-roofed cottage to some early Cape Breton homes, a blacksmith's shop, a school and a store, this is an interesting restoration site that celebrates the Gaelic experience in Nova Scotia. There is an increasing awareness among many Cape Bretoners that the Gaelic language, which was the mother tongue of virtually all the Scots who immigrated here, should not be lost. The museum is making a concerted effort to increase the use of the language on the island. The village sits high above Barra Strait and there are spectacular views in all directions. There's lots of walking in the Highland Village and many things to see.

OFF THE BEATEN PATH
The Iona Peninsula
On the map you will notice what appears to be an island in the middle of Bras d'Or Lake. As far as we know, it doesn't have any name so we'll call

it the Iona peninsula, for the community of that name. Circumnavigation of this area takes only about one and a half hours. Iona and Little Narrows are the only villages. There are a few farms, some cottages, some lumbering operations and a gypsum mine, but not much else in the way of human activity. You'll probably see more kingfishers than people and it's doubtful you would pass more than two dozen cars along the way.

For the most part, the highway travels close to the shores of Bras d'Or. Although it is a short trip around, you'll see three different areas of Bras d'Or Lake — the main part of the lake from Iona to Estmere, the St. Patricks Channel around Little Narrows and Washabuck and the Great Bras d'Or from Washabuck back to Iona. All three shorelines are surprisingly different. St. Patricks is low-lying with many shallow inlets and marshes, often alive with waterfowl. Near Great Bras d'Or the highway rises dramatically to an excellent look-off over Maskells Harbour. From Iona to Ottawa Brook, farmland runs down to the waters of the open Bras d'Or. There are panoramic views across to Johnstown and Irish Cove. There are no paved roads through the interior of the peninsula and the communities you see on the map exist in name only. This is truly off the beaten path.

Point Aconi
Turn toward Point Aconi just before crossing St. Georges Channel and drive to the end of the road that follows the channel much of the way. Near the end, continue on the dirt road to Point Aconi lighthouse, one of the prettiest locations in the province. From here you can see from the tip of Cape Smokey to the cliffs of Glace Bay. The Bird Islands are also clearly visible offshore. Thankfully, the one thing you can't see is the Point Aconi Power Plant, which is obscured by trees. This is a good spot to get that great shot of a lighthouse.

WALKING TOURS
Baddeck
Even though there is no official walking tour, Baddeck is tailor-made for walking. Park near the government wharf and walk to the end of it. From here, there is a marvelous view of the harbour with the lighthouse on Kidston Island. In the distance, Beinn Bhreagh, the Bell estate where the great man is buried, sits on a hill overlooking the village. Nearer at hand you will see yachts and cruisers from all over North America. Leaving the wharf, tour Water Street with its boardwalk and fine cottages, and turn up Twining Street to Chebucto, the main street. Walk past the old Courthouse and Post Office to the Alexander Graham Bell Museum at the far end of town. It is a short walk from here back to your car.

ACCOMMODATIONS

Inverary Resort, Baddeck, 1-800-565-5660, www.inveraryresort.com
There are those who can remember when the Inverary was an inn — a charming building on a great property that ran right down to the shores of the Bras d'Or just outside Baddeck. Then it got written up in *Country Inns and Back Roads* and a number of other publications that specialize in romantic country inns. Naturally, a lot of people wanted to stay there, so, for better or worse, the Inverary started expanding — first a few cottages, then an annex here and there, then some motel units, and so on. Today the Inverary is anything but a small country inn. It has metamorphosed into a full-blown resort complete with indoor pool, convention hall, gift shops, two restaurants and a lot of things to do. Bikes, canoes and paddle boats can be rented. There is also tennis, a basketball court and volleyball. While this is no longer the place to go for a quiet Baddeck getaway, it is a great spot to take your family.

Lynwood Country Inn, 23 Shore Road, Baddeck, 1-877-666-1995, www.lynwoodinn.com
The Lynwood used to consist only of a lovely late-nineteenth century home at the outer edge of Main Street — a welcome alternative to the motels in Baddeck. There were only four rooms, each beautifully decorated with collectibles, reproductions and lots of colour. However, in 2002 the Lynwood followed the example of the Inverary and added a 27-room expansion modeled along the lines of the original house. The new rooms are fine, and you can still stay in the inn, but the small-inn charm is gone.

Silver Dart Lodge and MacNeil House, 257 Shore Road, Baddeck, 1-888-662-7484, www.silverdart.com
These two quite different sets of accommodation are both part of a large resort property on Shore Road on the south side of Baddeck. The Silver Dart is a series of motel units, while MacNeil House is a restored Victorian property. Both are set amid large, very well-maintained lawns and gardens. The MacNeil House contains six luxury suites, which are fully equipped with kitchen facilities, fireplaces, separate living room and large baths. They are expensive, but really closer to condo units than just suites. In addition to the gardens, there are woodland walking trails, a pool, children's play areas and generally lots to do. McCurdy's, the large restaurant, has a great view of the Bras D'Or Lakes and serves good food. In the summer, you'll be serenaded at dinner with lovely live Celtic harmonies. All in all this is a good spot for both families and couples.

Dundee Resort, West Bay, 1-800-565-5660, www.dundeeresort.com
Overlooking the west bay of the Bras d'Or Lakes is one of Nova Scotia's lesser-known resort destinations. It offers 60 hotel rooms and 39 cottages spread over a large facility. The main attractions are the 18-hole championship golf course and a large marina from which cruises of the Bras d'Or Lakes can be arranged. The dining room has yet to live up to the rest of

the resort, but there are several emerging operations close by that are worth checking out.

DINING

Inverary Resort, Baddeck, 1-800-565-5660, www.inveraryresort.com
The Inverary offers a couple of choices for dining. In the main building is Flora's, a Taste of Nova Scotia restaurant which means lots of local fare, especially seafood. The Lakefront restaurant offers a less formal setting right on the water's edge. Both are good choices.

**The Lynwood Inn, Baddeck, (902) 295-1995,
www.lynnwoodinn.com**
The dining room of the Lynwood Inn is formal in appearance, but the staff is welcoming and warm. The menu is limited, but makes good use of fresh local ingredients, such as chanterelles, blackberries and salmon. The desserts are unusual and tasty. The Lynwood offers a welcome alternative to the many run-of-the-mill restaurants in the Baddeck area.

**Rita's Tea Room, Big Pond, (902) 828-2667,
www.ritamacneil.com/tearoom.htm**
Fans of singer Rita McNeil will not want to miss her tea room/restaurant located in her former home in the tiny community of Big Pond on the shores of Bras d'Or Lakes. Admittedly an obvious play for the bus-tour crowd, the tea room is still a nice spot to have lunch. You can tour a room displaying some of Rita's many awards. It's also not unusual for Rita to be on hand; she's often in the kitchen.

FLEUR-DE-LIS TRAIL

The Fleur-de-lis Trail follows the east coast of Cape Breton Island, from the causeway to the Fortress of Louisbourg. Most of the communities in this area are Acadian settlements and the French culture is very much in evidence. Along the way, the trail explores the unspoiled scenery of Isle Madame, as well as passing through some of the most sparsely populated areas of Nova Scotia. Several stretches of the road have only recently been paved, but overall, the Fleur-de-lis Trail offers a very pleasant alternative to driving the busy Trans-Canada Highway up the centre of the island.

Not far from the beginning of the trail, at the Canso Causeway, is Port Hawkesbury (www.townofporthawkesbury.ca), an industrial community with a pulp mill and a deep-water port that can accommodate the largest ships in the world. Follow Highway 104 through largely uninteresting country as far as Louisdale and turn towards Isle Madame. The Fleur-de-lis Trail really begins in earnest once you cross the bridge over Lennox Passage to Isle Madame (www.islemadame.net).

Visitors are often looking for the "real Nova Scotia," and this corner of the province fits the bill nicely. This island of tightly knit communities maintains its ties with the traditional lifestyle associated with the fisheries.

Settled by French fishermen at least 250 years ago, there are indications of settlement much earlier. It became the centre for a number of traders from the Isle of Jersey who set up stations close to Arichat, which thrived until the early twentieth century. The lifeblood of the economy has always been fishing and continues to be so. The crab, lobster, shrimp, and mackerel fisheries are still thriving, although cod and other species ceased to be fished commercially in the 1990s.

The island is dotted with a number of Acadian villages of which Arichat (www.arichat.com) is the most significant. With a special pride in their French heritage, the local residents are among the friendliest and most outgoing people you'll meet anywhere.

After crossing the Lennox Passage Bridge, turn towards Arichat and tour the island in a counter-clockwise direction. A few kilometres on, look for the turn to Janvrin Island. This is a very pleasant drive through a number of small fishing communities. The island is named after one of the early Jerseymen. Here, the tranquil sheltered waters of the inner side of Isle Madame contrast markedly with the craggy and barren windswept shore you will see later on. Returning to the main road, there are very pretty views of the church at West Arichat and a number of reddish bluffs.

Arichat is the county seat of Richmond County and the largest town on the island. It has a wooden cathedral dating from 1837, a government wharf where fishing boats are often unloaded, and a small museum. Be sure to turn towards the water at the cathedral and you will find the route through the centre of town.

After Arichat, follow the signs to Petit de Grat and Sampsons Cove, both of which are very picturesque Acadian communities. Most of the small homes are reasonably new and are painted a variety of bright colours. The yards are often decorated with folk art, Acadian flags and symbols, which from a distance make these settlements extremely photogenic. Petit de Grat is on a smaller island with a number of dead-end roads, all worth exploring. One of the roads ends at Sampsons Cove, where you can park your car and continue on foot via a well-worn path to the shore through some very pretty lichen-covered granite boulders.

After touring Petit de Grat, return to Arichat and turn right at Route 320. At Pondville you will find a good swimming beach. To follow the shoreline, turn right at the sign to Rocky Bay. For the next 8 kilometres, you will enjoy peaceful landscape with quiet and sheltered harbours, such as D'Escousse and Poulamon.

Martinique has a picnic park, a lighthouse and a small beach with changing facilities for swimming. From here, it is a short distance to the Lennox Passage Bridge and the mainland.

On leaving Isle Madame, return to Highway 104 until Exit 47, which will take you to River Bourgeois. Leave the main highway and drive out to the church to admire the view of the villages across the water on Isle Madame.

Not far from River Bourgeois is St. Peter's (www.visitstpeters.com), one of Nova Scotia's oldest communities. It was founded in 1650 by Nicolas Denys and has had strategic significance for both the English and the French, as it stands on a portage between the Atlantic and the Bras d'Or Lakes. In the late 1800s a short canal was cut through the portage, making St. Peter's the usual gateway to that inland sea. The town offers a number of attractions including two museums and two parks, located on either side of the canal.

Shortly after crossing the bridge, make a right turn towards Grande Greve and Rockdale, watching for the sign to Chapel Cove. This scenic detour follows the coast as far as L'Ardoise. Next look for the Little Harbour Road, which leads to a panoramic seascape with a great view back to L'Ardoise. A few kilometres later, you will pass by Point Michaud Beach, one of the best on this coast. From here, a good road takes you cross-country to Grand River, about 12 kilometres away.

From Grand River to Framboise, you will travel through some of the least populated and wildest areas of Nova Scotia. Deer, moose and bear are not uncommon. The coastline is quite irregular, so you have only occasional glimpses of the sea, but there are a number of rugged side roads that lead to some of the least-visited beaches in the province.

At L'Archeveque, a short road leads to a cove, one half of which is a beach and the other half a colourful collection of fishermen's huts, boats, lobster and crab traps.

Fourchu has one of the few real harbours on this coast, and there is an array of wharves and boats on both sides of the bay. The lack of trees and somewhat bleak surroundings in the Fourchu area is reminiscent of a Newfoundland outport. Between here and Gabarus, look for a side road to Belfry Beach, one of the longest in the province and certainly among the most deserted. Gabarus has a pretty location with a lighthouse and a large fishing fleet. Not far past the government wharf you can follow a rutted road that eventually becomes little more than a path that makes a pleasant hike along the shoreline. All through this area, you will notice many signs in German advertising land for sale and new developments. It is ironic that Europeans seem to appreciate the unique beauty of this area more than Nova Scotians, who rarely venture into this part of the province.

As the crow flies, it is not far from Gabarus to Louisbourg, but to get there by car you must cut inland to Marion Bridge on the Mira River. Just before the river, turn right and follow the course of the river to Albert Bridge. From here take Highway 22 directly to Louisbourg.

As the fleur-de-lis is a French emblem, it's only logical that the Fleur-de-lis Trail should bring you to Louisbourg (www.louisbourg.com), the site of the eighteenth-century French fortress built to protect France's interests in the New World. However, Louisbourg is really two communities, the fishing town that has existed since colonial times, and the massive restoration of the fortress, several kilometres away.

The town of Louisbourg has long been a major port and fishing centre. The train station has been lovingly preserved and now operates as the tourist bureau and museum. On the tracks outside sit a number of restored rail cars that until recent times operated as the Sydney and Louisburg Railway. The main street has benefitted from a recent overhaul, and the building facades are uniformly well painted giving an impression of prosperity. Before leaving town, take a walk on the recently constructed promenade, which provides an interpretive history of the fortunes and failures of the area. And finally, don't miss a visit to the fortress, but allow yourself at least half a day to really get the flavour of the place.

Leaving Louisbourg, look for the turnoff to the Marconi Trail on your right, but before leaving town, be sure to drive to the lighthouse on the north side of the harbour. There are many photo opportunities along the way, of colourful fish shacks and the town's waterfront across the harbour. The lighthouse is part of the Louisbourg National Historic Site and was the site of the first lighthouse in North America. In our opinion, the present lighthouse is among the prettiest and most photogenic in the province. There are no power lines or fences to distract from the classic edifice, which stands guard against the elements at the mouth of the harbour. In addition, there is an unobstructed view of the fortress from the lighthouse area. The parking lot is the beginning of an interesting coastal hike.

BEACHES
Pondville, Isle Madame
This fine beach of dark sand and clear water has an old wharf at one end of the beach from which you can fish and watch the tide rush in to the salt marsh that backs onto the beach. The beach offers good birding, picnic tables and toilets, and it's not crowded.

Grande Greve

Turn right onto a dirt road exactly where the sign for Grande Greve is posted. Follow the road a couple of miles to a small sand beach. This is one of many interconnected beaches and inlets to be explored around St. Peter's Bay. On the way to Grande Greve Beach, you will pass an inlet where clam-diggers are often hard at work.

Point Michaud

This long broad crescent beach of hard-packed sand with offshore sandbars makes for great surf. Here, you can play in the waves, make sandcastles or hike a few kilometres out to Point Michaud. This is a wonderful beach that is literally right beside the road. It has a few facilities and fewer people.

Morrison Beach

This is a large sandy tract just outside Framboise, isolated, often cold and decidedly beautiful.

Belfry Beach

Despite the fact that this is one of the longest beaches in Nova Scotia, it is not easy to find. Look, or ask, for the unmarked Belfry Road not far north of Fourchu. At the end, you will come to an awe-inspiring beach. You can get out here and walk into an uninhabited wilderness. At the back of the beach is Belfry Lake, which is equally beautiful. In the fall, it is alive with migrating shore birds and waterfowl and is almost always deserted.

Kennington Cove

There are two beaches at Kennington Cove, which is within the confines of Louisbourg National Historic Site. One of them is supervised. Both are in small protected coves with reasonably warm water. On a hot day it's a great place to relax after you've spent four or five hours exploring the fortress.

CYCLING

Isle Madame

The Isle Madame area has the potential to be one of Nova Scotia's premier cycling destinations. Most of the island's roads follow the shoreline, many leading to secluded coves, beaches or tiny fishing communities, and are made even more attractive by the absence of heavy traffic. The island's terrain is gentle, and there are a number of places to stay, including a good motor inn, a campground and several B&Bs. Anyone serious about a cycling tour in Nova Scotia should consider a few days on Isle Madame.

HIKING

Lighthouse Trail, Louisbourg

This trail begins at the lighthouse parking lot just north of Louisbourg and follows the shoreline for almost 6 kilometres to the tiny community of Little Lorraine. The rocks in this area contrast sharply with the round polished granite of Nova Scotia's south shore. They are pre-Cambrian, over

600 million years old — the oldest rocks in Canada. They are extremely hard and resistant to erosion, resulting in angular rock faces. As an added bonus on this hike, the rocks are interlaced with beautiful bands of rose quartz and other inclusions.

The trail winds its way along the shoreline, mostly over the rocks but occasionally through cranberry bogs. Along the way, it passes a number of historic sites, including an old fort and the site of General Wolfe's landing to commence the siege of Louisbourg. At the end of the trail, you pass the site of the sinking of the *Astria*, where over 500 Irish immigrants lost their lives in a tragic shipwreck.

On the return, the views of Louisbourg lighthouse with the spire of the Governor's Palace in the background are among the many reasons that this is one of the most scenic coastal hikes in all of Nova Scotia. Note that the rocks are rugged and not suitable for young children or unleashed dogs.

HISTORIC SITES

The Fortress of Louisbourg, (902) 733-2280,
www.pc.gc.ca/eng/lhn-nhs/ns/louisbourg/index.aspx

This is Nova Scotia's top historical attraction, and no matter what your expectations, you're bound to be impressed. If you have been following the Fleur-de-lis Trail, you will have noticed that while this area is scenic, it is also harsh, bleak in some areas, often foggy, and always damp. The trees are stunted; the ocean is rough and relentless. Towns and services are few and far between. Really, it's the last place you'd expect to find an historical reconstruction on a scale equalled only by colonial Williamsburg in Virginia. Yet this is exactly what you find at the Fortress of Louisbourg.

By way of background, in 1713 France ceded mainland Nova Scotia to Britain after losing control of Port Royal. If you have already visited the Habitation and Annapolis Royal, you will know the history of these events. Still controlling Cape Breton, Prince Edward Island and, of course, Quebec, France decided to build the mother of all fortresses to make sure the rest of its North American possessions didn't go the way of Acadia. Louisbourg was chosen because of its proximity to the fishing grounds, its ice-free harbour and most importantly, its strategic location at the entrance to the Gulf of St. Lawrence. Nobody at the time seems to have paid much attention to the abysmal weather. Between 1713 and 1750, France built the largest fortified outpost in North America. One of the most oft-repeated stories about Louisbourg is how Louis XIV, concerned about the escalating costs of building Louisbourg, opined that he expected to see the walls of the fortress rising on the horizon as he sat in his palace at Versailles. While this is apparently a myth, when you visit the restoration you will understand King Louis' concerns. The fortress was actually much more than a military garrison. At any given time, there were as many fishermen and merchants, along with their wives and children, as there were soldiers living both within the walls of the fortress and just outside.

Although built and designed by some of the best military engineers of the day, as a fortress Louisbourg was ultimately a failure. Twice it came under siege, the first time in 1745, by New Englanders, and the second by the English under the command of that nemesis of the French, General Wolfe, in 1758. Both times it fell, largely because France had failed to provide the necessary naval support to prevent an invading force from getting close. Just as importantly, the long cold damp winters with no fresh fruit or vegetables led to disease and low morale. For many, garrison duty in Louisbourg was the equivalent of exile. The conditions were so harsh that in the winter of 1745–46, more than a thousand of the New Englander conquerors died of disease, starvation and cold. It seems to have been the ultimate pyrrhic victory.

In 1760 the British demolished the fortress and scattered the surrounding inhabitants. The site was abandoned for over 200 years until one of the largest restoration projects in history was undertaken by the Canadian government. Employing an army of archaeologists, planners, master workers and former coal miners, the fortress rose again, and now, about one-fourth of the original fortified city has been completely restored.

A visit to Louisbourg begins at the interpretive centre about 2 kilometres from the fortress. You then board a bus to be transported to the front gate. The first sight of the fortress as it comes into view across the bay is always impressive. One suddenly realizes the sheer magnitude of this place, with its Governor's Palace, dozens of private homes and seemingly miles of walls. It is hard to believe it ever could have been a heap of rubble.

There are 65 separate areas to explore, including the Governor's Palace, many fine colonial homes, taverns, barracks and storehouses. There are dozens of inhabitants to talk to, from the governor to the captain of the guard, and the lowest servants — even children. Follow the sounds of the drums to different daily events, such as musket and cannon firings. Have lunch at one of the several inns. Take a walk through the ruins to the graveyard, where the New Englanders who perished in that winter of 1745 are buried. Explore some of the backyards where there are vegetable and herb gardens.

There are numerous reconstructions and restorations of Colonial North America. This is the only one that features a French colonial city. Its origins unique, size impressive, history fascinating, setting beautiful, once visited Fortress Louisbourg won't soon be forgotten.

MUSEUMS

Le Noir Forge, Arichat, (902) 226-9364

Built in 1793 on the waterfront, this is the only surviving building of early Arichat. It was restored in 1967 as a centennial project, and contains a number of artifacts and implements related not only to blacksmithing, but also to the history of Isle Madame. The location itself is enough to recommend this small museum.

The Wallace MacAskill Home, St. Peter's, (902) 535-2531

A native of St. Peter's, Wallace MacAskill was one of Canada's foremost photographers. His early pictures of Peggys Cove were almost single-handedly responsible for spreading the fame of that tiny community. Almost 45 years after his death, MacAskill's photographs of traditional fishing and other Nova Scotia themes continue to sell well. Many people believe that nobody before or since has been able to capture the essence of Nova Scotia as well as MacAskill.

The museum preserves MacAskill's childhood home and contains many fine examples of his work. It is a fitting tribute to a man who has done so much to establish Nova Scotia's fame for natural beauty.

PARKS AND GREENSPACE

St. Peter's Canal National Historic Site and Battery Park, St. Peter's, www.pc.gc.ca/eng/lhn-nhs/ns/stpeters/index.aspx

These two parks, on opposite sides of the canal, are interesting spots to watch pleasure craft pass through the canal locks. They are also popular spots for mackerel and pollock fishing. St. Peter's Canal was completed in 1869 and has been in continuous use ever since, the only operational locks in Nova Scotia.

Crossing to the northern side of the canal, either by foot over the locks or by automobile, you enter Battery Park, which is located on a number of historic sites associated with St. Peter's. There is a short, but strenuous, trail to the site of Fort Grenville, where you can get a fine view of the town and the Atlantic Ocean. Battery Park has excellent camping facilities, some sites being right on the ocean's edge overlooking St. Peter's Bay. It also has a very picturesque lighthouse at the entrance to the bay.

Two Rivers Wildlife Park, Grand Mira Road, (902) 727-2483, www.tworiverspark.ca

With over 500 acres to explore this place is all about the kids. There are many types of native wildlife on display, a petting zoo, wagon and hay rides and a fishing pond so the little ones will be amused. For adults and kids there is swimming in the famed Mira River and hiking on the many trails. Two Rivers is a very popular place for Cape Bretoners to bring their families for a weekend afternoon. We think you'll like it too.

WALKING TOURS

Fortress of Louisbourg

This is probably the ultimate walking tour in Nova Scotia. Not only are you transported back to the year 1744 into a town ready for you to explore, but apparently a lot of the residents and inmates of the fort are there as well. The park service offers regular guided walking tours of Louisbourg, which can greatly enhance your appreciation of this historic site. If you don't like the structured format of a guided walking tour, pick up a map of the fortress and explore on your own.

ACCOMMODATIONS

L'Auberge Acadienne Inn, 2375 Highway 206, Arichat, 877-787-2200, www.acadienne.com

Not an inn, as the name suggests, this is a modern motor hotel designed from the front to look like a large manor. The rooms are clean and well-furnished, the staff very friendly and the dining room more than adequate. There is also a small intimate lounge, which occasionally features Acadian folk singers. L'Auberge Acadienne is conveniently located a short walk from the town wharf, the cathedral and Le Noir Forge. This is one of the best places to stay along the entire Fleur-de-lis Trail.

Salmon View Housekeeping Cottages, 1910 Soldier's Cove Road, Grand River, 1-877-676-0972, www.salmonviewlogcabins.com
Located in the tiny community of Grand River, these modern, well-equipped pine log cabins provide a comfortable spot to get away from it all. There are no nearby restaurants so bring your own supplies. These cottages are very popular with salmon fishermen and are quite reasonably priced.

Fortress View Suites, 7513 Main Street, Louisbourg, 877-733-3131, www.fortressview.ca
The Fortress View has five new suites right in the town of Louisbourg and an in-house restaurant which is not bad.

DINING
L'Auberge Acadienne, Arichat, (902) 226-2200, www.acadienne.com
The small dining room at L'Auberge Acadienne is gaily decorated with floral print wallpaper. The friendly waitstaff wear traditional Acadian garb without embarrassment or affectation. The menu is strong on seafood and traditional Acadian items. We can particularly recommend the chicken fricot, the meat pie, or the haddock done to perfection in a very light breaded coating. Small, delicious, hot baked loaves of bread are served with each meal. For an appetizer, mushroom caps stuffed with scallops are great. The wine list is minimal, but very reasonable. Try homemade pie or short-cake for dessert.

Fortress of Louisbourg, (902) 733-2280
The fortress has several choices. First you have to decide whether you belong in the lower-class tavern or the upper-class restaurant. At the Hotel de la Marine, you will be given a spoon no matter what you order and your choices are limited to fish, pea soup, beans and a few other staples. Only foods that were actually served in the 1700s are offered. It's a very interesting experience you don't want to miss. If you're not up for peasant food try the L'Epée Royale next door, if you are allowed in. Here there is real cutlery but no choice as each day one set meal is served, such as roast beef, fish of the day or pork en blanquette. Unfortunately, the prices have moved up a bit since 1745. Interestingly, the restaurants observe church tradition so that on Friday you can expect fish only.

MARCONI TRAIL

The Marconi Trail follows the coast from Louisbourg through a number of old fishing towns, to the mining communities of industrial Cape Breton, and ends in the Sydney area. It is named for the great inventor Guglielmo Marconi, who spent several years in the area and established a number of the first transatlantic communications sites, one of which is partially preserved at Glace Bay. If you have stayed overnight at Louisbourg, you can be in Sydney in 20 minutes via Highway 22 or you can spend an interesting day exploring this historic and picturesque trail. Louisbourg has much more to offer than simply the famous fortress and is described in more detail under the Fleur-de-lis Trail.

The Marconi Trail begins with a turn off Highway 22 just outside Louisbourg. Initially, it traverses an area of bogs and stunted spruce in a rather dreary drive to Main-à-Dieu, which despite its bleak appearance from afar is a charming Cape Breton fishing village up close and definitely worth the short detour off the main trail. There is an extensive boardwalk system along the beach just outside of town. Once in the village, be sure to follow the road around the circular cove to the Coastal Discovery Centre where there is a small fisheries museum and a lookoff from which you can watch the crab and lobster boats coming and going. This is also the starting point for a short walking trail to Moke Head. Along this shoreline you can see Scatarie Island with its lighthouse marking the treacherous Main-à-Dieu Passage that has claimed many ships and lives over the years.

From Main-à-Dieu the Marconi Trail follows the shoreline to Mira Bay, where the fabled Mira River empties to the sea. As you enter Port Morien, you catch the first glimpse of the cliffs that dominate this shoreline around to Sydney. A rather ordinary-looking community, it is the site of the beginning of one of North America's most important industries — coal mining. In 1720 the French first started mining the seams of coal that are clearly visible on the sides of the cliffs. Amazingly, you can walk to the very spot where it all began and see the remnants of the first French workings lying abandoned and unprotected. Park at the ball field across from the cairn and follow a short path to the shore. Not only can you see the old workings, but there is great beachcombing for industrial artifacts, as well as excellent fossil finds at your feet. The cliffs here have ledges that act as natural stairways, which allow you to get to the coal-bearing seams and the fossil-bearing strata that lie just above and below them, but great care must be taken around these cliffs.

At Donkin you enter what is usually referred to as "Industrial Cape Breton." The city of Sydney and the towns of Glace Bay, Dominion, Reserve Mines and New Waterford were recently amalgamated and named the Cape Breton Regional Municipality (www.cbrm.ns.ca). All of these communities came into existence because of coal and the products it generated, namely steel and electricity. However, the reliance on "king coal" has come to an end with the closure of the steel mill in Sydney and the mines that supplied it, and the unattractive and polluting power plants at Lingan and

Point Aconi now import coal. The subsidies that artificially buoyed the local economy and caused resentment both within and without Cape Breton are gone. These towns have had a hard and sometimes violent industrial history. They do not count among Nova Scotia's most attractive towns and their natural settings have been built over with industrial development, but there is a good side to the story. Rather than die economically, the region is reinventing itself with high-tech and education-based companies, which are finding the area a good place to do business. There is a definite air of optimism for the first time in decades.

Glace Bay, which follows shortly after Donkin, is a good example of the new spirit of industrial Cape Breton. The town has a definite spruced-up feeling that centres around the tiny, busy harbour and the walkway that flanks the creek that drains into the harbour. The restored Savoy Theatre is one of the premier venues to see and hear Cape Breton's legendary celtic music performers. The Miners' Museum and the Marconi Monument are both very worthwhile stops.

From Glace Bay you can take Highway 4 directly to Sydney or follow Highway 28 around the shoreline by the Colliery Route, which features the coal-mining history of the area. Frankly, after visiting the Miner's Museum you might have had enough of coal mines, but the seashore route is still worth it for the views from the cliffs that form the coastline of this area.

Once known for steelmaking and still known for the infamous tar ponds, one of Canada's most polluted sites, Sydney seems an unlikely tourist destination. However, it does have a world-class harbour and regularly hosts some of the world's largest cruise ships, which discharge passengers to stroll the boardwalk on the Esplanade or try their luck at the casino. Founded in the 1700s as an English settlement, Sydney has an attractive historic district that starts just north of the boardwalk. As the largest community in Cape Breton, it is the administrative, educational and financial centre of the island.

On leaving Sydney via King's Road, turn right at Keltic Drive where you will notice the unique plaid tourist bureau. From the community of Northwest Arm, Route 305 follows the shoreline of Sydney Harbour on a very pleasant drive through to North Sydney, which long has been the terminus of the Newfoundland ferry. The town has a varied industrial past centred around its port. There are a number of historical markers around the restored waterfront that make for an interesting short walk in the area. Just beyond North Sydney is the community of Sydney Mines, the last and most attractive of these Sydney Harbour communities. For an excellent view of the mouth of the harbour and the towns across the way, explore the Sydney Mines cemetery, which runs right down to the harbour cliffs. The town's tourist bureau is located in the old brick train station, which houses an exhibit of fossils found in the area.

BIRDING
Schooner Pond Head
Halfway between Port Morien and Donkin is the small community of

Schooner Pond. Look for a dirt road on the ocean side and take it as far as the steel gate, which leads to an abandoned coal mine. Whether the gate is open or closed, park here and make your way across the field and up the hill on a well-worn path to the top of the cliffs. From here it is an easy and beautiful walk to a kittiwake colony.

Along the way, you will note a number of unusual rock formations and tiny Flint Island with its lighthouse just offshore.

The kittiwakes are gone by August, but if you visit later, the area is frequented by migrating hawks and shore birds. It is a beautiful hike at any time of year.

CANOEING
The Mira River
The Mira is a very wide, slow-flowing river that is really an extension of the sea. Traversable in two to three days with no portages, the route passes through an historic inland supply route to Fortress Louisbourg. Along the way, old churches, deserted settlements and even the resting grounds of two sunken French ships may be seen. Campsites are plentiful and supplies may be purchased along the way.

HISTORIC SITES
Marconi National Historic Site, Timmerman Street, Glace Bay, (902) 295-2069, www.pc.gc.ca/lhn-nhs/ns/marconi/index.aspx
The great inventor Guglielmo Marconi was a major influence in industrial Cape Breton. Although many know that he made his first successful transatlantic wireless transmission from Signal Hill in St. John's, Newfoundland, most don't know that he was denied permission to set up a commercial operation there. Newfoundland's loss was Cape Breton's gain as Marconi sought out suitable sites for a commercial venture. He chose Table Head in Glace Bay from which he launched what eventually became a modern worldwide communications network. Later, Marconi's company set up transmission stations on a number of points found along the Marconi Trail and established the first ship-to-shore communications. While these stations are now long gone, the Marconi National Historic Site has on display many interesting artifacts from this period, and documents the history of early wireless communication. The Marconi site is not particularly easy to find, so you may have to ask for directions in Glace Bay.

MUSEUMS
Cape Breton Miners' Museum, 17 Museum Street, Glace Bay, (902) 849-4522, www.minersmuseum.com
Coal mines in Cape Breton were unique, extending many miles out under the water. It is safe to say that the Cape Breton Miners' Museum is one of the most revered in the province, run by retired miners who will guide you through an underground tour of the Ocean Deeps Colliery and answer questions you have about the industry. There is much more to the museum than simply the coal mine. There is also a miners' village and recently the

exhibit area was completely revamped, to explain the story of coal, from its formation millions of years ago to its extraction and use in industry. Typically, museums that feature industrial sites never sound too interesting at first, but, invariably, they surprise you. This museum is no exception and is a definite top attraction on the Marconi Trail.

Cossitt House, 75 Charlotte Street, Sydney, (902) 539-7973, www.museum.gov.ns.ca/ch/ and Jost House, 54 Charlotte Street, Sydney, (902) 530-0366
These two museums housed in Sydney's two oldest houses are almost across the street from one another in the city's historic north end. Jost House, operated by the local historical society, has a great collection of early mechanical toys as well as a room dedicated to the area's marine history.

Cossitt House is a provincial museum in the home of an early Anglican minister, Ranna Cossitt, who managed to get himself transferred to Yarmouth as a result of his political ambitions. Believed to be the oldest house in Sydney, Cossitt House is preserved and furnished largely in its original state. The house has a dark, dour interior, apparently in keeping with Cossitt's view of the human condition.

ROCKHOUNDING
Cliffs of the Marconi Trail
There are a number of different rockhounding opportunities along the Marconi Trail. The exposed cliffs from Morien Bay to Sydney are rife with fossils and numerous types of minerals. The area around Louisbourg is of interest because of the pre-Cambrian rocks, the oldest in Nova Scotia, which are interlaced with quartz veins and other collectible specimens.

SPECIAL EVENTS
Celtic Colours International Festival, 1-877-285-2321, www.celtic-colours.com
This fall music festival could be included under any Cape Breton trail as it is held at venues all around the island during the second week of October. Only recently established, it has quickly gained a reputation as a must-attend event for lovers of Celtic music. Attracting the best in Canadian and international talent, the festival usually coincides with the optimum fall foliage week in most of Cape Breton, especially the incomparable Margaree Valley. The combination of sight and sound is well worth a late season visit to Cape Breton. Glace Bay's Savoy Theatre is one of the best places to take in a concert. Celtic Colours is now the premiere Celtic music festival in North America.

WALKING TOURS
Sydney's North End
While Sydney may not be your first choice as a place to visit, its historic north end is of interest. Although no formal walking tour is available, pick up a copy of the Historic Sydney pamphlet, which lists a number of attrac-

tions including two museums and several churches. The tour is simplicity itself — park anywhere along the Esplanade, Sydney's waterfront street, and walk north until it ends. Turn right and then right again and return via Charlotte Street. Along the way you will pass St. Patrick's and St. George's churches, both of which have interesting cemeteries, and the Jost and Cossitt houses, the two oldest dwellings in the city. This walk, particularly if you include a walk along the harbourfront portion of the Esplanade, takes you by the best Sydney has to offer.

ACCOMMODATIONS

With the recent closing of the venerable Gowrie House in Sydney Mines, the choices of where to stay and eat just got a lot more restrictive. There are lots of motels, mostly just okay, but no great inns anymore.

Cambridge Suites, 380 Esplanade, Sydney, 1-800-565-9466, www.cambridgesuitessydney.com

Good value for your money, especially for families, these large suites with kitchen facilities are a practical solution when eating out loses its appeal. Located right on the waterfront, Cambridge Suites has a good exercise room opening onto a view of Sydney Harbour. Free internet and deluxe continental breakfast are included.

Delta Sydney, 300 Esplanade, Sydney, 1-800-268-1133 www.deltasydney.com

Also right on Sydney's waterfront, the Delta offers good accommodations and amenities, including a pool with a large indoor waterslide, which the little ones love. Like Cambridge Suites, the Delta fronts right on Sydney's boardwalk, so you can enjoy a morning walk or jog along the shores of Sydney Harbour. The dining room and lounge are both convenient, if not spectacular.

DINING

With the demise of Gowrie House we are embarrassed to say there is no restaurant that we know of in the Sydney area that rises above the average.

MARINE DRIVE

Marine Drive is one of Nova Scotia's longest scenic trails and certainly the least visited on the mainland. Stretching for several hundred kilometres from the Canso Causeway to Dartmouth, Marine Drive closely follows the shoreline of the Atlantic through an area most Nova Scotians refer to as the Eastern Shore. Up until recently, the economy along this shore was almost exclusively tied to the fishery; however, the Sable Island offshore gas pipeline comes ashore along this coast and has brought with it much-needed jobs.

Despite its length, there are no sizable towns along Marine Drive and accommodations and services can be scarce. However, Marine Drive offers some of Nova Scotia's wildest and most scenic country. The beaches are beautiful and uncrowded.

Many portions of this route cut across the base of peninsulas that jut out into the Atlantic. Communities tend to be located at the head of the harbours, but the best beaches and the wildest areas are inevitably at the ends of these peninsulas. It is well worth exploring many of the side roads, some of which are mentioned here.

Marine Drive begins at the Canso Causeway and follows the shoreline of the Strait of Canso until it reaches the shore of Chedabucto Bay.

Mulgrave (www.townofmulgrave.ca), not far past Aulds Cove, has the unfortunate circumstance of directly facing the heavy industries of Point Tupper across the strait, and as a result it is not unusual to see large ocean-going tankers at anchor. At Eddy Point you can drive down to the light-house on a gravel spit at the entrance to the Strait of Canso. From here you can see across to Janvrin Island and Isle Madame. You may even see a giant super-tanker passing through a rather narrow channel.

After rounding Eddy Point, the road travels a more inland route until reaching Port Shoreham, where you can enjoy the clear waters of Cheda-bucto Bay.

At Boylston, you will cross the mouth of the Milford Haven River, which you can view from the provincial campground located high on a hill overlooking the bay. Even if you are not camping, make sure that you drive up to the entrance of the campground for this beautiful view of the Milford Haven Valley and the upper reaches of Chedabucto Bay. At the scenic look-off there is a monument that commemorates the exploits of Prince Henry Sinclair of Orkney, who allegedly landed near here in 1398 before making his way further south. While most historians consider the Sinclair story to be a legend, obviously the people who paid for and erected this interesting memorial put more stock in it. At the picnic park at the foot of the hill, there is a small footbridge that crosses to an island in the river.

Shortly after Boylston, you arrive at Guysborough, a historic town that was populated principally by Loyalists in 1783. European settlement, how-ever, dates back to 1636 when Nicolas Denys founded a fishing station called Chedabucto. Guysborough is the administrative centre of Guysbor-ough County. It has a number of fine churches, especially St. Ann's with its beautiful spire, and there is an interesting museum in the Old Courthouse.

The waterfront has recently had a facelift with the development of Chedabucto Landing, which features a marina where you can rent kayaks or canoes and several other retail establishments built in an architectural style that complements this fine old town.

Leaving Guysborough, you can cut across the base of the Canso Peninsula to Larrys River, but you will miss some of the best scenery on the trail, so if you have the time, continue following the coast. Near Queensport, there is a very photogenic light station on a rock in the middle of the harbour. Where the road travels close to the water, you can see why Chedabucto Bay has long been considered one of Nova Scotia's great beauty spots.

Just past Half Island Cove, Marine Drive turns right to follow Route 316, while Highway 16 continues straight to Canso, which is described under Off the Beaten Path. The next communities are Whitehead and Lower Whitehead, both traditional fishing villages. Lower Whitehead has especially good views of Whitehead Harbour with its boulder-strewn granite shores lined with the rusty yellows and oranges of seaweed.

From the church at Port Felix, there is a marvelous view of the islands of Tor Bay spread out below. At Charlos Cove, there is a waterfront park with picnic tables where you can pause to enjoy the cove and beach. Larrys River is spread out on either side of a long narrow inlet joined by a scenic foot bridge. Shortly after, you come to Tor Bay, where the provincial park is definitely worth a stop. This was the site of the first transatlantic cable crossing, although all signs of that enterprise have long since disappeared.

Next is New Harbour, located at the mouth of the river of the same name. The sand flats here are often alive with shorebirds and herons during the fall and spring migrations. Marine Drive then follows the course of the river on a very scenic route as far as New Harbour West before cutting across to Coddles Harbour. Soon you come to the first of many fjord-like bays that penetrate the Eastern Shore. The twin communities of Goldboro and Isaacs Harbour face each other across the tranquil waters.

Goldboro is the landfall for the Sable Offshore pipeline, which runs underwater some 250 kilometres from gigantic platforms just off Sable Island, and the site of a newly opened gas plant. There is an interpretive centre at the large wharf, which was specifically constructed to land some of the larger components for the gas plant and pipeline. It explains the history of the area with an emphasis on mining, forestry, fishing and now natural gas. From the time the pipeline was first proposed and right up until its opening on January 1, 2000, there were concerns about how it would affect the environment, both onshore and off, and the slow-paced, friendly way of life in this area. Ten years into operation, it is pleasing to report that very little has changed, certainly not in a negative way. There does appear to be more prosperity, but little change in either attitude or environment. The gas plant is located well off Marine Drive and does not impair the view.

Marine Drive proceeds down one side of the bay to the headwaters and then back up for a short distance before cutting across to the next long bay at Country Harbour. Here you must take a short ferry ride, which is always an interesting diversion on any tour. If for some reason the ferry is not operating or the line-ups are too long, you can drive around via Country Harbour Crossroads.

Leaving the ferry, you will pass through an area of peat bogs before coming to the turnoff for Fishermans Harbour. Down a short side road, you'll find a small collection of fishing huts and a lighthouse on the tip of a gravel spit. Next is Port Bickerton, with the Nova Scotia Lighthouse Interpretive Centre. If you're content merely to look at the lighthouse, there is a good view from Beachview Road in Bickerton West.

At Port Hilford, where you'll see some of the few farms on this entire coast, you have a choice of continuing along Marine Drive, following the shore of Indian Harbour Lake to Sherbrooke, or taking a gravel road to Sonora. It's a pleasant dilemma because both routes are good choices, but we prefer the Sonora way. The pavement returns and the road to Sherbrooke follows the shores of the St. Mary's River on one of the most pleasant river roads in the province. As you enter Sherbrooke, you pass the sawmill, which is part of the Sherbrooke Village restoration.

Sherbrooke is quite different from the places you've been passing through since Guysborough. For one thing, it is well-treed and has a look of quiet prosperity. For another, its original economy was not based on fishing, but lumbering, mining and guiding. The prosperity originally dated from gold, which was mined extensively in Guysborough County during the 1800s. The St. Mary's River is a major salmon river and Sherbrooke has always been a guiding and outfitting centre as well. Just before entering town from Marine Drive you can stop at the St. Mary's River Interpretation Centre, which focuses on the history of these activities on the river. Most people, however, stop in Sherbrooke to visit the excellent village restoration.

Leaving Sherbrooke, you travel through the woods for about 16 kilometres before reaching the Atlantic again at Little Liscomb. A side trip down to the end of the road here will bring you to Indian Point, where you will find a deserted boulder beach and excellent views of Cape Gegogan and Tobacco Island on one side, and the many islands of Liscomb Harbour on the other.

Marine Drive then follows the shore to Liscomb Mills, where the highway crosses the Liscomb River. Just before the bridge, you can park and get out of your vehicle to enjoy this scenic river landscape with its series of small waterfalls or walk the Liscomb River trail.

The next villages are Marie Joseph, Ecum Secum and Necum Teuch, strange names, but traditional fishing communities. At Ecum Secum bridge, turn left and follow the side road to Mitchell Bay, where there is a beautiful Anglican church and cemetery overlooking the water. There are also excellent views of the dozens of small islands along this coast, which provide sea kayaking opportunities second to none. Stay on this road and it will take you back to Marine Drive. The main highway then follows the coast until Beaver Harbour. Here you can continue the shore views by taking the road to Sober Island, which loops around and rejoins the Marine Drive just outside Sheet Harbour. Sober Island is worth a side trip at least as far as the short bridge that connects it to the mainland.

Sheet Harbour (www.sheetharbour.ca) lies between the outflows of the East and West Sheet Harbour Rivers at the head of a long narrow bay. Coming into town, just before the bridge over the East River, turn left and follow the paved road to the sign for Ruths Falls. Park at the hydro station and walk down to where the falls spill over the dam. This is a great spot for a picnic.

Returning to Marine Drive and crossing the bridge, you will notice that Sheet Harbour has a fair number of amenities not found between here and Sherbrooke. In recent years the government has made an effort to make Sheet Harbour into a major port and chief supply depot for the Scotian Shelf gas platforms.

Just before crossing the West River, stop at the information centre by MacPhee House; there is a balcony that overlooks the rapids of the West River. You also have a view of what must be the world's only tavern in an oil tank! Just across the bridge is a small park with paths leading down to the rapids.

From Sheet Harbour, Marine Drive travels inland to Mushaboom Harbour, where a paved side road leads to Mushaboom. There are several very scenic fishing wharves and great views of the offshore islands down this road.

Shortly after Mushaboom, look for the entrance to Taylor Head Provincial Park with its excellent hiking trails. Marine Drive then follows the coast in a scenic drive through the tiny communities of Spry Harbour, Popes Harbour, Tangier and Murphys Cove to Ship Harbour, another long indented bay. The great number of buoys and markers in the sheltered waters of Ship Harbour bespeak the aquaculture industry that dominates this area. At Ship Harbour, turn left to follow the coast around to DeBaies Cove, Owls Head and then Clam Harbour, where there is yet another in the series of exceptional provincial parks on this coast. Clam Harbour is the best swimming beach on the Eastern Shore and the site of an annual sandcastle competition.

From Lake Charlotte, where you rejoin Marine Drive, it is a short distance to Musquodoboit Harbour. Along the way look for the Fishermen's Life Museum at Head of Jeddore. Musquodoboit Harbour is a small community at the mouth of the beautiful Musquodoboit River. It has a Railway Museum and more facilities than most of the communities in the area. From here Route 357 leads to the farming communities of the Musquodoboit Valley.

Shortly past Musquodoboit Harbour, look for Route 207 and a left turn towards Chezzetcook where, for a while, the highway follows the shore. The spire of St. Anselm's Church can be seen for many miles in all directions. This is the centre of life in the Acadian communities of Chezzetcook and Grand Desert. At Seaforth, take a short detour down Causeway Road to the Fishermen's Reserve. The reserve is a collection of fishermen's huts and shanties located at the tip of an island that is joined to the mainland by a causeway. It provides a good photographic opportunity of remnants of a traditional way of life. From Seaforth, Marine Drive passes right behind Lawrencetown Beach, popular with surfers, and past the road to Conrad Beach, popular with birders. Soon after, the trail enters the outskirts of Dartmouth; it is actually easier to visit this portion of Marine Drive in a daytrip from the Halifax area.

BEACHES

Port Shoreham
A long beach of coarse sand with very clear water, the beach faces the inner portion of Chedabucto Bay, so the water is usually very calm. This is the only beach with any type of facilities on beautiful Chedabucto Bay and it is definitely worth stopping here for a walk or a swim.

Clam Harbour
This is one of the best swimming beaches on Nova Scotia's entire Atlantic coast. The kilometre-long beach is composed of fine, hard-packed sand that slopes gently into the cool waters of Clam Harbour. A much warmer tidal stream cuts across the beach and empties into the harbour. Depending on the tides, this can be a gentle flow, easily forded, or a strong current requiring considerable care.

Every August, Clam Harbour is the site of a sand sculpture contest, which attracts upwards of 10,000 visitors. So perfect is the sand for this type of activity that the finest details of sandcastles and other sculptures stay in place for hours. The ingenuity of the entries is always amazing and entertaining. There is a children's division, so your youngsters can try out their latent architectural skills.

Clam Harbour is a supervised beach and has full facilities, including a canteen and showers. It's a big, friendly, family-type beach usually free of excessive crowds.

Martinique Beach
If your idea of a great beach is miles of sand pounded by crashing surf with nobody around, then Martinique Beach is the place for you. With a length of 5 kilometres, it is one of Nova Scotia's longest beaches and although only 40 minutes from Halifax, it is never crowded. On a sunny August weekend, there might be 200 people spread over the length of the beach. On weekdays, the beach is often virtually deserted. The province has wisely staggered the parking areas along the first mile of the beach so that no more than six or seven cars can park at any one of the small access lots. This minimizes damage to the fragile dunes that must be traversed by boardwalks to reach the beach, and it has the beneficial effect of limiting congestion at any particular area.

So what's the catch? The provincial tourist guides variously describe the water as refreshing, bracing or invigorating. These are polite euphemisms for cold as hell! While small children, who seem to be impervious to cold temperatures, may enjoy the water before mid-July, most normal adults will not. However, in late August and early September, the waters do warm up considerably and the beach is rarely crowded.

While swimming may be out for all but Polar Bear Club members, Martinique is a great place to stretch one's legs. After a walk to the rocky headland, you can return on the opposite side of the spit along the salt-water marsh, where from August on shorebirds and waterfowl congregate in considerable numbers. This is also one of Nova Scotia's most consistently rewarding birding hotspots.

Lawrencetown Beach
This is a full-service beach with washrooms and change houses. Boardwalks protect the dunes, which were at one time the site of gold-mining activity. This is a very exposed, windswept spot and not a great place for sunbathing or swimming, but it is a favourite of surfers who can be seen at all times of year. Offshore in their dark wetsuits, they can easily be mistaken for seals.

CYCLING
Musquodoboit Area Recreational Trails
This is a series of recently developed trails that start right in Musquodoboit Harbour at a well-posted parking lot just around the corner from the Musquodoboit Railway Museum. The portion of interest to biking enthusiasts is the 14.5-kilometres (one way) linear trail that follows the railbed of the *Blueberry Express* that ran between Musquodoboit Harbour and the upper Musquodoboit Valley. The trail is in excellent condition for bikes with few sandy or extremely gravelly spots, as it meanders its way past Bayers Lake to the banks of the Musquodoboit River and eventually to the foot of Gibraltar Rock. At each end of the trail there are short, but steep climbs to excellent look-offs. The trail has numerous covered picnicking areas and, unlike many other reclaimed railbed trails, this one is free of ATVs so it's a great place for a family bike outing.

BIRDING
Martinique Beach
The back side of Martinique Beach is a large wetland that attracts a great variety of waterfowl and shorebirds during the spring and fall migrations.

Conrad Beach
Turn at Conrad Road across from the Lawrencetown Community Centre and drive to the end of the road. The tidal marsh on the left is usually a good spot for migrating waterfowl and the occasional rarity such as snowy egrets. Willets breed here in the summer. The beach is frequented by shorebirds while offshore, loons, eiders and scoters are common. A bridle path through nearby woods offers an opportunity for spotting woodland species. The variety of habitats at Conrad Beach consistently produces rarities. This is one of the best places close to Halifax/Dartmouth to birdwatch.

CANOEING
The Musquodoboit Valley

The Musquodoboit Valley is close to three of Nova Scotia's most accessible rivers — the Musquodoboit, the Stewiacke and the Shubenacadie. The rivers are criss-crossed by many small roads so there are a lot of good put-in and take-out sites. If you don't have your own canoe, Meaghers Grant Canoe Rentals can help. It is not easy to find, so call first for directions — (902) 384-2513. Not only can you rent a canoe here, but the owner will be glad to drive you to any one of a number of put-in spots so that you can paddle downstream to your vehicle. The best time of year is late spring, while the waters are still high and the weather has warmed up some. Suffice it to say that there is no more pleasant way to spend a leisurely morning or afternoon than canoeing along the meandering waters of the Upper Musquodoboit. You will easily see or hear 30 or more species of birds among the many varieties of hardwoods and softwoods, as well as territory that is surprisingly wild. When the river is reasonably high, there are no rocks, rapids or other impediments for novice canoers.

GOLF

Osprey Shores Golf Resort, Guysborough, 1-800-909-3904, www.ospreyshoresresort.com

This nine-hole golf course is built on a peninsula extending into the upper reaches of Chedabucto Bay. The water is in view on every hole, and in play on three or four. Golfers have excellent views of the town of Guysborough and the islands of Chedabucto Bay. The course is not hard except for hitting the minuscule greens. Once you are on them, they're so small that you never have a long putt.

River Oaks Golf Club, Meaghers Grant, (902) 384-2033, www.riveroaksgolfclub.ca

This 27-hole layout is located in the heart of the beautiful Musquodoboit Valley. When it was constructed, great effort was made not to despoil the banks, marshes and small tributaries of the Musquodoboit River, which feature prominently in many of the holes. The effort was successful and chances are you will see more wildlife on this course than any other in the province. Not only are bald eagles, Canada geese, many species of duck and other wading birds common, but you might also come across otters, beavers, muskrats, deer or even moose. The most interesting feature is unquestionably the trout pond by the fourth tee. You can feed the always-hungry fish while waiting to tee off. The course sacrifices nothing in preserving the habitat. It is a very stiff challenge, particularly a number of holes that have water on both sides. With a friendly staff and reasonable green fees, this is a great alternative to the more expensive Halifax courses, and yet it's only a 40-minute drive from downtown. With the recent opening of a third nine-hole course, a small lodge has been opened, so it's now possible to stay and play.

HIKING
Guysborough Nature Trail, Guysborough
The Trans Canada Trail passes through the Guysborough area following the path of a railbed that was laid down in the late 1920s, but was never actually put into service. Different portions have been opened and more will continue to be over the next few years. The first to open was a 3.7-kilometre section that has been named the Guysborough Nature Trail. It is worth hiking for the magnificent view of Cook's Cove and Chedabucto Bay that you get from a field not far into the hike. The trail can be accessed just outside Guysborough at a well-signed location where it crosses the highway. Look for the large trail map to make sure you start on the proper side of the road. This portion of the trail ends at a bridge over the Salmon River in a quiet spot where the waters are inviting on a hot day. Notice the concrete abutments that were built for a bridge that was never completed. Legend has it that a disliked foreman, a latter-day Jimmy Hoffa, is entombed in one of them.

Chapel Gully Trail, Canso
This is a set of loop trails maintained by the Eastern Tip Trails Association that starts right in the town of Canso. The trailhead is easy to find by following signs through the town. There is ample parking. The trail consists of an outer loop that the trail guide alleges is 10 kilometres, but seems much shorter. There is an inner loop that is about half as long and, finally, a very short stroll that basically features the bridge that has been built across the head of Chapel Gully. Taking the outer loop in a counterclockwise direction will save the best for last.

The trail features an interesting growth of jack pine followed by a segment that gives tantalizing views of the ocean until you come upon French Cove, where you can swim in the very clear water. The trail then wends its way alongside Chapel Gully, which is actually an inlet and not a gully as we usually think of it. Near the end of the trail, a substantial footbridge crosses the gully and returns to the trailhead. This is not a trail that overwhelms one with its beauty, but over the course of the hour or so it takes to walk it, the subtle interplay of land and ocean on the easternmost tip of mainland Nova Scotia becomes more and more apparent. What is very impressive about this trail is the obvious effort and devotion the trail association has put in to build and maintain it. A substantial portion of the trail is boardwalk, and there are gazebos, picnic areas, look-offs and a great number of bird houses and bird feeders, some very whimsical.

Liscomb River Trail, Liscomb Mills
This is a gratifying, if somewhat rugged, hike along the banks of one of Nova Scotia's most scenic rivers, taking you to a suspension bridge, small falls and a fish ladder.

The well-marked trail goes up one side of the river and back the other. You can either begin behind the chalets at Liscombe Lodge or from the other side of the highway bridge that crosses the river. The trail from the chalets generally follows the course of the river for about 4 or 5 kilometres to the bridge. Along the way there are several marked salmon pools and many places to clamber on the rocks that stud the riverbed. In some places the river is wide and serene and at others narrow, rocky and very photogenic.

The suspension bridge, which crosses the river just in front of the narrow gorge through which the waterfall plunges, is always a hit with kids. Just across the bridge, be sure to turn left and follow the trail to an old dam, which has been converted to a trap-and-release station at the top of an extensive fish ladder. At certain times of the year you can see salmon resting at various spots in the ladder.

The trail returns to the highway along the riverbanks via a route that is not as rugged as the other side. Hiking boots are a must on this trail, as it contains innumerable rocks and roots, along with a number of potentially wet areas. On the way to the bridge the trail climbs sharply at least three times. For those who can't do the hike, there is a narrow dirt road on the north side of the highway bridge, which will take you to the old dam and suspension bridge. However, if you are in reasonably good shape, the hike is a lot more interesting and rewarding.

Taylor Head Provincial Park

Taylor Head Provincial Park is a hikers' paradise. There are a number of great coastal walks, including a hike from Bull Head to Psyche Cove, but, unquestionably, the star attraction is the Headland Trail to the tip of Taylor Head. This figure-eight trail connects with the Spry Bay Trail. You can take it in either direction from the last parking lot on the park road, but we prefer going clockwise. The first part of the trail passes through open fields, where old stone walls tell of former farming ventures. Shortly after, the trail enters a dense softwood forest, just above the shore. The forest floor is covered by various mosses and fungi, including the ethereal Indian pipe. Glimpses of the ocean are frequent. After 2 kilometres or so, you will notice the trees getting shorter and the vegetation sparser. Suddenly the trail comes out on a rocky shore and you are on a barren boulder-strewn headland. The sound, smell and ever-changing colours of the sea are omnipresent. On a sunny day the white of the granite boulders and the bleached skeletons of dead conifers are almost blinding.

The path returns on the open shoreline — on this side of the peninsula the barrens extend for several kilometres. There are cobble beaches, lots of seabirds, driftwood and lichen-covered glacial erratics. After the barrens end, you come to a bridge over a swampy cove; from there you can continue the loop along the shoreline or cut directly across to the parking lot.

The trip to Taylor Head takes a couple of hours each way. The path is always wet in some places and the hiker will require strong, waterproof hiking boots. You should take a pack with water and warm clothing. It's much colder out on the barrens than at the parking lot. The path is well maintained and signed and there are usually trail maps available at the trail head.

Musquodoboit Area Recreation Trails
This recent addition to the Trans Canada Trail system features something for everyone. The linear railbed trail is described under Biking, although it is very well suited for walkers as well, particularly those who are not up to the fairly strenuous trails that head up from each end of the trail.

From the Musquodoboit Harbour end of the trail, about a kilometre after crossing the river, two loop trails diverge. The Bayers Lake look-off is only a kilometre or so, although quite steep, and provides views of the lake. The Admiral Lake look-off trail is listed at 5 kilometres, but seems longer due to both the elevation change and the many often-slippery moss-covered rocks that must be negotiated. Like all Marine Drive hiking trails, good hiking boots are a necessity. The reward for perseverance is a tremendous view, first of Bayers Lake and later Admiral Lake, both far below. Much of the trail is through rich fern and moss-laden undergrowth, which spreads like a green carpet between the trees of a mixed forest. Warblers and other forest birds abound. In late July and August, blueberries blanket every open space. Munching on a handful while watching the old railbed snake alongside the river, you won't have any problem understanding why this was called the *Blueberry Express* line.

At the far end of the railbed trail is a short loop to Gibraltar Rock from whence there are excellent views of the Musquodoboit River valley. This is also a favourite spot for rock climbers, so don't be surprised if someone pops up from what looks like a sheer drop of several hundred feet.

Hikers with small children and pets should confine their explorations to the railbed trail.

HISTORIC SITES
Canso Islands National Historic Site, Union Street, Canso,
(902) 295-2069, www.pc.gc.ca/lhn-nhs/ns/canso/index.aspx
Grassy Island is a small treeless islet just off the town of Canso. From the shore, it looks like nothing more than an island pasture, yet until its destruction in 1744, this was once a bustling community of New England fishermen. On the mainland, a new interpretation centre gives you the history of this "forgotten settlement" by way of an audiovisual display, models and artifacts. The highlight is a trip to the island on a Parks Canada launch. Once on the island, you can take a self-guided tour or avail yourself of a free guided tour. It's quite fascinating to think that below your feet are the remains of large houses, taverns, a fort and even a church. The entire settlement was burned to the ground by the French in 1744 and lay abandoned for over 200 years. At a few bucks a person, this has to be the cheapest boat trip and guided tour available almost anywhere.

KAYAKING
Coastal Adventures, 84 Mason's Point Road, Tangier,
1-877-404-2774, www.coastaladventures.com
Scott Cunningham literally wrote the book, in fact a number of them, on ocean kayaking in Nova Scotia. His company, Coastal Adventures, is based

in Tangier, and takes advantage of the entire Eastern Shore for various sea kayaking expeditions. You can take one-day, weekend or week-long sea kayaking packages. You will have a chance to explore many of the hundreds of islands along this fascinating coast and visit forgotten settlements, seabird colonies and shipwreck sites. The only way to really experience the islands of the Eastern Shore is by kayak and this is the place to do it from.

MUSEUMS

The Old Court House, Guysborough, (902) 533-4008, www.guysboroughcountyheritage.ca

The Guysborough Courthouse was in use for over 130 years before being replaced by a modern complex in 1973. It is one of the oldest preserved courthouses in Canada and architecturally resembles a church more than a house of justice. The interior contains exhibits relating not only to the history of the courthouse, but all of Guysborough County as well. The two huge temperance banners on display set a sombre tone. Admire the messages and initials carved in the benches of both the spectators' gallery and the jury box. It seems perhaps that the jurists were sometimes dividing their attention between the proceedings and doodling.

Whitman House, 1297 Union Street, Canso, (902) 366-2170

The museum and tourist bureau is located in the former home of local merchant A.N. Whitman. While the museum contains little that cannot be found in most local museums, there are a couple of very interesting features. The first is the Widow's Walk, where there is a great view of the town and harbour, obscured only by the ever-present Irving oil tanks. The second is a room of folk art by a retired RCMP officer. His folksy murals of the town of Canso and ship replicas are especially good. A little let-up on the "Don't Touch" signs would be in order.

Sherbrooke Village, Sherbrooke, (902) 522-2400, museum.gov.ns.ca/sv/index.php

In the late 1960s the Nova Scotia Museum organization realized that portions of the town of Sherbrooke were so well preserved that with very few changes it could become a living museum of life in nineteenth-century Nova Scotia. Every day at 9:30 am this is exactly what happens: the gates are put across Upper Main Street and Sherbrooke goes back to the past. All told, the village is made up of over 80 historic buildings and almost an equal number of private homes that are maintained in the style consistent with the illusion of life in the 1800s. About 25 are open for viewing. It is very much a living museum — the Court House was used up until 2000 — the old school is now the town library, the post office is still the town post office and the old telephone exchange works and serves the village. Most of the people you will see and meet are in period costume, conducting their affairs much as they would have a hundred years ago.

The village itself is beautiful to look at, beginning with its location on the banks of the St. Mary's River, through its marvellously detailed architecture (this was not a poor community) to the old saw mill, which looks as if it were made for calendars or jigsaw puzzles, to the little knoll where the church, school and temperance hall (now the Legion!) hold domain over this little town.

Our favourite time to visit is very early in the morning, before the gates go down, while no-one else is around and not much is moving except the horses, ducks and geese. The illusion that you have somehow slipped back into the past is very strong. You forget about the harsher aspects of life in those days and are overwhelmingly drawn to the simplicity and apparent lack of stress of life long ago. Yes, you can believe those really were the good old days. Suddenly it is 9:30, the gates go down, the other visitors arrive and it's now time to go visit the building interiors where up until now you've been window shopping.

A visit to Sherbrooke Village requires at least a half day to really enjoy it. Children love it as well.

Fisherman's Life Museum, 58 Navy Pool Loop, Jeddore, (902) 889-2053, museum.gov.ns.ca/flm/

Where other provincial museums in Halifax and Lunenburg concentrate on what might be considered the larger aspects of the fishing industry, this museum focuses on the life of one fisherman. James Myers was an inshore fisherman hand-lining from his own dory in the waters around Jeddore Bay. The Myers lived a simple life, supplementing their meagre fishing income with a small farm operation. After James' death, his son Irvin occupied the house and, believe it or not, raised 13 daughters here. Despite a lack of what most of us would consider the absolute essentials, it is apparent that this was a happy household and one that did not need material goods or wealth to enjoy a successful life.

Musquodoboit Railway Museum, Musquodoboit Harbour, (902) 889-2689

You can't miss this museum dedicated to documenting and preserving the history of the railway in this province and, in particular, the Musquodoboit Valley line. If you somehow miss seeing the brightly painted station you surely will not fail to notice the collection of old rail cars right beside the highway in the middle of this small community. Housed in one of the few old-style train depots still remaining, this is an interesting collection of railroad memorabilia. There are also several old railway cars to explore. The Musquodoboit Valley Railway has long been decommissioned, but recently, portions have been reopened to the public as part of the Trans Canada Trail, which you can access directly from the parking lot. It is good to know that something very useful has come from our wholesale abandonment of the railway system in this and other Atlantic provinces.

OFF THE BEATEN PATH

Canso, www.townofcanso.ca

Canso may be the oldest European settlement in Canada, and perhaps all of North America. There is evidence that Europeans, particularly the French and the Basques, were making annual visits to fish here, perhaps 100 years earlier than 1605, the first recorded date of settlement in North America. Canso's fortunes have certainly been linked to the area's rich fisheries for more than 400 years. While this has produced economic prosperity, it has also brought war and conflict. In the 1700s, Canso was regularly attacked by first the English, then the French, and finally the Americans under the noted privateer John Paul Jones. Canso survived and it is a great irony that today it again faces a crisis of survival — there are no more fish to fight over. Rampant over-fishing has shut down most of the Atlantic fishery and with it, Canso's livelihood.

The road into Canso offers little until Hazel Hill, where you will notice a large abandoned brick and stone building. This was the former site of the Transatlantic Cable Office. From the 1880s to the 1920s, Hazel Hill was a major telegraphic centre employing dozens of people who occupied the large homes in the area. Technology advanced and Hazel Hill slowly declined.

Canso is not particularly attractive, there being little evidence of the antiquity of the place, but there is much to see and do in the area. The Canso Islands National Historical Site explains the story of the early Canso fishery and offers an opportunity to visit one of the bay's islands. There is also the Whitman House Museum.

After visiting these sites, take Union Street to where it ends and follow a rugged dirt road to Glasgow Head. Along the way, there is a magnificent view of the mouth of Canso Harbour with its fine lighthouse and many islands. Shortly after, you will come to a delightful secluded cove with a gravel beach. From here you can continue to explore on foot. Alternatively, you can walk the Chapel Gully Trail to French Cove and Chapel Gully.

Moose River Gold Mines
If you have an interest in gold mining or media history, you might consider this side trip, which begins in Tangier. Moose River Gold Mines is truly off the beaten path, lying 37 kilometres off Route 7 on a road that is very rough in spots and offers no services to speak of. Nova Scotia has a long history of gold mining with the most productive mines located in the backwoods of the Eastern Shore. Moose River Gold Mines was one of the best producers, but today it is remembered for the events of a 10-day period in 1936, when three prominent Toronto businessmen were trapped underground after the main shaft collapsed. What made the event particularly noteworthy was the convergence of the media from around North America upon this remote community. While rescuers from all of the province's other mines worked desperately to drive a new shaft toward the trapped men, reporters broadcast live radio reports to rapt listeners across the nation. Today, we take these CNN-type broadcasts from around the world as a given, but in 1936 it was novel and exciting. Some might call it the first media frenzy. Many believe it was the professionalism of J. Frank Willis' riveting live accounts of the rescue efforts that first gave the

Canadian Broadcasting Corporation recognition as an important part of Canadian daily life.

Ultimately, two of the three men were brought up alive, one having died seven days into the ordeal. Very little remains of the mine disaster site, which has been made into a small provincial park. A cairn marks the site of the rescue shaft. Today, it is difficult to imagine that this tranquil and remote place was once the scene of so much activity. Within the confines of the original schoolhouse, the community maintains a small museum which documents the disaster, the history of gold mining in this area and other local events. We note from the guest book that it gets about two visitors a day in the busy season.

With the recent rapid rise in the price of gold, efforts are underway to reopen gold mines in the area.

Bays of the Eastern Shore

Not far from Dartmouth a series of four long bays with equally long names - Chezzetcook, Petpeswick, Musquodoboit and Jeddore - bisect the Atlantic coast for a distance of about 30 kilometres. Marine Drive cuts across the base of the peninsulas and connects the head of one bay to the next. To really appreciate this beautiful coastline, you must drive out to the end of the peninsulas to where they meet the open sea. The best of these side roads are as follows:

East Chezzetcook: a paved road with great views of Chezzetcook Harbour that ends at a sand and stone beach about a kilometre in length, which is almost certain to be deserted. A path along the shore leads to the rugged coastal rocks at Meisners Head, where even on the calmest day the surf will be crashing.

East Petpeswick: a pleasant drive along the eastern side of Petpeswick Inlet, ending at the spectacular Martinique Beach and Game Sanctuary.

West Jeddore: a drive along the western shore of Jeddore Harbour takes you to a prosperous, well-kept lobster fishing community.

Ostrea Lake and Pleasant Point: a drive along the eastern side of Musquodoboit Harbour to Pleasant Point, which is not dramatic but has many excellent sea vistas.

The Musquodoboit Valley, www3.ns.sympatico.ca/mvta/

The Musquodoboit Valley is one of Nova Scotia's principal farming areas. Its gentle green rolling hills make for some of the finest pastoral scenery in the province. In fact, Joseph Howe toured the area in the 1800s, long before Confederation, and he thought it was just about one of the nicest areas he had seen in his travels around the province. Not a lot has changed in the last 150 years. There are probably no more people living here now than there were in Joe Howe's time. There are a number of small communities, including the pretty village of Middle Musquodoboit. If you are staying in Halifax and don't have time to take the Marine Drive, a circular day trip featuring the Musquodoboit Valley makes an interesting alternative. Simply follow the Marine Drive to Musquodoboit Harbour and turn inland on Route 357 as far as Middle Musquodoboit. Then follow Highway 224 to Shubenacadie and return to Halifax on Route 2.

PARKS AND GREENSPACE
Black Duck Cove Day-Use Park, Little Dover
This small park is well worth seeking out just to see the very unusual rock formations that are found about midway along the short trail that circumnavigates the park. The park is reached by turning toward Little Dover off Route 16 just before Canso. After passing through the fishing village you will come to the parking lot from whence you can depart for a short stroll around the area, go for a swim or just do some beachcombing. The beach is fine grayish-white sand in a protected cove, so it's warmer than most along this coast. The Coastal Trail passes behind the beach on a boardwalk until it reaches the mouth of Black Duck Cove. Shortly after, you will notice an unusual jumble of granite slabs that at first appearance seems to be some type of man-made conglomeration, maybe a collapsed version of Stonehenge. On closer inspection it proves to be a clearly natural phenomena. Somehow the combined forces of water, ice and wind have pried loose these huge chunks and piled them up in a haphazard fashion. Even without these peculiar rock formations, the area bears a resemblance to the granite outcroppings at Peggys Cove, which explains the signs urging extreme caution due to the possibility of rogue waves.

Tor Bay Atlantic Provincial Park, Tor Bay
Many years ago the Canadian government, recognizing the great natural beauty of the Eastern Shore, tried to establish a national park to preserve some of the best spots. For one reason or another, the plan didn't go ahead, but it did spur the Nova Scotia government to establish a series of provincial parks, which has done wonders to both protect and advertise the scenic attractions of Marine Drive.

Tor Bay is an area of great natural beauty that stretches from Whitehead to the community of Tor Bay, and includes a number of fishing communities in between. The park is located on a narrow isthmus that joins Berry Head to the mainland. Within the park, there are a number of habitats, of which unquestionably the most spectacular is a string of crescent-shaped sand beaches interspersed with rocky headlands. There is a small boardwalk that circles a bog and connects to the beaches. There are change houses, but we've never been here when the air temperature was warm enough to consider swimming. The beaches are really made for walking, birding and beachcombing. There are seldom many people around this wonderful park.

Taylor Head Provincial Park, Taylor Head
Taylor Head Provincial Park occupies a point of land that juts into the Atlantic like a thrust spear. Although the park has a fine sand beach, its real attraction is the hiking trails. There simply is no better spot on the entire Atlantic coast of Nova Scotia to walk the hard granite shores and witness the cataclysmic meeting of land and sea that makes this shoreline so beautiful

and so formidable. Most of the coastline of the park is traversed by a series of well-maintained footpaths. The Headland Trail to the tip of Taylor Head is not to be missed.

SPECIAL EVENTS

Stan Rogers Folk Festival, Canso, 1-888-554-7826, www.stanfest.com
Along with Celtic Colours, this is one of two major music festivals that have sprung up in the past decade. Given his many songs about the sea and Maritime life, most people are surprised to learn that the late, great folk singer Stan Rogers hailed from Ontario and not the East Coast. However, Stan spent much of his too-short life travelling in and writing about Atlantic Canada. As a tribute to Stan, this festival kicked off in the small town of Canso in 1998. Nobody expected it to be the huge overnight success it has become. Stan had many friends and admirers among other folk artists, and many of them jumped at the opportunity to sing his and other folk songs in this quintessential Maritime community as a tribute to the man and the people he sang about. The festival, which kicks off on the Canada Day weekend, is extremely popular, so you must book well in advance to arrange accommodations. However, if you are lucky enough to get there, we are sure you will agree with the accolades this festival has been receiving.

SPECIAL INTEREST

The Nova Scotia Lighthouse Interpretive Centre, Port Bickerton, (902) 364-2000
With its long and varied coastline, it is not surprising that Nova Scotia has a great many lighthouses — over 160 in fact. What is surprising, given that some of these lighthouses could be considered among Nova Scotia's most well-known attractions, is that up until a few years ago there was no one centre focusing solely on lighthouses. That deficiency was remedied with the opening of the Nova Scotia Lighthouse Interpretive Centre in two buildings that once comprised the Port Bickerton light complex. To get there, follow the signs down a dead-end, very narrow road not far off Marine Drive. The principal building is identical in design to the much-photographed Queensport lighthouse, which you will have passed if coming from Cape Breton to Halifax. Housed within is a well-laid-out display about lighthouses in Nova Scotia, including a series of binders with photographs of all of those 160 lights. You can climb to the top for a great view of the entrance to the harbour, although the actual light has long since been removed. A secondary building houses a nice collection of miniature replicas of some of the better-known lighthouses in the province.

The interpretive centre staff are both knowledgeable and enthusiastic. As a bonus, there are a number of short walking trails that will take you along the shore to Initial Point or through a springy carpet of bunchberries and moss.

Willy Krauch's Smoke House, Tangier, (902) 772-2188
Connoisseurs of smoked salmon have long recognized that the Nova Scotia variety is among the best. For many years, Willy Krauch and his sons have

operated a smoke house in Tangier, from where their products are shipped all over the world. Now you can buy the products right at the smoke house, any day of the week, almost all year. The Krauchs offer not only smoked salmon, but smoked mackerel and eel as well. If you are not familiar with the delights of smoked fish, this is the place to give them a try.

WILDERNESS AREAS
Waverley-Salmon River Long Lake Wilderness Area
The Eastern Shore is fortunate to have the largest concentration of designated Wilderness Areas in Nova Scotia. Most are very inaccessible and have had no improvements to attract visitors. This Wilderness Area is the exception.

While most people may believe that wilderness is necessarily remote and inaccessible, think again. Only 20 minutes from downtown Halifax, the Crowbar Lake Trail Systems provides a memorable opportunity to hike through genuine wilderness featuring old growth forest, pristine lakes and sensational views. These trails access the southern portion of the 8,710 hectare (21,500 acre) Waverley-Salmon River Long Lake Wilderness Area.

One of 33 provincially designated, protected wilderness areas, this area features a series of undulating and sometimes barren granite ridges, offering spectacular views. In between lie a series of streams and lakes. The steady ups and downs makes for exhilarating, if rugged, hiking. Working with the Province, a local trail group, known as The Porter's Lake and Myra Road Wilderness Area Association, have constructed a series of looped trails that allow hikers of all abilities the chance to observe at least part of this unique area. The trails have been constructed with a minimum of disturbance to the land so that in places it is difficult to tell whether sections of the trail are natural or manmade. As an added bonus, the trail system starts right off a paved road in West Porter's Lake, making access easy for any type of vehicle.

The first trail is the Porter's Lake Loop which at only 1.4 kilometre may seem short, but requires a very rugged ascent to the top of the first ridge. Those who make the climb will be rewarded by a grand view of Porter's Lake. On the way is a small pond which is set in a natural bowl between ridges and surrounded by wildflowers. It is a scenic jewel and not typical of anything else on the trail system. A boardwalk makes sure that your presence won't disturb the fragile bog, full of pitcher plants, that skirts the pond. For those wishing to really get into the wilderness the Spriggs Brook Trail leads to two more loops that can extend the hike from four to six hours if you are up for it.

About 2.8 kilometres from the trail head is a well constructed wooden bridge over the brook that is an idyllic spot for a picnic amid the dappled shade of overhanging branches. From here the trail follows the stream for a short while providing the opportunity to see a beaver, muskrat or maybe even an otter, all of which are denizens of this wilderness area. 1.5 kilometres after the bridge, the trail climbs to a vantage point from which there are fine views of Granite Lake, far below. Descending to the shore reveals a true wilderness lake set majestically between two high ridges. There are a number of places to swim, fish or just contemplate the peaceful surroundings.

Next up is the West Lake loop, a 16-kilometre circuit from the parking lot, including portions of the Porters Lake loop and all of Spriggs Brook trail. It is rugged and has more than a fair share of steep ascents and descents, but it will definitely reward those who are up to the challenge. Portions of this trail follow the shoreline of the lake through old growth pine forest on a carpet of pine needles. The Crow's Nest viewpoint is also a highlight of this trail.

ACCOMMODATIONS
DesBarres Manor Country Inn, 90 Church Street, Guysborough, (902) 533-2099, www.desbarresmanor.com
Located immediately adjacent to the historic courthouse, the DesBarres Manor is easily the grandest residence in Guysborough and deserving of the appellation mansion. Originally the home of the area's pre-eminent businessman, it was built in a style closer to what you find in Annapolis Royal than in eastern Nova Scotia. The large rooms are appointed with antiques throughout. The entire manor has been completely renovated to include very large and modern bathrooms along with new windows that open easily to allow cross-breezes in the corner rooms. The grounds are pleasant with a gazeboed deck out back, providing shade and a quiet place to read. A good continental breakfast is included. Evening dining is by reservation. Chedabucto Landing, the heart of tourist activity in Guysborough, is close by on the waterfront, although down quite a steep hill. The DesBarres is definitely the best inn for many miles around.

SeaWind Landing, 159 Wharf Road, Charlos Cove, 1-800-563-4667, www.seawindlanding.com
This is one of the few quality places to stay between Guysborough and Sherbrooke. Sea Wind Landing is located on an oceanfront property that offers private beaches, seaside walks and terrific views of this seldom-visited coastline. The main building houses five rooms decorated with antiques and collectibles, two parlors for gathering, Internet access or reading, and a dining room. Eight larger rooms are located in a newer building a short distance away, each with a private entrance and balcony, some with panoramic views as well. The inn is the ultimate in peacefulness and tranquility. We can't help but observe from the guestbook that SeaWind Landing is visited by an astounding number of Americans, Germans and Ontarians, relative to the few Nova Scotians who record their presence. Frankly, it's our loss.

Liscombe Lodge, 2884 Highway 7, Liscomb Mills, 1-800-665-6343, www.liscombelodge.ca
Located near the mouth of the Liscomb River, this large complex is made up of hotel units, a small meeting area, a recreational complex that has an

indoor pool and best of all, a series of excellent cabins right along the shores of the Liscomb River. Chalets 1 to 10 overlook the falls and rapids of the river in one of the prettiest accommodation settings you'll find anywhere.

Liscombe Lodge is a full-service resort with a dining room and a marina. You can make use of canoes to explore the area below the falls or you can hike upriver and try your luck in some of the trout pools. This is a good base from which to explore the Eastern Shore, especially Sherbrooke Village.

DINING
What Cheer Tearoom, Sherbrooke Village
As the name implies, this is a cheerful restaurant in the old Sherbrooke Hotel, a part of the Sherbrooke Village Restoration. It serves traditional fare for lunch, such as beans, stew and pea soup as well as sandwiches. It also serves breakfast.

Riverside Room, Liscombe Lodge, (902) 779-2307
The dining facilities at Liscombe Lodge weren't always up to the level of what one expects from a full-service resort, but in recent years there has been a great improvement. The Riverside Room overlooks the Liscomb River near where it meets the Atlantic. From your table, you can watch canoeists, kayakers or fly fishermen, or observe the antics of the many small birds that are attracted to the feeders set up just outside. The menu is fairly safe and traditional, with an emphasis on seafood, particularly planked salmon.

Seafood on Marine Drive
Marine Drive is one of the best places to find fresh seafood anywhere in the province, although you won't find any particularly grand restaurants. The area is home to excellent clam mud flats, a large aquaculture industry and an inshore fishery that provides fresh haddock and, of course, lobsters. Some of the best bets are clams, mussels, fish and chips, lobster rolls and chowders, which are usually served in small roadside take-outs or even from mobile canteens. It's difficult to make a specific recommendation because these places are seasonal and tend to open and close quicker than we can keep track. Make sure you ask for what is fresh and you will not go wrong, despite the lack of decor.

INDEX

1001 Golf Holes You Must Play Before You Die, 288

Abercrombie Golf Club, 272
AbitibiBowater Pulp and Paper Mill, 147, 177
Acadia University, 200, 206, 215, 216
Acadia, 19-23
Acadians, 22-23, 37, 127, 150–151, 163, 181, 208, 212, 224, 233
architecture, 42
cemetery, 50
dykes, 199, 206, 223
expulsion of, 22-23, 180, 200, 208, 212, 226, 240
music, 63
regions, 270, 284, 306, 322
returning from exile, 164, 181
settlements, 21, 224, 242, 256, 306
accommodations, 33–35
Bras d'Or Lakes, 304
Cabot Trail, 295–296
Ceilidh Trail, 281
Evangeline Trail, 194–196, 217–219
Fleur-de-lis Trail, 312–313
Glooscap Trail, 231, 252–253
Halifax/Dartmouth, 109–111
Kejimkujik Scenic Drive, 178–179
Lighthouse Route, 141–142, 169–171
Marconi Trail, 318
Marine Drive, 336
Northumberland Shore, 265–267, 275
types of, 34–35
Acton's Grill and Café, 220
Admiral Lake, 328
Admiral Rock, 227
Advocate Beach, 237
Advocate Harbour, 235
Age of Sail Heritage Centre, 236, 242
Agricola Street, 105
airport, 32
Alderney Landing, 103
Alexander Graham Bell Museum, 298, 302
Alexander Keith's Nova Scotia Brewery, 95, 101
Alexander, Sir William, 20
Allendale, 148
amazon.ca / amazon.com, 32
American Revolution,

147–148
Amethyst Cove, 59
Amherst, 254, 258, 260, 264
Amherst, General Jeffrey, 23
Amherst Golf and Country Club, 258
Amherst Point Migratory Bird Sanctuary, 237, 241
Amherst Point, 241
Amherst Shore Country Inn, 265, 267
Amherst Shore Provincial Park, 255, 262
Amos "King" Seaman School Museum, 242, 246
Anatolia, 119
Anderson, Gerrard, 232
Anglo-French rivalry, 21–23
Angus L. Macdonald suspension Bridge, 68
Anna Leonowens Gallery, 106
Annapolis River, 203
Annapolis Room, 197
Annapolis Royal, 21, 183, 184, 185, 188, 193, 195, 196, 198
Annapolis Royal Golf and Country Club, 185
Annapolis Tidal Generating Station, 199
Annapolis Valley, 42, 46, 50, 64, 65, 157, 180, 192, 199–201, 203
Anne Murray Centre, 247, 250
Anthony Provincial Park, 223
Antigonish, 270, 272, 272, 274, 275, 276
Antigonish Golf Course, 273
Antigonish Harbour, 270
Antigonish highlands, 17
Antigonish Landing, 272
Antigonish movement, 270
Antigonish Victorian Inn, 275
Antigonish Wildlife Management Area, 272
antiques, 29, 40-41, 105, 136
Apple Blossom Festival, 215
Apple River, 236
aquaculture, 322
Arcadia, 151, 184
Archelaus Smith Museum, 161
architecture, 42-43, 63, 81, 102, 126, 127, 131, 139, 147, 159, 169, 192, 210, 231, 233, 254, 329
Ardmore Tea Room, 123
Argall, Samuel, 207–208
Argyle, 151
Arichat, 306, 311, 312, 313
Arisaig, 269

Fossil Cliffs, 274
Picnic Park, 274
Army Museum, 81
Art Gallery of Nova Scotia, 84
Western Branch, 188
Artisans in Stone of Pictou County, 275
arts, crafts and folk art, 29, 43-44, 85, 105, 137, 140, 224
Ashburn Golf Club, 76
Aspotogan, 126
Aspy Bay, 286, 293
Aspy Valley, 285, 287
Athens Restaurant, 123
Atlantic Film Festival, 94
Atlantic Jazz Festival, 93
Atlantic View Motel and Cottages, 142
Attica Furnishings, 105
auctions, 41
Aulds Cove, 271, 275
Austrian Inn, 196
Autoport, 87
Avon River, 201
Avon Valley Golf Course, 205
Avondale, 226
Avonport, 201
Aylesford, 215

B&Bs (bed-and-breakfasts), 35
Baan Thai, 120
Baccaro, 150
Baccaro Point, 162
Back Pages, 108
Baddeck, 283, 298, 300, 301, 303, 304, 305
Baddeck Bridge, 301
Baddeck Forks, 301
Baddeck Harbour, 299
Baie Ste.-Marie Ocean Front Cottages, 194
Baile Langan Log Cottages, 231
Balancing Rock trail, 186, 189
Ballantynes Cove, 270
Balmoral Grist Mill, 260
Balmoral Mills, 260
banking, 31
Barrington, 150
Barrington Meeting House, 160
Barrington Museum Complex, 160
Barrington Passage, 150
Barrington Woolen Mill, 160
bass fishing, 53, 55, 72, 203, 223, 228, 233, 234
Bass River, 233
Battle of Culloden, 269

Bay of Fundy, 17, 45, 47, 59–60, 63–64, 91, 181, 193, 199, 202, 205, 212, 222, 227, 240, 241, 249
Chignecto Ship Railway, 255
in Natural Wonders of the World competition, 222
tidal turbine, 245
Bay St. Lawrence, 293
Bayers Lake lookoff, 328
Bayfield, 270
Bayfield Provincial Park, 271
Bayport Plant Farm, 135
Bayside, 75
Bayswater Beach, 128
Beach Meadows, 147
beaches, 30, 44-46, 86, 134, 146, 148
Bras d'Or Lakes, 300
Cabot Trail, 286–287
Ceilidh Trail, 277–278
Evangeline Trail, 183, 201–202
Fleur-de-lis Trail, 308
Glooscap Trail, 236–237
Halifax/Dartmouth, 70–71
Kejimkujik Scenic Drive, 175
Lighthouse Route, 128, 151–154
Marine Drive, 323
Northumberland Shore, 257, 271–272
Bear Cove, 181
Bear River, 182, 190–191
Beaver Harbour, 321
Beechville, 75, 80
Beinn Bhreagh, 299
Belfry Beach, 45, 307, 309
Bell Bay Golf Club, 300
Bell Island, 161
Bell, Alexander Graham, 298, 302, 303
Belle Côte, 284
Belliveau Cove, 183
Ben Eoin, 299
Benacadie, 299
Bertossi, Maurizio and Stepha- nie, 112, 113, 115
Berwick, 204
Berwick Heights Golf Club, 204
Best Western Glengarry, 231
Beulach Bann Falls, 285
Bible Hill, 224
bicycle touring, *see* cycling
Big Bras d'Or, 300
Big Intervale, 283
Big Island, 271, 272
Big Pond, 299, 305

Big Tancook Island, 128, 129, 132–133
biking, *see* cycling, mountain biking
Billard, Allan, 58
Birchtown, 149, 167
Bird Island Boat Tours, 300
Bird Islands, 300, 303
Birding in Metro Halifax, 71
Birding Sites of Nova Scotia, 48
birding, 30, 47-48, 151, 163, 190, 212, 265, 308, 328
Bras d'Or Lakes, 300
Evangeline Trail, 184, 202–203
Glooscap Trail, 225, 237
Halifax/Dartmouth, 71, 91
Lighthouse Route, 128, 154
Marconi Trail, 315–316
Marine Drive, 324–325
Northumberland Shore, 257, 272
Birds of Nova Scotia, 48, 202
Bish World Cuisine, 113
Bishop, Elizabeth, 233
Bishop's Landing, 101, 104, 113
bistros, 115–116
Black Cultural Centre, 70, 85
Black Duck Cove Day Use Park, 333
Black Harbour, 126
Black settlers, 24, 149, 258
Black Loyalist Interpretive Centre, 167
Black Point Beach, 153
Black Rock, 245
Blomidon, 211, 212
Blomidon Inn, 218, 219
Blomidon Provincial Park, 213, 214
Bloody Creek massacre, 211
Blue Rocks, 133
Blue Sea Corner Beach, 262
Blueberry Express, 324
Bluenose Ghosts, 85
Bluenose Golf Course, 130
Bluenose II, 84, 127, 132
Bluenose, 26, 127, 132
Bluff Wilderness hiking trails, 77–78
Boardwalk Café, 198
boat tours, 48–49, 135, 162, 281, 300
Halifax/Dartmouth, 71–72
Bon Portage Island, 49, 154
Bookmark, 32, 107
bookstores, 107–108

Borden, Robert, 201
Boscawen Inn, 142
Boscawen, Admiral Edward, 23
Boston bluefish, 52
Boularderie Island, 298, 300
Boutilier, Ralph, 140
Boutiliers Point, 80, 125
Bowater Mersey Pulp and Paper Company, 147
Boylston, 319
Braeshore, 266, 267
Bramber, 223
Bras d'Or Lake, 302
Bras d'Or Lakes, 60
Bras d'Or Lakes Scenic Drive, 298–305
Bread and Roses, 196
Brewery Market, 101, 104
Bridgetown, 199, 214, 216
Bridgewater, 130, 146, 156, 166
park system, 165
Brier Island, 48, 63, 184, 185, 190
Brier Island Lodge, 194, 197
Brier Island Oceanographic Study Research Group, 193
Brier Island Whale and Seabird Cruises, 194
Brightwood Golf and Country Club, 77
Broad Cove Concert, 280
Broad Cove (Lighthouse Route), 147, 162
Brookfield, 224
Brooklyn, 147, 223, 226, 227
Brothers Islands, 244
Brown, Geoff, 59
Brule Fossil Centre, 260
Burnside, 70
Burntcoat Head lighthouse, 223
Bush Island, 161

Cable Wharf, 101
Cabot Landing Provincial Park, 293
Cabot Links, 56
Cabot Strait, 63
Cabot Trail, 17, 46, 283–297, 302
Cabot, John, 19, 20, 283, 293
Cabot, Sebastian, 19
Caddell Falls Lookoff, 224, 225
Café Chianti, 118
Caledonia, 174
Cambridge Suites, 110, 318

Cameron Beach, 45, 257
Camp Hill Cemetery, 73
campgrounds, 135
Canada Creek, 212
Canadian Heritage River, 49, 177, 287
Canadian Wildlife Service, 257
Canning, 213
canoeing, 49-50, 174, 269
  Cabot Trail, 287
  Evangeline Trail, 203
  Halifax/Dartmouth, 72
  Kejimkujik Scenic Drive, 175
  Marconi Trail, 316
  Marine Drive, 325
  Northumberland Shore, 258
Canso, 19, 320, 328, 329, 330–331, 334
Canso Causeway, 16, 277, 306, 319
Canso Islands National Historic Site, 328, 331
Cap Le Moine, 284
Cape Breton, 45, 277–318
  music, 62
  whale-watching, 63
Cape Breton highlands, 17, 283
Cape Breton Highlands National Park, 58, 284–285
Cape Breton Miners' Museum, 315, 316
Cape Breton Regional Municipality, 314
Cape Chignecto Provincial Park, 58, 239–240, 248
Cape Clear, 292–293
Cape d'Or, 245–246, 248
Cape Gegogan, 321
Cape George, 269
Cape Islander, 163
Cape Mabou Highlands, 278
Cape Negro, 150
Cape North, 59, 285, 292, 294
Cape Sable, 132
Cape Sable Historical Society, 161
Cape Sable Island, 48, 150, 154, 163
Cape Smokey, 286, 287
Cape Smokey Hiking Trail, 290
Cape Smokey Provincial Park, 286, 290
Cape Split, 59, 206–207, 212, 213
Cape St. Mary's, 181, 183
Capeview Restaurant, 197
Capstick, 294

Caribou Island Beach, 257
Caribou, 256, 259
Caribou/Munroes Island Provincial Park, 259
Carleton House, 114
Carters Beach, 148, 153
Cartier, Jacques, 19
Casino Nova Scotia, 95
Ceilidh Trail, 277–282
ceilidhs, 62, 277, 280
Celtic Colours International Festival, 62, 317
Celtic music, 62, 317. *See also* music
Celtic Music Interpretive Centre, 280
cemeteries, 50, 138, 147, 161, 169, 212, 216, 222, 234, 245, 315
  Halifax/Dartmouth, 73–74
  Lighthouse Route, 128–129, 154
  Evangeline Trail, 184, 203
  Northumberland Shore, 258, 275
Centennial Trail, 165
Central Economy, 247
Centrelea, 211
Centreville, 189, 204
CFB Greenwood, 200
Chameau, 50
Champlain, Samuel de, 19-20, 91, 168, 207, 245, 248
Chapel Cove, 307
Chapel Gully Trail, 326, 331
Chapel Hill Museum, 150
Chapin Brothers Family Folk Concert, 135
chapters.indigo.ca, 32
Charlos Cove, 320, 336
Charlotte Lane Café and Crafts, 172
Cheapside Café, 85, 124
Chebogue Peninsula, 184
Chebogue salt marsh, 151, 184
Chedabucto Bay, 319, 320, 323, 325, 326
Chedabucto Landing, 320
Cheelin, 119
Cherry Hill Beach, 152
Cherry Hill, 147
Chesapeake, 73, 74
Chester, 94, 126, 130, 136, 138, 140, 143
Chester Basin, 131, 143
Chester ferry, 128, 132
Chester Golf Course, 56, 130
Chester Playhouse, 138
Chester Race Week, 136

Cheticamp Island, 284
Cheticamp, 284, 294, 295
Cheverie, 223
Chez Christophe, 197
Chezzetcook, 322, 332
Chignecto National Wildlife Area, 237
Chignecto Ship Railway, 255
Chimney Corner, 277
Chives Canadian Bistro, 113
Church of Our Lady of Sorrows, 102
Church Point, 182
churches, 274, 306, 321
  Covenanters' Church, 200
  Mabou Catholic, 279
  replica, 273
  St. Andrew's Presbyterian, 139
  St. Ann's, 319
  St. George, 212
  St. James United, 233
  St. John's Anglican, 139
  St. Margaret's, 294
  St. Mary's, 181
  St. Ninian's, 270
  St. Paul's, 81
  St. Peter's, 270
  St. Pierre, 284
  Ste-Anne-du-Ruisseau, 151
  three most-photographed, 126
  Trinity Anglican Church (Liverpool), 168
  Trinity Church (Digby), 193
  Trinity Church (Middleton), 200
  Zion Evangelical Lutheran Church, 140
Churchill House, 201, 216
Citadel Hill, 17
Citadel, *see* Halifax Citadel
Clam Harbour, 322, 323
Clancy, Dave, 51
Clare Golf and Country Club, 185
Clare region, 181, 191
Clark, Wayne, 61
Clarksville, 226
Classic Boat Festival, 136
Clementsport, 183
Cleveland Beach, 125, 128
clothing, 106–107
Clyde River, 149, 155
Coady Institute, 270
The Coast, 70
Coastal Adventures, 61, 328
Coastal Discovery Centre, 314
Coastal Nova Scotia, 17

Coastal Trail, 289
Cobequid Interpretive Centre, 238
Cobequid Mountains, 17, 65, 234, 244, 247
Cobequid Bay, 224
Cod, 53
Coffinscroft, 150
Colchester Historical Museum, 225
Cole Harbour, 71, 79, 88
Cole Harbour Heritage Farm, 88
Cole Harbour Heritage Park, 79
Colliery Route, 315
Collins, Enos, 73, 148
Colonel Locke's Beach, 169
Colwell Brothers, 107
Comeau, Paul, 197
confederation, 26
Conrad Beach, 322, 324
Conrod, Gary, 47
Consulate Inn, 267
Cook's Cove, 326
Cooke, Graham, 56, 76, 77, 259
Cooper's Inn, 171
Cornwallis, 182
Cornwallis, Colonel Edward, 68
Cossit House, 317
Country Harbour, 321
country inns, 35
Cove Motel, 275
Cow Bay, 87–88
Coyle House, 160
Creamery Square Heritage Centre, 256, 260
credit cards, 31
Creighton, Helen, 85
Crescent Beach (LaHave), 146, 151, 161
Crescent Beach (Lockeport), 148
Cribbons Point, 270, 272
Crocker, William S., 138
Croft, Eric, 140
Crombie House, 275
cross-country skiing, 65, 80, 240, 266
Crowbar Lake Trail System, 335
Cruising Nova Scotia from Yarmouth to Canso, 61
cruising permit, 60
crystal, 108
Crystal Cliffs, 270
Crystal Crescent Beach, 70, 86

CSS *Acadia*, 83, 101
Cumberland County Museum, 255, 260
Cunard, Samuel, 26, 83, 101
Cunningham, Scott, 61, 328
Currency exchange, 31
Customs regulations, 60
Cut Steakhouse and Urban Grill, 117
cycling, 30, 46-47, 58–59, 134, 150, 163, 213
  Cabot Trail, 287
  Fleur-de-lis Trail, 309
  Halifax/Dartmouth, 75
  Lighthouse Route, 129
  Evangeline Trail, 184, 203
  Marine Drive, 324
  Northumberland Shore, 258
Cyprus Walk booklet, 199, 216

d'Anville, Duc, 21
da Maurizio, 104, 112
Darling Lake, 184
Dartmouth, 70, 72, 76, 77, 85, 91, 103, 104, 111, 121, 323
Dartmouth Commons, 103
Dartmouth Ferry, 72
Dartmouth Heritage Museum, 85
Dartmouth Heritage Walk, 103
Dartmouth Lakes, 72
Dartmouth Crossing, 70
Dauphinee Inn, 143
Day, Frank Parker, 126
de Monts, Sieur, 19, 207
Deadman's Island, 74
DeBaies Cove, 322
Debert, 243
deCoste Centre, 257
Deep Brook, 182
Deerfield, 184
deGarthe, W.E., 98
Degooyer, Kermit, 59
Delaps Cove, 182, 205, 212
Delaps Cove Wilderness Trails, 205, 212
Delta Barrington, 109
Delta Halifax, 109
Delta Sydney, 318
Denmark, 261
Denys, Nicolas, 307, 319
Denys Basin, 300
DeRazilly, Isaac, 146
Derby Point, 299
DesBarres Manor Country Inn, 336

DesBrisay Museum, 156
Devil's Bend Trail, 238
Devils Island, 88
Dharma Sushi, 119
Dickey, R. B., 255, 260
Digby Neck, 63, 184, 189–190, 193
Digby Pines Golf Resort and Spa, 185, 192–193
Digby, 182, 185, 192, 195, 197, 198
Diligent River, 235
Dill, Howard, 201, 215, 222
Dingwall, 295, 296
dining, 36-38
  Cabot Trail, 297
  Ceilidh Trail, 281–282
  Glooscap Trail, 231–232, 253
  Evangeline Trail, 196–198, 219–221
  Fleur-de-lis Trail, 313
  Halifax/Dartmouth, 111–124
    Chinese, 119
    family dining, 123
    fish & chips, 120
    Greek, 118–119
    Italian, 118
    Japanese, 119
    pizza, 120
    pubs and taverns, 121
    Thai, 120
    Turkish, 119
    vegetarian, 122
  Kejimkujik Scenic Drive, 179
  Lighthouse Route, 143–145, 171–173
  Marine Drive, 337
  Northumberland Shore, 275–276
Discover Mcnabs Island, 89
Discovery Centre, 95
District of Clare, 181
diving, 50–51
  Lighthouse Route, 129
Dr. Elizabeth LeFort Gallery, 284, 292
Doers' & Dreamers' Travel Guide, 32, 49, 50, 51, 60
Domaine de Grand Pré, 217, 220
Dominion Chair Company, 233
Donkin, 314
Dory Rip, 246
Dory Shop Museum, 159
Doucet, Anna and Jacques, 194
Driftwood Park Retreat, 253
Dublin Shore, 146

Ducks Unlimited Canada, 229, 237, 257
Dugger's Quality Men's Wear, 107
Duke of Kent, 42, 81, 200
Duncans Cove, 86
Duncreigan Country Inn, 281
Dundee, 299, 301
Dundee Golf Course, 301
Dundee Resort, 304
Dunns Beach, 271
Dunvegan, 277
Durty Nelly's, 122
Eagle Crest Golf Course, 204
Earltown, 267
East Bay, 299
East Berlin, 147
East Chezzetcook side road, 332
East Coast Outfitters, 92
East Ferry, 189
East Ironbound Island, 126
East Petpeswick side road, 332
Eastern Passage, 75, 87–88
Eastern Shore, 45, 57, 65, 87, 319–337
Eaton, Cyrus, 255
Eatonville Day Use Area, 58, 240, 248
Economy, 234, 238
Economy Falls, 238
Economy Mountain, 234
Economy River Wilderness Area, 251
Economy Shoe Shop Café and Bar, 116
economy, 24, 25, 27, 132, 146, 148, 157, 182, 189, 255, 306, 319, 321
Ecum Secum, 321
Eddy Rebellion, 24
Eddy, Jonathan, 24
Eden Golf Club, 203
Église St. Pierre, 284
Eisenhauer, Collins, 44, 140
Ellenwood Park, 184
Englishtown, 286, 298
Ericson, Leif, 18
Escarpment Trail, 238
Eskasoni, 299
Estia, 118
Eureka, 273
Euro Pizza, 120
Evangeline, 22
Evangeline Beach, 46, 202
Evangeline Trail, 180–221
Evergreen House, 85
Explore More! Cape Breton, 58

Fair Exchange program, 31
Fairview Lawn Cemetery, 74
Falmouth, 50, 205
family accommodations, Lunenburg area, 142
family vacations, 51
Feltzen South, 134
ferry service, 32, 72, 101, 128, 132, 146, 189, 190, 256, 259, 286, 298, 315, 321
festivals, 51–52, *see also* Special events
Fiasco, 115
Fid Resto, 112
Fiddlin' Whale Tours, 295
Firefighters' Museum of Nova Scotia, 187
Fireworks Gallery, 105
First Baptist Church, 254
fish hatchery, 174, 274, 283, 287
fish ladder, 174, 327
Fisheries Museum of the Atlantic, 51, 59, 132
Fisherman's Cove, 87
Fisherman's Life Museum, 322, 330
Fishermans Harbour, 321
Fishermen's Reserve, 322
Fishing Cove, 285
fishing, places for, 19, 52–55, 72, 86, 91, 92, 126, 146, 203, 223, 228, 283, 287, 291, 293, 312, 321
Five Islands, 234, 235, 239, 244, 247
Five Islands Provincial Park, 239, 247
Fleming Park, 86, 91, 103
Fleur-de-Lis Trail, 306–318
Fleur de Sel, 145
Flinn, Craig, 113
Flora's (craft shop), 294
Flora's Dining Room, 305
Fo'c'sle, 139
folk art, *see* Arts, crafts and folk art
Folk Art in Canada, 140
footbridge, 255, 273, 319, 320, 327
Foreign Affair, 107
Fort Anne National Historic Site, 183, 184, 186
Fort Cumberland, 24
Fort Edward National Historic Site, 201, 209
Fort McNab, 88
Fort Needham, 102
Fort Ogilvie, 101

Fort Point Lighthouse Park, 165
Fort Point Museum, 146, 156
Fort Point, 146
Fort Ste-Marie-de-Grace, 146
Fortress of Louisbourg, 21, 23
Fortress of Louisbourg National Historic Site, 21–23, 51, 308, 309, 310–311, 312, 313
Fortress View Suites, 313
fossils, 17, 152, 233, 241, 248, 274, 314, 315
Four Points by Sheraton Halifax, 110
Four Seasons Retreat, 252
Fourchu, 307
Fox Harb'r Golf Resort & Spa, 56, 259
Fox Harbour, 255, 259
Fox Harbour Provincial Park, 257, 262
Fox Point, 126
Fox River, 236
Framboise, 307, 309
Franey Mountain, 290
Frankaleen Beach, 300
Frasers Mills, 274
Freeman's Little New York, 123
Freeport Whale and Seabird Tours, 194
Freeport, 190
French Cove, 326, 331
French Mountain, 284, 287
French Village, 75, 97
Fries and Co., 120
Fuller, Alfred C., 187
Fundy coast, 211–212
Fundy Geological Museum, 235, 241
Fundy Shore Ecotour, 222, 247
Fundy Trail Snowmobile Club, 65

Gabarus, 308
Gabrieau, Mark, 276
Gabrieau's Bistro, 276
Gaelic College of Celtic Art and Culture, 286, 294
galleries,
Acadia University, 216
Anna Leonowens, 106
Art Gallery of Nova Scotia, 84, 188
Cumberland County Museum, 260
Elizabeth LeFort, 292
Fireworks, 105

Gingerbread House Inn, 219
Houston North, 140
Joy Laking, 249
Lyghtesome, 275
Mary E. Black, 43, 95
Roger Savage, 166
Zwicker's, 106
Gambo Abbey, 285
Garrison Cemetery, 184
Garrison House Inn, 196, 198
Gaspereau River, 213
Gaspereau Valley, 213–214
Gathering of the Clans, 263
Genealogy, 225
geocaching, 55
geography, 16–17
Geological Highway Map of
Nova Scotia, 17, 60
George, Eldon, 250
Georges Island National His-
toric Site, 82
Georges River, 299
German cemeteries, 50, 128
German settlers, 126, 127
Gesner, Abraham, 73
ghost stories, 85, 188, 196
Gilberts Cove, 182
Gingerbread House Inn, 219
Glace Bay Miners' Museum,
315, 316
Glace Bay, 314, 315, 316
Glauser, Kathleen and Roland,
172
Glen Arbour Golf Course, 76
Glen Haven, 97
Glen Margaret, 97
Glendyer Station, 279
Glenghorm Beach Resort, 296
Glenholme, 233
Glenora Distillery, 277, 280,
281
Glenora Inn, 281
Glenville, 277, 280, 281
Glooscap, 213, 214, 222, 234
Glooscap Heritage Centre, 229
Glooscap Trail, 222–253
gold mining, 135, 176, 321,
324, 331–332
Goldboro, 320
Goldmines Trail, 176
Golf, 30, 55–56
Bras d'Or Lakes, 300–301
Evangeline Trail, 185,
203–205
Glooscap Trail, 225, 237–238
Halifax/Dartmouth, 75–77
Lighthouse Route, 130,
154–155
Marine Drive, 325

Northumberland Shore,
258–259, 272
Government House, 42
Grand Desert, 322
Grand Étang, 284
Grand Lake, 72, 77, 92
Grand Narrows, 299
Grand Pré National Historic
Site, 200, 208
Grand Pré, 200, 202, 208,
217, 220
Grand River, 307, 313
Grande Greve Beach, 309
Grandview Golf & Country
Club, 76
Granite Springs Golf Club, 75
Granville Centre, 199
Granville Ferry, 199, 209
Granville Mall, 104
Grassy Island, 328
Graves Island Provincial Park,
55, 134
Gravestone Carving and
Carvers in Nova Scotia, 50
Great Bras d'Or Channel,
299, 303
Great Village, 233, 244
Green Bay, 147, 161–162
Greenhill Lookoff Provincial
Park, 274
Greenwing Legacy Interpretive
Centre, 229
Grohmann Knives, 264
Grosses Coques, 197
Grosses Coques Beach, 181
Groundfish, 52
Group of Seven, 162, 274
Guide to Craft and Art in
Nova Scotia, 43
Gulf of St. Lawrence, 57, 63,
277, 284, 295
Gulf Shore, 255, 265
Gulf Shore Beach, 257
Gunning Cove, 149
Guysborough Courthouse, 320
Guysborough Nature Trail,
326
Guysborough, 319–320, 325,
326, 329, 336

Habitation, see Port Royal
National Historic Site
Hacketts Cove, 97
haddock fishing, 52
Haliburton, Thomas Chandler,
201
Haliburton House, 59, 201,
209
Halibut Bay, 86

halibut fishing, 52
Halifax, the First 250 Years,
70
Halifax Citadel National
Historic Site, 43, 80
Halifax Explosion, 69, 74, 102
Halifax Stanfield International
Airport, 32
Halifax International Busker
Festival, 93
Halifax Marriott Harbourfront
Hotel, 109
Halifax waterfront, 101
Halifax, 46, 68–124
explosion, 69, 74, 102
founding of, 22, 68
Halifax–Dartmouth ferry, 72
Hall, William, 201, 217
Halliburton House Inn, 110
Halls Harbour Lobster Pound,
212, 219
Halls Harbour, 212, 219
Hammond Street cemeteries
(Shelburne), 154
Hammonds Plains, 76
Hangman's Beach, 88
Hank Snow Country Music
Centre, 59, 166
Hants County, 226, 227
Hantsport, 201, 216
Harbourview Inn, 195
Harbourville, 212
Hardy, Ann, 37
Harmonized Sales Tax (HST),
31
Hartlen Point Forces Golf
Club, 75
Hartlen Point, 75, 87
Haus Treuburg, 281
Havre Boucher, 270
Haynes, Michael, 58
Head of St. Margaret's Bay,
80, 125
Headland Trail, 327
Heather Beach, 45, 257
Hebert, Louis, 208
Hebron, 194
Hector, 24, 62, 264
Hector Heritage Quay, 257,
264
Hector National Exhibit
Centre, 261
Hemeon's Beach, 153
Hemlocks and Hardwoods
Trail, 176
Heritage Models, 250
Heritage Conservation Dis-
trict, 223
heritage streetscape, 169

Hermans Island, 127
Herring Cove, 85–86
Highland Games, 274
Highland Road, 292–293
Highland Scots, 24, 261
Highland Village, 233, 302
highlands, 17
Highlands Links, 56, 287–288
highways, 100-series, 33, 46
  Highway 1, 180–183,
  199–201
  Highway 2, 224, 233–235
  Highway 3, 92, 125–127,
  146–151
  Highway 4, 247, 315
  Highway 6, 255–257
  Highway 7, 273–274
  Highway 8, 174
  Highway 12, 133
  Highway 14, 133, 222, 226
  Highway 16, 320
  Highway 19, 277, 279
  Highway 22, 308, 314
  Highway 28, 315
  Highway 101, 180–183,
  199–201
  Highway 103, 97, 125–127,
  146–151
  Highway 104, 233, 269–271,
  306, 307
  Highway 106, 269
  Highway 201, 211
  Highway 207, 322
  Highway 209, 235–236
  Highway 215, 223–224
  Highway 224, 333
  Highway 236, 224, 226
  Highway 305, 315
  Highway 309, 154
  Highway 316, 273–274, 320
  Highway 320, 307
  Highway 326, 261
  Highway 332, 88
  Highway 333, 96–100
  Highway 340, 188
  Highway 347, 273
  Highway 349, 86
  Highway 357, 322, 333
  Highway 358, 213
  Highway 366, 255–256
  Highway 374, 273
Hiking, 30, 56–58, 71, 212,
  228, 234, 270, 296
  Bras d'Or Lakes, 301
  Cabot Trail, 288–292
  Ceilidh Trail, 278–279
  Evangeline Trail, 185–186,
  205–207
  Fleur-de-lis Trail, 309–310

Glooscap Trail, 238–241
Halifax/Dartmouth, 77–80
Kejimkujik Scenic Drive, 176
Lighthouse Route, 155
Marine Drive, 326–328
Northumberland Shore,
  259–260
Hiking Trails of Nova Scotia,
  58
Hiking Trails of Cape Breton,
  58
Hilden, 224
Hillcrest Cemetery, 129
Hillsdale House, 196
Hines, Sherman, 158
Hinterland Adventures and
  Gear, 49
Hirtles Beach, 134
Historic Acadian Village, 168
Historic Cyprus Walk, 199,
  216
Historic Dock Street (Shel-
  burne), 159, 160
Historic Gardens (Annapolis
  Royal), 183, 191
historic Halifax walking tour,
  102
Historic Properties, 101, 104,
  148
historic sites
  Bras d'Or Lakes, 302
  Evangeline Trail, 186–187,
  207–209
  Fleur-de-lis, 310–311
  Halifax/Dartmouth, 80–83
  Lighthouse Route, 130–131,
  156
  Marconi Trail, 316
  Marine Drive, 328
history, 17–27, 68
HMCS Sackville, 84, 101
hooked rugs, 284, 292, 294
Hopewell, 273
Horseshoe Cove, 245
hostels, 35
hotels and motels, 34
Houses of Nova Scotia, 43
Houston North Gallery, 140
Howe, Joseph, 26, 73, 81
Howell, Michael, 220
Hubbards, 75, 80, 125–126,
  135
Hunters Mountain, 293
Hunts Point Beach Cottages,
  170
Hunts Point, 148, 170, 171
Hurricane Juan, 78, 79, 88,
  89, 90
Hydrostone area, 102

Hydrostone Market, 103,
  120, 124

Il Mercato, 115
immigration, 20, 24, 27
  museum of, 82
Indian Brook, 286
Indian Harbour, 97, 100
Indian Point, 126
Ingomar, 149
Ingonish Beach, 45, 286, 296
Ingonish, 285, 286, 295, 296
Innlet Café, 143
International Dory Races, 136
International Tuna Competi-
  tion, 53, 164
Inverary Resort, 304, 305
Inverness Beach, 45, 278
Inverness, 56, 62, 277, 278
Iona, 299, 302
Iona Peninsula, 302
Irish Cove, 299
Irving Environmental Centre
  and Botanical Gardens, 215,
  216
Isaacs Harbour, 320
Isle Madame, 21, 306–307,
  309
Isthmus of Chignecto, 16
Italian restaurants, 118

J. W. Doull, Bookseller, 108
Jake's Landing, 175, 176
James House Museum and Tea
  Room, 199
James I, 20
jane's on the common, 124
Janvrin Island, 306
Jazz festival, 93
Jeddore, 322, 330
Jennifer's of Nova Scotia, 106
Jerry Lawrence Provincial
  Park, 91
Jitney Trail, 265
Joe's Scarecrow Village, 284
Joggins, 17, 60, 236, 249
Joggins Fossil Centre, 236, 249
Joggins Fossil Cliffs, 236, 249
John Daly Antiques, 105
John's Lunch, 121
Johnston, Dennis, 112
Johnstown, 299
Jones, John Paul, 331
Jordan Bay, 149
Jordan Falls, 149
Jordan Ferry, 149
Jost House, 317
Jost Winery, 64, 262, 264
Joudrey Trail, 214

Joy Laking Gallery, 249
Joyce, Christopher, 105
Judique, 280
Julien, Didier, 143
Julien's Pastry Shop, 143

Karsdale, 211
Kaulbach House Historic Inn, 142
Kayak Cape Breton, 302
Kayaking, 30, 61, 92, 161, 163, 269, 302, 321, 328
campsites at Cape Chignecto, 248
upper Bay of Fundy, 241
Keith, Alexander, 73, 95
Kejimkujik National Park, 59, 174, 176
canoeing, 49, 174
petroglyphs, 229
Kejimkujik Scenic Drive, 174–179
Kejimkujik seaside adjunct, 148, 155
Kellys Mountain, 286, 298, 299
Keltic Lodge, 296
Kempt, 178, 179
Kempt Head, 299
Kennetcook, 226
Kennington Cove beaches, 309
Kenomee Canyon Wilderness Trail, 251
Kentville, 200, 214, 216
Kentville Agricultural Centre, 200, 205, 214
Kentville Ravine, 205
Ken-Wo Golf Course, 204
Ketch Harbour, 86
Keyzlar, Martin, 115
Kick Ass Shoes, 107
Killam Brothers Shipping Office, 187
King, Andrew, 112
King's-Edgehill School, 201, 217, 222
King of Donair, 123
King Wah, 123
Kingsburg, 134
Kingston, 204
Knoydart, 269
Krieghoff, Cornelius, 274

L'Archeveque, 307
L'Ardoise, 307
L'Auberge Acadienne, 312, 313
L'Auberge au Havre du Capitaine, 194
Laceby family, 220, 265, 267

LaHave, 156, 157, 171
LaHave Bakery, 171
LaHave ferry, 146
LaHave Islands Museum, 157
LaHave Islands, 49, 151, 161
LaHave River, 134, 146
Lake Ainslie, 280
Lake Charlotte, 322
Lake O'Law, 283
Lakeside, 125
Laking, Joy, 249
Lane's Privateer Inn, 169
LaPlanche River, 258
Larrys River, 320
Laurie Park, 92
Lawley, David, 58, 284
Lawlor Island, 87, 89
Lawrence, Governor Charles, 22, 23, 201
Lawrence, William D., 225
Lawrence House Museum, 223, 225
Lawrencetown Beach, 46, 323, 324
Le Caveau Restaurant, 217, 220
Le Festival Acadien de Clare, 191
Le Noir Forge, 311
Le Village historique acadien, 168
LeFort, Elizabeth, 284, 292
Leonowens, Anna, 106
Lequille, 175
Lescarbot, Marc, 208
Lewis, Everett, 140
Lewis, Maud, 85, 140
Lewis Lake Provincial Park, 75
Life How Short, Eternity How Long, 50
Light, Joanne, 17
Lightfoot Tower, 138
Lighthouse Route, 125–173
Lighthouse Trail, 309
lighthouses, 76, 86, 88, 96–98, 125, 126, 147, 150, 154, 157, 162, 163, 168, 181, 183, 185, 189, 212, 223, 234, 236, 246, 259, 270, 277, 284, 300, 303, 307, 308, 314, 316, 319, 321, 331
museum, 262, 321
reconstructed, 160, 223
Lily Front Motel and Cottages, 142
Lime Hill, 299
Liscomb Harbour, 321
Liscomb Mills, 321, 326, 336, 337

Liscomb River Trail, 321, 326
Liscombe Lodge, 336, 337
Little Dover, 333
Little Harbour, 148, 153
Little Liscomb, 321
Little Narrows, 303
Little River, 189
Little School Museum, 158
Little Tancook Island, 133
Liverpool Golf Club, 154
Liverpool Packet, 25, 148
Liverpool, 147–148, 157, 158, 165–169
Loch Broom, 273
Lockeport, 148, 158, 168
Londonderry, 243–244
Lone Sheiling, 285
Long Cove Point, 147
Long Island, 235
Long Lake Provincial Park, 92
Long Pond, 216
Longfellow, Henry Wadsworth, 22, 180
lookoffs, 146, 224, 246, 278, 283, 290, 291, 292, 293, 298, 299, 303, 314, 319, 328
Lord Nelson Hotel, 111
Lordly Manor, 138
Lorneville, 265, 267
Lothar's Café, 172
Louis Head, 148
Louis XIV, 310
Louisbourg, 21–23, 308, 310–311, 313
Louisdale, 306
Lower Deck, 122
Lower Prospect, 100
Lower Rose Bay, 134
Lower Selma, 223
Lower Shubenacadie River, 225
Lower Whitehead, 320
lowlands, 16
Loyalists, 24-25, 40, 42, 149, 160, 182, 319
black, 149, 160, 167
cemeteries, 50
Dutch, 151
Lucy, 148
Lumsden Dam, 213
Lunenburg, 50, 127, 129, 130, 132, 136, 137, 139, 140
accommodations, 141
area, 129
dining, 144
Lunenburg Academy, 130
Lunenburg Bike Barn, 129
Lunenburg Fisheries Museum, see Fisheries Museum of the

Atlantic
Lunenburg Folk Harbour
   Festival, 137
Lunenburg Marine Park, 129
Lunenburg Town Walking
   Tours, 140
Lyghtesome Gallery, 275
Lynwood Country Inn, 304,
   305

M&W's Restaurant, 179
Mabou, 62, 277, 279,
   281–282
Mabou Catholic Church, 279
Mabou Coal Mines, 279
Mabou Harbour, 278, 279
Mabou Highlands, 57, 278
Mabou hiking trails, 278, 279
MacAskill, Angus, 59, 298
Maccan, 236
MacDonald Museum, 200,
   209
MacDonald, Clyde, 275
MacDonald, J.E.H., 162
MacDonald, William, 209
MacKay, Donald, 26, 159
MacKenzie Mountain, 285
mackerel fishing, 53, 126,
   146, 312
Mackinnon's Brook, 279
MacLean, Grant, 70
MacLeod, Alistair, 277
MacMaster, Buddy, 280
MacNeil House, 304
MacPhee House, 322
MacPhersons Mills, 273
Maders Cove, 127
Magnolia's Grill, 144
Mahone Bay, 60, 126–127,
   131, 136, 139, 140, 141
Mahone Bay Settlers' Museum,
   131, 139
Mahone Bay islands, 17
Main-à-Dieu, 314
Maitland Bridge, 175, 178
Maitland, 26, 223, 230
Major Point Beach, 183
Malagash Peninsula, 64, 256,
   262, 264
Malagawatch, 299
Malignant Cove, 269
Maple Inn, 252
Mapleton, 235
Maps and More, 49, 73, 108
Marble Mountain, 299, 300
Marconi, Guglielmo, 314, 316
Marconi National Historic
   Site, 315, 316
Marconi Trail, 314–318

Margaree, 62
Margaree Forks, 283
Margaree Harbour, 277, 283
Margaree River, 54, 287
Margaree Salmon Museum,
   287, 292
Margaree Valley, 283, 295, 297
Margaree Wilderness Area, 293
Margaretsville, 212
Marie Joseph, 321
Marine Drive, 319–337
Maritime Museum of the
   Atlantic, 51, 59, 74, 83, 101
Markland, 18
Markland Coastal Resort, 296
Marriott Courtyard Halifax,
   110
Martello tower, 90
Martinique Beach and Game
   Sanctuary, 323, 324
Martinique (Isle Madame),
   307
Mary Ann Falls, 285
Mary E. Black Gallery, 43
Masstown, 253
Masstown Market, 253
Maughers Beach, 88
Mavillette Beach, 181, 183,
   197
Maybank, Blake, 48
Mayer, Lothar, 172
McBroom, Tom, 300
McCulloch, Thomas, 261
McCulloch House, 261
McCurdy's, 304
McElmon's Pond Wildlife
   Sanctuary, 237, 243
McGowan Lake, 174
McKelvie's, 117
McLachlan, Sophia, 129
McLachlan House, 142
McNabs Island, 88–89
McNeil, Dugger, 107
McNeil, Rita, 305
McNutt's Island, 162
Meaghers Grant, 325
Meaghers Grant Canoe Rent-
   als, 325
Meat Cove, 57, 293–294
Medway River, 54
Melmerby Beach, 45, 269, 271
Melville Island prison, 74
Merigomish, 271
Merigomish Harbour, 269
Merrymakedge, 175
Mersey River Chalets, 178
Mersey River Trail, 176
Meteghan, 181, 191
Meteghan River, 194

Mi'kmaq, 18, 20, 207, 211,
   213, 214, 224, 229, 256, 299
artifacts, 167
petroglyphs, 175
quillwork, 84, 229
Michelin Tire, 146
Middle Head Trail, 289
Middle River, 283
Middle River Wilderness Area,
   293
Middleton, 199, 209
migratory birds, 47, 79, 165,
   184, 190, 202–203, 237,
   257, 272, 286, 316, 320, 324
Milford Haven Valley, 319
Milford House, 178
Mill Village, 146
Mills Brothers, 106
Mills Falls Trail, 176
Milton, 174, 177
Minas Basin, 45, 223
Minudie, 242
Minudie Peninsula, 246
Mira River, 314, 316
Mitchell Bay, 321
Money Point, 59
Monks Head, 271
Montbeliard Protestants, 126,
   127, 256
Moose Island, 59, 235
Moose River Gold Mines, 331
Morden, 212
Morris Island, 163
Morrison Beach, 309
Mosaic, 124
Moshers Point lookoff, 146
Mosherville, 226
Mount Martock, 133
Mount Olivet Cemetery, 74
Mount Uniacke, 201, 207, 210
mountains in Nova Scotia,
   16–17, 199, 222, 244, 251,
   285–286
Mountain Bike Nova Scotia,
   59
mountain biking, 58–59, 92,
   176
movie setting, 159
Muir-Cox Shipyard, 160
Mulgrave, 319
Murphy's Fish and Chips, 232
Murphy's on the Water, 71–72
Murphys Cove, 322
Murray, Anne, 247, 250
Museum of Industry, 269, 273
museums, 18, 59, 135, 149,
   150, 151, 174, 183, 189,
   200, 226, 227, 233, 256,
   269, 300, 306, 307, 314,

320, 322
Bras d'Or Lakes, 302
Cabot Trail, 292
Evangeline Trail, 187–188, 209–211
Fleur-de-lis Trail, 311
Glooscap Trail, 225–226, 241–243
Halifax/Dartmouth, 83
Lighthouse Route, 131–132, 156–161
Marconi Trail, 316–317
Marine Drive, 329–330
Northumberland Shore, 259–262, 273
Mush-a-Mush, 128
Mushaboom, 322
music, 62–63, 135, 137, 166, 280, 282, 295
fais dodo en Acadie, 191
Musquodoboit area trails, 324, 328
Musquodoboit Harbour, 322, 330
Musquodoboit Railway Museum, 322, 330
Musquodoboit River, 325
Musquodoboit Valley, 322, 325, 332
Myers family, 330

Nappan, 236
National Philatelic Centre, 270
Native people, see Mi'kmaq
A Nature and Hiking Guide to Cape Breton's Cabot Trail, 58, 284
Necum Teuch, 321
Neils Harbour, 285
Neptune Theatre, 61, 100
New Brunswick, 32
New Edinburgh, 194
New England Planters, 23, 40, 147, 199, 200, 203, 224, 226
cemeteries, 50, 212
New Glasgow, 269, 272, 274, 275
New Harbour, 320
New Minas, 200, 204
New Ross, 131, 133
Newfoundland ferry, 32, 315
Newport Landing, 42, 226
Nicholson, Colonel Francis, 21, 22
No Great Mischief, 277
Noel, 223
Normaway Inn, 295, 297
Norris, Joseph, 44, 100, 140
Norse explorers, 18

North East Margaree, 292, 293
North End Halifax, 10
North Highlands Community Museum, 286, 292
North Hills Museum, 209
North Mountain (Annapolis Valley), 17, 211, 213
North Mountain (Cape Breton), 285
North River Falls, 291
North River Provincial Park, 291
North Sydney, 315
Northport Beach, 257
Northumberland Fisheries Museum, 262
Northumberland Links, 56, 259
Northumberland Shore, 254–282
cycling, 258
Northumberland Strait, 29, 44, 254, 257, 262
Northwest Arm (Halifax), 91
Northwest Arm (Cape Breton), 315
Northwest Cove, 126
Not Since Moses Race, 235
Nova Scotia, 158
Nova Scotia Agricultural College, 224
Nova Scotia Art Gallery Shop, 106
Nova Scotia Bicycle Book, 47
Nova Scotia Bird Society, 48
Nova Scotia Centre for Craft and Design, 43, 95
Nova Scotia College of Art and Design, 106
Nova Scotia Country Music Hall of Fame, 167
Nova Scotia duck tolling retrievers, 164
Nova Scotia Exhibition, 224
Nova Scotia Festivals and Events Guide, 51
Nova Scotia Folk Art Festival, 137
Nova Scotia Gem & Mineral Show, 249
Nova Scotia Golf Guide, 56
Nova Scotia International Tattoo, 93
Nova Scotia Lighthouse Interpretive Centre, 321, 334
Nova Scotia Museum of Industry, 269, 273
Nova Scotia Museum of Natural History, 18, 84

Nova Scotia tartan, 160
Nova Scotia Yachting Association, 61
Nova Scotian Crystal, 108
Nova Shores Adventures, 241

O'Connor, D'Arcy, 138
O'Dell House Museum, 188
O'Neil, Pat, 58
Oak Island, 17, 126, 137
Oak Island Gold, 138
Oak Island Resort and Spa, 141
Oakfield Golf Club, 77
Oakfield Park, 92
Oaklawn Farm Zoo, 215
Ocean Explorations, 194
Oceanstone Inn and Cottages, 100
Oktoberfest, 263
Old Barns, 224
Old Burying Ground (Amherst), 258
Old Burying Ground (Chester), 138
Old Burying Ground (Halifax), 73
Old Burying Ground (Wolfville), 203
Old Burying Ground at Mush-a-Mush (Mahone Bay), 128
Old Covenanters Church, 42, 200
Old Court House (Guysborough), 329
Old Meeting House, 147
Old Schoolhouse, 211
Old Stone House, 226
Old Triangle Irish Alehouse, 121
Onslow, 243
Onyx, 114
Opa Greek Taverna, 118
Orangedale, 300
Order of Good Cheer, 20, 208
Osborne, 148
Oshan Whale Cruise, 295
Osprey Ridge Golf Club, 130
Osprey Shores Golf Resort, 325
Ostrea Lake side road, 332
Ottawa House, 235, 242
Our Lady of Guadalupe shrine, 299
Our Lady of Sorrows shrine, 277
Ovens Natural Park Oceanview Cottages, 142
Ovens Natural Park, 60, 134

Overton, 180
Owls Head, 322
Oxford, 263

Paddle East Canoe and Kayak, 72
Paddy's Head, 97
Paleo-Indians, 17–18, 244
Paradise, 203
Paragon Golf Club, 204
Park Place Ramada Renaissance, 111
Parkdale-Maplewood Community Museum, 157
Parkers Cove, 212
parks and greenspace, 147, 148, 320, 322
  Evangeline Trail, 191, 214
  Glooscap Trail, 227, 247–248
  Halifax/Dartmouth, 89–92
  Kejimkujik Scenic Drive, 177
  Lighthouse Route, 134–135, 165
  Marine Drive, 333
  Northumberland Shore, 262, 274
Parrsboro, 59, 222, 235, 242, 244, 250, 251, 252
Parrsboro Golf Course, 237
Parrsboro Rock and Mineral Shop, 250
Partridge Island, 245
passport, 30
Patterson, Robert, 209
Pavilion 22, 104
Pearson Peacekeeping Centre, 182
Peggy's Cove, trip to, 96–100
Pelton-Fuller house, 187
Pennant Point, 71, 78, 86
Penner, Judith, 61
Penney, Allen, 43
Pentz, 146
Pepperell, William, 21
Perkins, Simeon, 158
Perkins House, 157
Petit de Grat, 306
Petit Passage, 189
Petite Passage Whale Watch, 194
Petite Rivière, 146, 147
Petpeswick Bay, 332
Phil's Seafood, 123
Philips Mountain, 283
Pictou, 42, 256–257, 261, 262, 264, 265, 267, 269
Pictou Academy, 262
Pictou County, 273
  stonecutters, 275
Pictou Lodge Resort, 266

Pier 21 National Historic Site, 82, 101
Pine Grove Park, 177
Pinkney's Point, 164, 184
Pioneers' Cemetery (Brooklyn), 147
Pipers Cove, 299
piping plover, 151, 156
Pirate's Cove Whale Cruises, 194
Pleasant Bay, 285, 295
Pleasant Point, 148
Pleasant Point side road, 332
Pleasantville, 146
Point Aconi, 303, 315
Point Michaud Beach, 45, 307, 309
Point Pleasant Park, 62, 90, 102
Point Prim, 182
Pollett's Cove/Aspy Bay Wilderness Area, 64, 285
pollock fishing, 52, 126, 146, 312
Polly's Cove, 99
Pomquet, 270
Pomquet Beach, 271
Pondville, 307
Pondville Beach, 308
Popes Harbour, 322
Port aux Basques–North Sydney ferry, 32, 315
Port Bickerton, 321, 334
Port Clyde, 150
Port Felix, 320
Port George, 212
Port Greville, 236
Port Greville Beach, 236
Port Hawkesbury, 306
Port Hilford, 321
Port Hood, 277, 281
Port Hood Beach, 45, 277
Port Joli, 155
Port L'Hébert Pocket Wilderness, 165
Port LaTour, 150, 162
Port Lorne, 212
Port Maitland, 181
Port Medway, 147
Port Medway Lighthouse Park, 147
Port Morien, 314
Port Mouton, 153, 156
Port Royal, 20-21, 183
Port Royal National Historic Site, 43, 51, 199, 207–208
Port Shoreham, 323
Port Williams, 212, 219
Portaupique, 233

Portree, 283
ports of entry, 60
Portuguese Cove, 86
Prescott House, 59, 209
prices, 30
Prince Edward Island ferry, 32, 48, 256, 260
Prince George Hotel, 109
Prince's Lodge rotunda, 42
Princeport, 224
Princes Inlet, 127
privateers, 25, 148, 331
Prospect, 99
Province House, 42, 81
Public Gardens, 89, 102
Pubnico, 150
Pugwash, 255, 259, 263
Pumpkin Festival, 215

Quaker House, 85, 103
quality of life, 27
Quarterdeck Beachside Villas, 170
Quarterdeck Grill, 152, 172
Queen Anne Inn, 196
Queen Elizabeth II Health Sciences complex, 69
Queens County Museum, 157
Queensland beach, 125, 128
Queensport, 320

Raddall, Thomas, 70
Rafting, tidal bore, 230
Rails to Trails, 75, 200
Rainbow Haven Beach, 70, 71, 88
rating system for accommodations, 34
Red Shoe Pub, 282
Redgrave, Pat, 198
Reed's Head Park, 169
Refugee Cove, 240
Reid, Don, 248
rentals
  bicycles, 75, 129, 177
  canoes/kayaks, 175, 320, 325
  sailboats, 60
reservation system, 34
restoration project, 43, 321
retrievers, Nova Scotia duck tolling, 164
Rhubarb Grill, 100
Rissers Beach, 146, 152
Ristorante aMano, 118
Rita's Tea Room, 305
River Hebert, 236, 250
River Hills Golf and Country Club, 155
River John, 256, 258

River Oaks Golf Club, 325
River Road, 273
Riverport Peninsula, 134
Riverside Room, 337
Riverview Cottages, 252
Riverview Park, 165
Rob's Rock Shop, 60
Roberta, 299, 302
Robie Tufts Nature Centre, 202
Rockbound, 126
Rockdale, 307
Rockhounding, 59–60, 190, 202, 212, 222, 244, 248, 274, 317
Rocky Bay, 307
Roger Savage Gallery, 166
Rogers, George, 61
Rogers, Stan, 334
Rose Bay, 135
Roseway, 149
Roseway River Cottages, 171
Rosewood Cottages, 141
Ross, Captain William, 131
Ross Bridge, 283
Ross Farm, 51, 131, 133
Ross Ferry, 299
Rossignol Cultural Centre, 167
Ross-Thomson House, 159
Round Bay Beach, 153
Route, see Highway
Rover, 148
Royal Nova Scotia International Tattoo, 93
Rubenstein, Lorne, 56
Rudder's Seafood Restaurant and Brew Pub, 196
Rushtons Beach, 45, 257
Ruths Falls, 322
Ryan Duffy's, 117
Ryan, Dennis, 108
Ryan's Fancy, 108

Sable Island, natural history of, 84
Sable Offshore pipeline, 320
Sable River, 148
Saege, 116
Saguenay, 50, 129
Sailing, 60–61
    lessons, 61
St. Andrews, 274
St. Andrews Channel, 299
St. Andrew's Presbyterian Church, 139
St. Ann's, 286, 294
St. Ann's church (Guysborough), 319
St. Ann's Harbour, 286

St. Anselm's Church, 322
St. Bernard, 181
St. Croix Island, 19
St. Francis Xavier University, 270
St. George Church, 212
St. George's Church, 318
St. Georges Bay, 53, 270, 271
St. James United Church, 233
Saint John–Digby ferry, 32
St. John's Anglican Church, 139
St. Margaret, 294
St. Margaret's Bay Rails to Trails, 80
St. Margaret's Bay, 60, 80, 97
St. Mary's Bay, 182
St. Mary's Church, 181
St. Mary's River, 54
St. Mary's River Interpretation Centre, 321
St. Ninian's Cathedral, 270
St. Patricks Channel, 298, 303
St. Paul's Church, 42, 81
St. Peter's Church, 270
St. Peter's Canal National Historic Site and Battery Park, 60, 312
St. Peter's, 307, 311, 312
Ste-Anne-du-Ruisseau, 151
Salamat, Tahir, 115
Salem Pioneer Cemetery, 258
salmon fishing, 54–55, 72, 228, 274, 283, 287, 291, 292, 295, 321
Salmon Pools Trail, 288
Salmon View Housekeeping Cottages, 313
Salt Marsh Trail, 79, 88
Salt Mountain Trail, 301
saltwater fishing, 52–55
Salvador, Martin Ruiz, 145
Salvatore's, 120
Sambro, 70, 78, 85–86
Sambro Island lighthouse, 71, 78
Sampsons Cove, 306
Samson, Garvie, 56
Sand Hills Beach, 150, 154
Sand River, 236
Sandford, 180, 184
Sandy Cove, 189
Sandy Point, 149, 163
Saraguay Club, 103
Satisfaction Feast, 122
Saul, Suzanne, 105
Savage, Roger, 162, 166
Savoy Theatre, 315, 317
Scarecrow Festival & Antique

Fair, 136
Schooner Books, 108
Schooner Pond Head, 315–316
Scots Bay, 201, 206, 213
Scotsburn, 266
Scott Walking Tours, 58
Scottish Pines Log Cottages, 265
Seabright, 97
sea caves, 135
sea kayaking, see kayaking
Sea Kayaking in Nova Scotia, 61
seafood, 116–117, 337
Seafoam, 256
Seaforth, 322
Seagull Pewter, 263
Seahorse Tavern, 122
Seal Island Bridge, 298
Seal Island, 49, 150, 154
Seaman, Amos, 242
Seaside Shanty, 143
SeaWind Landing, 336
Second Peninsula, 127, 133
self-government, 26
Shag Harbour, 150
Shakespeare by the Sea, 62, 101
Shand House, 201, 210
Shannon, 74
shark fishing, 54
Shearwater, 87
Shearwater Aviation Museum, 87
Sheet Harbour, 322
Shelburne, 24, 149, 154, 159, 165, 169, 171, 172
Shelburne County, 154
Shelburne County Genealogical Society, 160
Shelburne County Museum, 149, 159
Shelburne Harbour Boat Tours, 162
Shelburne River, 49, 177
Shelburne Whirligig Festival, 166
Sherbrooke, 329
Sherbrooke Village, 51, 59, 321, 329, 337
Sherman Hines Museum of Photography, 158
Ship Harbour, 322
Ship's Company Theatre, 235, 251
shipbuilding, 25, 148, 149, 159, 160, 242, 256
shipwrecks, 50–51, 83, 88,

92, 161, 163, 286, 292, 295, 310, 316
Shipwrecks of Nova Scotia, 51
Shirley, Governor William, 21, 22
shopping
  Halifax/Dartmouth, 104–108
  Lighthouse Route, 140
Shore Club, 135
Shubenacadie, 224, 229
Shubenacadie Canal, 70, 72, 91, 103
Shubenacadie River, 224, 225, 325
Shubenacadie River Adventure Tours, 230
Shubenacadie River Runners, 230
Shubenacadie Tidal Bore Rafting, 230
Shubenacadie Wildlife Park, 224, 229
Shubie Park, 91
Shulie, 236
Silver Dart Lodge, 304
Simpson, Norman, 35
Sinclair, Prince Henry, Earl of Orkney, 18-19, 319
Sinclair Inn Museum, 188
Sir Sandford Fleming Park, 86, 91, 103
Sissiboo River, 182
skiing, cross-country, 65, 80, 266
Ski-Tuonela, 65
Skyline Trail, 288–289
Slocum, Joshua, 190
Smiley's Provincial Park, 227
Smith and Rhuland Shipbuilding Works, 140
Smith, Archelaus, 161
Smith, Scott, 56
Smiths Cove, 182, 196
smoked fish, 334
Smugglers Cove Provincial Park, 181, 191
Snow, Hank, 63, 147, 166
snowmobiling, 65
snowshoeing, 65
Sober Island, 322
Sobey, Frank, 274
Sonora, 321
South Maitland, 224, 230
South Milford, 178
South Shore Exhibition, 166
South Shore, 45, 125–173
Southampton, 235
special events, 235, 322

Ceilidh Trail, 280
Evangeline Trail, 191, 215
Glooscap Trail, 249
Halifax/Dartmouth, 93–95
Lighthouse Route, 136–137, 166
Marconi Trail, 317
Marine Drive, 333
Northumberland Shore, 274
Spencers Beach, 236
Spencers Island, 236
Spring Garden Road, 105
Springhill, 235, 243, 246, 250
Springhill Miners' Museum, 59, 243, 246
springwater, 234
Spry Bay Trail, 327
Spry Harbour, 322
SS Atlantic, 51, 99
SS Atlantic Memorial Park, 99
Stan Rogers Folk Festival, 334
Stanfield, Robert, 73
Stanfield Factory Outlet, 224, 230
Stanley, 226
Stayner's Wharf Bar & Grill, 121
steakhouses. 117
Stellarton, 269
Stevens, Clarence, 71
Stewiacke, 224
Stewiacke River, 54, 325
Stewiacke River Park, 228
Stewiacke River Valley, 226–227
Stonehame Lodge & Chalets, 266
Stonehurst (North and South), 133
Stories, 115
Storm, Alex, 50
Strait of Canso, 277, 319
Studio Rally map, 43
Sugar Moon Farm, 267
Sullivan's Pond, 91
Summerville Beach Retreat Chalets, 170
Summerville Beach, 148, 152, 170, 172
Summerville, 223
Sunrise Trail, 254–282
Sunrise Trail Museum, 260
Sunshine on Main Café, 276
Surettes Island, 163, 184
surfing, 45
Sutherland Steam Mill, 261
Swissair Flight 111 memorial, 97
Sydney, 314, 315, 317, 318
Sydney & Louisburg Railway,

308
Sydney Mines, 315
Syperek, Victor, 114

Tall Ships, 94
Tallahassee, 87
Tancook Island, see Big Tancook, Little Tancook
Tangier, 322, 328, 334
Tantallon, 97
Tantramar marshes, 254, 258
Tatamagouche, 256, 260, 263
Tattingstone Inn, 218
taxes, 31
Taylor Head Provincial Park, 322, 327, 333
Tempest World Cuisine, 220
Terence Bay, 99
Terence Bay Wilderness Area, 103
Terre-Noire, 284
That Dutchman's Farm, 253
The Bistro, 275
The Chickenburger, 123
The Dingle, 91
The Fireside, 123
The Islands Provincial Park, 165
The Keg, 117
The Knot, 144
The Lakes Golf Club, 56
The Lookoff, 213
The Mull Café and Deli, 281
The Nova Scotian, 26
The Pergola, 220
The Pools, 206, 214
The Port Pub, 219
The Press Gang, 114
The Seaside, 171
The Unicorn, 107
The Week The Women Went, 256
theatre, 61–62, 235
  Glooscap Trail, 251
  Halifax/Dartmouth, 100–101
  Lighthouse Route, 138
theme park, 191
Theresa E. Connor, 132
Thomas Raddall Research Centre, 158
Thomas Walters & Sons Marine Blacksmiths, 140
Thomas' Cove Coastal Preserve, 247
Thompson, Dale, 93
Thompson, John, 74
Thompson, Stanley, 56, 77, 287
Three Sisters Interpretive

Centre, 240, 248
tidal bore, 227–228, 230, 236
Tidal Bore Park, 224, 225, 227, 230
Tidnish, 255
Tidnish Dock Provincial Park, 255
Tim Hortons Children's Camp, 256
Timberlea, 125
Titanic, 83, 161
graves, 74
Tiverton, 186, 189, 193
Tobacco Island, 321
Tobeatic Wilderness Area, 49, 64, 177
Tomavinos, 120
Toney River, 256
Topmast Motel, 142
Tor Bay, 320, 333
Tor Bay Atlantic Provincial Park, 320, 333
touring, 33, 46
bicycle touring companies, 47
ornithological, 47
Tourist Industry Association of Nova Scotia (TIANS), 34
tourist information, 31–32
tower, 90, 138, 150, 214, 234, 290
Town Clock, 42, 81
Tracadie, 270
Train Station Bike & Bean, 75
Trans Canada Trail, 57, 65, 79, 258, 279, 326, 328
Trans-Canada Highway, 33, 270, 283, 298, 301
transportation, 32
Trask, Deborah, 50
Treaty of Paris, 23
Treaty of Utrecht, 21, 186
Treaty of Versailles, 25
tree sculptures, 231
Trellis Café, 143
Trenton, 269
Trenton glassware, 40, 269, 273
Trinity Anglican Church (Liverpool), 168
Trinity Church (Digby), 193
Trinity Church (Middleton), 200
trout fishing, 53, 72, 203, 228
Truro, 224, 225, 228–232
Truro Golf Course, 225
Truro Raceway, 224
Tufts, Robie, 48, 202
tuna fishing, 53–54
Tupper, Sir Charles, 242, 254

Tupperville, 211
Tusket Falls, 184
Tusket Islands, 49, 163, 164
Tusket, 151
Two Islands Road, 244
Two Rivers Wildlife Park, 312

UFO incident, 150
Uisge Ban Falls, 301
Uktobok Trail, 151
UNESCO World Heritage Site, 127, 236, 248
Uniacke Estate Museum Park, 201, 210
trails, 207
Uniacke House, 42, 210
United Empire Loyalists, see Loyalists
Université Sainte-Anne, 181
uplands, 16-17
Upper Clements Theme Park, 191–192
Upper Economy, 252, 253
Upper Stewiacke, 227
Urban Cottage, 105
Urbania, 231

Valleyview Provincial Park, 214
Veteran's Memorial Park, 233
Victor Emmanuel Nature Tours, 48
Victoria Beach, 182, 199, 211
Victoria Park, 225, 228
Victoria's Historic Inn, 217
Vinland, 18, 64
Vinton, Robert, 276
visa, 30

W. E. deGarthe Memorial, 98
Walk Historic Halifax, 70
walking tours, 63
Bras d'Or Lakes, 303
Evangeline Trail, 192, 216–217
Fleur-de-lis Trail, 312
Glooscap Trail, 231
Halifax/Dartmouth, 101–103
Lighthouse Route, 138–140, 168–169
Marconi Trail, 317–318
Northumberland Shore, 264–265
Wallace Bay, 257
Wallace MacAskill Home, 311
Wallace, 255, 258, 262
Walton Pub, 232
Walton, 223, 232
War of 1812, 25
Warden of the North, 70

Wards Falls Trail, 239
Warren Lake Trail, 289
Warren Lake, 286
Wasson Bluffs, 248
water clock, 200
waterfalls, 238, 240, 285
Waterfalls: Nova Scotia's Masterpieces, 58
Waterside Beach, 257
Waverley–Salmon River Long Lake Wilderness Area, 335–336
weather, 27-29
Wedgeport, 164
Wedgeport Peninsula, 53, 164–165
Wedgeport Sport Tuna Fishing Museum and Interpretive Centre, 164
Wentworth Valley trails, 240
Wentworth Valley, 241, 247
West Advocate, 237, 253
West Baccaro, 162
West Bay, 299, 304
West Berlin, 147
West Dover, 99
West Jeddore side road, 332
West Mabou Beach, 277
West Pennant, 103
West Pubnico Golf and Country Club, 155
West Pubnico, 150, 155, 168
Western Head, 162
Western Shore, 126, 141
Westin Nova Scotian, 110
Westport, 190, 193, 195, 197
Westville, 269
Weymouth, 182
Whale Cruisers Ltd., 295
Whale-watching, 63–64, 190, 193, 284, 295
What Cheer Tearoom, 337
Where to Eat in Canada, 37, 120, 172
White Point (South Shore), 148, 154, 169
White Point (Cape Breton), 285
White Point Beach, 169
White Point Beach Resort, 169
White Star Line, 26
Whitehead, 320
Whitman House, 329
Whitman Inn, 178
Whycocomagh, 298, 301
Whycocomagh Provincial Park, 301
Wild Blueberry & Maple Centre, 263
Wild Blueberry Harvest

Festival, 235
wilderness areas, 64
  Glooscap Trail, 251
  Halifax/Dartmouth, 103
  Kejimkujik Scenic Drive, 177
  Marine Drive, 335–336
wildlife parks, 224, 229, 312
Wile Carding Mill, 156
William D Lawrence, 26,
  223, 225
Willy Krauch's Smoke House,
  334
Windsor Agricultural Exhibi-
  tion, 215
Windsor Hockey Heritage
  Centre, 216, 217
Windsor, 201, 209–210, 216,
  217
windsurfing, 61, 152, 271
wineries, 64–65, 217, 262, 264
Wineries and Wine Country
  of Nova Scotia, 65
Winery Association of Nova

Scotia, 65
Winsby's, 107
winter sports, 65
Wolfe, General James, 23
Wolfville, 200, 202, 203, 206,
  215, 216, 217–220
Wolfville dykes, 206
Wood, Sean, 65
Wood Islands–Caribou ferry,
  32, 256
Woodland Trail, 214
Woods Harbour, 150
World Heritage Site, 127,
  236, 248
Wreck Cove, 293

Yamamoto, Hideki, 119
Yarmouth, 32, 42, 46, 180,
  187–188, 192, 194, 196–197
Yarmouth area salt marshes,
  184
Yarmouth County Museum
  and Archives, 187

Yarmouth County, 184
Yarmouth Light, 180, 188
York Redoubt National His-
  toric Site, 82, 86
Your Father's Moustache, 122
youth hostels, 35

Zion Evangelical Lutheran
  Church, 140
Zwicker's Gallery, 106

READERS RESPONSE FORM

Send to:
Formac Publishing Company Limited
5502 Atlantic Street, Halifax,
Nova Scotia   B3H 1G4

or:
Dale Dunlop and Alison Scott
maritexp@ns.sympatico.ca

Re: Exploring Nova Scotia, Sixth Edition

On_____, I/we visited the following place(s) recommended in Exploring Nova Scotia. Here are my/our comments:

Place(s):_____
Comments:_____
_____
_____
_____

I/we have no personal connection to the place(s) commented upon.

Name:_____
Address:_____
_____
_____